Music and Ex

Music and Expression

Robert Weiss
Southern Illinois University

 Wm. C. Brown Publishers

Book Team

Editor *Meredith M. Morgan*
Developmental Editor *Dean Robbins*
Production Editor *Michelle M. Campbell*
Photo Editor *Mary Roussel*
Permissions Editor *Vicki Krug*
Visuals Processor *Kenneth E. Ley*

 Wm. C. Brown Publishers

President *G. Franklin Lewis*
Vice President, Publisher *George Wm. Bergquist*
Vice President, Publisher *Thomas E. Doran*
Vice President, Operations and Production *Beverly Kolz*
National Sales Manager *Virginia S. Moffat*
Advertising Manager *Ann M. Knepper*
Marketing Manager *Kathleen Nietzke*
Managing Editor, Production *Colleen A. Yonda*
Production Editorial Manager *Julie A. Kennedy*
Production Editorial Manager *Ann Fuerste*
Publishing Services Manager *Karen J. Slaght*
Manager of Visuals and Design *Faye M. Schilling*

Cover design by Sailer & Cook Creative Services

Cover image by Liz Kathman Grubow

The credits section for this book begins on page 399, and is considered an extension of the copyright page.

Consulting Editor Frederick W. Westphal

. . . .

To my wife, Jan,
and my daughters,
Heather and Meghan

. . . .

CONTENTS

Section Two

Expression

Section Three
Cultural Context

14 Baroque *217*

15 Classical *253*

16 Romanticism *273*

CORE LISTENING EXAMPLES

. . . .

F rom the soothing lullabies you were sung as infants to the dignified strains of "Pomp and Circumstance" that ushered you through high-school graduation, you have no doubt experienced the expressiveness of music countless times throughout your lives. What's more, by the time you entered college most of you had already been exposed to a great variety of musical styles—by parents, classroom teachers, chorus, band or choir directors, private piano or violin instructors, or siblings and peers. In fact, if you think for a moment, you will probably realize that you have heard rock and roll, rhythm and blues, new age, soul music, folk music, country western, and jazz—not to mention religious music, classical music, and, of course, "elevator music."

Indeed, with all this exposure, most of you by this time have developed a decided preference for one kind of music or another. You may even know quite a bit about it, including information about its

> composers (who wrote it),
> performers (who plays it),
> timbre (the sounds of the instruments used),
> tempo (is it fast? or slow?),
> rhythm (the pattern in which you tap your feet, snap your fingers, clap your hands, sway your shoulders, pat the steering wheel, or nod your head when you listen to it).

In other words, you "appreciate" it.

And since you know so much about the music styles you "appreciate," why spend an entire semester being submerged in music you don't necessarily want to "appreciate"—music that may never find its way into your tape or CD collection? Because music is EXPRESSIVE. Consequently, all kinds of music have something to say to us—if we know how to listen. However, just as with foreign languages, if we don't learn how to listen to musical styles we find "foreign"—if we don't pay attention to what's being communicated (and how)—we can hear all our lives but never understand. More specifically, directed listening to a broad range of musical styles can help you to:

Enrich your current listening experiences. Since the same listening skills apply, regardless of the style of music you listen to, the more you listen attentively to unfamiliar music, the more you learn about listening to the music that is already familiar to you.

Discover new avenues of musical enjoyment. As much as we think we "know what we like," we should also be aware that to a large extent we like what we know. That is, the more we know, the more we like; and expanding listening horizons means expanding listening enjoyment.

Broaden cultural understanding. In many ways, music is a product of society. Just as musical choices reflect notable differences from one generation to the next in our own culture, the styles of traditional music from other past as well as present cultures teach us a lot about the way people interact with each other and with their environments.

Improve the quality of your life. The more we understand about the methods and manners by which music influences us, and has influenced us over the years, the more we can use it to our own advantage—as a tool to soothe us, relieve stress, motivate, manipulate, and otherwise enrich our personal lives.

While these rather ambitious goals may more accurately describe challenges for long-term development than goals to be accomplished in a single semester, significant progress toward them can be made in a short period by:

Learning to recognize and identify the individual characteristics or elements of music in order to understand how it is created;

Learning how those individual elements—both singularly and in combination—can affect the listener;

Becoming comfortable with terminology/vocabulary that will help you articulate and clarify what you are hearing;

Exposing yourself to new styles and sources of music.

Such are the skills and techniques a textbook and directed listening regimen can provide to a willing learner. Indeed, if you apply these skills and techniques with a continuing awareness of the common thread that runs through all music—expressiveness—then even a single semester of "music appreciation" can significantly expand your cognitive universe.

To ease the task somewhat, this text uses several methods to build skills and inspire progress toward both the short- and the long-term goals that have been proposed. The first chapter will suggest some different ways in which music is expressive as well as different ways in which you might listen to music. The remaining chapters of Section I will focus on understanding the basic elements of music and how to identify them as you listen. Section II examines more specifically how those musical elements are used expressively. Section III is a brief chronological review of how those same elements have been used and developed in various cultural contexts from Pre-Renaissance times through the twentieth century, including a quick look at the less familiar traditions of non-Western music.

In order to provide you with an efficient way to identify musical elements, examine how they can be used expressively, and view those same elements within a cultural context, a set of seventeen musical selections (provided on the tapes with this text) are used as a *core of listening examples* throughout the text. Every one of these examples is cited in each section at least once, and usually more often, in order to help familiarize you with a broad range of styles within a manageable selection of musical works. While these listening selections will be supplemented in class, the core examples provided on the cassette tapes will provide a convenient way to compare, contrast, and review the observations you make and the discoveries you unearth as you survey the world of Music and Expression.

One additional musical example was originally intended to be a core example and included on the tapes which accompany this text. The *Threnody: To the Victims of Hiroshima* by Penderecki is used throughout the text but only two recordings of this work exist and neither could be obtained for use on the tapes. I hope that the instructor will be able to obtain a recording of this work to augment the classroom listening experiences.

Acknowledgments

I owe sincere thanks to numerous individuals who made this project possible. Catherine McHugh's love of teaching and concern for students have served as an inspiration to my own work. Dean Brown and Patricia Dusenbury provided significant advice and research assistance. Robert Roubos, Director of the School of Music at Southern Illinois University at Carbondale, and the faculty there gave me encouragement and answered numerous questions over the past several years.

Nancy Stemper worked with the manuscript in its roughest form and made remarkable contributions in grammar, style, and clarity. Her work was invaluable in producing a consistent and readable text.

I have great respect for and wish to thank Raphael Kadushin, Meredith Morgan, and all of the staff at Wm. C. Brown Company who were most understanding, as well as generous in their time and expertise. Thanks also goes to the thousands of students who have endured my trial and error methods over the past eighteen years.

My appreciation for honest reactions and superb advice goes to the reviewers of the manuscript, whose comments constantly challenged me to make significant corrections and improvements:

Hugh Albee, Palm Beach Jr. College

Ann C. Anerson,
  University of Minnesota–Duluth

Paul Hilbrich,
  University of Wisconsin–Eau Claire

Kenneth Keaton,
  Florida Atlantic University

William L. Kellogg,
  University of Southern Colorado

Alan Luhring, University of Colorado

Roy V. Magers, Winthrop College

Rodney Boyd, Washburn University

Charles F. Schwartz,
  East Carolina University

Anthony Thein, Mayville State College

Larry Warkentin, Fresno Pacific College

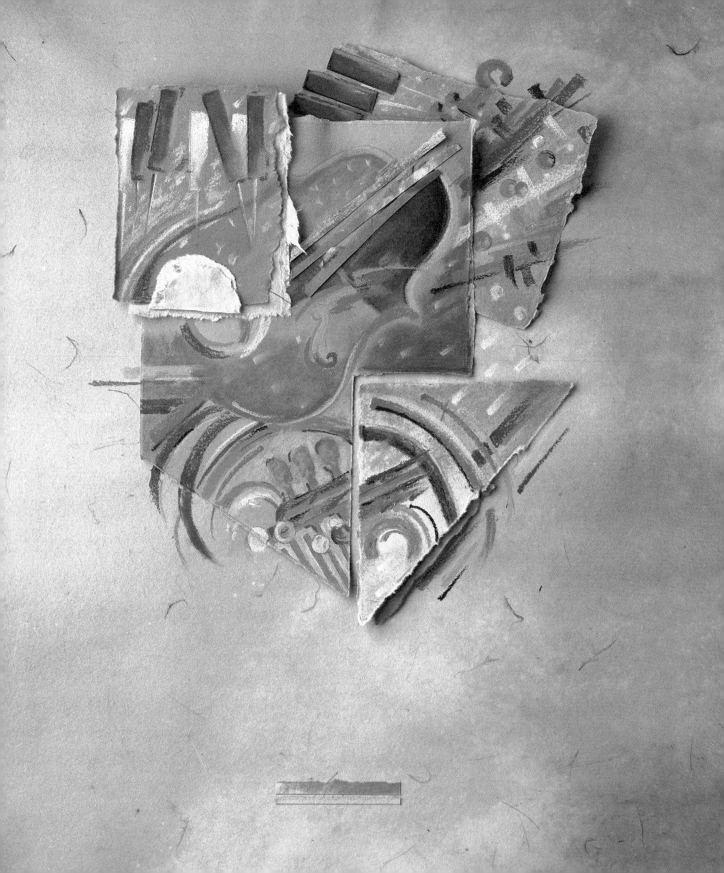

Elements

CHAPTER ONE

Musical Expressiveness

Preview of Terms and Concepts

Music, like language, is **expressive.** However, the manner in which musical meaning is expressed differs from that of spoken language in that spoken language is **denotative;** it points to an object with a word. Music, on the other hand, is primarily **connotative;** it conveys meaning through personal associations.

    Vocal music makes use of both methods of expression.

    Program music uses extramusical associations in the form of a title, story, or written comments from the composer to help convey meaning.

    Absolute music avoids all extramusical associations.

    Music listening may take place in any of three modes: **subconscious,** purely **technical,** and **insightful.** Expressive interaction with music can be experienced by a **composer,** a **performer,** or a **listener.** The musical selections that you seek out on radio, attend at concerts, or purchase on recordings reveal your **musical preferences, appreciations,** and **values.**

M usic is expressive. Listen to the following three examples. What do each of these express and how?

Listening Guide
Expressiveness

. . . .

B. Smith: Lost Your Head Blues
H. Berlioz: Symphonie Fantastique
          V. Dream of the Witches' Sabbath
          (Listen to the first few minutes of this work)
J. S. Bach: Prelude in C Major

As representative examples of vocal music, program music, and absolute music, respectively, these selections may be equally expressive, but each in a different way.

Lost Your Head Blues	Vocal music
Symphonie Fantastique	Program music
Prelude in C Major	Absolute music

Vocal Music

The expressiveness of **vocal music** is most immediately obvious through the presence of words (also referred to as text or lyrics). The words for "Lost Your Head Blues" are obviously very direct in expressing sadness, rejection, and loneliness.

"Lost Your Head Blues"
by Bessie Smith

I was with you baby when you did not have a dime.
I was with you baby when you did not have a dime.
Now since you got plenty money you have throw'd your good gal down.

Once ain't for always, two ain't for twice.
Once ain't for always, two ain't for twice.
When you get a good gal you better treat her nice.

When you were lonesome I tried to treat you kind.
When you were lonesome I tried to treat you kind.
But since you've got money, it's done changed your mind.

I'm going to leave baby, ain't going to say good-bye.
I'm going to leave baby, ain't going to say good-bye.
But I'll write you and tell you the reason why.

Days are lonesome, nights are long.
Days are lonesome, nights are so long.
I'm a good old gal, but I've just been treated wrong.

Notice in addition, however, that the "low-down" feeling expressed by the lyrics is conveyed by the music as well. The overall sound is slow and plodding. The cornet imitates the very mournful character of the voice as it answers each line, and the voice itself adds to the feeling of dejection by sliding to pitches. Even without lyrics, you could probably recognize quite accurately the mood of this selection, but together, the words and music provide a double avenue of expressiveness.

Meaning: Language and Music

While music and language are both symbolic systems used to convey meaning, the notion of music as a "universal language" is not technically accurate, in that music does not communicate in the same direct way that language does. Language provides us with symbols—words—for daily communication. These symbols are denotative; they have a direct correlation to objects, events, or ideas that are defined through shared experiences. The word "cat," for example, denotes a mammal in the family *Felidae.* The addition of adjectives—my pet cat—may further narrow the number of possible shared experiences to the perception of a small furry animal with specific coloration and markings.

The symbolism in music also communicates—but in a much less direct manner. Where verbal language is denotative, music is primarily connotative—it conveys meaning through personal associations with the symbol. Musical sounds (for the most part) simply do not have assigned meanings in the same way that words do. Thus, while a violin may be played in such a way as to imitate the purr or whine of a cat, there is not a fixed musical symbol for cats. The pitches, rhythms, and harmonies that constitute symbols have no fixed meanings that can be looked up in a dictionary. In fact, except for obvious "imitations" of extramusical sounds (e.g. purring cats, car horns, or thunder), music has no literal meaning at all.

Rather, music symbolizes the composer's, performer's, or listener's conception of the realm of human feeling. The movement through time of musical sounds can parallel personal affective (sentimental or emotional) experiences. Human feelings such as those denoted by the words joy, sadness, hope, despair, and love have personal significance beyond what can be described in words. Life experiences make these feelings truly individual to each person. Music (and the other arts) provide a uniquely human way to symbolize these feelings.

Denotation is the process of conveying meaning through shared experiences or universally understood signs.

Connotation is the process of conveying meaning through personal associations.

Having emphasized this primary difference between music and language, we must also note that music can be denotative just as language can be connotative. The repeated association of a particular selection of music with an object, event, or idea, for example, will result in a denotative relationship. Thus to generations of radio listeners and television viewers the *William Tell* Overture conjured an immediate image of the Lone Ranger. Similarly, words can have personal, emotional associations. To a person who loves cats, the word "cat" may connote warm, positive feelings. For an individual who dislikes cats, the same word will generate distasteful, negative feelings.

Product marketing is one field where music frequently is used denotatively in that advertisers often utilize catchy tunes for product identification. These are very limited applications of musical denotation, resulting from numerous associations of the tune with the product. Nonetheless, you need only to listen to television network identifications or familiar commercial jingles to hear music being used denotatively. (Listen especially to commercials for cars and soft drinks.) While denotative assignment does occur occasionally in serious music for listening, this is the exception rather than the norm and music remains primarily connotative.

As we observed in the first musical example, when words are put to music both denotation and connotation may take place. In addition to the meaning carried by the words, the music may reflect and support the text, supplement the meaning of the text, or, in some special cases, even contradict the meaning of the text.

The text of a good poem can stand alone. Read the following example aloud.

I Hear America Singing
by Walt Whitman

I hear America singing, the varied carols I hear,
Those of mechanics, each one singing his as it should be blithe and strong,
The carpenter singing his as he measures his plank or beam,
The mason singing his as he makes ready for work, or leaves off work,
The boatman singing what belongs to him in his boat, the deckhand singing on the
    steamboat deck,
The shoemaker singing as he sits on his bench, the hatter singing as he stands,
The woodcutter's song, the plowboy's on his way in the morning, or at noon intermis-
    sion or at sundown,
The delicious singing of the mother, or of the young wife at work, or of the girl sewing
    or washing,
Each singing what belongs to him or her and to none else,
The day what belongs to the day—at night the party of young fellows, robust, friendly,
Singing with open mouths their strong melodious songs.

If you have read aloud and with expression, then you have made use of some musical elements, even without the help of instruments or accompaniment. The pace and timing of your recitation and the rise and fall of your voice are aspects of speech that are similar to musical rhythm and melodic movement. These musical elements are the primary constituents of expressive reading.

If possible, listen to the musical setting of a poem and notice if the music supports the text by emphasizing important words and following the natural rhythmic inflection of the words. These characteristics are common in songs that use poetry for a text, and examples abound in everything from fourteenth century songs to the popular music of Paul Simon and Art Garfunkel.

Some vocal works employ texts that carried a significant meaning long before they were put to music. The biblical passages that are repeated in George Frideric Handel's *Messiah,* for example, originated hundreds of years before that composer set them to music so effectively. Listen to the expression of joy in the following excerpt.

George Frideric Handel
(FREED-rick HAHN-dl)

Listening Guide

Vocal Music

· ·

 G. F. Handel: Messiah

"Glory to God"
(Voices with orchestral accomp.)

Glory to God, in the highest,
and peace on earth,
goodwill towards men.

Bright and quick-moving.
Orchestra supports voices, adds fast-moving ornamental lines, and ends movement with
material borrowed from the voices.

Other vocal works may tell moving stories complete unto themselves. Read the following text of Schubert's song *Erlking.* Although very brief, this is a gripping and powerful account of a young boy dying in his father's arms.

Listen to Schubert's musical setting of this story, which is based on the text by Goethe. Even though you may not understand the German, try to hear four characters present in the drama—narrator, son, father, and Erlking (a legendary elf king who symbolized death)—who should be evident in the subtle changes of the voice.

Goethe (GEHR-teh)

Listening Guide
Vocal Music with a Story

· ·

  F. Schubert: Erlking

> *Narrator:* Who rides so late through night and wind? It is the father with his child; He folds the boy close in his arms, he clasps him securely, he holds him warmly.
> *Father:* My son, why do you hide your face so anxiously?
> *Son:* Father, don't you see the Erlking? The Erlking with his crown and train?
> *Father:* My son, it is a streak of mist.
> *Erlking:* Dear child, come, go with me! I'll play the prettiest games with you. Many colored flowers grow along the shore; My mother has many golden garments.
> *Son:* My father, my father, don't you hear the Erlking whispering promises to me?
> *Father:* Be quiet, stay quiet, my child; The wind is rustling in the dead leaves.
> *Erlking:* My handsome boy, will you come with me? My daughters shall wait upon you; My daughters lead off in the dance every night, And cradle and dance and sing you to sleep.
> *Son:* My father, my father, don't you see there, the Erlking's daughters in the shadows?
> *Father:* My son, my son, I see it clearly; The old willows look so gray.
> *Erlking:* I love you, your beautiful appearance delights me! And if you are not willing, then I shall use force!
> *Son:* My father, my father, now he is taking hold of me!
> *Narrator:* The father shudders, he rides swiftly on; He holds in his arms the groaning child, He reaches the courtyard weary and anxious: In his arms the child is dead.

The popular vocal music of today is expressive of topics, feelings, and values of younger audiences. The most common subjects are love, rebellion against parents or government, and political issues or patriotism. Other themes include novelty tunes, dance backgrounds, and reflections of a carefree attitude about life.

On yet another level, the combination of vocal music and drama in the form of operas and musical theater has long been a source of entertainment. Subjects have included everything from serious religious themes to lighthearted and whimsical comedies. Obviously, vocal music continues to be a very popular form of musical expression.

Program Music

Music does not need a text to convey concrete images. Instrumental compositions (works for instruments without voices) sometimes rely only upon stories, titles, or written comments from the composer to help the listener understand the extramusical connections that are intended. These instrumental works with associations outside of the music are called **program music.**

Instrumental music that is descriptive of some extramusical object or idea is called program music.

Animals, scenes of nature, battles, poems, literary stories, and historical events have all provided inspiration for program music. Some composers have attempted to produce realistic sounds with instruments to imitate thunder and lightning, birdcalls, running water, and battle scenes. Other programmatic techniques have relied upon the creation of a more general mood or atmosphere.

The programmatic work in the first listening assignment of this chapter—*Symphonie Fantastique*—provides both a title and notes by the composer to suggest extramusical associations. Without the program notes you may not have made the same specific connections as the composer, but your general perception of the mood and feeling of the music would probably have been similar.

Read the description of the young man's nightmare in the Listening Guide which follows and then listen to the entire fifth movement of this programmatic symphony by Hector Berlioz. How does the music suggest or express the composer's program even without a vocal text?

Listening Guide
Program Music

. . . .

 H. Berlioz: Symphonie Fantastique
V. "Dream of the Witches' Sabbath"

He sees himself at a witches' sabbath in the midst of a hideous crowd of ghouls, sorcerers, and monsters of every description, united for his funeral. Strange noises, groans, shrieks of laughter, distant cries, which other cries seem to answer. The melody of his loved one is heard, but it has lost its character of nobleness and timidity; it is no more than a dance tune, ignoble, trivial, and grotesque. It is she who comes to the sabbath! A howl of joy greets her arrival. She participates in the diabolical orgy. The funeral knell, burlesque of the *Dies irae* ("Day of wrath"). Witches' dance. The dance and the *Dies irae* combined.

Dies Irae
(DEE-ays EE-ray)

This movement is the culmination of a longer work based upon a program provided by the composer. In addition to musical "groans and shrieks," a melody is assigned to represent the woman who is the object of the young man's spurned affections, and an old melody is borrowed to create another fearful association. The term *"Dies irae"* refers to a melody from a traditional religious vocal work used at funerals—the requiem mass. The text of this section is a terrifying warning of the coming of Judgment Day—"Day of wrath, day of doom." Such specific associations give a very detailed description of the composer's programmatic intentions.

Requiem
(REH-kwee-em)

Absolute Music

Instrumental music that has no intended association with extramusical ideas is called **absolute music.** Some composers would insist that their music should be listened to solely for the sake of the music itself. The twentieth-century composer Igor Stravinsky stated that his music had a life of its own, with no other meaning than its own purely musical existence.

Igor Stravinsky
(EE-gor Strah-VIN-skee)

Absolute music is instrumental music that has no extramusical associations.

Titles of absolute music are usually descriptive of the music itself. While examples such as sonata, fugue, concerto, and symphony provide no hint of external relationships, they do give some suggestion of form or organization to be expected.

Sonata (soh-NAH-tah)
Fugue (fewg)
Concerto (kohn-CHEHR-toh)

Listening to absolute music requires the ability to focus on sound for the sake of sound. This does not mean that your own personal experiences and interpretations of musical sounds will not or should not result in a perception of expressive feelings. However, those feelings and perceptions will probably be more difficult to put into words and are likely to vary greatly from one listener to the next.

The example of absolute music in your first listening assignment—Prelude in C Major by Johann Sebastian Bach—contained no vocal text or descriptive title to indicate what the composer had in mind. The term "prelude" simply implies one piece that precedes another piece. Rather than trying to connect the musical sounds with external symbols, you should listen to the time and sound relationships created by the music itself. The following example is similar.

Johann Sebastian Bach (YO-hahn Se-BASS-tee-ahn BAHK)

Listening Guide
Absolute Music

. . . .

 J. S. Bach: Fugue in C Major (WTC I)

The term "fugue" refers to a technique of composition resulting in interesting musical relationships—but there are no extramusical references provided by the composer. (More specific information on the fugue will be given in later chapters.)

Modes of Listening

We do not always listen to music in the same way. Using records or the radio as background to studying or doing chores is not the same as sitting in a concert hall with all of your attention focused on the performance. Even in a formal concert setting, your mode of listening may vary from a conscious perception of expressive aspects, to technical observations, or even daydreaming as the music retreats to the background. These three distinct modes of listening can be described respectively as *insightful, technical,* and *subconscious.*

Subconscious Listening

Sometimes music is used simply to help set a particular mood. The pianist playing at a nice restaurant provides pleasant sounds rather than a formal concert. Your selection of a particular album of music to play at the end of a long and strenuous day might be a reflection of your state of mind rather than a desire to focus on the music. Since this music is not the primary focus of your attention, it is called **background music.**

> Music that is intended to provide a mood or atmosphere rather than to be the primary focus of attention is called background music.

Background music is clearly functional, but requires no conscious thought. Companies that provide piped-in music depend upon this subconscious level of listening to achieve specific results. Elevators and dentists' offices frequently play soothing music to cover the silence and to reduce stress. Supermarkets play sedately paced music to slow you down, the theory being that if you spend more time in a store, you will buy more. Since the 1930s, factories and offices have used background music, not to entertain their employees, but to motivate them to be more productive.

Different situations call for different listening modes.

Top: Columbia Artists Management.
Bottom: © UPI/Bettmann Newsphotos.
Opposite page: © Mark Antman/The Image Works, Inc.

Through the use of an "ascending program," the pace of the music is increased at mid-morning and mid-afternoon—times when workers usually are starting to feel lethargic. In fact, studies have shown that this reduces worker fatigue and increases accuracy and productivity. Music has been known to assist in everything from dieting to increasing milk and egg production on farms—all without musical study or even conscious attention to the sound.

Technical Listening

Technical listening focuses on the formal relationships of the musical sounds. This mode of listening may result in your identification of the musical form or awareness of specific changes in any of the elements of music that will be introduced in the next two chapters (i.e., melody, harmony, texture, timbre, or rhythm).

Timbre (TAM-ber)

Technical listening focuses on the formal relationships of the musical sounds.

Most music instruction relies solely on this mode of listening to develop appreciation. However, while it is an important learning tool (and will be used as a major part of this text), technical observation should not be the only mode of listening you develop.

Insightful Listening

Music is an artistic medium capable of symbolizing emotional experiences. Music becomes expressive and meaningful when you as the listener associate the musical sounds you hear with personal feelings or experiences you have had. Such feelings and experiences reflect complex combinations of memories, moods, and emotions unique to each individual that cannot be expressed clearly or adequately by words. The result is that music gives humankind a mode of expression that transcends the limitations of language.

Given this, the listener who concentrates only on the formal relationships of sound may find the experience intellectually interesting, but he will fall short of appreciating the real purpose of music as an art form. Musical expressiveness is a function of much more than mathematical relationships of time and sound. Indeed, these formal relationships do open avenues of expression for human emotions, but in order to *utilize* this avenue of expression, the listener must combine technical

Background music can be used in the workplace to increase worker accuracy and productivity.
©UPI/Bettmann Newsphotos

perceptions with personal observations and/or reflections in a process of *imaginative perception.*

The goal, then, of insightful listening is perception of meaning. At the beginning of this chapter you were asked to listen to how meaning was expressed in three different pieces of music. Although it may be difficult or impossible to put this meaning into exact words, by using imaginative perception you, as a listener, can try to share the composer's insight into the realm of human feeling. Again, exercise the use of *imaginative perception,* which combines *technical listening* and *personal experience.* The result can be a very rewarding experience that is unique to music listening.

Insightful listening utilizes technical listening and personal experience through imaginative perception to realize expressiveness and meaning in music.

Personal Experience
        \
        Imaginative Perception ⟶ **Insightful Listening**
        /
Technical Listening   (Perception of meaning)

Of course, perception of sound events in the abstract may be an enjoyable activity in much the same way as is putting together a picture puzzle. Identification of individual pieces and their proper places in the whole can be very satisfying. But there is potential for a greater reward in the perception of music than in the completion of a jigsaw puzzle. Putting pieces in the right places to match a picture on a box top requires no creative thought—just accurate perception accompanied by abundant trial and error.

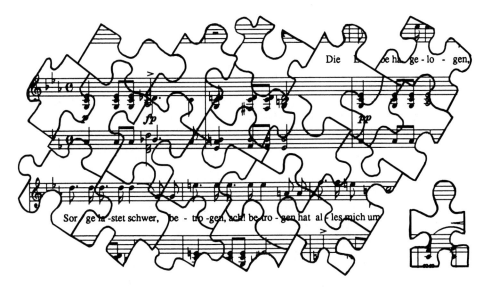

The accurate perception of music, however, can be enriched by the addition of imagination based on personal life experiences. The unique perspective that each listener brings to a musical composition leads to an equally unique imaginative musical perception.

Composer, Performer and You, the Listener

Expressive interaction with music is realized for the *composer* in the creation of a work and for the *performer* in the interpretation and re-creation of a work. As a *listener* your interaction begins when you select *which* music you want to hear. If you engage in insightful listening, you begin to attach feelings or images of feelings to the musical experience through imaginative perception. This is not a passive activity. In effect, you—the listener—are sharing the composer's insight into the realm of human feeling as interpreted and re-created by the performer.

Self-Expression and Listening

The focus of this text is music listening. As a listener, your choice of music may be based at times upon a very specific rationale and at other times merely upon whim and chance. What are your musical *preferences*—the choices you make? They might be very broad ("classical" music or "rock and roll") or quite narrow (Beethoven sonatas or Beatles albums). Preferences are frequently revealed in your expression of opinion. What music do you *appreciate*—not only choose but "understand"? What music do you *value*—by affirming that appreciation with repeated actions?

Preference. An act of choosing one thing over another (enjoyment)

Appreciation. Preference accompanied by an awareness of salient characteristics

Value. A choice made freely from alternatives that is cherished and affirmed to others through repeated actions

---

As you can see, various pieces of music may fall into different categories for each listener. Over a period of time your musical values may change. Do you own any recordings that you played frequently when you first bought them, but to which you rarely listen anymore? These seldom-used recordings may reflect your change of musical values.

Why do you like some music and dislike other music? How do you decide if you like a piece or not? Why do you tire of some pieces and never seem to tire of others? Have you ever thought about what influences your musical preferences, appreciations, and values?

Research indicates that two of the strongest influences on your musical preferences are (1) repetition and (2) perception of approval by someone who is significant to you. This means that your musical choices are frequently determined simply by your repeated exposure to certain pieces (hence the importance of air time for a song trying to climb the "Top 40") and by the opinions of friends and authority figures (i.e., anyone from disc jockeys to respected musicians or teachers).

Think about your own musical preferences, appreciations and values. To what extent can you honestly say they reflect totally independent and objective consideration? Do you see repetition and approval by others as having a significant role in the development of your musical choices?

By developing your modes of *technical and insightful listening,* you will have a better understanding of your own *musical preferences, appreciations,* and *values.* Music listening can become less frequently a mere *subconscious activity,* and the *imaginative perception* of music can open to you a new range of experiences through the *expressiveness of music.*

CHAPTER TWO

Time

. . . .

Preview of Terms and Concepts

Music is a temporal phenomenon, i.e., it exists in **time.** Musical **rhythm** is the duration of sound and the illusion of movement of that sound in time.

The most obvious aspect of rhythm is **beat** or steady pulse. The steady beat may have a fast or slow **tempo** (speed of the beat).

Musical notation of rhythm assigns time values to **notes** and **rests** *to indicate different lengths of sound and silence.*

Time signatures and **measures** help to organize these notes and rests into recognizable patterns.

The grouping of beats through **accents** (emphasis) results in **meter.**

usic is a temporal phenomenon; it exists in time. The duration and illusion of movement of music in time is called *rhythm*—from the Greek word *rhyth- mos* meaning measured motion.

Life is full of measured motions or rhythms. Your heartbeat, regular breathing, the rise and set of the sun, the change of seasons—each provides a different level of movement. **Musical rhythm** is created by the illusion of movement through changes of sounds in time. These rhythmic similarities of life and music provide some clues to the power of music to reflect and symbolize the realm of human feelings (as discussed in Chapter 1).

Musical rhythm is the duration of sound and illusion of movement of that sound in time.

Music has an illusion of movement through time rather than through space. However, while we generally think of movement through time in terms of *unit* measures with absolute values (for example, seconds, minutes, hours, etc.), the movement of music through time is more often perceived in terms of *rhythmic* activity or motion. Listen to the following example and compare the feelings of motion among the different musical instruments as created by the rhythmic activity.

Listening Guide
Motion

· ·

 C. Ives: The Unanswered Question

Strings. Very slow-moving and static; remain constant throughout.

Trumpet. Enters with the same musical material seven times; moves moderately fast compared with the strings.

Flutes. Most active of the three; enter six times, each time more active than the previous time.

Beat

The most obvious aspect of rhythm is beat or pulse, which is usually steady. If you will listen to any march or popular dance tune, you will easily detect a strong steady beat. Even though there may not be any single instrument playing just the steady beat, there is a feeling of cohesiveness and regularity of pulse in these kinds of music.

The easiest way to detect the beat is to move to it. Tap along with the steady beat in several of the following examples.

Listening Guide
Steady Beat

· ·

W. A. Mozart: Symphony No. 40 in G Minor
          I. Allegro molto

L. van Beethoven: Symphony No. 3
          I. Allegro con brio

F. Schubert: Erlking

B. Smith: Lost Your Head Blues

Wolfgang Amadeus Mozart (VULF-gahng Ah-mah-DAY-oos MOHT-zart)

Allegro (ah-LEH-groh)

Franz Schubert (Frahntz SHOO-bert)

As you can hear, each of these selections, like most music that is familiar to us, has a fairly strong and obvious steady beat. Even without a dominant marchlike drumbeat or captivating dance beat, the pulse of the music is a constant factor providing a sense of rhythmic security and cohesiveness.

Since the steady beat provides a common unifying factor for most musical works, pieces without such a pulse must rely upon some other musical element or elements to hold them together. As you become more aware of how all of the elements of music can be used, you will be able to hear alternative methods of unification. For now, try listening to several of the following examples that *lack* a steady beat. See if you can perceive what contributes unification or organization for these examples.

Listening Guide
Absence of Steady Beat

· ·

J. Coltrane: Ascension
K. Penderecki: Threnody: To the Victims of Hiroshima
P. Grainger: Lincolnshire Posey (opening section)
E. Varèse: Ionisation
E. Varèse: Poème Électronique
V. Ussachevsky: Of Wood and Brass

Penderecki (PEN-de-retz-kee)

Figure 2.1
Today, metronomes may be mechanical or electronic.

Photo courtesy of MIDCO International, reprinted by permission.

Tempo

Tempo (TEM-poh)

The speed of the beat, referred to as **tempo,** can be described in several ways. Very general terms such as fast, medium, and slow provide the most basic of comparisons for the casual listener. Composers and performers make use of much more specific Italian terms, but even these are only *relative* indications open to various interpretations. The most exact way to measure tempo is with a metronome marking, which refers the performer to an absolute time ratio for determining the speed at which the beat should be counted (for example, M.M. = 120). The abbreviation M.M. stands for Maelzel's Metronome, a clocklike machine that can be set to tick at various speeds. The number indicates how many beats per minute the machine should be set to tick (fig. 2.1). This figure may vary from approximately 40 to over 200.

Tempo is the speed of the beat. It can be indicated by either general descriptive terms or by a precise number of beats per minute.

Common Italian Terms Used to Indicate Tempo

Largo	extremely slow, broad
Lento	very slow
Adagio	slow ("at ease")
Andante	"walking" tempo
Moderato	moderate
Allegro	fast ("cheerful")
Presto	very fast

Adagio (ah-DAH-jyoh)

These Italian terms are commonly used in the titles of works and sections of works (i.e., movements) to indicate tempo. Additional terms may also be used to further indicate the style in which the music is to be performed or to describe its form. For example, the following titles of movements give considerable information about each piece before you even hear it.

Mozart: Symphony No. 40 in G Minor

    I.   Allegro molto (very fast)
   II. Andante (walking tempo)
 III. Menuetto. Allegretto (in the style of a minuet dance; not quite as fast as allegro)
 IV. Finale. Allegro assai (very fast)

Andante (ahn-DAHN-teh)

Allegretto (ah-leh-GRET-toh)

Finale (fee-NAH-leh)

Assai (ah-SAHY)

Haydn: Trumpet Concerto in E♭

    I. Allegro (fast)
   II. Andante (walking tempo)
 III. Allegro (fast)

Beethoven: Symphony No. 3

    I.   Allegro con brio (fast, with brilliance)
   II. Marcia funebre. Adagio assai (in the style of a funeral march, very slow)
 III. Scherzo. Allegro vivace ("joke," extremely fast)
 IV. Finale. Allegro molto (very fast)

Funebre (feu-NE-bruh)

Vivace (vee-VAH-cheh)

Scherzo (SKEHR-tzoh)

Notation of Rhythm

The notation of musical rhythm within a piece is accomplished with a system of symbols that include note heads, stems, flags and beams, dots, rests, bar lines, and meter (or time) signatures.

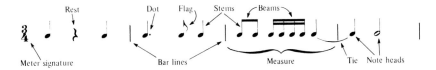

Most rhythms can be understood in relation to the quarter note (♩ or ♪), which is usually given a value of one beat. Other note values in relative proportion are as follows:

♩   =   quarter note   =   1

♩·   =   dotted half note   =   3

♩   =   half note   =   2

𝅝   =   whole note   =   4

Note values shorter than the quarter note are indicated with flags.

♪   =   eighth note   =   ½

♬   =   sixteenth note   =   ¼

Two or more notes of the same value occurring in succession can also be written with beams.

♪ ♪   may also be written   ♫

♪♪♪♪   may also be written   ♫♫

♪ ♪♪   may also be written

Ties are used to join the value of two notes into one sound. (A single sound lasts for the value of the two notes.)

𝅗𝅥   𝅘𝅥   𝅝   𝅗𝅥   ♩   ♪

2   +   1   =   3   4   +   2   =   6   1   +   ½   =   1½

Dots are used to increase a note length by half its value.

𝅗𝅥·   =   𝅗𝅥 ___ 𝅘𝅥   =   3

2   +   1

♩·   =   ♩ ___ ♪   =   1½

1   +   ½

♪·   =   ♪ ___ ♬   =   ¾

½   +   ¼

For each note value there is a **rest** of equivalent value to indicate *silence* for the same length time.

▬	whole rest	= 4		⸲	eighth rest	= ½
▬	half rest	= 2		⸲	sixteenth rest	= ¼
⸲	quarter rest	= 1				

Musical rhythms are usually felt in groupings of 2, 3, 4, 5, or 6 steady beats of time. This grouping of beats—called **meter**—is notated by the use of a meter signature and measures (sometimes called **bars**) separated by bar lines.

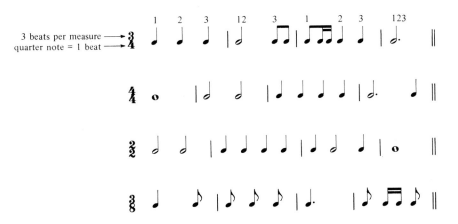

The meter signature (also called a **time signature**) is not an indication of a fraction; rather, the top number tells how many *beats* to count in each measure and the bottom number tells which *note value* is assigned one beat.

Look at the rhythmic notation for the "Star Spangled Banner." Tap a steady beat as you say the words in proper rhythm. Notice which words are the same length as a steady beat and which are longer or shorter than the steady beat.

Meter is the grouping of beats.
An accent is a stress or emphasis on a particular beat.

Listening for Meter

Beats are usually grouped into patterns of twos, threes, fours, or sixes. Other group-ings, such as fives, sevens, and larger numbers, are utilized less frequently. Each of these groupings, or *meters* as they are termed in music, is delineated by emphasis or stress called an accent.

Meter is a very powerful aspect of rhythm. Experience how meter can alter the feeling of a rhythm with the following experiment:

Clap the following series of twelve steady beat quarter notes without accents.

Now try the same number of beats but with a louder clap on those indicated with the > (accent mark) above.

Compare this grouping of two with the following grouping of three.

Even this simple steady beat has a different feel when grouped by accents into twos and threes.

Now try the same thing with a rhythm pattern. First practice (if you need to do so) clapping the following steady beat (of quarter notes).

Next clap a pattern of sounds twice as fast (of eighth notes).

Now practice switching back and forth between the two patterns without pausing.

Be sure to keep the pulse steady as you switch between the two. (It may be helpful to say "one" for the steady beat or quarter note pattern and "one-and" for the faster eighth note pattern.)

Now try applying your basic rhythm reading skills to this simple rhythm. Clap the following pattern (or listen to someone clap it) without meter or grouping.

Next apply the following accents as they are indicated to created groupings of two (duple) and three (triple).

Even though the rhythm is the same in the two preceding examples, the change in grouping or meter gives them a considerably different effect.

Meter has an equally strong influence on the music to which you listen. Practice listening for the meter in the following examples. Find the steady beat (by tapping along if that helps) and then try to feel where regular emphasis occurs—every second, third, or fourth steady beat. Note that groupings of two (duple) and four (quadruple) may have only subtle differences that are not always identifiable by ear.

Listening Guide
Meter (groupings of 2, 3, and 4)

· ·

		Grouping or Meter
	J. S. Bach: Prelude in C Major	4
	J. S. Bach: Fugue in G Minor	4
	J. S. Bach: Cantata 140	
	I. Chorus	3
	F. Haydn: Concerto in E♭	
	I. Allegro	4
	II. Andante	3
	III. Allegro	2
	W. A. Mozart: Symphony No. 40 in G Minor	
	I. Allegro	4
	III. Menuetto	3

Franz Joseph Haydn
(Frahntz YO-sef
HAHY-dn)

[cassette icon] **L. van Beethoven:** Symphony No. 3
          I. Allegro con brio   3

Ludwig van Beethoven (LUHD-vig fahn BAY-toh-ven)

[cassette icon] **F. Schubert:** Erlking   4

[cassette icon] **B. Smith:** Lost Your Head Blues   4

Listening Guide
Duple and Triple

· ·

[cassette icon] **A. Gabrieli:** Ricercar on the Twelfth Tone

Gabrieli (Gah-bree-EL-ee)

Ricercar (REE-cher-kar)

This work for four brass instruments changes between quadruple and triple meter several times. (Because of the very active rhythm, the quadruple meter may be easier to count by twos rather than by fours.)

Timing	Meter	Description
0′00″	quadruple	Starts with trombones imitated by trumpets
0′50″	triple	New melody, slightly faster; trombones begin, imitated by trumpets
1′10″	quadruple	Brief transition back to . . .
1′20″	triple	Same melody as previous triple section
1′40″	quadruple	Brief transition back to . . .
1′50″		Opening melody, stays in quadruple to end (2′20″)

All of the examples above represent what is called **simple meter** and use time signatures such as $\frac{2}{4}$, $\frac{3}{4}$ and $\frac{4}{4}$. **Compound meter** adds another level of rhythm to the feeling of grouping. Count the following steady pattern several times at different speeds with an accent where indicated (emphasize "1" more than "4"):

$$\overset{>}{1} \quad 2 \quad 3 \quad \overset{>}{4} \quad 5 \quad 6 \qquad \overset{>}{1} \quad 2 \quad 3 \quad \overset{>}{4} \quad 5 \quad 6$$

If the pattern is counted slowly, you can feel the grouping in six. If counted very quickly, you may start to hear the broader grouping of twos with each of those subdivided into threes.

Try feeling compound meter with the rhythmic notation for one of the following songs. As you sing or say the words in time, tap the steady beat in a broad two and then in a moderate six.

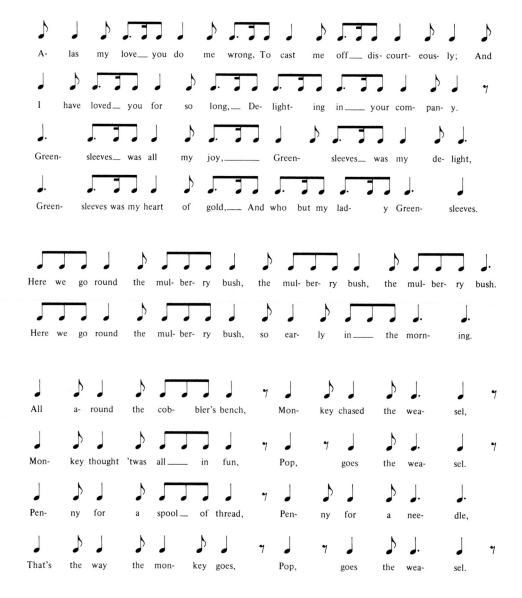

A- las my love___ you do me wrong, To cast me off___ dis- court- eous- ly; And

I have loved___ you for so long,___ De- light- ing in ___ your com- pan- y.

Green- sleeves___ was all my joy,_____ Green- sleeves___ was my de- light,

Green- sleeves was my heart of gold,___ And who but my lad- y Green- sleeves.

Here we go round the mul- ber- ry bush, the mul- ber- ry bush, the mul- ber- ry bush.

Here we go round the mul- ber- ry bush, so ear- ly in ___ the morn- ing.

All a- round the cob- bler's bench, Mon- key chased the wea- sel,

Mon- key thought 'twas all ___ in fun, Pop, goes the wea- sel.

Pen- ny for a spool ___ of thread, Pen- ny for a nee- dle,

That's the way the mon- key goes, Pop, goes the wea- sel.

While the meter signature in these examples indicates six beats per measure, with the eighth note counted as one beat, a quicker moving tempo will make the dotted quarter feel like the main beat and the eighth notes like subdivisions in threes.

Besides $\frac{6}{8}$, the most common examples of compound meter are $\frac{9}{8}$ and $\frac{12}{8}$. The meter $\frac{9}{8}$ can be felt in a moderate- to quick-moving group of nine or a broad group of three. The meter $\frac{12}{8}$ can be felt in similar groupings of twelve or four. When $\frac{6}{8}$, $\frac{9}{8}$, or $\frac{12}{8}$ meter are felt in two, three, and four, respectively, there is an underlying triple subdivision of each beat. This is the characteristic that distinguishes compound meter from simple meter.

The following time signatures are referred to as compound because their basic steady beat note value is divisible by three.

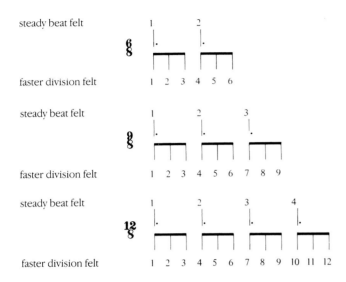

steady beat felt

faster division felt

steady beat felt

faster division felt

steady beat felt

faster division felt

Simple meter is a grouping of beats with note values divisible by two.
Compound meter is the accented grouping of beats in multiples of discernible three-count subdivisions.

Listen to the following examples that use the compound meter. In each of these the tempo is fast enough that you will probably hear in the first two pieces groupings of two beats and in the third piece groupings of three beats. Try to listen also for the subdivision of each broader beat into threes, thus accounting for the full six or nine beats you see in the time signature.

Listening Guide
Compound Meter

. . . .

B. Smetana: The Moldau (opening section)   6/8

J. S. Bach: "Gigue" from Partita No. 5 in G Major   6/8

J. S. Bach: Jesu, Joy of Man's Desiring   9/8

Bedrich Smetana
(BAYD-rik
SMEH-teh-nuh)

Gigue (zheeg)

Partita (par-TEE-tah)

When you attend a live program of music performed by a group of musicians led by a conductor, you might enjoy *watching* for meter. One way in which the conductor may choose to lead the group is to show the meter through conducting motions. Common beat patterns for simple meters are as follows:

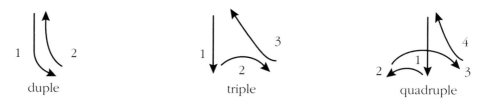

duple   triple   quadruple

Notice that the strongest beat of each pattern—the first one—is always given in a downward motion. (Hence, it is called the "downbeat.") Compound meter in a slow six would use this pattern:

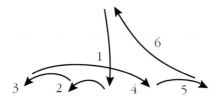

From the conductor's viewpoint, the first beat is always down and the last beat is always up from the right. Try beating some of these patterns along with recordings to *feel and see* the groupings of beats.

Additional Listening

Duple or quadruple meter
Most "Top 40" songs
S. Joplin: The Entertainer
G. F. Handel: "Halleluia" from *Messiah*
G. F. Handel: "Glory to God" from *Messiah*
L. van Beethoven: Symphony No. 5, I.
J. S. Bach: Brandenburg Concerto No. 5 in D Major, I.

Triple meter
Any piece titled "Waltz"
J. S. Bach: Passacaglia in C Minor

Compound meter
J. S. Bach: Fugue in G Major (WTC, Bk. 1)
W. A. Mozart: Symphony No. 40 in G Minor, K. 550, II.
A. Vivaldi: Concerto for Violin and Orchestra in E, op. 8, no. 1, III.

Passacaglia
(pah-sah-KAHL-yah)

Antonio Vivaldi
(An-TOH-nee-oh
Vee-VAHL-dee)

Other Meters (Optional)

The sequential combination of a grouping of two with a grouping of three on a regular basis results in a grouping of five. This somewhat unconventional meter can occur as either of the following patterns:

$$\overset{>}{1} \quad 2 \quad 3 \quad \overset{>}{4} \quad 5 \qquad \overset{>}{1} \quad 2 \quad \overset{>}{3} \quad 4 \quad 5$$

(most common)

Listening Guide
Groupings of Five

. . . .

D. Brubeck: Take Five $(3 + 2)$
P. Hindemith: "Fugue No. 2 in G" from Ludus Tonalis
A. Lloyd-Webber: "Everything's Alright" from Jesus Christ Superstar $(3 + 2)$
P. I. Tchaikovsky: Symphony No. 6 in B Minor, op. 74
            II. Allegro con grazia $(2 + 3)$
G. Holst: The Planets, Op. 32,
         "Mars, the Bringer of War" $(3 + 2)$

Hindemith
(HIN-de-mit)

**Peter Ilich
Tchaikovsky** (EEL-yitch
Chahy-KAWV-skee)

Grazia (GRAH-tzee-ah)

Over the years composers have experimented with various other meters—sometimes with unusual results. Listen to as many of these examples as you are able to find.

Listening Guide
Meters Other Than 2, 3, 4, 5, or 6

. . . .

Dave Brubeck: Unsquare Dance $(2 + 2 + 3 = 7)$
            (see also other early albums by Brubeck for many additional
            examples of unusual meter)
Dave Brubeck: Unisphere ($\frac{10}{4}$)
Riegger: New Dance (mostly $\frac{7}{4}$)

Some music changes meter almost continually to create a constant feeling of the unexpected. This kind of changing meter can be very complex and difficult to follow as a listener—at least on a technical basis. Listen to some of these examples and notice the unpredictable occurrence of accents as a result of rapidly changing meters.

Listening Guide
Changing Meters

. . . .

Celesta
(cheh-LESS-tah)
Copland (KOH-pland)

I. Stravinsky: L'Histoire du Soldat (The Soldier's Tale)

B. Bartok: Music for Strings, Percussion and Celesta, I.

A. Copland: Music for the Theatre, II. Dance

D. Brubeck: Blue Rondo a la Turk

L. Bernstein: West Side Story, ''Symphonic Dance''

B. Bartok: Mikrokosmos, Vol. V, No. 126

CHAPTER THREE

Sound

(Pitch, Dynamics)

. . . .

Preview of Terms and Concepts

Pitch refers to the highness or lowness of sound.

Musical notation uses a **staff, clef, key signature, sharps** and **flats.**

A succession of pitches and time values with a sense of cohesiveness results in a **melody.** Pitches sounded together produce **harmony.** The relationship of melody to other melodies or harmony is described as **texture.**

The volume (loudness or softness) of musical sound is described as **dynamics.**

I n addition to duration, or rhythm, musical sounds generally exhibit pitch, timbre and volume. Together, these characteristics constitute the fundamental tools with which the composer can manipulate sounds in the creative process of musical composition. Musical notation is the shorthand used to communicate on paper the specific intentions of the composer with regard to these four basic characteristics, so that the music is performed in a manner as close to the composer's original idea as possible (fig. 3.1).

Figure 3.1
Musical score of Beethoven's Symphony No. 3.

Pitch

Pitch refers to the highness or lowness of sound. Definite pitch (i.e., pitch that can be duplicated exactly from one time to the next) is acoustically determined by the number of vibrations or cycles per second (cps) being produced by a given musical instrument. Some percussion instruments such as drums or cymbals produce indefinite pitches, which do not maintain a constant number of vibrations per second. These sounds are perceived by the ear more generally—as high or low without being identifiable by a specific pitch name.

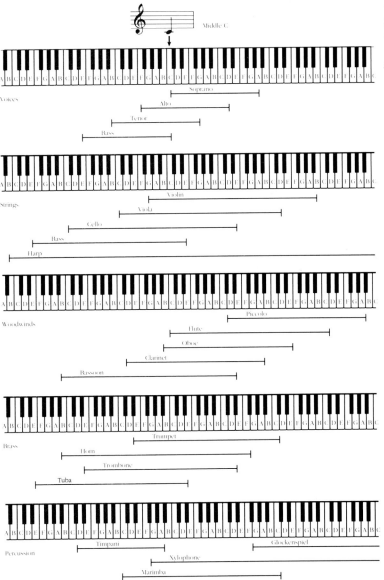

Figure 3.2
Comparison of instrument ranges on piano keyboard.

Notation of Pitch

The notation of musical pitch uses the rhythmic symbols called notes (described in Chapter 2) on a **staff,** with **clef signs, ledger lines, key signatures, sharps** and **flats,** as shown below in Figure 3.3.

Figure 3.3
Grand staff with terms.

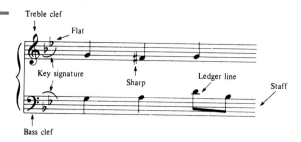

Notes are placed on the lines or in the spaces of a **staff** (plural is **staves**), which consists of five horizontal lines.

The staff can be extended with **ledger lines** to indicate pitches above or below it.

The pitch range of the staff is determined by a **clef sign** at the beginning. The two most common clefs are called **bass** and **treble.**

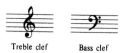

The treble clef or "G clef" wraps around the "G line" to indicate G above middle C. (Middle C is located near the middle of the piano keyboard.)

Treble clef with G

The bass clef is also referred to as the "F clef" because the two dots in its clef sign are placed on either side of the "F line" below middle C.

Bass clef with F

While the piano makes full use of both clefs, other instruments may use the treble or bass clef depending upon how high or how low they generally play. Figure 3.4 shows the relationship of the bass and treble clefs to the piano keyboard.

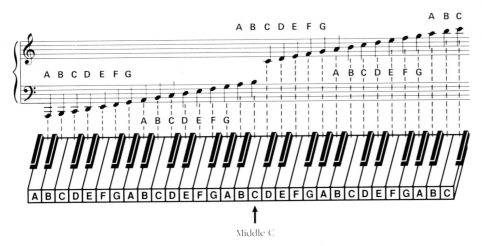

Middle C

Figure 3.4
Keyboard and staff.

The distance from one adjacent piano key to the next produces the pitch relationship called a **half step.** The distance between two half steps is called a **whole step.**

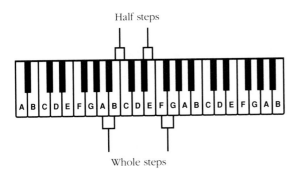

Half steps

Whole steps

In notation a pitch can be raised one-half step by placing a sharp sign (♯) in front of it and lowered one-half step by placing a flat sign (♭) in front of it. The **key signature** at the beginning of the staff indicates which pitches are to be played throughout with sharps or flats (fig. 3.5). When a sharp appears on a particular line or

Figure 3.5
A musical score with symbols indicating both pitch and rhythm.

Beethoven SYMPHONY NO. 3, Eulenburg Edition
© 1987 Ernst Eulenburg Ltd.
All Rights Reserved
Used by permission of European American Music
Distributors Corporation, agent for Ernst Eulenburg Ltd.

space of the staff directly to the right of the clef sign, all the notes that appear on that line or space are to be automatically played (or sung) a half step higher. (Key will be explained further within the context of harmony later in this chapter.)

Notation of pitch	**Notation of rhythm**
staff	measures
clef signs	bar lines
pitches	notes and rests
key signature	time signature
sharps	beams, flags, dots, ties
flats	tempo markings

All of these symbols work together to create a visual representation of music. While they may seem very precise, these "performance instructions" really provide only part of the information required. As you proceed through this book, you will see that many other factors contribute to the final performance of a musical score and thus to the ultimate expressiveness of a work of music.

Melody

Melody is a succession of pitches and time values, usually with a sense of cohesiveness. This *horizontal* movement in music, which can be seen in the following example, is sometimes referred to as the "melodic line."

The melody or tune of a piece is often one of the first musical elements that attracts our attention—as well as the one most easily remembered when the piece is over. If someone were to ask you "how a piece goes," you might reply by singing or humming a bit of the melody.

A melody can be . . .
    smooth (conjunct) or jagged (disjunct)
    performed by one instrument or shared by several instruments
    isolated or performed with other melodies
    rhythmically active or static
    complex or simple.

Listening Guide
Melody

. . . .

S. Barber: Adagio for Strings	*smooth (conjunct)*	
B. Smetana: The Moldau (river theme)		
A. Webern: Three Songs, 1. Schatzerl Klein	*jagged (disjunct)*	**Anton von Webern** (AHN-tohn fun VAY-bayrn)
C. Ives: The Unanswered Question (solo trumpet)		
Paul Winter Consort: Eagle	*single melody alone*	
Gregorian Chant (any example)		
J. S. Bach: Fugue in C Major, WTC Bk. I	*several melodies (3)*	
F. Schubert: Erlking	*melody performed by a single voice (with accompaniment)*	
L. Beethoven: Symphony No. 3 I. Allegro con brio	*melody shared by many instruments*	
I. Stravinsky: Greeting Prelude		
K. Penderecki: Threnody: To the Victims of Hiroshima	*no melody*	
E. Varèse: Poème Électronique		
J. S. Bach: Prelude in C Major, WTC Bk. I		
F.J. Haydn: Trumpet Concerto in E♭ II. Andante	*simple melody*	
C. Debussy: Prelude No. 8		**Claude Debussy** (Klohd Day-byoo-SEE)
J. S. Bach: Fugue in C Major, WTC Bk. I	*complex melody*	
H. Berlioz: Symphonie Fantastique V. Larghetto; Allegro		**Berlioz** (BAYR-lee-ohz) **Larghetto** (lahr-GEH-toh)

A single work will usually incorporate and alternate a variety of these melodic characteristics in order to create contrast and interest.

Listening Guide
Melodic variety

· ·

 B. Smetana: The Moldau

0′00″
Conjunct, swirling melody. Two flutes (two streams) very rhythmically active, leading
to . . .
1′00″
Broad, sweeping melody. Strings (river) present strong, full sounding, main melody
2′45″
Disjunct, arpeggiated melody. Horn calls (hunting horns), mixed with swirling sound;
more disjunct than previous melody
3′45″
Rhythmic melody. Light, dancelike (peasant wedding dance); becomes heavier and
more accented, then returns to lighter sound
5′30″
Slow, shimmering melody. Rhythmically static strings with gentle swirling melody of
flute (reflection of moonlight in water), in sharp contrast to previous melody; brass
fanfare leads back to . . .
7′45″
Smooth, broad melody. Strings present the main melody again
8′30″
More complex melody. Full orchestra combines to create exciting, rhythmically active
climax
9′45″
Main melody. Returns in major key and much faster
10′10″
Majestic melody. Brass chorale

Gradual disappearance of swirling melody and rhythmic activity
Two strong chords give feeling of completion (11′40″)

Harmony

Two or more pitches sounded together produce harmony. If you think of melody as a
horizontal aspect of music (melodic line), then it is logical to call harmony a *vertical*
aspect.

Harmony is a very difficult element of music to explain fully without becoming extremely technical. The discussion here will thus be confined to relatively broad concepts and characteristics, some of which can be identified by the following descriptive terms:

Consonant	Dissonant
Functional	Non-functional
Simple	Complex
Diatonic	Chromatic
Tonal	Atonal
Active harmonic rhythm	Static harmonic rhythm

In order to discuss these broader concepts, some specific terms need to be understood: **interval, chord, triad, scales.**

Two pitches sounded together produce a sound that can be described and labeled by the **interval** or distance between the two pitches.

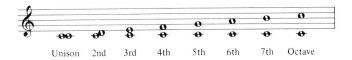

Unison   2nd   3rd   4th   5th   6th   7th   Octave

Three or more pitches sounded together produce a **chord.** The particular intervals present in a chord determine the quality of the chord or its name. The most commonly used chord is the **triad**—a three-note chord constructed with thirds.

Triads

These triads can be used to harmonize a melody—adding a sense of depth to its forward movement.

Triads are generally very **consonant** or stable sounding. As you add more pitches to each triad, the result is less consonance and greater **dissonance**—instability.

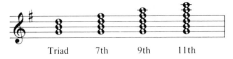

Triad   7th   9th   11th

Consonance and dissonance are relative terms. Consonance is a stable sound that generally pleases the ear; dissonance is less pleasing to the ear. It is interesting to realize, however, that what we consider to be consonant today was thought to be dissonant in Medieval times. Furthermore, a chord perceived to be dissonant in one context may be perceived as consonant when surrounded by even more dissonant chords in a different context.

Functional harmony, a term used to describe a universal system of relationships among chords, has been used in Western music since the Baroque time period. In functional harmony a **pitch center** (also called the **tonic pitch** or **keynote**) is established through a system of chords that progress toward a feeling of repose and stability. The central chord in this feeling is built on the tonic pitch and is called the **tonic chord.** Music with a pitch center is called **tonal** or described as having **tonality.** Listen to someone play the following two progressions. Our familiarity with Western functional harmony makes the second progression more satisfying, as it ends on the pitch center (G) for this tonality (G major).

Tonality is a feeling of pitch center—a melodic and harmonic "home base" to which the music returns.

Scales

In creating music, tonality is achieved by using a framework—a set of pitches arranged in order from low to high (or high to low) to form a **scale.** Scales provide the basic materials for constructing almost all musical compositions. The two most common kinds of scales used in Western music are the **major** scale and **minor** scale. Each scale is built with a particular but constant pattern of half steps (the distance from one pitch to the next closest pitch) and whole steps (the interval of two half steps together), which creates a unique sound discernible to the ear as either major or minor.

For both major and minor scales the pattern of half and whole steps repeats every eight notes to form **octaves.** Figure 3.6 demonstrates the sequence of steps within any given octave for each type of scale.

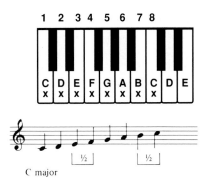

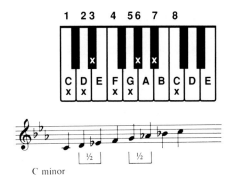

Figure 3.6
The major scale has half steps between the 3rd and 4th and the 7th and 8th scale degrees. Half steps in the minor scale are found between the 2nd and 3rd and the 5th and 6th scale degrees. All other scale degrees are a whole step apart.

When a particular scale is used as the basis for the melody and harmony of a musical composition, the sharps or flats used in that scale are placed at the beginning of each musical staff in the **key signature.** Musical pieces that use a certain scale are said to be "in the key of" that scale (i.e., "in the key of C major"). This indication of key can also be seen in titles of compositions, such as *Symphony in G Minor* and *Prelude and Fugue in C Major.*

Major and minor scales are both **diatonic.** This means that there are seven *different* pitches within the octave and the scale has two half steps and five whole steps. (While octaves are so-named because of their eight pitches, the last pitch is, in most respects, a repetition of the first.) The C major scale contains the following seven **diatonic** pitches—C D E F G A B. If any pitches other than these seven are used in the key of C major, they are referred to as **chromatic.** (A third type of scale, consisting of 12 different pitches within the range of an octave—all separated by equal half steps, is called a **chromatic scale.**) Usually, the greater the use of chromatic pitches, the more complex and dissonant the music becomes. This can create tension and instability, which resolve with the return to diatonic pitches and the pitch center or tonic.

A series of pitches arranged in order from low to high or high to low is called a scale.
A diatonic scale consists of seven different pitches per octave including two half steps and five whole steps.
Pitches outside of the diatonic scale are called chromatic.
A chromatic scale consists of twelve pitches all separated by equal half steps.

Sometimes these chromatic pitches are used to move to a new pitch center thus creating a change of pitch centers—**modulation.**

Twentieth-century music has experimented with increased dissonance, sometimes to the point of avoiding a pitch center altogether. This music is called **atonal,** which means absence of tonality.

Harmony can also be perceived as relatively active or static, a characteristic determined by the rate at which chords change. Frequent chord changes give a feeling of **active harmonic rhythm,** while relatively few chord changes result in **static harmonic rhythm.** Active or static harmonic rhythm can contribute to the overall perception of motion in a piece of music.

A change of pitch centers is called a modulation.

Music that has no pitch center is called atonal.

Music may be perceived to be harmonically active or static, depending upon how frequently the chords change.

Listen to the following musical examples to compare general harmonic differences.

Listening Guide
Harmony

· ·

T. Morley: My Bonnie Lass **G. F. Handel:** Messiah, "Glory to God"		*predominantly consonant, tonal, mostly diatonic*
H. Berlioz: Symphonie Fantastique **F. Chopin:** Prelude No. 4 in E Minor, Op. 28 **W. A. Mozart:** Requiem, K. 626		*greater use of dissonance but tonal (more chromatic)*
K. Penderecki: Threnody: To the Victims of Hiroshima **A. Schoenberg:** A Survivor from Warsaw		*atonal, very dissonant*
F. Chopin: Polonaise in A♭ Major		*active harmonic rhythm*
J. S. Bach: Prelude in C Major **B. Smith:** Lost Your Head Blues **R. Wagner:** Das Rheingold, "Prelude"		*static harmonic rhythm*

Frédéric Chopin
(FRED-er-rick SHOH-pan)

Schoenberg
(SHEHRN-bayrg)

Polonaise
(poh-loh-NEHZ)

Richard Wagner
(REE-kard VAG-ner)

Texture

The relationship of a melody to other melodies or harmony is called **texture.** Just as different kinds of threads can be woven together to create various textures, melody and harmony can be combined in different ways to create a variety of textures. The four kinds of musical texture generally found in Western music are **monophonic, polyphonic, homophonic** and **nonmelodic.** (A fifth texture—heterophonic—will be described in Chapter 18.)

    Monophonic texture consists of a single melody without accompaniment. For centuries this was the only kind of texture used, but today it usually occurs in brief passages only—for contrast or emphasis. Note that this texture is defined by the presence of a single melody—not by the number of instruments or voices performing that melody. The following melody remains monophonic, regardless of whether one person sings it or one hundred people sing it.

The texture of fabric is determined by the material used and how the threads are woven together.
© The Bettmann Archive

Graphically, this could be represented by a single line that follows the contour of the melody.

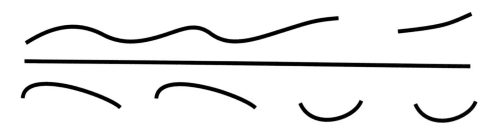

As soon as a second melody is added, the texture changes. **Polyphonic texture,** usually the most complex kind, occurs when two or more melodies are played or sung at once. The melodies must be rhythmically independent and have relatively equal interest. The same children's tune becomes polyphonic when sung as a round, with the second and third repetitions of the melody line overlapping the first. Notice that the melodies are not moving rhythmically at the same time and are of equal interest.

Graphically, this could be represented by several contoured lines stacked on top of one another.

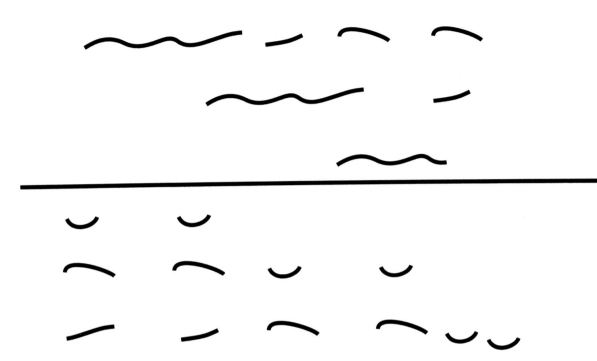

The most common kind of texture, **homophonic,** consists of melody with accompaniment. The accompaniment in its simplest form may consist of block chords or broken chords. Block chords sound all pitches simultaneously; broken chords (also called **arpeggios**) separate the individual pitches of the chord into a rhythmic pattern. The same musical example used above would look like this in the homophonic textures just described:

The next example is a graphic representation of these textures.

Increasing or decreasing the rhythmic activity of the chords does not change their role as accompaniment. All of these variations may sound quite different from one another, but they still preserve the relationship of melody to accompaniment called homophonic texture.

Non-melodic texture, a somewhat unusual form, is traditionally reserved for interludes or transitions between sections of a larger work to provide contrast. Thus, while some twentieth-century works ignore melody throughout (focusing instead on other elements—such as rhythm or timbre), there are few examples of *wholly* nonmelodic works from earlier periods. One such work, however—the J. S. Bach *Prelude No. 1 in C Major*—provides a clear illustration of nonmelodic texture in a tonal setting. This work consists entirely of a series of broken or arpeggiated chords that sustain interest through their harmonic movement. The simple, repetitious rhythm and the absence of a melody allow the harmony to remain central to the listener's attention.

Texture is the relationship of a melody to other melodies or harmony.
Monophonic texture consists of a single melody without accompaniment.
Polyphonic texture occurs when you have two or more melodies at once. The melodies must be rhythmically independent and have relatively equal interest.
Homophonic texture consists of a single melody with accompaniment.
Nonmelodic texture is musical sound without melody.

Listening Guide
Texture

. . . .

Gregorian Chant (any example)   *monophonic texture*
F. Haydn: Trumpet Concerto in E♭
              (cadenza found near the end of the first movement)

Cadenza (kah-DEN-zah)

Janis Joplin: Mercedes Benz

J. S. Bach: Fugue in G Minor — *polyphonic texture*

J. S. Bach: Cantata No. 140 — **Cantata** (kahn-TAH-tah)
    I. Chorus

J. S. Bach: Cantata No. 140 — *homophonic texture*
    VII. Chorale — *block chord*

G. F. Handel: Messiah
  No. 15 "And the angel said unto them" — *sustained block chords*
  No. 16 "And suddenly there was with the angel" — *broken chords*

J. S. Bach: Prelude in C Major — *nonmelodic*

K. Penderecki: Threnody: To the Victims of Hiroshima

Most composers draw upon a mixture of textures to create interest and variety. Listen to the following musical example and notice the important role taken by texture changes in creating an exciting and varied work.

Listening Guide
Changing Textures

. . . .

G. F. Handel: Messiah, No. 17 "Glory to God"
  (S A T B represent soprano, alto, tenor, and bass voices, respectively.)

Glory to God, Glory to God in the highest,	*S A T, homophonic*
and peace on earth,	*T B, monophonic*
Glory to God, glory to God, Glory to God in the highest	*S A T, homophonic*
and peace on earth,	*T B, monophonic*
goodwill towards men. (many repetitions)	*B T A S entrances, polyphonic, imitative*
Glory to God, glory to God in the highest,	*S A T B, homophonic*
and peace on earth,	
goodwill towards men. (many repetitions)	*imitative, polyphonic, repetitious*

Dynamics

The term used to describe the volume of musical sound (loudness or softness) is **dynamics.** Abbreviations for Italian terms are frequently used to indicate dynamics and changes within dynamics. Some of the most common include:

Mezzo (MET-zoh)

Forte (FOR-teh)

Fortissimo
(for-TEE-see-moh)

Crescendo
(kreh-SHEN-doh)

Decrescendo
(deh-kreh-SHEN-doh)

pp	pianissimo	very soft
p	piano	soft
mp	mezzo piano	medium soft
mf	mezzo forte	medium loud
f	forte	loud
ff	fortissimo	very loud
<	crescendo	gradually louder
>	decrescendo	gradually softer

CHAPTER FOUR

Sound
(Tone Color/Timbre)

. . . .

Preview of Terms and Concepts

Timbre or **tone color** refers to the characteristics of musical sound that enable distinction between voices, instruments, or combinations of instruments. Musical timbre is usually identified as a particular **voice, instrument, family of instruments** or combination of these in conventional or unconventional **ensembles.**

Timbre (TAM-ber)

Timbre and **tone color** are collective terms for those characteristics that enable distinction between different voices, instruments, or combinations of instruments. While all sound (musical as well as nonmusical) is generated by vibrations, timbre is a function of how those vibrations are generated. In music, then, gross differences in timbre distinguish different families of instruments. More subtle but still perceptible differences distinguish specific instruments within those families. Table 4.1 indicates the main families of instruments, the method by which they produce their vibrations, and the main instruments in each family.

Viola (vee-OHL-lah)
Cello (CHEL-loh)

Table 4.1 Families of Instruments

Family	Characteristics	Main instruments
String	have strings bowed or plucked	violin viola cello string bass harp guitar

Woodwind	*Most* have a reed
	  (single or double)
	  (vibration of reed starts air column vibration)
	wood (or metal)
	wind blown
		piccolo
		flute
		oboe
		English horn
		clarinet
		saxophone
		bassoon

Brass	metal cupped or funnel-shaped mouthpiece wind blown (vibration of lips starts air column vibration)	trumpet French horn trombone tuba

Percussion	struck	*melodic* or *nonmelodic*
		timpani snare drum
		xylophone cymbals
		chimes bass drum
		marimba triangle
		bells gong
		                    castanets
		                    wood blocks

Keyboard	sound controlled by a keyboard	piano organ harpsichord
Voice	human vocal production	soprano mezzo-soprano alto tenor baritone bass
Electronic	electronically produced, altered, or amplified	amplified versions of traditional instruments sound synthesizers

Listening Guide
Instrument Families

. . . .

S. Barber: Adagio for Strings — *String family*
W. A. Mozart: Theme and Variations for Wind Instruments — *Woodwind family*
A. Gabrieli: Ricercar on the Twelfth Tone — *Brass family*
E. Varèse: Ionization — *Percussion family*
T. Weelkes: As Vesta Was Descending — *Voices*
F. Chopin: Polonaise in A♭ Major — *Keyboard*
M. Babbitt: Composition for Synthesizer — *Electronic*

String Family

The most common sound from the string family today is that produced by drawing a bow across the string to create a very smooth and almost voicelike quality. String instruments began as plucked instruments. However, it was not until the latter part of the eighth century that bowing became common. Nor were the earliest string instruments made with the hollow body construction necessary to produce the big tone that was finally realized with the introduction of the Greek kithara.

The Middle Ages saw a rise in the use of the "troubadour fiddle," which was both bowed and hollow-bodied. From this fiddle came the viols of the Renaissance and the early Baroque. Modern-day violins appeared in the late 1400s. Their sound production was much improved over that of the viol family, due to stronger construction that included a curved back and a tilted neck. It was only a little more than 200 years later, in the early 1700s, that string instruments still considered to be among the finest were first made by Italian families with famous names such as Amati, Guarnerius, Ruggeri, and Stradivarius.

The rich, singing quality of these modern instruments is achieved by drawing a bow across the strings, causing them to vibrate in a particular pitch. More than one pitch can be sounded at once (called double or triple stops) by drawing the bow across two or three of the strings at once. Changes in pitch are produced when the left hand shortens the length of the strings by pressing them down at various places on the fingerboard. Rocking each finger placement slightly adds warmth or "vibrato" to the tone. Musical variety and accents can be achieved with pizzicato, plucking the strings, or glissando, sliding the finger smoothly on the string. A slight change in the overall sound can be accomplished by using a mute—a device placed on the bridge to deaden some of the vibrations.

A man playing Kithara—a design on an ancient Greek amphora (jar).
The Metropolitan Museum of Art, Fletcher Fund, 1956.

Baroque (Bah-ROHK)
Viol (VAHY-uhl)

Bass viola da gamba.
© The Bettmann Archive

The Juilliard String Quartet.

Photo courtesy of Colbert Artists Management, Inc.

The harp is one of the oldest string instruments. While each individual string can be plucked, the most striking and characteristic timbre is that of the harp "glissando," produced when many of the strings are brushed in succession with a broad motion to create a dramatic and beautiful sweep of sound. While there are many works written for solo harp, you are more likely to hear harp solos as brief interludes in larger orchestral works, where the instrument lends a distinctive color to the full orchestral timbre.

The guitar, while occasionally used in the orchestra, is more frequently played as a solo instrument or as an accompaniment for voice. Like the harp, the strings of the guitar are plucked (or brushed) rather than bowed. Spanish in origin, the guitar was primarily an "amateur's" instrument until the early nineteenth century. At that time, virtuoso players further developed various performance techniques, and the music of Bach, Mozart, and other well-known composers was transcribed for the instrument. Amateur enthusiasts continued to flourish throughout the nineteenth century, including among their ranks such well-known romantic composers as Hector Berlioz and Franz Schubert. Largely through the performances of virtuoso Andres Segovia and a proliferation of original works for the instrument by composers such as Heitor Villa-Lobos, Joaquin Rodrigo, Mario Castelnuovo-Tedesco and Manuel Ponce, the guitar has gained tremendous popularity in the twentiety century as well.

Heitor Villa-Lobos
(AY-tor VEE-yah
LOH-bohs)

Listening Guide
String Family

. . . .

P. I. Tchaikovsky: Violin Concerto in D, Op. 35
L. van Beethoven: Violin Concerto in D, Op. 61
F. Mendelssohn: Violin Concerto in E Minor, Op. 64
J. Brahms: Violin Concerto in D, Op. 77

virtuoso concerti for violin

J. S. Bach: Partita No. 2 for Unaccompanied Violin

use of double and triple stops

J. Brahms: Concerto in A Minor, Op. 102

"double concerto" for violin and cello

B. Bartok: Concerto for Viola and Orchestra
P. Hindemith: Trauermusik

solo works for viola and orchestra

J. Brahms: Sonata for Cello and Piano
(No. 1 in E Minor, Op. 38
No. 2 in F Major, Op. 99)
S. Barber: Concerto for Cello and Orchestra

solo works for cello and orchestra or piano

Figure 4.1
(a) *The clarinet mouthpiece with single reed and the chalumeau mouthpiece from which it developed;* (b) *double reeds* (left to right): *modern bassoon reed, early bassoon reed, modern oboe reed, early oboe reed.*

Photo courtesy Conn Band Instruments.

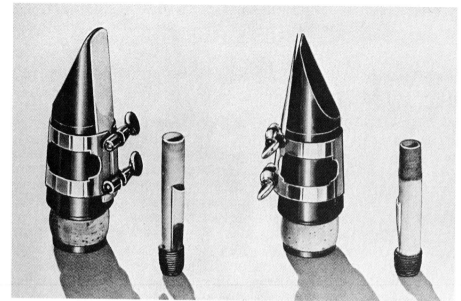

(a)

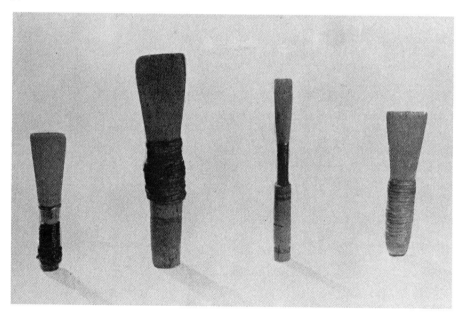

(b)

C. Saint-Saëns: Carnival of the Animals
   "The Elephant"

   *the string basses in a rare
   soli section*

Camille Saint-Saëns
(Kah-MEEL San-SAHNS)

M. Ravel: Introduction and Allegro for Harp and
   Strings
C. Debussy: Prelude to "The Afternoon of a Faun"

works featuring the harp

M. Castelnuovo-Tedesco: Concerto in D Major
J. Ibert: Entr'acte for Flute and Guitar
H. Villa-Lobos: Prelude No. 1 in E Minor

works featuring the guitar

Ibert (ee-BAYR)

Woodwind Family

With the exception of the flute and piccolo, all of the woodwind instruments produce their sound with the help of a small piece of vibrating cane called a **reed.** Single reeds, used for clarinets and saxophones, are clamped on a mouthpiece. Double reeds, used for oboes and bassoons, consist of two pieces of cane wrapped together (fig. 4.1).

The flute is the oldest wind instrument known. Indeed, the principle of blowing across the opening of a cane tube probably dates back long before recorded history. Plato's writings refer specifically to the pipes of Pan, and Socrates even went so far as to accuse those primitive pipes of having an adverse effect on the morality of women. Nonetheless, this ancient instrument has recently been revived and promoted with recordings of popular music. (See recordings by Gheorghe Zamfir.)

While the Latin name for flute, *tibia,* refers to the ancient practice of making flutes from the shinbone of animals, the modern flute is made of metal, usually silver. Sound is produced when air is blown across a hole in its side. Between the ancient pan pipes and our modern version with numerous complex mechanisms for improving fingerings and intonation, the flute went through many adjustments. During the 1500s, two kinds of flutes were popular—the *flauta dolce* (sweet flute, known today as the recorder; fig. 4.2) and the *flauta transverso* (transverse flute, played in the same manner as our modern flute). In order to appreciate the differences between the two flutes, it may be interesting for you to compare recordings of baroque music that include examples of both, sometimes within the same piece.

In 1847, the famous flutist Theobald Boehm, of the Royal Bavarian Court Orchestra, designed the instrument that is the prototype of the modern-day flute. Boehm's design was a significant departure from earlier models in that it was fashioned from metal rather than wood and shaped in a cylinder rather than a cone. Boehm also developed a revolutionary new fingering system that allowed the performer to play more easily in many different keys with excellent intonation. Thanks largely to him, today's flute is one of the most agile and versatile instruments in the symphony orchestra.

Figure 4.2
The recorder family including soprano, alto, tenor, and bass recorders.
© Trophy Music Company

Dolce (DOHL-cheh)
Boehm (Baym)

Elements

The modern family of flutes includes three additional instruments of various sizes (fig. 4.3). Most common is the piccolo, which is about half the size of a regular flute and "sounds" an octave higher. Larger flutes include the alto flute (called the "flute d'amour" during the eighteenth century) and the rarely used bass flute, which sounds an octave below the regular flute.

The clarinet is a single-reed woodwind instrument (fig. 4.4). Although its predecessor, the *chalumeau,* dates back to early Greece, it was almost 1700 before that instrument was improved sufficiently to make it useful on a regular basis by serious composers. Because its improved sound so resembled that of the "clarion" (a high-pitched brass instrument popular at the time), the chalumeau became known as a clarionette (for "small clarion"). Mozart was one of the first major composers to recognize the usefulness of the clarinet in an orchestral setting and even wrote a concerto for it. With many subsequent improvements in the fingering system (similar in effect to what Boehm did for the flute), the modern clarinet makes a dramatic and sonorous contribution to the orchestral woodwind section. It has also become an important member of the symphonic band, frequently playing a role equivalent to the violins in the orchestra.

The clarinet family includes two commonly used larger instruments—the *bass clarinet* and *contrabass clarinet.* These are pitched one and two octaves, respectively, below the clarinet.

Figure 4.3
Modern piccolo and flute (bottom) *and earlier forms.* (1) *panpipes,* (2) *bone flute,* (3) *Chinese flute,* (4) *eighteenth century boxwood flute with four keys.*

Photo courtesy Conn Band Instruments.

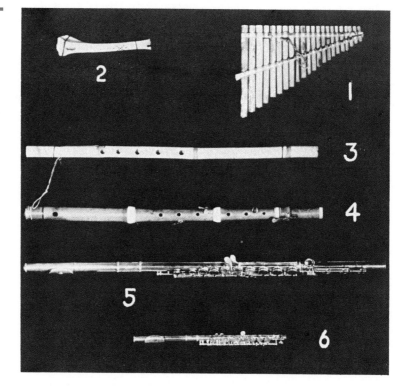

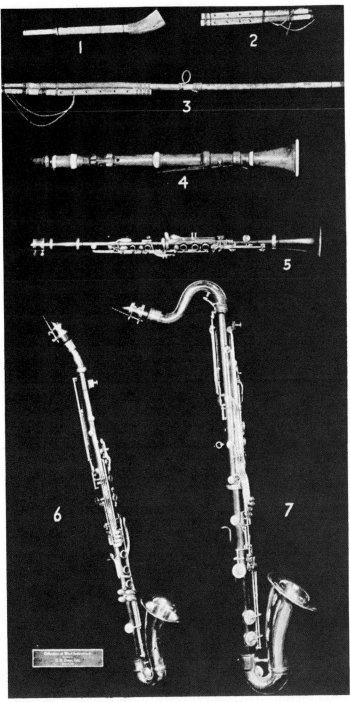

Figure 4.4
Modern B♭ clarinet (5), alto clarinet (6), bass clarinet (7) and earlier forms of the instrument: (1), (2), and (3) primitive chalumeaus, and (4) boxwood clarinet with five brass keys.
Photo courtesy Conn Band Instruments.

Figure 4.5
*Alto, tenor, and baritone
saxophone.*
Photo courtesy Conn Band
Instruments and Selmer-Ludwig
Company.

Although the saxophone is also a single-reed instrument, it is not technically classified among the orchestral instruments (fig. 4.5). The saxophone is a relatively recent invention, dating back only to 1840 when Adolphe Sax first experimented with putting a clarinet mouthpiece on a now obsolete brass instrument called the ophicleide. The result was a unique blend of the brass and reed sound that has immortalized the name of its inventor. While Sax envisioned this instrument becoming a standard part of the orchestra, that notion failed to catch on except, to a limited extent, in France. Instead, the symphonic band and jazz band became the primary homes for the whole family of saxophones, including the soprano, alto, tenor, and baritone.

Ophicleide
(AHF-i-kleed)

The primary double-reed woodwinds include oboe, English horn, and bassoon. While these instruments have an Oriental heritage, which traveled to Europe with the crusaders, primitive double-reed shawms have also been found in ancient Egyptian tombs dating back to 3700 B.C. The name oboe came from the French *hautbois* (or "high wood"), referring to the high pitch of the instrument as well as to its wooden construction (fig. 4.6). Larger shawms developed into the English horn (an alto oboe) and the bassoon (producing an even deeper nasal tone). Bach, Haydn, Mozart, and Beethoven all made increasing use of these double-reeds, giving them an important place in the woodwind section of the orchestra. A larger version of the bassoon, which sounds an octave lower, is called the contrabassoon (fig. 4.7). This huge instrument requires a great deal of breath control and adds a unique low sound to the orchestral timbre.

Hautbois (oh-BWAH)

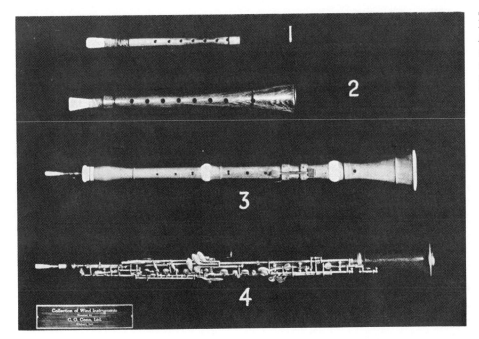

Figure 4.6
*Modern oboe (4) and
earlier versions of the
instrument.*
Photo courtesy Conn Band
Instruments.

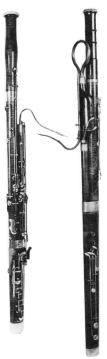

Figure 4.7
*Modern bassoon and
contrabassoon.*

Listening Guide
Woodwind Family
. . . .

J. S. Bach: Sonata in A Minor for Unaccompanied Flute   *flute*
C. Debussy: Prelude to "The Afternoon of a Faun" (opening)
C. Ives: The Unanswered Question

W. A. Mozart: Concerto in A Major for Clarinet and Orchestra,   *clarinet*
         K. 662
C. Saint-Saëns: Carnival of the Animals, "Fossils"

G. F. Handel: Concerto in A Minor for Oboe   *oboe*
J. Sibelius: The Swan of Tuonela   *English horn*
W. A. Mozart: Concerto in B Flat Major for Bassoon and Orches-   *bassoon*
         tra, K. 191

Jan Sibelius (Yahn
See-BAY-lee-uhs)

Brass Family

Brass instruments, with their cup- or funnel-shaped mouthpieces and flared bells, probably find their ancestors in animal horns, nautilus shells, or even simple pieces of hollowed-out wood. The basic concept of a bell shape that amplifies the vibrations created by buzzing the lips in the mouthpiece, remains essentially the same in the trumpet, French horn, trombone, and tuba. The main differences among these instruments are in their sizes, the shape of their tubing (i.e., the passage through which blown air travels), and the method used by the performer to manipulate the length of tubing.

Trumpets of various kinds have been around for centuries (fig. 4.8). From their role in court and martial functions to their popularity in the jazz idiom, trumpets have been versatile and well-received instruments. The ancestors of the trumpet were single, straight tubes. Unique among these was the zinke or cornetto popular in the fifteenth and sixteenth centuries. This instrument, originally made of wood and covered with leather, had six finger holes and a thumb hole and was played through a wooden, cup-shaped mouthpiece. Despite a rather harsh tone, the German zinke and English cornetto enjoyed great popularity. When technological progress enabled the air tubes of these instruments to be bent and curved, the modern trumpet began to take shape. First came a buglelike, conical bore version with no valves. The keyed bugle was invented around 1800 but was short-lived due to the appearance of the piston valve in 1815. The cornet is similar to the trumpet, but again has a conical bore. The cylindrical bore of the trumpet, with its more piercing tone, became the orchestral choice and has remained so today.

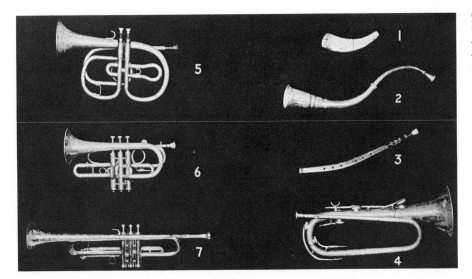

Figure 4.8
Modern trumpet (7) *and several earlier versions of the instrument.*
Photo courtesy Conn Band Instruments.

The French horn is a remarkably versatile instrument equally at home with the brass and woodwind families. While the funnel-shaped mouthpiece, flared bell, modern valve design, and metal construction put this instrument in the brass family, where it can achieve the bold brassy sound of trumpets and trombones, the conical bore contributes to a sonority that blends well with woodwinds. Its versatility is underscored by the common role the instrument plays in both the brass quintet and woodwind quintet—both important small ensembles in their respective families. Originally designed for loud outdoor, over-the-shoulder signals, the horn has had a long and broad history—from the Hebrew *shofar* used in religious services and made from the horn of a ram to the hunting and signal horns of England. It finally received recognition as an orchestral instrument in France—thus the name by which we now know it. With the move "indoors," the horn's player turned the bell down under his arm and placed his hand inside it to partially muffle the strident tone to blend with the softer indoor instruments. Since the instrument was still a "natural" horn in those early years—with no valves to manipulate the air flow—placing the hand in the bell was also the only way the player could produce a complete set of pitches necessary to play melodies. The invention of the rotary valve in 1827 was accepted in some countries as an improvement over the piston valve on which the trumpet relied, and the piston valve remains the most common in America today.

The trombone began as a "big trumpet"—the literal meaning of its name in Italian (fig. 4.10). While the slide mechanism used to change pitch allowed for greater chromatic alterations than natural trumpets and horns without valves, most early use of the instrument was limited to doubling choral parts in order to strengthen them. This blending with voices was possible in those early years since the English "sackbut" (literally meaning "pump") had a much smaller bell than the modern-day trombone. The trombone's orchestral debut did not occur until Beethoven wrote the instrument into the fourth movement of his renowned Fifth

Figure 4.9
Natural horn (right) *and modern French horn.*
Photo courtesy Conn Band Instruments.

Figure 4.10
Bass trombone with double rotary valve attachment.
Photo courtesy G. Leblane Corporation.

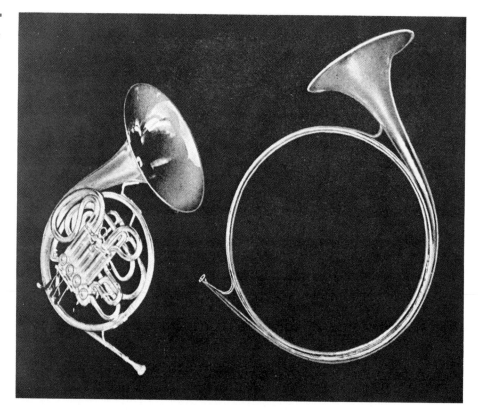

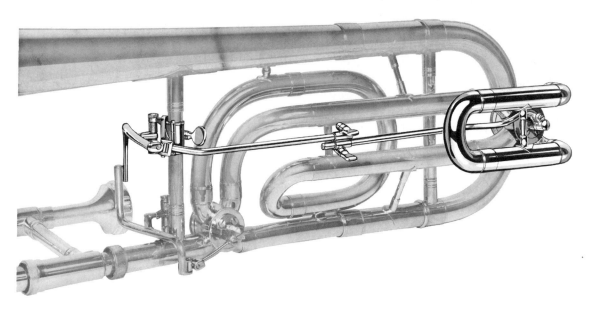

Brass section of the modern orchestra.
© Stock Boston/Frederick D. Bodin

Symphony, by which time the standard orchestra had grown considerably. Today the modern tenor and bass trombones add power to the orchestra's brass section and are an important part of the symphonic band, as well as a popular instrument of the jazz idiom. One technique that distinguishes the trombone among brass instruments is the "glissando." This is a "smear" or smooth connection of notes made possible by moving the slide without articulating the individual notes. The glissando is generally limited, however, to comic effects and to being occasionally used in jazz. While it continues to rely principally upon the slide to alter its sound, the modern tenor trombone frequently is augmented by a single rotary valve to allow for greater agility and a few additional pitches. The bass trombone usually has double rotary valves to assist with flexibility in the lower range.

The tuba, largest of the brass instruments, probably came from a bass member of the cornetto family called the serpent. A keyed version of this metal instrument, the ophicleide, appeared in the early nineteenth century. The invention of the piston valve in 1815, however, sparked a series of "bass horn" designs that eventually resulted in the modern tuba. The sousaphone is a variation on the tuba (fig. 4.11). Designed by and named after John Phillip Sousa, the famous bandmaster, it originated in 1898 as a convenient way for the tuba player to carry the instrument in parades.

The trombone section, front row, of a jazz band.
Photo courtesy of Paul Tanner.

Figure 4.11
Sixteenth century serpent
(1) and late nineteenth
century sousaphone (2).
Modern sousaphones
have their bells turned
toward the front.
Photo courtesy Conn Band
Instruments.

Listening Guide
Brass Family

. . . .

C. Ives: The Unanswered Question   *trumpet*
F. Haydn: Trumpet Concerto in E♭

B. Smith: Lost Your Head Blues   *cornet*

W. A. Mozart: Concerto in D Major for Horn and Orchestra,   *French horn*
             K. 412
P. I. Tchaikovsky: Symphony No. 5 in E Minor
                   II. Andante cantabile, con alcuna licenza (first theme)
B. Britten: Serenade

Andante
(ahn-DAHN-teh)

Cantabile
(kahn-TAH-bee-leh)

R. Wagner: Tannhäuser, "Overture"   *trombone*
P. Hindemith: Sonata for Trombone and Piano
W. A. Mozart: Requiem, K. 626, "Tuba mirum"

R. Vaughan-Williams: Concerto for Tuba and Orchestra   *tuba*
H. Berlioz: Symphonie Fantastique
                   V. ("Dies irae" section)

Percussion Family

The very first musical instrument was probably a drum from the percussion family. It is not hard to imagine our earliest ancestors striking a hollow log to accompany ceremonial dancing or to send signals. Stretching an animal skin over a hollow object would be the next logical step, and is not far removed from the timpani or kettledrums of today.

The percussion family is widely diverse and generally includes anything that is struck. One of the best ways to classify the different kinds of percussion instruments is by their capability to produce an actual pitch. **Melodic percussion** includes those instruments that produce regular vibrations and therefore identifiable pitches. While some of these instruments might be tunable, such as timpani, others have their pitches permanently set and usually are constructed in a keyboard similar to the piano. Included in this category are the xylophone, orchestra bells, and tubular chimes among others. **Nonmelodic percussion** includes instruments that produce irregular vibrations resulting in sounds that may be described as generally high or low but that cannot be identified as specific pitches. These include the snare drum, cymbals, bass drum, gong, triangle, castanets, and wood blocks to name a few.

Percussion instruments were initially treated primarily as military instruments and were seldom used in orchestras. Beethoven was one of the first composers to recognize the potential for percussive timbre—particularly that of the timpani, which he used in many innovative ways. Today percussionists are called upon to play some extremely unusual, if not unlikely, instruments, including sirens, whistles, brake drums, wind machines, and cannons.

Example of melodic and nonmelodic percussion instruments.
Courtesy of Ludwig Industries, Inc.

The percussion family also includes several instruments that could be described as "keyboard." The celeste is one such instrument; the percussionist or pianist plays a set of orchestra bells with a small keyboard. The piano itself is another keyboard percussion; it produces sound from strings that are **struck** by felt hammers when a key is depressed. The role of a piano as a percussion instrument is further understood when you consider that it is traditionally a part of the "rhythm section" in jazz.

Listening Guide
Percussion Family

. . . .

M. Ravel: Bolero   *snare drum*
C. Saint-Saëns: Danse Macabre   *xylophone*
I. Stravinsky: Symphony of Psalms (finale)   *timpani*

E. Varèse: Ionization   *percussion ensemble*
B. Bartok: Sonata for Two Pianos and Percussion

In addition to these four orchestral families, the classifications of keyboard and electronic are useful in describing some remaining instruments.

Keyboard Instruments

While the piano and the celeste are technically considered percussion instruments, they can also be classified as keyboard. Other fairly common non-percussive instruments that fall into this category include the organ and the harpsichord.

The pipe organ has been called the "king of instruments" because of its potential for range of tone color and dynamic contrast (fig. 4.12). Its sound is produced by forcing wind through one or more pipes, which are actually sophisticated whistles ranging in size from a few inches to thirty-two feet long. They can be made of metal or wood and some have reeds similar to the woodwind instruments. Knobs called "stops" are used to couple an entire set or "rank" of one kind of pipes to a keyboard or pedal board, which is played with the feet. By connecting several ranks of pipes to a keyboard at once, almost infinite combinations of tone colors are possible.

Every pipe organ is an individual instrument with different kinds and numbers of ranks of pipes. Different performances of the same work for pipe organ will vary not only with performer interpretation but also with choice of pipes (registration) and construction design of the particular instrument used.

Figure 4.12
Large pipe organ with five manual console. Mormon Tabernacle, Salt Lake City, Utah.

Photo courtesy of The Church of Jesus Christ of Latter-Day Saints.

The harpsichord is a keyboard instrument that produces its sound by plucking strings with small plectra made of quills, hard leather, or plastic (fig. 4.13a). Larger harpsichords have two keyboards and several sets of strings that can be coupled together by the use of stops similar to those found on the organ (fig. 4.14). The strings can also be dampened to create a sound similar to the lute. Dynamic changes cannot be produced by key pressure, as the harpsichord's strings are plucked in the same way regardless of pressure. However, the coupling of sets of strings and the use of a lever to vary the distance between the plectra and the strings make rather abrupt changes in dynamics possible. Although the harpsichord is not a common keyboard instrument today, it was especially popular in the baroque era and still generates significant interest among musicians performing music of that stylistic period.

Figure 4.13
(a) *Closeup of harpsichord mechanism;* (b) *cutaway view of a single key in a grand piano action.*

(a) Smithsonian Institution, (b) Yamaha International Corporation.

(a)

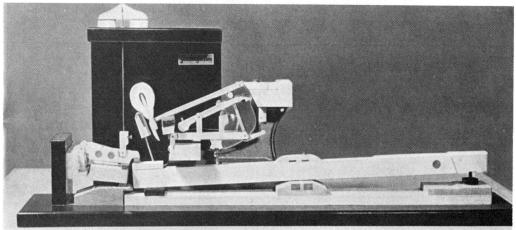

(b)

Figure 4.14
Ornate double manual harpsichord made in 1650.

The Metropolitan Museum of Art, The Crosby Brown Collection of Musical Instruments, 1889.

Listening Guide
Keyboard Instruments

. . . .

 J. S. Bach: Prelude and Fugue in C Major

Compare recordings of this work on piano and harpsichord (The recording on your cassette tape uses a harpsichord.)

C. Ives: Variations on America   *pipe organ*

J. S. Bach: Toccata and Fugue in D Minor   **Toccata** (toh-KAH-tah)

 J. S. Bach: Fugue in G Minor ("Little")

P. I. Tchaikovsky: Nutcracker Suite, "Dance of the Sugar-Plum Fairy"   *celeste*

Electronic Instruments

Twentieth-century electronics and computerization have brought many innovations to musical sound production. Just as the Boehm system of fingering and the invention of the valve radically changed the course of orchestral instrument development, new instruments and sound-producing techniques are being designed today that have revolutionized the world of music, particularly the "popular" genre. Synthesizers, computers capable of digital sampling, and amplified versions of traditional instruments continue to redefine our concept of musical sound (fig. 4.15).

Genre (ZHAHN-rah)

Figure 4.15
Synthesizers.
Courtesy ARP Instruments, Inc.

Voice Types

Human voices, while not considered part of the orchestral families above, are very important instruments with distinctive ranges of pitch, which define their musical roles. The most common classifications of vocal ranges are as follows:

Female	**Male**	
Soprano	Tenor	High voices
Mezzo-soprano	Baritone	Medium voices
Alto or contralto	Bass	Low voices

In addition to these basic categories, voices are sometimes labeled with additional descriptive characteristics. Operatic roles frequently call for one of the following particular kinds of voices.

Additional Selected Classifications of Voices

Lyric soprano	Lighter sound with emphasis on beautiful tone
Lyric tenor	
Dramatic soprano	Heavy, powerful voices
Dramatic tenor	
Basso profundo	

Coloratura
(koh-loh-rah-TOO-rah)

Coloratura soprano	Great flexibility and agility, especially in the high range

---

Listening Guide
Most Common Voice Types

. . . .

J. S. Bach: Cantata No. 140
      I. Chorus   *soprano, alto, tenor, bass*
G. F. Handel: Messiah
      Nos. 14–16   *soprano*
      "Glory to God"   *soprano, alto, tenor, bass*
W. A. Mozart: Requiem
      "Tuba mirum"   *bass, tenor, alto, and soprano solos*

F. Mendelssohn: Elijah
                "O rest in the Lord"   *mezzo-soprano*

J. Brahms: Alto Rhapsody   *alto*

G. F. Handel: Messiah
                "Every valley"   *tenor*

F. Schubert: Erlking   *baritone*

G. F. Handel: Messiah
                "The people that walked in darkness"   *bass*
                "But who shall abide"

Conventional Ensembles

Since the 1700s composers have frequently chosen to write for fairly standardized groupings of instruments. Even though considerable variety and overlap exist today, some large ensembles and smaller chamber ensembles continue to be popular media.

Chamber groupings include an infinite variety of instrumental combinations, with separate parts written for each player. While some combinations have maintained their popularity for many years, such as the string quartet (two violins, viola, cello), composers continue to write for almost any combination of instruments. The number of players in any given chamber ensemble is identified by the following terminology:

Number of Performers	Description
2	duet
3	trio
4	quartet
5	quintet
6	sextet
7	septet
8	octet
9	nonet

Larger ensembles generally have fallen into the categories of **band** and **orchestra. Marching band, concert band, symphonic band,** and **wind ensemble** are all terms that describe the common groupings of wind and percussion instruments. The symphony and chamber orchestras use these wind and percussion instruments in smaller numbers and place greater emphasis on a large string section. These ensembles will be discussed further in Chapter 9.

Marching band.

© Howard Dratch/The Image Works, Inc.

Large concert band.

Courtesy of the University of Illinois at Urbana-Champaign.

Large bands of 100 or more players frequently march in parades or in creative formations on the football field.

Concert or symphonic bands, usually with fewer than 100 players, perform a wide range of literature in formal concerts.

Wind ensemble.

Courtesy Eastman School of Music,
Rochester, N.Y.

The wind ensemble is similar to the concert or symphonic band in instrumentation, but it is much smaller in size. With one player on a part, this ensemble is essentially comprised of the wind and percussion sections from the full symphony orchestra.

Modern symphony orchestra.

The symphony orchestra combines many different timbres in one ensemble. With large numbers of strings (violin, viola, cello, bass) and a smaller group of wind and percussion instruments, this is a very versatile instrumental medium.

Voices can also be combined with instruments, usually an orchestra, to create a very powerful and expressive performance medium.

Listening Guide
Large Ensembles

· ·

G. Holst: Suite for Band in E♭   *concert band*
P. Hindemith: Symphony for Band in B♭

L. van Beethoven: Symphony No. 3   *orchestra*
H. Berlioz: Symphonie Fantastique
B. Britten: Young Person's Guide to the Orchestra

Gabriel Fauré   **G. Fauré:** Requiem   *orchestra and chorus*
(Gah-bree-EHL Foh-RAY)   I. Introit and Kyrie
J. S. Bach: Mass in B Minor
          "Cum sancto Spiritu"

CHAPTER FIVE

Organization

Preview of Terms and Concepts

The organization of musical sound events is called **form** and can be described according to aspects and degrees of **unity** and **variety.** Some pieces adhere to conventional forms, which make use of **sectional, multimovement, variation,** or **contrapuntal** procedures. Others have a continuous unfolding of ideas called **free form.**

ost objects have shape or a plan. Interesting and recurrent designs can be found both in nature and man-made creations.

Painters work with the elements of color, texture, line, and perspective to create beautiful and expressive visual art. Architects use space and mass within a particular environment along with color, texture, and light to design attractive, functional, and expressive structures. The poet draws upon language, imagery, meter, and acoustical devices to imbue words with greater expression and meaning. Rhythm and movement are the expressive tools of the dancer. Using rhythm, melody, harmony, timbre, and dynamics, the composer builds an expressive musical composition. The painter, architect, poet, dancer, and musician start with a set of basic elements or materials, which they then arrange in meaningful ways to create their art. In this chapter we will look only at *musical* forms, but aspects of these basic principles of organization can be seen also in each of the other art forms mentioned.

Form is important to the painter, draftsman, writer, dancer, and composer.

(*top left*) © David M. Grossman, (*top center*) © Joseph Nettis/Photo Researchers, Inc., (*top right*) © AP Wide World Photos, Inc., (*bottom left*) © Dan Chidester/The Image Works Inc., (*bottom right*) © Harriet Gans/The Image Works, Inc.

Principles of Organization

The most basic elements of musical organization are **unity** and **variety.** Simple **repetition** provides a strong feeling of cohesiveness or unity; but since too much repetition quickly becomes boring, variety is often introduced through **contrast** or **development. Variation** is a mixture of both unity and variety.

Principles of Organization

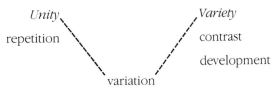

Unity   *Variety*

repetition   contrast

                     development

          variation

(a) *The principle of repetition can be seen in the architecture of row houses;* (b) *most urban areas have large contrasts in architectural styles;* (c) *the architecture of houses in a subdivision can be viewed as variations on a basic theme.*

(a) © S. Oristaglio/Photo Researchers, Inc. (b) © Alan Carey/ The Image Works, Inc. (c) © George W. Gardner/The Image Works, Inc.

(a)

(b)

(c)

To experience various effects of repetition and contrast in music, try the following experiment. First, select a familiar melody from the following list and hum it.

Marine's Hymn
All Through the Night
Au Clair de la Lune
Drink to Me Only with Thine Eyes
Twinkle, Twinkle Little Star
O Christmas Tree (O Tannenbaum)
Deck the Halls
The Ash Grove
Oh Susanna

Notice that the melody has four lines or phrases. The first, second, and fourth lines are identical, while the third is different. Lowercase letters are usually assigned in the following manner to represent the relationship of lines.

a   a   b   a

Now try humming your selected melody through, but change the contrasting "b" line to another "a." The result would be represented as: a a a a. As you can easily hear, it doesn't take long for repetition to create a sense of boredom.

The discussion of musical form in this chapter will begin with a look at traditional organizational patterns. Of course, not all musical selections fit neatly into pre-existing molds; greater interest lies in how a composer has stretched or altered a traditional form. However, by becoming familiar with some of the most basic forms as they are introduced in this chapter, you can better perceive departures and innovations in other musical examples and more easily follow larger and more complex compositions. (Additional ones will be described as they evolve chronologically in Section III—The Cultural Context.)

Sectional Forms

Because music is a temporal phenomenon—it exists in time—aural memory is critical to the perception of musical form. You must compare what you hear at the moment to what came before and be prepared to compare it to what follows. This comparison is least difficult when the music has been written with simple sectional forms. While sections of such music may differ in length, they are usually delineated by a feeling of rhythmic pause. Contrasting sections within a single piece (longer than a single melodic line) are conventionally labeled by *capital* letters (A, B, C) with the addition of a some kind of superscripted or subscripted marking (A_1 A^1 A') to identify sections that differ only slightly. This text will use subscripted numbers ($A A_1 A_2$) to identify slight variations between sections and lowercase letters to indicate subsections. Subsection markings are especially useful in longer works in order to make a more accurate comparison of sections. The following is one example of what this system might reveal:

A	B	A	Main sections
a a$_1$ b a$_2$	c c$_1$	a a$_1$ b a$_2$	Subsections

Music written in sectional form may also have opening and closing sections called introduction and coda, respectively. These do not alter the basic shape of the form. The introduction does what the name suggests, and the coda (an Italian word meaning "tail") serves to give a feeling of finality and cohesiveness to the work.

Strophic Form

Strophic (STROH-fik)

The most basic of all sectional forms—**strophic**—is found in vocal music where the text is written in units called stanzas or strophes. (Most of the songs listed on page 87 use this form.) Since the same music is repeated for each section, the form is diagrammed A A A . . ., depending upon the number of stanzas in the text. Because of the amount of repetition inherent in strophic form, it is reserved for works that are relatively short and uncomplicated.

Listening Guide
Strophic Form

· ·

F. Schubert: Das Wandern (The Wanderer)
F. Schubert: Who is Sylvia?

Many songs in strophic form that may be familiar to you are church hymns, holiday carols, and patriotic songs. Examples include "Amazing Grace," "Beautiful Savior," "Silent Night," "O Little Town of Bethlehem," "America the Beautiful," and "My Country, 'Tis of Thee."

Binary Form

A simple sectional form that also provides contrast is **two-part** or **binary form.** This can be diagramed in its most basic format as A B. Since the immediate repetition of a section is not considered to be an alteration of the basic form, other versions of binary form include the following:

A   A   B

A   B   B

A   A   B   B

Listen to the following examples of binary form. Notice the differing methods of contrast between the "A" and "B" sections, the balance and symmetry achieved by some, and the creation of a feeling of a need for change in the example that repeats the "A" sections.

Listening Guide
Binary or Two-part Form

· ·

F. Chopin: Prelude in C Minor, op. 28, No. 20	A B B
C. Saint-Saëns: Carnival of the Animals "Turtles"	A B
J. S. Bach: Prelude in C Minor, WTC, Bk. 2	A A B B
G. C. Menotti: Amahl and the Night Visitors "Shepherds Dance"	A B

Ternary Form

A simple way to add greater unity to binary form is to repeat the "A" section after the "B" section. This becomes ternary or three-part form, which is diagramed A B A. The balance and symmetry of this form is so popular that it is one of the most frequently used forms in both simple and complex versions. Again, since the immediate repetition of any section does not alter the basic form, several variations exist; the most common variation is A A B A.

Listen to the following examples of ternary form. As the "A" section is repeated, you will probably feel the need to move on to contrasting material. Pay special attention to the feeling of unity and balance provided by the return of "A" following the "B" section.

Listening Guide
Ternary or Three-Part Form

· ·

F. Chopin: Prelude No. 15 in D♭ Major	A B A_1
W. A. Mozart: Symphony No. 40 in G Minor III. Menuetto. Allegretto	A A B A
C. Saint-Saëns: Carnival of the Animals "The Swan"	A B A

| **Serge Prokofiev**
(SAYR-gay
Pro-KOHF-ee-ef) | **S. Prokofiev:** Classical Symphony in D Major
III. Gavotta. Non troppo allegro
R. Vaughn-Williams: Fantasia on Greensleeves
L. Bernstein: West Side Story
"Tonight" | A   A   B   A₁

A   B   A

A   B   A |

Listening Guide
Ternary Form

. . . .

F. Haydn: Trumpet Concerto in E♭
    II. Andante   A   A   B   A   (coda)

Timing	Section		Description
0'00'	A	a	Strings, smooth ascending and then descending melody (triple meter, A♭ Major)
0'15"		a₁	Repetition of "a," but second half slightly altered
0'30"	A	a	Trumpet plays "a" with string accompaniment
		a₁	Trumpet continues
1'00"	B	b	Strings begin contrasting melody, which is picked up and continued by the trumpet; modulation to distant key (C♭ Major)
1'30"		c	Static trumpet line, returns to E♭ Major with transition back to . . .
2'00"	A	a	Trumpet plays "a" with string accompaniment
2'15"		a₁	Trumpet continues as above
2'30"	Coda		Material borrowed from "b" and "a" brings the movement to a quiet close (3'10")

Rondo Form

An extension of ternary leads to **rondo** form. With the addition of a contrasting section in between two simple ternary structures, you have a seven-part rondo—A   B   A   C   A   B   A. Sometimes the final two sections are omitted for a five-part rondo—A   B   A   C   A. The melody of the returning "A" section is referred to as the rondo theme. Especially in seven-part rondos, this entire "A" section need not be repeated every time. In order to avoid too much repetition, just a segment of the rondo theme is sometimes presented to give a feel for the return of the section before proceeding to the next.

Listen to the following example of rondo form. Notice that the "A" section is not performed in its entirety every time. Two additional sections mentioned earlier—introduction and coda—are also present. These are common in longer forms.

Listening Guide
Rondo Form (seven-part)

· ·

F. Haydn: Trumpet Concerto in E♭
     III. Allegro

Timing	Section	Description
0'00"	Intro	Main theme (A) played softly by violins; fast tempo

Theme A

Timing	Section	Description
0'10"		Main theme repeated by orchestra, louder
0'22"		B theme played by violins; transition

Theme B

Timing	Section	Description
0'38"	A	Trumpet enters with main theme (A); repeats; transition
1'08"	B	Trumpet and violins alternate B theme in new key; transition
1'48"	A	Trumpet plays main theme
2'05"	C	Trumpet plays main theme in relative minor key (C)
2'38"	A	Trumpet plays main theme in original key, some imitation by the violins

Timing	Section	Description
2'55"	B	Trumpet and violins play B theme together
3'27"	A	Trumpet plays first part of main theme; transition with trilled notes
4'05"	Coda	Pause, after which trumpet plays part of main theme softly; closes with crescendo and full-sounding chord.

Multimovement Structures

Some musical compositions consist of several self-contained sections of music called **movements** between which there is usually an extended pause. The forms that we have discussed so far can be used for any one of the movements, but many additional forms (which will be introduced in Section III) are also used for these extended works. Since each of the movements in a multimovement work—regardless of its structure—is considered to be just a part of the total composition, in a live concert it is appropriate to wait until the end of the entire composition before acknowledging the performance with applause.

Musical compositions containing two or more self-contained sections (called movements) are referred to as multimovement structures. These movements are identified by the order in which they occur (i.e., First movement, Second movement), by their form (i.e., rondo), or by their tempo (i.e., slow movement, allegro).

The following are examples of multimovement structures. Notice that the titles of the movements give you considerable information about what you can expect to hear in each selection.

Con Brio
(kohn BREE-oh)

L. van Beethoven: Symphony No. 3
   I.   Allegro con brio
   II. Marcia funebre. Adagio assai
   III. Scherzo. Allegro vivace
   IV. Finale. Allegro molto

Agitato (ah-jee-TAH-toh)
Appassionato
(ah-pah-see-oh-NAH-toh)

H. Berlioz: Symphonie Fantastique
   I.   Largo; Allegro agitato e appassionato assai
   II. Allegro non troppo
   III. Adagio
   IV. Allegretto non troppo
   V.   Larghetto; Allegro

F. Haydn: Trumpet Concerto in E♭
    I. Allegro
   II. Andante
  III. Allegro

W. A. Mozart: Symphony No. 40 in G Minor
    I. Allegro molto
   II. Andante
  III. Menuetto. Allegretto
  IV. Allegro assai

In addition to the symphonies and concerto listed above, other common multimovement forms include the suite, quartet, and sonata in instrumental music and the mass, song cycle, oratorio, cantata, and opera in vocal music. These will be individually introduced later in Section III.

Suite (sweet)

Listen to all three movements in the following example. Notice that there is a sense of balance and symmetry achieved by alternation of tempo among the movements and that the forms of each movement are all somewhat related. While a single movement could stand alone, the three movements complement each other and create a cohesive structure for a longer composition.

Listening Guide
Multimovement Structures

. . . .

F. Haydn: Trumpet Concerto in E♭

I. Allegro	fast tempo sonata-allegro form (This form will be introduced in a later chapter.)
II. Andante	moderate tempo ternary form (A A B A)
III. Allegro	fast tempo rondo form (Intro A B A C A B A coda)

Variation Forms

Variation, as a principle of organization that provides both unity and contrast, can be imposed by sections or as a continuous technique. Sectional variation, usually called **theme and variations,** begins with the statement of a familiar or original theme and proceeds with several restatements of the theme, each with alteration of selected elements. These alterations may incorporate one or more aspects of rhythm, harmony, timbre, or texture. The form can best be diagramed A A$_1$ A$_2$ A$_3$ A$_4$ and so on, depending upon the number of variation sections.

Continuous variations, as found in the **passacaglia** and **ground bass,** are based upon a repeated bass line. Melody, harmony, timbre, texture, and rhythmic patterns may all change, while the bass line remains intact. This type of variation keeps going without stopping for ther entire selection or movement. (See Chapter 14 for a listening example of passacaglia.)

Listen to the following example of variation form. Notice the assortment of ways in which musical elements are changed to create variety, while still maintaining an identifiable melody.

Listening Guide
Theme and Variations

· ·

L. van Beethoven: Variations on "God Save the King"

Beethoven used the theme and variation form extensively, both for independent works for piano (20 altogether) and as the form for movements of his symphonic works.

The theme for this piano work may also be known to you as "America." Follow the major changes in elements listed below by using the timings or humming the original melody along with the variations.

Timing	Section	Key Elements and Their Changes	
0'00"	Theme	Beat—steady	Dynamics—constant
		Tempo—moderate	Meter—triple
		Key—major	Timbre—mid-range of the piano
		Texture—block chord homophonic	
		Form—a a b b ("a" sections are six measures each and "b" sections are eight measures each)	
1'07"	Variation 1	Melody—extra pitches added	
		Beat—varies slightly	
		Dynamics—softer	

Timing	Section	Key Elements and Their Changes
2'00"	Variation 2	Melody—disguised within many other notes Tempo—faster at times Dynamics—vary slightly Rhythm—constantly running 16ths
2'50"	Variation 3	Texture—broken chord homophonic Melody—"ornamented" Rhythm—pause at the end of each section
3'34"	Variation 4	Dynamics—many sudden changes and accents Timbre—contrasts of low and high range of piano
4'22"	Variation 5	Key—minor Tempo—slower Melody—notes added to make groups of three; smooth, connected Dynamics—softer, with some changes between sections Texture—broken chord homophonic
5'44"	Variation 6	Meter—duple (marchlike) Key—returned to major Rhythm—short notes (uses dotted 8th & 16th) Dynamics—loud
6'40"	Variation 7	Tempo—faster Rhythm—very active, constantly running 16th notes in accompaniment Timbre—mostly mid to upper range of piano until end of section, when it descends to lower range
7'30"	Coda	Tempo—slow then changes to fast Key—changes key (F Major to C Major) Dynamics—soft gradually to loud Timbre—uses wide range of piano

Contrapuntal Procedures

Another continuous process for organization of a musical composition, contrapuntal procedure, refers to the use of polyphonic texture, rather than sections, to build an interesting structure. This includes familiar procedures such as the canon and round. Rounds such as "Three Blind Mice," "Frere Jacques," and "Row, Row, Row Your Boat" demonstrate the principle of imitation found in both rounds and canons. **Imitation** is the immediate restatement of a melodic idea by a different part or voice.

The main difference between rounds and canons is that each voice of a round must begin on the same pitch. Canons retain the use of melodic imitation but can become much more complex by starting each voice on a different pitch, as well as by incorporating other contrapuntal devices such as turning voices upside down (inversion), running a melody backward (retrograde) or elongating the rhythmic values of a voice (augmentation).

The most important contrapuntal procedure is the **fugue.** Imitative techniques are based on a melody that is called the **subject.** The subject is usually introduced by itself and, then, combined with a countersubject and introduced in each voice to be used in the composition. Additional contrapuntal techniques are used but are beyond the scope of this text. In spite of the fugue's complex nature, you will probably be able to follow many of the entrances of the themes in the suggested example if you follow the listening guide.

Listening Guide
Contrapuntal Procedures—Fugue

. . . .

J. S. Bach: Fugue in G Minor ("Little")

Because of the polyphonic texture, fugues can be very complex and difficult to listen to on a purely technical basis. With several melodies playing at once, you may have difficulty determining where to focus your attention. To follow this initial listening guide for the Fugue in G Minor, try to listen just for the beginning of the subject as it is passed around among the four voices. First become familiar with the subject by playing the opening of the fugue several times (i.e., where the subject is performed by itself and then introduced in each of the other three voices of the texture). Use the score or graphic representation below to help you recognize the subject. Finally, listen to the entire fugue several times. Don't be concerned with trying to hear everything, just listen for the subject as it is presented five more times after the first four appearances.

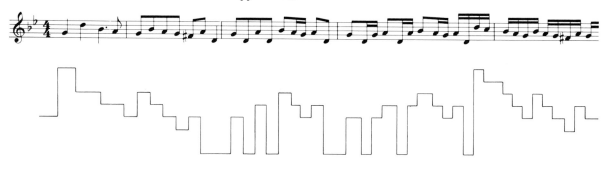

Free Forms

Some compositions do not fall into conventional structures. This does not mean they lack organization. Rather, they either offer a continuous unfolding of ideas or depend upon some extramusical aspect for organization.

Each of the following titles suggests both a free form and a particular style:

Toccata literally means "touch piece." This is usually a keyboard piece that is meant to demonstrate brilliant technique. It is played in a relatively free rhythm, tempo, and meter.

Fantasia is a fantasy piece. As the title suggests, a free and fanciful wandering discourse is usually the result.

Etude is a study piece that is used to practice a particular technique. In addition to this educative role, these works frequently are artistic and musically appropriate for concert performance.

Prelude is an introductory type of piece. While it was originally meant to come before another piece, more recent composers have used it as a separate entity.

Vocal songs with a continuous change of ideas and moods that do not match the repetition found in strophic form are frequently **through-composed.** This vocal free form provides significant opportunity for diversity and creativity on the part of the composer, in that the music can evolve to match changes in the text.

Listening Guide
Free Forms

. . . .

Extra-Musical Associations

K. Penderecki: Threnody: To the Victims of Hiroshima (see Chapter 17)

B. Smetana: The Moldau (see Chapter 16)

C. Debussy: Prelude to the Afternoon of a Faun

C. Saint-Saëns: Carnival of the Animals

C. Ives: The Unanswered Question (see Chapter 17)

Through-Composed Vocal Works

T. Weelkes: As Vesta Was Descending

F. Schubert: Erlking (see text on page 10)

Instrumental Free Forms

J. S. Bach: Prelude in C Major, WTC Bk. 1

J. S. Bach: Toccata in F Major

R. Vaughan-Williams: Fantasia on a Theme of Thomas Tallis

Listening Guide

Through-Composed

· ·

T. Weelkes: As Vesta Was Descending

The music for this work is composed without repetition of themes or a feeling of sections. Follow the text below and notice how the composition has a continuous flow from beginning to end.

> As Vesta was from Latmos hill descending,
> she spied a maiden queen the same ascending,
> attended on by all the shepherds swain,
> to whom Diana's darlings came running down amain.
> First two by two, then three by three together,
> leaving their goddess all alone, hasted thither,
> and mingling with the shepherds of her train with mirthful tunes her presence
>   entertain.
> Then sang the shepherds and nymphs of Diana,
> Long live fair Oriana!

In summary, the organization of musical sounds can be very complex or quite simple. Perception of form in music is dependent upon your ability to recognize sound relationships in time. While it may not be necessary for you to identify the form of a piece of music in order to enjoy listening to it, the recognition of structure may assist you in discovering additional musical relationships. This may be especially important when listening to very long works.

In addition to the mental road map that the use of form provides, you may find an interest in the variety of ways in which different composers manipulate and alter traditional forms. Expectations established by common methods of organization are sometimes fulfilled and just as often foiled. At its best, the identification of form can help you to become more perceptive of the expressiveness of music. At its worst, form recognition can become an end unto itself. Use your knowledge of musical forms to increase your perceptiveness rather than restrict it.

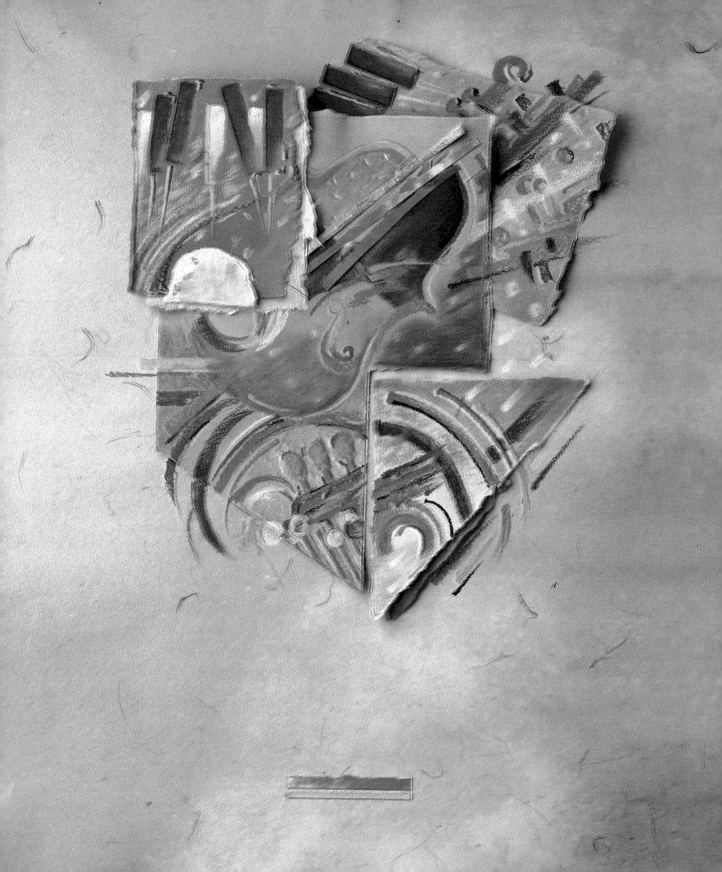

Expression

Music is   sound   organized   expressively   in time.

Pitch Timbre Dynamics   Form   Meaning   Rhythm

Music is expressive. Through the expressive organization of sound in time, a composer symbolizes the realm of human feeling. You, the listener, share the composer's insights as interpreted by the performer.

As previously discussed in Chapter 1, perception and analysis of the elements of music in isolation do not automatically lead to an understanding of the expressiveness of music. These elements must be synthesized and perceived within a perspective that includes both your own personal experience and the cultural context of the composer. You also must be willing to let your own feelings and experiences become an active part of the listening process—a process of imaginative perception.

Just as each listener will bring a different background to the same listening experience, so too will the perspective of any individual vary with each listening. The combination of your own personal experiences, feelings, and mood at any given time provides many complex variables. What you are thinking about and how you feel as you listen to music will affect the way in which you perceive it. Also, as a particular piece of music becomes more familiar, you become more keenly aware of its different elements and their relationships to one another. A very complex work may continue to provide new insights with every listening.

A study of the expressiveness of music requires a certain amount of personal investment. As your study of music continues through analysis of expressive aspects, allow your own feelings to play a part in the process.

In addition to your structured listening, think about how the music in your regular listening repertoire is expressive. Do you find each and every listening experience to be different, even with familiar pieces? Do some selections hold up better than others and retain their interest and fresh perspective even when repeated several times? What helps a musical composition to "stand the test of time"? Are there any popular pieces today that you believe will be "classics" in the future?

As you read about the mechanics of expression described in Section II, ask yourself which of them you detect in your favorite listening selections. Remember, however, that the expressiveness of music cannot be perceived through mechanical analysis alone. You must provide the human element of feeling. Let your imaginative perception work on all of the music to which you listen.

CHAPTER SIX

Motion

Preview of Terms and Concepts

The rhythm and progression of musical events can give an illusion of **motion.** This is usually done through manipulation of **tempo,** alternation of **tension and release,** or **programmatic imitation.**

Some of the expressive tools used to create this motion are **consonance** and **dissonance, climax and resolution, expectation and fulfillment, unfamiliarity and familiarity, loudness and softness, rubato,** and **static and active rhythm.**

T he rhythm and progression of musical events in a piece create an illusion of **motion.** This motion can be a powerfully expressive tool. While it is primarily an aspect of rhythm, motion may be suggested by something as obvious as a steady beat or as subtle as a sense of progression or change in one of the extra-rhythmical elements.

A time-lapse photo taken at night creates a still-picture visual illustration of motion.
© James F. Shaffer

Whether obvious or subtle, however, the perception of motion in music is a result of temporal relationships—changes through time. The only physical movements involved are vibrations and their resultant sound waves, which are the acoustical components of musical pitch. Thus the expressive movement described in this chapter is an illusion created by changes in musical elements over time, as can be demonstrated by the simple exercise that follows.

Clap a series of eight steady beats.

/ / / / / / / /

This very basic rhythmic pattern should sound rather static—unchanging. Now try the same series of beats, but add a gradual increase of volume for four beats followed by a gradual decrease in volume for four beats.

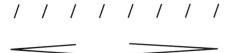

These very simple changes in dynamics should give you a greater sense of motion or movement than when you played eight equal sounds. The same principle can be demonstrated by holding a single pitch on a musical instrument for eight beats. While the pulse may not be audible, the illusion of motion should still be evident in the growth and decay of sound. (Additional listening examples for dynamic changes will be given in chapter 7.)

While these examples are simple, the illusion of motion in music can also be very complex. Contributing to this phenomenon is a sense of continuity, regularity, direction, and succession of events. At any moment in a musical composition one *or more* elements may be contributing to the illusion. Furthermore, motion may be created with gradual changes in an element over a long period of time (for example, the gradual dynamic changes indicated by crescendo or decrescendo) or there may be several much quicker changes.

Listening Guide
Motion Enhanced by Dynamics

· ·

M. Ravel: Bolero

The entire work is based on four alternating melodies and a rhythm played by the snare drum throughout. Variety is achieved by a constantly changing timbre and gradual growth in dynamics from a very soft solo flute at the beginning to the loud, full orchestra at the climactic conclusion.

The sequence of the themes (with two measures between each) is as follows:

a	b	a	b	c	d	c	d
a	b	a	b	c	d	c	d
a	b	a	b	c	d	c	d
a	b	a	b	c	d	c	d
a	b	c	d	coda			

Music that lacks any sense of continuity, regularity, direction, or progression of events may also appear to have less motion. Deliberate omissions of such characteristics are found more frequently in contemporary music, which may break away from conventional compositional techniques. Profuse repetition, seemingly random events, or a lack of melodic movement are all techniques that may reduce the illusion of motion.

Listening Guide
Limited Perception of Motion

. . . .

T. Riley: In C   *Example of "minimalist" music. Changes in timbre are very subtle and occur over a long period of time. Rhythm is chantlike and incessant. Melodies are fragmented.*

B. Eno: Ambient 1   *Repetitious, but lacks regularity of rhythm and long melodic lines. Sounds are somewhat unpredictable due to lack of constant pulse.*

Tempo

The rate at which the beat of music occurs (i.e., its tempo) can greatly affect your perception of motion. When the frequency of beat approximates an average pulse rate the music is considered to be "moving" at a moderate speed or tempo. Relative gradations of fast and slow have been assigned to appropriate variations of this speed. However, regardless of its tempo, a feeling of steady beat alone may not always be sufficient to create a sense of motion; changes in the tempo are more conducive to expressive motion.

Accelerando, Rallentando and Rubato

Accelerando
(aht-chel-leh-RAHN-doh)

Rubato (roo-BAH-toh)

Even gradual changes in tempo can help to create significant movement in music. Speeding up (accelerando) and slowing down (ritardando, rallentando) are the two most obvious and direct ways in which such tempo changes can occur.

Rubato ("to rob") is the slight fluctuation of tempo for expressive purposes. Time is taken from some notes and given to others so that the speed of the beat is altered to convey a subtle feeling of holding back or pushing ahead. These very quick and frequent changes are not usually notated in the musical score. Considerable experience and performing sensitivity is thus required in order to know when to insert them effectively. As a result, interpretations vary from performer to performer, and appropriate degrees of rubato can vary greatly. Many examples are found in music of the romantic era and later.

Active and Static Rhythm

The interaction of tempo with other rhythmic movement can also suggest more motion or less motion with a result that is described as **active** or **static rhythm.** The most common relationships are combinations of fast tempos with active rhythm and slow tempos with static rhythm. However, rhythmic activity may also vary independently of tempo. A slow tempo can thus be accompanied by quick rhythmic values.

Listening Guide
Motion—Tempo and Rhythmic Activity

. . . .

Use of Rubato

F. Chopin: Polonaise in A♭ Major

C. Debussy: Prelude No. 8

Gradual tempo changes

Edvard Grieg (ED-vard Greeg)

E. Grieg: Peer Gynt Suite No. I "In the Hall of the Mountain King"	*accelerando*
R. Gliere: "Russian Sailors Dance" from The Red Poppy	*variations in tempo*
H. Villa-Lobos: "Little Train of the Caipira" from Bachianas Brasileiras No. 2	*accelerando & ritardando*
D. Shostakovitch: "Pizzicato Polka" from Ballet Suite No. 1	*tempo & dynamic changes*

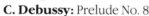

Active rhythm

J. S. Bach: Brandenburg Concerto No. 5
        I. Allegro
        II. Affettuoso

*Both of these movements are
rhythmically active despite
tempo differences.*

Static rhythm

F. Haydn: Symphony No. 101
        II. Andante

C. Ives: The Unanswered Question

*Strings—rhythmically static
Flutes—rhythmically active
The solo trumpet balances the
two with moderate movement*

Tension and Release

Motion can also be powerfully and expressively suggested in music by alternately *creating and releasing tension.* Many different elements, both singularly and in various combinations, can be used to produce expressive effects of movement under this umbrella. Resulting changes may occur repeatedly in rapid succession or over a long period of time.

Moreover, the involvement of more than one element may contribute to several levels of motion. Even as rhythm remains fairly static, dynamics and harmony may be creating expressive motion. Strong and sweeping motion can be created by involving several elements. A more subtle feeling of motion may result when fewer elements are utilized.

Tension and release can be thought of as the basis for organization of these musical elements in order to create expressive motion. The elements discussed in this section are listed below:

Tension	**Release**
dissonance	consonance
loudness	softness
climax	resolution
expectation	fulfillment
unfamiliar	familiar

Dissonance and Consonance

In chapter 3 you were introduced to harmony and the relative terms of dissonance and consonance. The instability and tension of dissonance resolving to the stability of consonance provides a feeling of movement. Listen to the series of dissonances created and resolved in the following example.

Listening Guide

Dissonance Moving to Consonance

. . . .

J. S. Bach: "Toccata" from Toccata and Fugue in D Minor

Part of the drama of this work is achieved through strong dissonances, created by piling up a very dense chord, which is then resolved.

> Three short opening statements
>
> Dissonant chord built and resolved
>
> Two short running figures
>
> One longer running figure; ends on a low note that provides the basis for . . .
>
> Dissonant chord built and resolved
>
> Several running passages alternating with strong block chords
>
> The work culminates in one last dissonant chord in the full organ which is resolved before beginning the fugue

Sometimes harmony is relied upon almost exclusively to create the motion in a piece of music. The following example is static with regard to rhythmic movement and lacks any real melody to give a feeling of direction. The composer relies upon a gradual change of harmony and gentle increase of dissonance to create a feeling of movement.

Listening Guide

Movement through Harmonic Change

. . . .

 J. S. Bach: Prelude in C Major   *Movement through harmonic change and resolution at the end*

Loudness and Softness

Dynamics (which will be discussed more fully in the next chapter) create a general sense of tension with an increase in loudness and relieve that tension with a decrease in loudness. As demonstrated at the beginning of the chapter, this can also contribute to a feeling of motion.

Listening Guide
Movement through Dynamic Change

· ·

A. Honegger: Pacific 231
S. Barber: Adagio for Strings   See outline on page 112.

Climax—Resolution

Most temporal arts have a point of climax. This usually occurs near the end of the work after a lengthy buildup. A comparatively brief period of resolution follows. The twentieth-century composer Barney Childs has suggested that this pattern can be represented by what he calls a narrative curve.

From Barney Childs, "Times and Music: A Composer's View," in *Perspectives of New Music,* 15:2, p. 195, Spring-Summer 1977. Copyright © 1977 University of Washington, Seattle, WA. Reprinted by permission of the publisher and author.

This broad view of tension and release can be perceived in a three-hour play, two-hour movie, or a half-hour television drama. Novels and short stories, as well as operas and art songs, frequently fit this stylized representation of life itself. There are numerous exceptions to this pattern, however, that provide interesting alternative models of organization.

Movement toward a climax in a musical work may be achieved through the use of one or more of the basic elements. Resolution reflects a fairly quick change in those elements. In a short work the resolution may occur very quickly and the piece may end. In a large work a substantial coda may be used to balance the resolution with the preceding long build to a climax. The following listening example provides a sample of climax and resolution based on the narrative curve.

Listening Guide
Narrative Curve

. . . .

S. Barber: Adagio for Strings

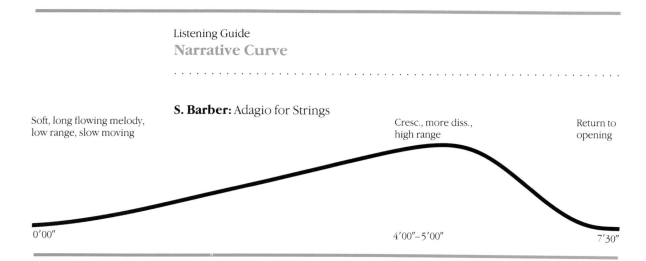

Soft, long flowing melody,
low range, slow moving

Cresc., more diss.,
high range

Return to
opening

0'00"   4'00"–5'00"   7'30"

While the narrative curve is a familiar pattern for climax and resolution, it is not the only one used by composers. Nor do composers usually set out intentionally to create a work to fit this particular pattern. Other creative and organizational factors are more likely to allow the composition to evolve as the composer proceeds. Listen to the following musical works and compare these aspects of climax and resolution: (1) elements used to create the climax; (2) balance between climactic buildup and resolution; (3) similarity of structure to Childs' narrative curve.

Listening Guide
Climax and Resolution

. . . .

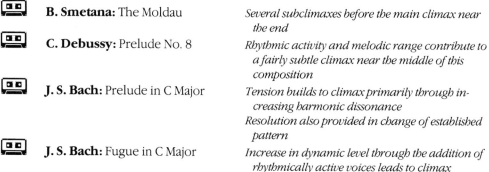

B. Smetana: The Moldau

Several subclimaxes before the main climax near the end

C. Debussy: Prelude No. 8

Rhythmic activity and melodic range contribute to a fairly subtle climax near the middle of this composition

J. S. Bach: Prelude in C Major

Tension builds to climax primarily through increasing harmonic dissonance
Resolution also provided in change of established pattern

J. S. Bach: Fugue in C Major

Increase in dynamic level through the addition of rhythmically active voices leads to climax
Resolution by decreased activity and density

Expectation and Fulfillment

After some experience with listening, certain musical events set up expectations. We begin to anticipate what will come next, based upon our experiences with the past. If none of our expectations are fulfilled, we become frustrated. Frustrations frequently result in dislike and avoidance.

Composers also play upon those expectations. The "deceptive cadence" is named after the feeling of surprise created by this particular harmonic movement. This cadence usually leads to an extension of a phrase by delaying an expected resolution to the tonic chord.

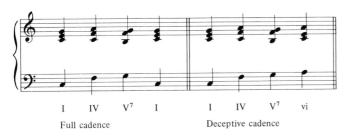

Sometimes composers set up rhythmic, harmonic, or dynamic expectations only to enjoy surprising us. Anticipation of certain elements can create a sense of forward motion. That motion may become disturbed, irregular, or uneven if expectations are not fulfilled as anticipated. The following examples demonstrate two more ways in which composers play with our expectations.

Listening Guide
Expectation and Fulfillment (or Nonfulfillment)

. . . .

F. Haydn: Symphony No. 94 in G Major ("Surprise")

II. Andante   *Rhythmically static but dynamic surprise is "set up" even more dramatically by decrease in volume*

P. D. Q. Bach: Howdy Symphony (Vanguard Records–VSD 79443)

II. Andante con mojo

Rhythmic and humorous misplacement of some notes

(The composer P. D. Q. Bach is actually the humorous invention of Peter Schickele. While Schickele has studied serious composition and earned dergees from Swarthmore College and Juilliard School of Music, he is best known for his creation of the fictitious composer P. D. Q. Bach and the composition of numerous "spoofs" on music of all kinds.)

Unfamiliar—Familiar

Similar to the phenomenon of expectation and fulfillment is the use of familiarity to create expressive motion. The introduction of new and contrasting material in a composition may create tension, which is resolved by the return of something familiar. This can most easily be seen in the basic ternary form A B A. The return of the "A" section achieves a balance simply in its familiarity. The rondo form extends this same principle, as the rondo theme (A) becomes a unifying factor for an extended work (A B A C A B A).

To the extent that we expect and hope for the return of something familiar, the resolution or nonresolution of our anticipation may greatly affect our perception of expressive motion. Listen to the third movement of the Haydn *Trumpet Concerto.* Try to be sensitive to the role of the rondo theme (A) as it relates to the contrasting material. The constant return of this theme should create a feeling of comfortable recognition. (See the listening guide in pages 91–92 of chapter 5.)

The ritornello form in Baroque concerto grosso functions in much the same way. The **ritornello** theme (meaning "return") provides comfortable recognition of a familiar melody as well as strength of instrumental timbre, when the entire ensemble returns—after the "freer" sounding material of the group of soloists. (This form will be examined more closely within its cultural context in Section III.) In the following musical example focus your listening on the alternation of the familiar (ritornello theme played by the whole orchestra—**ripieno**) with the unfamiliar (new material presented by the group of soloists—**concertino**). While the rhythmic activity of this work provides expressive motion throughout, the alternation of the familiar ritornello theme with new material works on a broader level to lead you through the fairly long movement.

Listening Guide
Familiarity in Ritornello

· ·

J. S. Bach: Brandenburg Concerto No. 5 in D Major
        I. Allegro

| Ripieno | Ritornello theme introduced by the whole orchestra; strong, homophonic texture |

Concertino	Flute (or recorder) and violin soloists accompanied by basso continuo—harpsichord and cello (harpsichord also provides solo material); polyphonic, imitative
Ripieno	Brief statement of beginning of ritornello theme
Concertino	Flute and violin continue
Ripieno	Slightly longer statement of ritornello theme
Concertino	Orchestra joins to accompany soloists
Ripieno	Very brief statement grows out of accompaniment of previous section
Concertino	Flute and violin featured
Ripieno	Brief statement
Concertino	Longer section that settles into alternation between flute and violin; texture thins, with harpsichord playing equal role, and eventually leading to trills in violin and flute
Ripieno	Return to ritornello theme provides relief to the tension created at end of previous section
Concertino	Begins with new material, but ends up similar to first section by solo group
Ripieno	Almost complete statement of ritornello theme
Concertino	Soloists featured but builds into . . .
Ripieno	Short statement
Concertino	Extended section in which the harpsichord eventually takes over; long solo includes arpeggios and brilliant runs that create tension to lead back into . . .
Ripieno	Final strong statement of ritornello theme

Programmatic Imitation

In addition to creating perceptions of motion in an abstract sense, music can imitate real life. As a temporal phenomenon, music is naturally capable of imitating many different life rhythms. The most basic aspect of rhythm—beat—is sometimes compared to the most basic rhythm of human physiology—the heart beat.

Music can also imitate events in nature. Listen to Smetana's *Moldau*. The fast-moving notes at the beginning of the piece are meant to mimic the movement and sound of swirling water. Near the end of the piece when the river theme returns, the sound becomes even more dramatic as if to signify more turbulent water. Other sounds depict scenes and a landscape that are a source of great nationalistic pride to the composer. By listening to the music, you can probably imagine a moving scene similar to the one envisioned by the composer.

Listening Guide
Imitation of Motion in Nature

. . . .

B. Smetana: The Moldau

Timing	Instruments	Description
0'00"	2 flutes	Two swirling springs, gradually growing in size until they become . . .
1'07"	violins	the flowing river
3'00"	french horns	Hunters' horns sounding in a thick woods
4'00"	rhythmic strings	Peasant wedding celebrated with song and dance in a grassy pasture
6'00"	muted strings	"Moonlight—Nymph's Revels"
		Reflected on the surface are fortresses and castles—witnesses of bygone days of knightly splendor and the vanished glory of martial times
8'40"	violins	The river theme returns and grows in intensity, depicting the seething rapids near Prague
11'15"	brass	A triumphal chorale
12'05"	(diminuendo)	The river vanishes into the horizon. (12'45")

St. Vitus' Cathedral in Prague overlooks the Moldau River.

© The Spectrum Colour Library

Composers from all periods have enjoyed creating moving "soundscapes" that provide an illusion of motion through programmatic imitation. The forces of nature are especially common sources of inspiration for soundscapes, which are usually accompanied by a title or notation in the score to give an indication of the composer's intended subject. Through imaginative perception, you too can share these moving landscapes for the ear.

Listening Guide
Musical "Soundscapes"

. . . .

F. Chopin: Prelude op. 28, No. 15, "Raindrop" (same steady tone)

F. Grofe: Grand Canyon Suite, "Cloudburst"

F. Mendelssohn: Fingal's Cave Overture (ebb and flow of waves depicted by melodic direction)

O. Respighi: The Pines of Rome
The Fountains of Rome
Roman Festivals
These three programmatic symphonies use nature and human achievement as points of departure to describe both the landscape and Roman life.

Ottorino Respighi
(Oh-toh-REE-noh Res-PEE-gee)

B. Britten: "Peter Grimes," *Four Sea Interludes*

C. Debussy: "La Mer," Play of the Waves (shorter movements)

E. Grieg: Peer Gynt, Suite No. 1, "Morning" (sunrise depicted with rising melodic register)

N. Rimsky-Korsakov: Tsar Saltan, "Flight of the Bumblebee"

CHAPTER SEVEN

Dynamics

. . . .

Preview of Terms and Concepts

Dynamics describe the loudness and softness (volume) of musical sound. Dynamic contrasts are achieved when a set number of instruments plays louder or softer (changing their **intensity**) or when the number of instruments playing at once is altered (changing the **density**). **Terraced dynamics** are sudden changes. **Crescendo and decrescendo** indicate a gradual increase and decrease in volume, respectively.

Accents are points of emphasis. **Dynamic accents** are created with louder sounds, and **agogic accents** are created with longer sounds. Accents can be regular or irregular and, when used in normally unaccented places, can create **syncopated** rhythm.

Changes in dynamics frequently support and enhance changes in other musical elements or in sections of form.

C hanges in dynamics (loudness and softness) play an important role in the expressiveness of music. These changes can be effected in a variety of different ways and to a seemingly infinite number of degrees. Dynamic nuance can be indicated on a score by the composer and then receive further elaboration through the interpretation of a conductor or performer.

The most basic change—the simple movement from soft to loud or the reverse—can be accomplished through an adjustment in **density** (number of instruments) or in the **intensity** of individual instruments. Thus, increasing the number of performing instruments or voices will usually result in an increase of volume—an especially popular method of achieving dynamic contrast during the Baroque era, when it was first referred to as **terraced dynamics.** In addition to providing dynamic contrast, increasing the number of performers gives a fuller, denser sound. In fact, modern recordings frequently result in a compression of dynamic range so that the change of density may be more obvious than any true dynamic change. Listen to several of the following selections and focus on how changes in density create dynamic contrasts.

Listening Guide
Dynamic Changes through Density

. . . .

M. Praetorius: "Der Lothringer"
(Musical Heritage Society The Recorder, Vol. 1
    OR 287)

Recorder consort; individual instruments have very limited dynamic range
Dynamic changes are made with alternation of large and small groups (terraced dynamics)

J. S. Bach: Brandenburg Concerto No. 5
        I. Allegro

Terraced dynamics; alternation of soloists (violin, flute, harpsichord) with orchestra (See outline on pages 114–115 of chapter 6.)

W. A. Mozart: Symphony No. 40 in G Minor
        III. Menuetto

Trio section (B) contrasts with fuller "A" sections (See a more detailed outline of this ABA form in chapter 15.)

M. Moussorgsky: Pictures at an Exhibition
          "Promenade"

*Alternation of single instru-
ment (trumpet) with orchestra*

Modeste Moussorgsky
(Moh-DEST
Moo-SORG-skee)

M. Ravel: Bolero

*Gradual addition of instru-
ments throughout the entire
work to achieve crescendo*

L. Van Beethoven: Symphony No. 7
          II. Allegretto

*Each of the four statements of
the theme (abb) increases in
volume through the addition
of instruments as well as
increased intensity*

Whether channeled through individual instruments or ensembles, change of dynamic **intensity** is also a powerful tool for expressiveness: melodic shapes can be enhanced by appropriate dynamic nuance; textural and timbral changes can be highlighted by accompanying dynamic alterations; harmonic dissonance and consonance are frequently intensified through dynamic crescendo and decrescendo; rhythmic interest can be dramatically focused and heightened with dynamic emphasis; and structural relationships of form receive clarification through dynamic contrasts.

The extent to which individual instruments can achieve dynamic contrast varies considerably from one to the next. Woodwind and string instruments as a whole are more limited in their dynamic range than are members of the brass and percussion families, and composers frequently consider these differences when specifying numbers and combinations of instruments performing together. This does not mean, of course, that a narrow range of dynamic contrast necessarily limits expressive capability. Relative changes in instruments that are generally softer or have a narrow dynamic range can be as effective as more marked changes in louder or more broadly ranged instruments.

Listen to several of the following examples that highlight dynamic changes of intensity. Try to identify some of the following differences: (1) gradual and sudden differences; (2) dynamic range achieved in different instrumental families; (3) use of dynamics to enhance other musical elements (melodic contour, dissonance and consonance, timbral changes, rhythmic activity, form).

Listening Guide
Dynamic Changes through Intensity

. . . .

R. Schumann: Fantasy Pieces, op. 12, No. 2
        "Aufschwung" (Soaring)

Many subtle changes in dynamics add expressive movement to the melodic line

G. F. Handel: Messiah
        No. 17. "Glory to God"

Changes in both density and intensity occur as the number of voice parts changes

F. Haydn: Trumpet Concerto in E♭
        II. Andante

Subtle crescendo and decrescendo shade the melodic line

F. Schubert: Erlking

*Dynamic changes follow changes in characters portrayed
(See text, page 10 of chapter 1.)*

B. Smetana: The Moldau

Numerous changes in dynamics highlight changes of sections and provide subtle shaping to melodic lines

F. Chopin: Prelude in C Minor, op. 28

Changes in sections are accompanied by dynamic changes (abb)

Accents

Accents are merely points of emphasis. **Dynamic accents** produce emphasis through marked changes in volume. As with other dynamic changes, these can be achieved by assigning individual instruments to play accents or by orchestrating sudden changes in the number of instruments playing at once.

Percussion instruments frequently serve to highlight other elements, especially rhythm, through dynamic accents. Listen to almost any march and you will generally hear the bass drum and snare drum provide a steady beat pattern, while the cymbal may highlight the melodic contour with dynamic changes and accents. Nonmelodic percussion such as these are rarely given extended solos, but they can be utilized effectively to add a distinctive timbral change and dynamic accent to melodic instruments.

Accents may occur at expected (predictable) or unexpected (unpredictable) places in the music. They therefore may result in either the reinforcement of a regular rhythm and meter or the creation of syncopation—an accent in a normally unaccented place. Emphasis placed on the regular grouping of beats can give metrical strength and can be achieved with duration of notes as well as volume. Emphasis created with duration is called an **agogic accent.**

Listen to examples of different kinds of accents as found in the following selections. Notice how dynamic emphasis provides an important expressive tool. Notice also that accents are sometimes added sparingly for contrast and at other times abundantly as a central part of composition.

Listening Guide
Accents

. . . .

Regular, metrical accents
G. Holst: The Planets op. 32,
　　　　"Mars, the Bringer of War"

Dynamic accents of intensity in the accompaniment highlight the meter (5)

J. P. Sousa: Stars and Stripes Forever

Duple meter is strengthened by percussive accents; cymbals highlight the melodic line

Syncopation
W. A. Mozart: Symphony No. 40 in G Minor
　　　　III. Menuetto. Allegretto

Metrical accents in the accompaniment provide interesting counterpoint with the syncopation of the first theme

H. Berlioz: Symphonie Fantastique
      V. "Dream of a Witches' Sabbath"   *Strong accents are used, especially*
      Larghetto; Allegro   *during "The witches round*
                                                                            dance"

B. Bartok: Music for Strings, Percussion and Celesta

      II. Allegro
      IV. Allegro molto   *Both of these movements are dra-*
                                                              matic, active works with numer-
                                                              ous syncopated accents
                                                          Definite and indefinite pitched
                                                              percussion (snare drum, cym-
                                                              bals, tom-tom, bass drum, tam-
                                                              tam, timpani, xylophone) pro-
                                                              vide a wide range of dynamic
                                                              interest
                                                          The piano and harp also are
                                                              treated percussively

Irregular, changing accents

I. Stravinsky: Le Sacre Du Printemps ("The Rite of Spring")
      II. Sacrificial Dance   *Harsh, percussive accents explode*
                                                              in unpredictable sequence as the
                                                              meter changes almost every
                                                              measure

A. Copland: El Salón México   *Mexican dance hall rhythms create*
                                                              an exotic and at times frantic
                                                              pace; meter changes add to the
                                                              excitement

Many musical works, especially longer ones, employ most if not all of these expressive dynamic nuances. Listen to the following section of Beethoven's *Symphony No. 3.* Observe the many dynamic changes and use of accents.

Listening Guide
Expressive Dynamics

. . . .

L. Van Beethoven: Symphony No. 3
I. Allegro con brio

*Many dynamic changes both subtle
and dramatically quick
Change of sections in the form
(sonata-allegro) is usually accompanied by dynamic change*

Timing		
0'00"	*ff*	Two loud accents on the downbeats of the first two measures
0'03"	*p*	Low strings—add high strings
		Main theme in low strings—add high strings

Main theme

p

woodwinds
alternation of strings and woodwinds
strings with syncopated accents, crescendo

0'42"	*f*	Full orchestra with main theme
0'52"	*p*	Three-note motive passed around

Three note motive

oboe-clarinet-flute-strings
strings, crescendo

1'15"	*f*	Strings with accented chords
1'36"	*p*	Woodwinds, strings, woodwinds
		soft, short notes with crescendo
2'12"	*f*	Full sound, strong chords, syncopated accents
2'40"	*mf*	Strings, crescendo with accents
3'03"	*p*	Main theme leads to the next section

Vincent van Gogh, "The Starry Night," 1889. Oil on canvas, 29" × 36¼". Collection, The Museum of Modern Art, New York. Acquired through the Lillie P. Bliss Bequest.

Plate 1
The turbulent lines and dramatic colors of Starry Night *create a shimmering illusion of motion.*

Georges Seurat, "Sunday Afternoon on the Island of La Grande Jatte," oil on canvas, 1884–86, 207.6 × 308 cm, Helen Birch Bartlett Memorial Collection.

Plate 2
Tiny dots of color create a visual texture strikingly different from that achieved with brush strokes.

José Orozco: "Zapatistas" (1931) Oil on canvas, 45" × 55". Collection, The Museum of Modern Art, New York.

Plate 3
Repetition of line creates a visual rhythm.

Pollack, Jackson (1912–1956) "Autumn Rhythm," oil on canvas, 105" × 207", The Metropolitan Museum of Art, George A. Hearn Fund, 1957.

Plate 4

Listening to absolute music requires the ability to focus on sound for the sake of sound. Without identifiable objects, abstract art provides a similar experience visually. The spontaneous and chaotic nature of this work keeps the eye from coming to rest for very long on any one part.

CHAPTER EIGHT

Phrasing

Preview of Terms and Concepts

A **phrase** in music can be compared to a sentence in prose. A musical phrase contains a complete musical idea.

      Cadences provide the punctuation for the "musical sentences" or phrases. A cadence, usually marked by a rhythmic pause, is the combination of harmony, rhythm, and melody that creates a feeling of completeness, either full or partial. A pair of phrases with a question and answer format called **antecedent and consequent** is called a **period.**

      Phrases may be **shaped** expressively by **rubato** and **dynamics.** These tools may help to emphasize **melodic contour, motion, direction,** and **patterns.**

A **phrase** is a musical sentence—a complete thought usually marked by a rhythmic and/or harmonic pause called a **cadence.** Just as sentences are combined to create paragraphs and chapters, phrases are the building blocks for larger musical sections. The skillful and sensitive shaping of a musical phrase can be one of the most expressive tools available to a performer.

A **cadence** is to a musical phrase what punctuation is to a sentence. Just as commas and periods help to organize thoughts and ideas by inserting pauses or stops, cadences mark points of rest in musical ideas. Without proper punctuation the meaning of some sentences would be altered. Consider the following example of a parenthetical phrase set off by commas.

Bowzer, says my father, is a fine family pet.
Bowzer says my father is a fine family pet.

Similarly, without consideration for cadences, musical phrases can sound run together and can lose some of their intended balance and meaning.

Some cadences give just a partial feeling of rest, as you might sense from a comma in a sentence. Other cadences are more final sounding, similar to a period at the end of a sentence.

Read the text to the following song. Notice where you feel partial resting spots and where they are more complete.

Streets of Laredo

As I walked out in the streets of Laredo,
As I walked out in Laredo one day,
I spied a young cowboy all wrapped in white linen,
All wrapped in white linen as cold as the clay.

Now listen to the melody and accompaniment without the text. While each line is a phrase, the endings of the first three phrases do not sound as final as the fourth phrase.

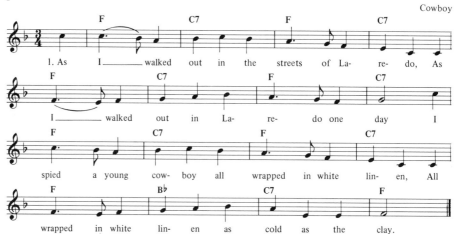

The first three phrases end with an **incomplete** cadence and the fourth phrase with a **complete** cadence. The feeling of punctuation, either partial or full, is produced by movement of the melody, text, harmony, and rhythm. Separate the elements by clapping the rhythm, reading the text, playing the chords, and playing the melody, each in isolation. While each individual aspect of the song supports the feeling of four phrases, the combination of all four elements produces an even more powerful system of phrase and cadence.

Harmonically, the feeling of complete cadence is produced by ending the phrase on the central chord of the key—the tonic or I chord (F major in this example). Any other chord at the end of a phrase (frequently the dominant—V—or subdominant—IV) results in an incomplete cadence. Melodically, the same principle applies. Ending a phrase on the tonic pitch ("F" in the example above) produces the strongest feeling of complete cadence. Rhythmically, a pause is characteristic of any cadence. Sometimes, but not always, a longer pause is found with a complete cadence than with one that is incomplete.

Phrases are very important in vocal music as a means to support and enhance the text. The very simple example above provides a clear and concise introduction to vocal phrases. Now apply these same principles of phrasing through melody, text, harmony, and rhythm to the following more complex example. (The translation of this text can be found on page 10 of chapter 1.)

Listening Guide
Phrasing and Cadences in Vocal Music

· ·

 F. Schubert: Erlking (*Erlkönig*)

Narrator:	Wer reitet so spät durch Nacht und Wind?	incomplete
	Es ist der Vater mit seinem Kind;	incomplete
	Er hat den Knaben wohl in dem Arm,	incomplete
	Er fasst ihn sicher, er hält ihn warm.	complete
Father:	"Mein Sohn, was birgst du so bang dein Gesicht?"	incomplete
Son:	"Siehst, Vater, du den Erlkönig nicht?	incomplete
	Den Erlenkönig mit Kron' und Schweif?"	incomplete
Father:	"Mein Sohn, es ist ein Nebelstreif."	incomplete
Erlking:	"Du liebes Kind, komm, geh mit mir!	incomplete
	Gar schöne Spiele spiel' ich mit dir,	incomplete
	Manch bunte Blumen sind an dem Strand,	incomplete
	Meine Mutter hat manch gülden Gewand."	complete
Son:	"Mein Vater, mein Vater, und hörest du nicht,	incomplete
	Was Erlenkönig mir leise verspricht?"	incomplete
Father:	"Sei ruhig, bleibe ruhig, mein Kind:	incomplete
	In dürren Blättern säuselt der Wind"	complete

Erlking:	"Willst, feiner Knabe, du mit mir gehn?	incomplete
	Meine Töchter sollen dich warten schön;	incomplete
	Meine Töchter führen den nächtlichen Reihn	incomplete
	Und wiegen und tanzen und singen dich ein,	complete
	Sie wiegen und tanzen und singen dich ein."	complete
Son:	"Mein Vater, mein Vater, und siehst du nicht dort	incomplete
	Erlkönigs Töchter am düstern Ort?"	incomplete
Father:	"Mein Sohn, mein Sohn, ich seh' es genau:	incomplete
	Es scheinen die alten Weiden so grau."	complete
Erlking:	"Ich liebe dich, mich reizt deine schöne Gestalt.	incomplete
	Und bist du nicht willig, so brauch' ich Gewalt."	complete
Son:	"Mein Vater, mein Vater, jetzt fasst er mich an!	incomplete
	Erlkönig hat mir ein Leids getan!"	complete
Narrator:	Dem Vater grauset's er reitet geschwind,	incomplete
	Er hält in Armen das ächzende Kind,	incomplete
	Erreicht den Hof mit Muhe und Not;	incomplete
	In seinen Armen das Kind war tot.	
		delayed complete cadence in accompaniment

Most of the phrasing in the example above follows a pattern of complete cadences where there are periods in the text and incomplete cadences where there are commas. Textual phrases that end in a question mark are also accompanied by incomplete cadences, as if to suggest completion will come with the answer to the question.

Complete and incomplete cadences are an important part of recitatives in vocal music. While the rhythm of the recitative is quite free, it must still contain appropriate phrasing to reflect the meaning and natural rhythm of the text. Listen to the recitative sections from Handel's *Messiah,* included on your tapes. Note the regular use of strong cadences to add stability to the otherwise rhythmically free phrases.

Listening Guide
Cadences in Vocal Recitative

. . . .

G. F. Handel: Messiah, Nos. 14, 16

There were shepherds abiding in the field,	incomplete
Keeping watch over their flocks by night.	complete
And lo! the angel of the Lord came upon them,	incomplete
and the glory of the Lord shone round about them,	incomplete
and they were sore afraid.	delayed complete cadence in accompaniment

And suddenly there was with the angel
a multitude of the heav'nly host
praising God, and saying:

incomplete
(incompleteness re-
solved on the down-
beat of next section—
"Glory to God")

Musical Periods (antecedent and consequent)

Sometimes the melodic and harmonic movement of a pair of phrases gives a sense of question and answer. Listen to the following familiar melody or hum it to yourself without the words.

This question-and-answer pair of phrases is referred to as a **period** and consists of an **antecedent** phrase, marked by an incomplete cadence, and a **consequent** phrase, marked by a complete cadence. Even though the words are identical in both phrases of this example, the melodic movement of the first line creates a sense of expectation, which is resolved by the second line. The following example consists of an antecedent phrase followed by a consequent phrase that is repeated.

Listening Guide
Antecedent and Consequent

. . . .

F. Chopin: Prelude No. 20 in C Minor, op. 28

Rhythm throughout, until the final chord, is the same pattern of

A—antecedent	four measures in slow quadruple meter, *ff*
B—consequent	four measures, soft (*p*)
B—consequent	repetition, softer (*pp*)
Final chord	

In a longer work, periods are used to build larger sections or entire movements of music. The following example uses a musical period with a repeated consequent as the unifying basis on which the first part of a movement is constructed. Note that the rhythm of the antecedent and consequent remains the same, as the melody and harmony change. Each statement of the period is varied slightly by the timbre (instrumentation) of the main melody and the countermelody.

Listening Guide

Musical Periods (antecedent and consequent)

· ·

L. van Beethoven: Symphony No. 7
II. Allegretto (first section)

soft chord—woodwinds and horns

Antecedent   **Consequent**   **Consequent** (softer)
violas, cellos, basses

Antecedent   **Consequent**   **Consequent** (softer)
melody in 2nd violins; countermelody in violas and cellos; accompaniment in basses

Antecedent   **Consequent** (crescendo)   **Consequent** (louder)
melody in 1st violins; countermelody in 2nd violins; accompaniment in violas, cellos,
  and basses; bassoons and oboes added on repeat of consequent

Antecedent   **Consequent**   **Consequent** (diminuendo)
full orchestra; melody in woodwinds and horns; countermelody in 1st violins; accompaniment in other strings, trumpets, and timpani

The ♩ ♫ ♩ ♩ rhythmic motive is used throughout the remainder of the movement. The theme returns boldly with a running countermelody and then is passed among all of the instruments to quietly end the movement.

Antecedent

Consequent

Expressive Shaping of Phrases

With or without a text, musical phrases can be emphasized and clearly identified through the use of rubato and dynamic shadings. Both of these elements can help to enhance the alternation of tension and release. By creating more tension in the middle of the phrase and release at the end, the feeling of cadence can be anticipated and confirmed as an even stronger point of partial or more complete rest.

This kind of musical "shaping" of the phrase may be indicated in the score by the composer, but is more often the interpretive addition of the performer or conductor. Performances of the same work by different artists may vary greatly according to how they treat the phrases. Thus, truly outstanding performers are often praised for their artistic and musical phrasing. Popular ballads performed by different singers with varying degrees of ability can provide very clear examples of phrasing. Listen to Frank Sinatra, Nat King Cole, Barbra Streisand, Al Jarreau, Maureen McGovern, Sandi Patti, Julio Iglesias, or Whitney Houston sing a popular ballad. If you compare any of their performances with one of a less experienced singer, you should be able to hear the differences in their ability to "shape the phrase."

Conventional phrases generally last about the length of one natural breath. The song at the beginning of this chapter—"Streets of Laredo"—uses the most common phrase length of four measures. Twelve-bar blues form, another common example, is based on three phrases—also of four measures each. (Listen to "Lost Your Head Blues" on your tape.) Of course, not all works utilize traditional or even consistent phrase length; nor are the beginnings and endings always as clear as in the examples presented so far. Such variety in phrase length and clarity, however, can provide significant interest in itself.

Listen to the recording of the Debussy prelude found on your cassette tapes. Not only are the phrases varied in length and less obvious in definition, but considerable freedom is possible in each performance of this work. If you are able to compare this performance to the same work recorded by different artists, you most likely will find many differences in interpretation.

Listening Guide
Uneven Phrases

. . . .

C. Debussy: Prelude No. 8 (Book 1) "La Fille aux cheveux de lin"
(The Girl with the Flaxen Hair)

Extensive use of rubato
Lack of a strong metrical feel
Varying and uneven phrase lengths
Few strong, complete cadences
Numerous subtle dynamic shadings
Movement sustained by repeated melodic ideas
Interesting melodic contours, emphasized by rubato and dynamic nuances

---

Compare this example with any of those in the following group (in which you should hear an emphasis on more regular, even phrases). Note that melodic contour, rubato, and dynamics are very important in the expressive shaping of these regular phrases as well. While these works may lack the spontaneous sound of the Debussy example, they are also dependent upon the musical interpretation of phrases to give them life and feeling.

Listening Guide
Regular and Expressive Phrases

· ·

F. Haydn: Trumpet Concerto in E♭
    II. Andante

The orchestra and trumpet frequently trade melodic phrases.

W. A. Mozart: Symphony No. 40 in G Minor
    III. Menuetto.

Longer phrases are used to balance shorter ones.

B. Smetana: The Moldau

Phrase length and shape vary by section. The broad contours of the long, sweeping phrases of the first main theme are contrasted with those which follow.

Some works are so melodically fragmented that an attempt to search for phrases would be futile and inappropriate. Others may provide no opportunity for cadential pause, as they continuously spin forward with rhythmic motion. The following two examples are separated by 300 years of time and stylistic conventions, but they share an absence of strong rhythmic pause for cadence. In the case of the Penderecki composition, a lack of melodic cohesiveness necessary for phrases is also evident.

Listening Guide
Lack of Cadential Pause

. . . .

K. Penderecki: Threnody: To the Victims of Hiroshima

> Clusters of pitches
> Percussive sounds
> No cohesive progression of pitches to form a melody
> Dynamic changes rather than melodies shape large sections
> Dissonant harmonies and rhythmic activity create tension
> Simple unison pitches and dynamic changes provide some release

J. S. Bach: Fugue in C♯ Major

> Continuous rhythmic drive without pause until end
> Smooth entry and exit of melodic voices
> Individual melodic lines have cadences, but overlap each other to keep overall
> rhythm driving ahead
> Harmonically, there are feelings of cadence, but these are brief and not reinforced
> with a rhythmic pause.
> Ends with strong, complete cadence

Musical phrases provide important structure and syntax to larger musical forms. The manner in which a composer uses phrases greatly affects the overall sound of the composition. Sensitive interpretation of phrases by performers is crucial to the achievement of an expressive realization of the musical score. Awareness of musical phrases can guide the listener to a more emotionally meaningful experience through imaginative perception.

CHAPTER NINE

Timbre

Preview of Terms and Concepts

Timbre is the quality or characteristic of the musical sound, usually identified as a particular instrument or **medium** (conventional combination of instruments). Timbre can vary with **families** of instruments, number of instruments (**density**), and manner in which the instruments are played (**articulation**). The composer's choice of timbre or changes of timbre within a piece can greatly affect the expressiveness of the musical sound.

B esides melody, one of the most distinctive and memorable elements of music is timbre. When you recall a favorite tune, you probably do so with a particular instrument or singer in mind. What are your favorite instruments, singers, or musical groups? Timbre probably influences the selection of music to which you listen.

The source of musical sound may have a strong impact upon other musical elements as well: The prominence of a melodic line can be enhanced by featuring it on a powerful instrument that stands out from the accompaniment; harmony can sound even more euphonious when played on instruments that blend together very well; a percussive instrument or style of playing may highlight some aspect of musical rhythm. As the preceding examples illustrate only a few of the potential effects of timbre, it is easy to see that composers and arrangers have many decisions to make and possibilities from which to choose when deciding the medium or timbre for which to write.

Homogeneous Grouping

Instruments from the same family or those that produce their sound in similar ways can achieve a very pleasing blend. The string orchestra is an excellent example of how this timbre has been used effectively. By combining the violin, viola, cello, and string bass, the composer can produce a unified sound that has the timbre of a single family of instruments, the range of four different instruments, and the power of a group as large as the stage can hold. Listen to several of the following examples and

The string orchestra creates a homogeneous tone color.
© Beringer/Dratch/The Image Works, Inc.

focus on these aspects of the homogeneous timbre: (1) similarity of tone colors and the resulting blend of sound; (2) the exploitation of range made possible by the use of several instruments in the same family; (3) the power achieved by a unified sound.

Listening Guide
Homogeneous Grouping

. . . .

Strings
S. Barber: Adagio for Strings

String orchestra—violin, viola, cello, bass

R. Vaughan Williams: Fantasia on a Theme
by Thomas Tallis
H. Villa-Lobos: Bachianas Brasileiras No. I

Eight cellos and soprano—part of the music for the voice has no text; it is used as an instrument similar to the strings

String Quartet
B. Bartok: Quartet No. 5
L. van Beethoven: Quartet No. 2 in G Major

Vocal Ensembles
T. Morley: My Bonny Lass

Vocal ensemble (a cappella)— soprano, alto, tenor, bass

T. Weelkes: As Vesta Was Descending
J. Brahms: Part Songs for Women's Voices, Op. 17   *Soprano, alto*

Brass and Woodwind Ensembles
G. Gabrieli: Canzonas

Brass ensemble—modern recordings use trumpets, horn, trombone, tuba

A. Gabrieli: Ricercar on the Twelfth Tone
F. Poulenc: Sonata for Trumpet, Trombone,
and Horn
W. A. Mozart: Theme and Variations for Wind
Instruments   *Flute, oboe, clarinet, bassoon*

Heterogeneous Grouping

Combining different families of instruments can create interest and variety. While several fairly standardized mediums continue to be used by composers, the twentieth century in particular has brought about greater flexibility and variety of timbral combinations. The most common mixed ensembles are the orchestra, band, and orchestra with chorus.

Orchestra

The orchestra as we know it today did not become standardized until the nineteenth century; although the word "orchestra" dates back to ancient Greece, when it designated the area in front of the stage where the Greek chorus danced and sang. With the emergence of opera in the early seventeenth century as an important form of musical and dramatic entertainment, the group of instruments used for accompaniment became known as the orchestra. The specified instrumentation of these seventeenth-century ensembles varied greatly among composers and compositions.

The orchestras of Bach and Handel in the early eighteenth century varied according to which instrumentalists were available and depended heavily upon a keyboard (organ or harpsichord) and a low melodic instrument (bassoon or cello) to highlight the bass line and fill in the harmonies. This combination of keyboard and low melodic instrument was called **basso continuo.**

The timbral resources of the modern symphony orchestra provide a rich source of musical sounds for the composer to manipulate in seemingly infinite combinations.
Courtesy of the New York Philharmonic

During the eighteenth century the orchestra grew in size and became more standardized, until the ensemble specified in later works of Haydn and Mozart and earlier compositions of Beethoven became identified as the ''classical'' orchestra. The nineteenth century saw the growth of this instrumental medium not only in size but also in popularity. The instrumentation and repertoire of that period remain an economic staple for major symphony orchestras today. As you listen to representative examples of orchestral music from both centuries, focus on the following main differences.

1. *Size.* Sheer numbers alone can have a dramatic impact on dynamic capabilities. This is especially true of earlier instruments that were limited in their individual dynamic potential.
2. *Instrumental families.* Strings are the common factor. Woodwinds were added next, with brass and percussion coming still later.
3. *Blend versus contrasting color.* Large numbers of double reeds and brasses were sometimes used for outside performances.
4. *Emphasis on melody and bass line.* Basso continuo was an important part of the early orchestra.

Listening Guide
Orchestral Timbre

. . . .

J. S. Bach: Brandenburg Concertos

Bach called these works "Six Concertos with Various Instruments." While originally scored for seven to thirteen instruments, modern performances usually multiply instruments on each part to produce a small chamber orchestra.

G. F. Handel: Royal Fireworks Music

The first performance of this work used nine trumpets, nine horns, twenty-four oboes, twelve bassoons, one contrabassoon (a new instrument at the time), timpani, and drums. Handel later added strings. Modern performances usually reduce the number of woodwinds proportionally.

Classical Orchestra

W. A. Mozart: Symphony No. 40 in G Minor
            I. Allegro

Scored for flute, two oboes, two clarinets, two bassoons, two horns, and strings.

L. van Beethoven: Symphony No. 3
                I. Allegro con brio

Scored as above but with a second flute, three horns, two trumpets, and timpani.

Nineteenth-Century Romantic Orchestra

B. Smetana: The Moldau

Piccolo, two flutes, two oboes, two clarinets, two bassoons, four horns, two trumpets, three trombones, tuba, timpani, bass drum, triangle, cymbals, harp, and strings.

H. Berlioz: Symphonie Fantastique
            V. Larghetto; Allegro

Piccolo, two flutes, two oboes, English horn, two clarinets, four bassoons, four horns, two cornets, two trumpets, three trombones, two tubas, four timpani, bass drum, snare drum, cymbals, bells, two harps, and strings. (See listening guide that follows.)

Listening Guide
Power, Range and Variety—Expanded Orchestra

· ·

H. Berlioz: Symphonie Fantastique
            V. "Dance of the Witches' Sabbath"
            (Witches' Round Dance section)

Timing

5'00"	Strings with syncopated brass interjections; becomes polyphonic
5'20"	Woodwinds join strings for fourth phrase of the string melody
5'30"	Short string phrases lead to large dynamic contrasts in strings
5'45"	Woodwinds take lead in imitative polyphonic texture with strings; brass interjections continue

6'00"	Brass $\sqrt{3}$ rhythm alternates with falling woodwind line and string ornamentation (four times)
6'20"	Thin texture—mixture of string, woodwind, brass (softer)
6'37"	Low strings (with horn), timpani, building, horn interjections, crescendo with full orchestra joining to create strong, syncopated rhythm
7'25"	Woodwinds/strings briefly
7'35"	Rhythmic string melody against majestic brass melody, strings change to flurry of runs
7'54"	Sudden change: shimmering strings; woodwind and string accents
8'00"	*Col legno* (on the wood) in strings; woodwind with trilled melody
8'15"	Thin texture—woodwind melody
8'20"	Sudden full orchestra chord alternated three times with trilled woodwinds
8'26"	Shimmering string crescendo to full chord
8'35"	Many dramatic chords, interjections, leading to conclusion by full orchestra (9'13")

Band

Ensembles that use the term "band" in their title include everything from concert or symphonic bands to jazz bands to rock bands. While exact instrumental composition varies significantly, this term usually indicates an ensemble that does not use strings as its primary timbre.

The concert or symphonic band has gained popularity in schools as an outgrowth of the military band. Dominated by woodwinds, brass, and percussion, these organizations function primarily as concert performing ensembles rather than military marching units. The instrumentation nonetheless reflects their original designation for outdoor performances. While marches remain an important part of the concert band repertoire, major composers in this century have recognized the expressive potential of the concert band and thus have written in a wide range of styles for elementary and professional bands.

The jazz band is a fairly recent phenomenon. Its flexible instrumentation usually includes a rhythm section (piano, bass, and drums), saxophones, trumpets, and trombones. Rock bands are essentially an extension of smaller "combo" versions of jazz bands. The rhythm section remains the same (with the possible substitution of a synthesizer for piano), and the electric guitar (or other more recent electronic counterpart) assumes the lead harmonic and melodic roles. Rock bands are frequently augmented with other traditional band, orchestral, folk, or even non-Western instruments.

*The term "band" may be
used in the description of
ensembles that are
actually quite different.*

(a)

(b)

(c)

Listen to several different examples of band music (concert, jazz, rock). Use the following criteria to focus on the expressive aspects of timbre in each example.

1. *Families.* Usually brass, woodwind, and percussion. Jazz and rock idioms have a rhythm section. If the ensemble is large, then woodwinds may be found in greater numbers to balance the dynamic capabilities of the brass and percussion.

2. *Size.* Listen not only for the total number of instruments playing but also for the use of soloists versus whole sections of instruments.

Listening Guide
Band Timbre

. . . .

Concert or Symphonic Band

J. Sousa: Stars and Stripes Forever

P. A. Grainger: Lincolnshire Posy

R. Vaughan Williams: English Folk Song Suite

P. Hindemith: Symphony in B♭

W. Schumann: Chester

R. R. Bennett: Suite of Old American Dances

Schumann
(SHOO-muhn)

Jazz Band

Compositions by any of the following jazz musicians should provide good examples for comparisons.

Louis Armstrong, Fletcher Henderson, Duke Ellington, Woody Herman, Harry James, Tommy Dorsey, Dizzy Gillespie, Dave Brubeck, John Coltrane.

Rock Bands

In addition to the following, see current play lists for more up-to-date groups.

Beatles, Jefferson Airplane, Rolling Stones, Blood Sweat and Tears, Grateful Dead, Stevie Wonder, Bruce Springsteen, Elton John.

Orchestra and Chorus

Since the introduction of seventeenth-century opera, composers have frequently chosen orchestras to accompany choral works. The combination of these two ensembles results in a uniquely powerful and expressive timbre. The singing quality of the strings blends easily with voices or creates dramatic contrast. Brass, woodwind, and percussion also provide support or contrast for the vocal timbre. Listen to examples of this combination and observe the following:

1. *Balance.* How do the voices balance with the orchestra? Is there an equilibrium in their roles or is the orchestra used primarily as accompaniment?
2. *Size.* How large or small are the two mediums?
3. *Families.* Do particular families of instruments support the voices while others work mainly to provide contrast? How do all of the various timbres work to achieve blend or contrast?

Listening Guide
Chorus and Orchestra

· ·

G. F. Handel: Messiah
             "Glory to God"

Glory to God,	
glory to God in the highest,	Orchestra supports vocal parts and adds a line of running 16th notes
and peace on earth,	Unison chorus and orchestra
	Two measure orchestra interlude
Glory to God,	Similar to opening
glory to God,	
glory to God in the highest,	
and peace on earth,	Unison chorus and orchestra
	One measure orchestra interlude
goodwill towards men.	Staggered entrances in imitative counterpoint; voices supported by orchestra
	Brief 16th-note run leads to next entrance
Glory to God,	Similar to opening
glory to God in the highest,	
and peace on earth,	Unison voices and orchestra
	One measure orchestra interlude
goodwill towards men	Imitative counterpoint between altos and tenors, changes to alternation of "goodwill" between sopranos and other voices, returns to imitative counterpoint in all voices; all supported by orchestra
	Orchestra ends movement by briefly continuing imitative counterpoint of last section; several soft chords lead to strong cadence

The combined orchestra and chorus create a powerful timbre.
© The Bettmann Archive

Listening Guide
Chorus and Orchestra

. . . .

J. S. Bach: Cantata No. 140, Wachet auf, ruft uns die Stimme
　　　　I. Chorus

W. A. Mozart: Requiem
　　　　Dies Irae

L. Beethoven: Symphony No. 9,
　　　　IV. Presto

J. Brahms: German Requiem
　　　　VI. How Lovely Is Thy Dwelling Place

H. Berlioz: Requiem Mass,
　　　　Dies Irae

K. Penderecki: Passion According to St. Luke
　　　　I. Chorus

I. Stravinsky: Symphony of Psalms
　　　　I. Psalm 38

C. Orff: Carmina Burana
　　　　1. O Fortuna

Articulation and Style

The manner in which instruments are played can vary, depending upon the designation of style by the composer. The "envelope" of each note—the way in which it is attacked or begun, how long it is held, and the manner in which it is released—is described by a vocabulary of various **articulations** available to the composer and performer. Standard Italian terms are used to indicate the most common of these articulations, some of which are: staccato—short and detached; legato—long, smooth; marcato—marked, accented; tenuto—sustained, full value.

Some twentieth-century composers have searched for new timbres using traditional instruments. These new sounds are created through the use of "extended techniques." By avoiding extensive instructions and, sometimes, graphic notation, composers have invented many unique ways to produce and organize sounds. Some of these techniques involve attaching additional materials to an instrument, such as those required for a "prepared" piano. Others simply ask for unusual articulations or percussive effects on various parts of wind and string instruments.

Recent advances in electronic technology have led to additional areas of experimentation for composers and performers. Digital sampling and computer manipulation of synthesized sound have opened whole new fields of timbre and articulation for creative musical composition. A composer searching for just the right expressive timbre can now experiment far beyond the human limits of traditional instruments.

The following example (first examined in chapter 1) uses traditional instruments (52 strings), but many unique and almost electronic or mechanical timbres have been created through extended techniques. Timbre plays a very important part in depicting the horror and trauma of nuclear war that is presented by this piece. The following techniques are used throughout: tone clusters—dense groups of pitches sounded together; glissando—sliding from pitch to pitch; whistles—shrill and unsteady squeals of sound produced by placing the finger next to where the bow is drawn across the string; percussive noises—tapping and scraping the wooden part of the instrument; pizzicato—plucking the strings.

Pizzicato
(pee-tzee-KAH-toh)

Listening Guide
Extended Performance Techniques

· ·

K. Penderecki: Threnody: To the Victims of Hiroshima

Time	
0'00"	Several staggered entrances of clusters—all high pitched at first, then interspersed with lower ones; all fade to soft, vague sound
0'55"	Pops, clicks, and scratching noises; builds in intensity
1'45"	Sudden change to soft unison; separates and returns to unison; fades to silence

2'05"	Low glissandos; several sustained sounds; accented entrances
3'00"	High-pitched cluster grows in intensity; glissandos; sudden stop; low cluster
3'40"	Sudden loud clusters, build through entrances of additional instruments; glissandos both up and down and fade to silence
4'20"	Dramatic staggered entrances; low cluster takes over with glissandos; steady tones; fade; silence
5'20"	Pops, tremolos, whistles, pizzicatos, glissandos, random-sounding entrances; activity increases; high cluster grows predominant and changes to high tremolos and whistles
7'30"	Sudden change to soft, vague clusters
7'40"	Sudden entrance of dense, low clusters; fade to end

Change of Media: Transcriptions and Arrangements

While composers generally specify a particular timbre for each composition, the search for new works or compositions by a certain composer will sometimes lead a performer to adapt an existing composition for a different instrument or ensemble. A work that is "rewritten" with only a change in timbre is called a **transcription.**

Just as translating books from one language to another opens new fields of literature, transcription can open a whole new area of musical literature to an instrument or ensemble with an otherwise limited repertoire. In addition, transcriptions provide excellent study pieces for students looking for practice in particular styles or techniques. Some famous composers have engaged in transcribing their own music, or that of other composers, for new mediums. Franz Liszt, a famous nineteenth-century composer who was also an accomplished pianist, transcribed all nine Beethoven symphonies for solo piano.

Another level of timbral change, which generally takes more liberty with the original work, is the **arrangement.** Instead of merely accommodating new instrumentation, this process may include altering the rhythm, form, or other elements, while still preserving some recognizable characteristics of the original melody. Jazz tunes are frequently "arranged" for combos, big band, or even symphony orchestras. Popular songs find their way into almost every conceivable medium, especially when they have enjoyed financial success. Johann Sebastian Bach demonstrated his admiration for the works of Antonio Vivaldi by arranging several of that composer's concertos for harpsichord, organ, and orchestra with four harpsichords.

Arrangements, like transcriptions, can expand the musical life of a single composition or melody. When done musically and tastefully, these processes can yield interesting and worthwhile compositions. Nonetheless, some melodies survive this change more easily than others. Many of today's popular songs become so strongly identified with their original artist that attempts by other groups to sing or play the song may never be as successful as the first. This is frequently due to unique performance characteristics of the original artist, which can play as important a part in the success of the song as the work itself. Usually, a popular composition that is strong musically can survive numerous arrangements and versions by other artists. These are the songs that last for many years and become known as "standards" in the commercial music industry.

Listening Guide

Transcriptions and Arrangements

. . . .

J. S. Bach: Fugue in C Minor

Compare a piano or harpsichord version of this work with transcriptions as available by Wendy Carlos for synthesizer and the Swingle Singers for voices.

J. S. Bach: Toccata and Fugue in D Minor
Passacaglia and Fugue in C Minor
Fugue in G Minor

Organ works transcribed for orchestra

M. Moussorgsky: Pictures at an Exhibition

Originally written for piano. Maurice Ravel's orchestration of the piano piece is now better known than the solo work.

Purcell (PER-sehl)   **H. Purcell:** "Dido's Lament" from Dido and Aeneas

This aria from the seventeenth-century opera has been arranged for string orchestra by the famous conductor Leopold Stokowski.

E. Satie: Gymnopedie

Numerous transcriptions and arrangements of this simple tune exist. (Blood Sweat and Tears, Canadian Brass Quintet, James Galway with Cleo Laine)

For some unique, frequently humorous, but always expertly played arrangements of well-known orchestral works, listen to recordings by a pair of musicians who call themselves the Cambridge Buskers. Dag Ingram on accordian and Michael Copley on recorder, flute, and various other instruments have recorded some lighthearted versions of the classics. (*A Little Street Music,* Deutsche Grammophon 2536 414; *The Cambridge Buskers Handel Bach,* Deutsche Grammophon 2415 469-1)

CHAPTER TEN

Form

Preview of Terms and Concepts

Insightful listening is dependent upon the recognition of technical elements through **imaginative perception** to find meaning in music. Understanding the **coherence of form** and developing an awareness of significant relationships of musical sounds, through the basic principles of tension and release, can help improve this imaginative perception.

Musical form, defined in chapter 5 as the organization of musical sound events, is not just a hollow structure into which a composer pours a musical work. Throughout history, musical forms have developed and evolved as a result of the needs and creative ideas of composers. Forms that are recognized today as standards in the musical repertoire were not usually chosen through a conscious effort by composers. Because of the coherence they offered to musical expression, various forms grew from the logical development of musical ideas in the imagination of creative human beings. For listeners, form provides **coherence** across a broad plane to our perception of the musical motion of tension and release. Without such coherent perception, it is difficult for the listener to maintain interest in anything but the briefest musical composition.

The rhythm and changing of musical events that give an illusion of motion can also be perceived from a broader perspective of the overall shape or plan of the musical work. These same basic principles of tension and release, introduced in chapter 6, lead to the building of a structure that gives a particular work coherence.

dissonance	consonance
loudness	softness
climax	resolution
expectation	fulfillment
unfamiliar	familiar
variety	unity

The American composer Aaron Copland described this musical motion in terms of a line with direction.

> The prime consideration in all form is the creation of a sense of the *long line* . . . That long line must give us a sense of direction, and we must be made to feel that that direction is the inevitable one. Whatever the means employed, the net result must produce in the listener a satisfying feeling of coherence born out of the psychological necessity of the musical ideas with which the composer began.

Since music is a temporal phenomenon, aural memory is important for the listener who seeks to comprehend a musical work in its entirety. Form becomes increasingly important when the composer is dealing with several musical ideas within a single piece or extensively developing one or more ideas. Simple repetition, as found in strophic form, may be so obvious and easily identified that the form is fairly insignificant compared to the text or smaller aspects of tension and release found in the individual elements. Very short works don't require complex forms. The principles of organization (repetition, contrast, and variation) may only be important at the level of the motive or phrase.

Most people have a fairly limited memory based on a single hearing of a musical composition. Generally, the number of items that can be recalled by the average adult after one hearing is about seven. (Hence, phone numbers are seven digits long.) What does this mean for a first time listener trying to enjoy a very complex composition? While music listeners need not identify the form of every piece in order to enjoy it, longer works may become more enjoyable if their overall structure is perceived. Each listener will have a different perception of a work, based upon his or her previous musical experiences, perceptual acuity, imagination, and emotional state at the moment. Repeated listenings, especially of complex works, will produce different listener responses. Awareness of musical form can help you to organize your listening and lead to greater insights into the musical relationships of repetition, contrast, and variation as created by the composer.

Awareness and Utilization of Form

1. On the first listening get a feel for the overall movement of tension and release.
2. On subsequent listenings identify specific elements (melodic, rhythmic, timbral, textural, harmonic) that are repeated either exactly or slightly altered.
3. Compare your observations of tension and release with repetition of elements to determine patterns of unity, contrast, and variation.
4. If you identified patterns of unity, contrast, and variation, do they fit any of the standard forms with which you have become familiar (that is, binary, ternary, rondo, etc.)?
5. How does the shape of the piece (form) contribute to the musical expressiveness?

   Are you better able to follow the many musical relationships once you identify the form?
   Does the knowledge of form improve your perception of the musical work?
   Does the form provide a sense of cohesiveness?
   If unity is not provided by a conventional form, are there other musical elements that contribute to a feeling of cohesiveness?
   If no form is identifiable, what sustains your attention throughout the piece?

First try this procedure with some familiar works and, then, move to the unfamiliar. The symmetry, balance, and cohesiveness of the three-part form have made it one of the most common musical structures since the Medieval era. Compare the following ternary forms, which vary in size and complexity.

Listening Guide
Listening for Formal Cohesiveness

. . . .

A B A	**Minuet**	**Sonata-Allegro**
Simple ternary	*Expanded ternary*	*Large, complex ternary*
Haydn: Trumpet Concerto	**Mozart:** Symphony No. 40	**Beethoven:** Symphony No. 3
II. Andante	III. Menuetto	I. Allegro

A

	Minuet	Exposition
A a	a	First theme group
a_1	a	Transition
A a	a_1	Second theme
a_1	a_1	Closing theme

B

	Trio	Development
B b	b	Themes from exposition are
c	b	developed with a special new
	c	theme.
	b_1	
	c	
	b_1	

A

	Minuet	Recapitulation
A a	a	First theme group
a_1	a_1	Transition
		Second theme
		Closing theme

Coda		Coda
		Uses material from first theme, special new theme and closing theme.

Try making similar comparisons with other less familiar works. Then, using the five steps suggested on page 153, listen to new compositions for which you do not have a listening outline or any previous knowledge of form. Use your imaginative perception of expressive motion—tension and release, dynamics, phrasing, timbre, and function to comprehend the cohesiveness or formal structure of the work. It may require several listenings to become familiar enough with the work to hear, remember, and relate most of the musical elements. Complex works will continue to provide new insights with each listening. Truly great compositions of music can present fresh listening challenges with each repetition and reward the listener with continuous and renewed musical pleasure.

CHAPTER ELEVEN

Function

Preview of Terms and Concepts

In addition to being expressive, music can also be **functional** and serve an **extra-musical** purpose. Functional uses of music include **music therapy, background music, ceremonial music, entertainment,** and **dramatic support.** Some of these purposes utilize the expressive aspect of music and others employ primarily subconscious powers that music possesses.

W hile the main purpose of this text is to increase appreciation for music through imaginative perception, an understanding of other functions of music can be helpful in developing a fuller awareness of the ways in which music can affect you. Some of these functions, such as musical entertainment, may be obvious to you. But have you considered how you may be using music therapeutically? Are you aware of the many ways background music is used to manipulate your actions? What would movies and television be like without the dramatic support of music? Functional music plays a daily role in our lives.

Music that is used to support some other activity rather than performed for its own intrinsic value as a work of art is called functional music.

Physiological and Psychological Effects

"David Playing for Saul," an engraving by Lucas Van Leyden, 1508. 10 × 7¹/₄.

The Metropolitan Museum of Art, Rogers Fund, 1918.

Since early times music has been credited with magical and mystical powers. Tribal chants combined with rhythmic dances sustained primitive man's hope for good health, abundant harvest, triumph in battle, and fertility. The Hebrews evidently recognized the therapeutic powers of music, as witnessed in the following reference in the Bible:

> And it came to pass, when the evil spirit from God was upon Saul, that David took a harp, and played with his hand; so Saul was refreshed, and was well, and the evil spirit departed from him. (1 Sam. 16:14–23)

The Greek god Apollo presided over both music and medicine. The Greek doctrine of *ethos* even went so far as to identify the ethical character of specific scale patterns and how music should be used to train man's soul and mind. Melodies written with these scales were thought to be capable of strengthening or weakening not only youth, but whole armies of men. Observations and speculations such as these have continued and developed along with a more scientific approach to measuring the effects of music, especially on the mental responses of individuals. Today registered music therapists practice their changing and developing profession, which mixes art and medicine.

Music Therapy

The use of modern music therapy formally dates from World War II, when it was discovered that music elicited responses in comatose patients. Since then, music has been used in the treatment of cancer, mental illness, numerous forms of mental handicaps, and even as a way to reduce the levels of pain medicine necessary for patients recovering from heart surgery.

Numerous studies have been conducted to measure the relationships between exposure to different kinds of music and human physiological responses such as heart and pulse rates, blood pressure, respiration, galvanic skin responses, muscular and motor responses. While a variety of contradictory results have been compiled, the measurement methods and other external variables have been too diverse to yield firm conclusions. At this point the only clear deduction is that music does indeed cause physiological changes in the listener. However, the variety of the findings does not diminish the impact of music therapy but, rather, suggests the need for additional research in order to better predict results and prescribe appropriate uses of music.

Music in Special Education

Music education has adopted some aspects of music therapy to meet the needs of students with physical and mental handicaps. Special activities have been developed for children with learning disabilities, mental retardation, hearing, speech and sight handicaps, and the emotionally disturbed. While these educational programs usually focus on involving the student in music performance, music listening is always an aspect of the therapy as well (fig. 11.1).

The appreciation of music is not usually the primary objective of music education for students with physical and mental handicaps. Of equal or greater importance are objectives of personal development, which are sometimes achieved through music when many other avenues have failed. Some of these extramusical objectives include the development of:

1. A positive self-image (personal satisfaction and self-confidence);
2. Auditory discrimination (general listening skills);
3. Visual-motor coordination (movement related to sound);
4. Perceptual-motor skills (spatial relationships and muscular coordination);
5. Communication skills (appropriate use of language).

Music has been successful in reducing many physical and mental barriers. The enhancement of self-image and the development of personal and social skills have been proven to be valuable functions of music in education.

Synaesthesia

One specific area of music therapy that is very closely related to music listening through imaginative perception is **synaesthesia.** This phenomenon, in which the stimulation of one sense creates imagery in another, occurs in music in two ways: The subject may hear music and see or sense a color; and/or the subject may visualize images in response to music. Dr. Helen Bonny has developed a technique of music therapy called Guided Imagery and Music, which uses this association of music with colors and images. The process incorporates relaxation and music listening to reduce stress, resolve personal conflicts, and gain greater personal insight. As a music listening technique, an enhanced degree of concentration may be achieved that, along with relaxation, can lead to new levels of consciousness and a greater awareness of all aspects of the music.

Figure 11.1
*Arts for learning
conceptual model.
Modified from:* National
Committee, Arts with the
Handicapped. Arts
Resource and Training
Guide. *Washington, D.C.:
NCAH, p. 59.*

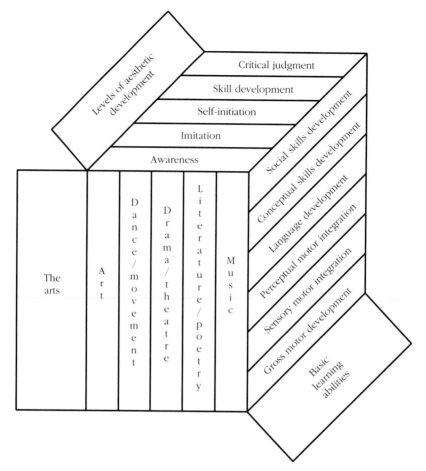

In a similar manner, program music relies upon the association of visual images in response to music. Absolute music can even be used in the same way any time you attach the memory of an event to a music stimulus. When you hear the title music to a favorite film or a melody that is associated with the first time you saw someone who is special to you, memories are stirred and images are visualized.

Most of us use music therapeutically to some degree. Just as the rhythmic rocking of a mother can soothe an upset child, so too can your own selection of appropriate rhythmic music provide relaxation and relieve stress. Your choice of a recording or radio station at any particular time probably reflects your "mood" at the moment or your desire to change that mood. Research studies have suggested that by starting with music which matches your current mood and then gradually changing the music, you can alter your own emotional state of being.

Some prominent composers have even written music with therapeutic functions in mind. The *Goldberg Variations* by J. S. Bach, while performed today as absolute music at formal concerts, were originally composed to soothe Baron von Kayserling on nights when he suffered from "melancholy thoughts" and insomnia.

Are there times when you depend upon music to help accomplish a particular goal? Can you identify specific musical selections you use to help relax or re-create memories? Do you ever seek a radio station with peppy music when you feel "down in the dumps"? Perhaps you use the "sleep" switch on your clock radio to help you go to sleep with music or an "easy-listening" station to relax after a long day. The therapeutic use of music is not restricted to hospitals and structured medical settings. The casual use of music to support or influence changes in mood is important to many people as they attempt to cope with daily pressures and stress.

Background Music

Not all music is meant to be listened to directly. Daily, we are bombarded by music piped into the office, elevator, grocery store, and over the phone while waiting. As harmless as this kind of music may seem, some of it is meant to be much more than just musical wallpaper. Subliminal manipulation with music has grown to be a diverse and profitable business. By knowing some of the ways in which music can be used to motivate people, you can be more aware of the potential manipulative effects, both positive and negative, that background music may have on you.

Industry

Music in the workplace has a long history of success. From the singing of the Egyptian slaves as they built the pyramids to the rhythmic cadences of black slaves as they toiled in the fields, music has helped to ease the burden of work. Modern day business managers continue to harness this powerful aspect of music through the sophisticated use of controlled music programs designed to motivate workers subliminally.

In 1922 General George Squier started Wired Radio, Inc., a competitor to the wireless radio. In 1934 General Squier combined the sound of the word "music" with the name of a new and popular camera—Kodak—and called his product "**Muzak.**" While the first customers of this piped-in music were households in Cleveland, Ohio, a series of experiments a few years later provided Muzak with the secret to its success.

An early test at the Stevens Institute of Technology in New Jersey claimed to show that properly programmed music in the workplace reduced absenteeism and early departures. In an effort to mask noise, eliminate arguments over the use of radios by various workers, and provide a motivating stimulus, industries incorporated "ascending programs" of music in many different factory settings. An **ascending program** of music is sequenced to grow progressively more stimulating. Studies have shown that workers slow down and reduce their productivity at mid-morning and mid-afternoon. By gradually increasing the pace of background music at these hours of the day, fatigue is greatly reduced. Some "easy listening" FM radio stations use the reverse of this process to program a more relaxing progression. Studies using such a "**descending program**" produced more worker errors and lower productivity.

Other Functions

Other uses of music in the marketplace are equally successful. Grocery stores have found that playing sedate music tends to slow down shoppers, who then spend more time in the store and, naturally, more money. Music is played in the waiting rooms of medical offices and claustrophobic places such as elevators to mask the silence and reduce stress.

The variety of ways in which music has been used for nonmusical purposes of subliminal psychological manipulation is large and continues to grow. Hitler used music to help win the German masses to Naziism. Advertisers on radio and television depend upon catchy tunes to carry their sales messages. Dieters have found music useful as well. Listening to lively melodies before meals can slow down gastric juice production and trigger the appestat (the part of the brain that regulates when you are full) so you do not feel as hungry. Music can also be a memory aid. Some multilevel parking garages have given each floor a movie title name and play the appropriate theme music to remind patrons where to find their cars. Obviously, we still do not understand all of the ways in which music can influence us.

Since music arranged specifically for use as background music is usually purchased as a service from a company or radio station, it is not commonly available on commercial recordings. The best places to hear Muzak or similar background music are retail businesses, workplaces, or over the telephone lines when your call has been placed on hold.

Listening Guide
Background Music
. . . .

Where do *you* hear background music? Try to be aware of music playing in any of the public places that you regularly frequent. Some of these may include:

Shopping mall
Grocery store
Factory
Professional office (doctor, dentist, bank)

What kind of music is used?

Records or tapes
Local radio station
    "Easy listening," Top 40, Classical?
Professionally produced, possibly with some subliminal motivation.

The following recordings are some of the few commercial releases of background music. Listening to some of these may give you a better idea of how background music is designed for unique purposes.

Listening Guide
Recorded Background Music

. . . .

B. Eno: Ambient 1 Music for Airports

Brian Eno's reaction to "canned" music, which he deemed uninteresting, led him to create music as an ambience—an atmosphere that is ignorable but still interesting. His music is intended to "induce calm and a space to think."

S. Halpern: Halpern Sounds

Steven Halpern has recorded several albums of music designed to promote or enhance specific activities. Some of these include: Creativity, Driving, Fitness and Exercise, Growing Plants, Massage, Pain Control, Productivity, Relaxation, Sleep, Starting the Day, Study and Learning, Weight Control.

Superlearning, Inc.

This company advocates a combination of relaxation and Baroque instrumental music with a tempo of 60 beats per minute to improve memorization skills. These recommendations are based on the research of a Bulgarian scientist, Dr. Georgi Lozanov, and described in the book *Superlearning,* by Sheila Ostrander and Lynn Schroeder with Nancy Ostrander.

Megalearning Institute

As advocates of sound support for accelerated learning, the researchers at the Megalearning Institute recognize the usefulness of Baroque music to support memorization; but they believe that not everyone enjoys listening to this style of music. Consequently, they have produced a series of tapes using electronic sound patterns that follow the characteristics of Baroque music. The electronic music is meant to mask environmental sounds, increase concentration, and induce relaxation by encouraging alpha state brain wave patterns with a tempo of 60 beats per minute. Relaxation and improved concentration lead to right-left brain integration, stimulation of visual memory, improved recall, and less fatigue.

Music in Ceremonies: Secular and Religious

Ceremonial music not only continues to be functional in rituals and proceedings to-day but also has provided the concert repertoire over the years with many works worthy of appreciation beyond their original intent and use. During the seventeenth and eighteenth centuries, music commonly was composed for celebrations. Wed-dings, funerals, anniversaries, announcements, and receptions involved elaborate ceremonies and equally elaborate musical accompaniment. The commissioning of musical works for specific occasions was a routine practice among members of certain social classes, and many composers greatly increased their income with such commissions.

For example, while J. S. Bach wrote more than three hundred cantatas for the various churches where he was employed, he also wrote several for weddings, birthdays, special appointments, and other celebrations. His *Cantata No. 208, Was mir behagt, ist nur die muntre Jagd* ("The merry chase, the hunt is my delight") was a work written in 1713 in honor of the birthday of Duke Christian of Saxe-Weissenfels. Bach reused the work for at least three other similar occasions by simply changing the names in the score.

Patriotic Music

Jean Sibelius (Yahn See-BAY-lee-uhs)

From the war dances of semicivilized cultures to the marches and ceremonial processionals of our modern-day armed forces, music has played an important role in motivating defense efforts and supporting group morale. The power of music to stir patriotic loyalties has long been recognized and effectively used. Hector Berlioz' famous *Funeral and Triumphal Symphony* was originally commissioned to celebrate the tenth anniversary of the July (1830) Revolution. Jean Sibelius wrote a suite, *Finland Awakes,* in 1899 for a patriotic fund-raiser to fight Russian oppression of the Finnish people. The suite's fourth movement, entitled *Suomi* (the Finnish name for Finland), was later separated from the suite, rewritten, and retitled "Finlandia." As the piece became identified with Finnish idealism, it became one of the composer's most popular works and played an important part in the stirring of strong patriotic feelings and actions. The chorale part of the work has since become the national anthem of Finland and the melody is commonly found in American hymnals.

Our own history of conflicts provides a long list of musical contributions to patriotic fervor. The Revolutionary War inspired the composition of "Yankee Doodle," as well as favorite hymn tunes such as "Chester" by William Billings. The words to our own national anthem, "The Star Spangled Banner," were written by Francis Scott Key during a naval battle in the War of 1812; and our Civil War spawned many popular tunes, including the "Battle Hymn" in the north and "Dixie" in the south. The best-known patriotic tunes from the world wars were "Over There" from World War I and "God Bless America" from World War II. The Vietnam War resulted in a proliferation of protest songs such as "Blowin' in the Wind" by Bob Dylan; "We Shall Overcome" has become a rallying invocation of the civil rights movement.

Public ceremonial music for secular events today is mainly confined to large athletic games. Within this context, however, even events like the World Olympics offer opportunities for the host country to promote nationalistic pride through musical presentations during opening ceremonies. While the longevity of these selections is yet to be determined, the fact that their performances are secondary in many ways to a multitude of other attractions suggests that the music may not stand very strongly on its own.

Religious Music

From the first use of musical chant in the worship of a supreme being to the modern composition of solo songs, anthems, and masses, religious music has had a prolific and varied history. The two main divisions of religious music are **liturgical**—music composed for a specific function in a religious ceremony—and **nonliturgical**—music with a religious theme but composed for concert purposes. While both categories share listening as a common mode of involvement, liturgical music also provides a means for congregational participation in the religious ceremony.

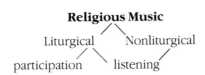

Religious Music

Liturgical   Nonliturgical

participation   listening

Liturgical music functions primarily to enhance congregational worship. While most of this music was and is meant to be performed by trained musicians, the sixteenth-century Protestant Reformation provided the impetus for the layperson to participate more actively in worship through singing. Calvinist churches in France and England introduced this concept with the metrical setting of psalms from the Old Testament of the Bible. Hymns became the preferred congregational music as familiar tunes were used with the texts of writers such as Isaac Watts and Charles Wesley. Martin Luther used popular secular tunes as the bases from which to write hymns, which he called chorales. Many of these early melodies remain in use today in the hymnody of Christian churches.

Familiar hymn melodies have also provided composers with a source of melodic material for liturgical music written specifically to be performed by trained musicians. Church cantatas for voices and instruments, and chorale preludes for organ were especially popular during the baroque era. Even though a congregation could not sing along with this more complicated form of music, knowledge of the hymn tunes upon which the pieces were based made the works more familiar and accessible to the listeners.

Two other important forms of liturgical music are the **mass** and the **motet.** As a celebration of the Eucharist (Holy Communion) in the Roman Catholic Church, the mass has been a dominant musical form since the time of Gregorian Chant. This re-enactment of the Last Supper includes two main sections: the Ordinary, which usually contains the same six subsections, and the Proper, which varies its component parts according to the season of the church year. The musical portions of the mass are divided as follows:

Kyrie (KEE-ree-ay)
Credo (KRAY-doh)
Sanctus (SAHNK-toos)
Benedictus (Beh-neh-DEEK-toos)
Agnus Dei (AHN-yoos DAY-ee)

Ordinary: Kyrie, Gloria, Credo, Sanctus, Benedictus, Agnus Dei
Proper: Introit, Gradual, Alleluia, Tract, Offertory, Communion.

The **motet,** which dates from the fifteenth and sixteenth centuries, is a short polyphonic composition for unaccompanied voices. The text, usually in Latin, was sometimes set to a traditional and simple plainsong but was always treated in a very elaborate form of contrapuntal imitation. Additional versions of the motet developed to include secular texts, solo works, and texts in the vernacular.

Settings of the mass and motet, as well as other liturgical forms, are also popular in the concert repertoire. Concert works that incorporate the title of "Mass" generally follow the six sections of the Ordinary as a musical setting.

Chiesa (KEEAY-sah)

An important form of instrumental liturgical music that continues to be performed at formal concerts is the *sonata da chiesa* or church sonata. This seventeenth-century baroque music was usually written for a trio of two treble instruments (such as violins) and keyboard. It originally served as "filler" music during times in the worship service when silent rituals were being conducted by the clergy at the altar. Today these works are performed more frequently outside of the church setting.

The principal form of nonliturgical music is the **oratorio.** This dramatic religious work is similar to opera, but it is performed without staging, costuming, or scenery. The text is usually a biblical story told by a narrator in recitative style. Solo arias, ensembles (duets, trios, quartets), and choruses, all accompanied by orchestra, provide a dramatic (and sometimes very lengthy) setting of the story. Oratorios called "Passions" are based specifically on the Easter story. These compositions were liturgical in origin, but they are frequently performed today as concert works.

Additional musical forms occasionally have incorporated religious themes with no liturgical function in mind. Operas, symphonic works, and solo songs have been composed over the years as sincere expressions of religious belief meant for the concert stage rather than a worship service.

Listening Guide
Ceremonial Music

Secular

E. Elgar: Pomp and Circumstance, March No. 1

J. S. Bach: Cantata No. 208, *Was mir behagt, ist nur die muntre Jagd* ("The merry chase, the hunt is my delight")

Patriotic Music

J. Sibelius: Finlandia

J. P. Sousa: Stars and Stripes Forever

H. Berlioz: Hungarian March from "The Damnation of Faust" (the setting of a Hungarian national melody)

S. Barber: Commando March

Liturgical Religious

 J. S. Bach: Cantata No. 140

Josquin Des Prez: Ave Maria (motet)

G. Palestrina: Pope Marcellus Mass

A. Corelli: Sonata da chiesa in E Minor, op. 3, No. 7

Nonliturgical Religious

 G. F. Handel: Messiah

J. S. Bach: St. Matthew Passion (an oratorio based on the Good Friday story)

J. S. Bach/C. Gounod: Ave Maria (Charles Gounod wrote his beautiful melody to fit with Bach's Prelude in C Major.)

Josquin Desprez
Zshahs-KAN Day-PRAY)

Giovanni Perluigo da Palestrina
(Jyoh-VAH-nee Pee-ayr-loo-EE-go dah Pal-eh-STREE-nah)

Music for Entertainment

Music brings people together. Making music, listening to music, and responding to music through dance are all ways of appreciating this art form that encourages group participation. Entertainment, diversion, relaxation, and amusement are important and prevalent social functions in our society, and all are well served by music.

While any style of music can provide entertainment (depending on the musical taste of the listener), some styles are more frequently associated with casual listening and social dances. Attempting to describe these styles of "recreational" music presents a dilemma in terminology. Terms such as classical, art, serious, folk, and popular, when used to categorize music, are not very precise and carry potentially negative connotations. To describe one kind of music as "serious" implies that other music is not serious. "Popular music" suggests an "unpopular" alternative. The term "classical" can be interpreted to mean "old music," music written during the "classical" era (1750–1809), or music that adheres to the artistic standards of the ancient Greeks and Romans.

Having acknowledged the limitations of such terminology, the following sections of text will nonetheless proceed to use three of the categories mentioned above (art music, popular music, and folk music) as a convenient, if imprecise, framework for further discussion.

Art music is composed by trained musicians, is written down, and usually requires some degree of study in order to be fully appreciated. Formal concert halls are the most common setting for performance of art music. A concert hall offers an optimal acoustic environment and focuses attention on the music with as few distractions as possible. This encourages the listener not only to be entertained but also to appreciate the music more fully as an expressive art form and to reflect upon personal responses to the music.

Popular music is usually written for commercial success. Composers and performers (frequently one and the same) strive to produce a product with immediate and broad market appeal. The message, as well as the musical style that delivers it, must therefore be current—a requisite that usually limits the potential of a piece of music to "stand the test of time." Unless the lyrics are "timeless" and cross-generational and the music is genuinely expressive and capable of withstanding numerous repetitions without becoming boring and stale, the immediacy of commercial music almost by definition limits the duration of its popular appeal.

Folk music is the indigenous musical expression of a particular culture, generally preserved over time through an oral, rather than written tradition. Folk music is predominantly vocal and usually is created and performed by musicians who have not necessarily had formal training in music.

While folk and popular music may find their ways to the concert hall, such a formal atmosphere is not necessary for their enjoyment. Popular music is more likely to be heard in an informal setting where listeners are also gathered to socialize. Folk music is best enjoyed when the listener is also an active participant. Singing or dancing is often a very appropriate and emotional response to folk music.

Breakdancing.
© UPI/Bettmann Newsphotos

Music for dance is an important function of both popular and folk compositions. Many folk dances grew out of planting and harvesting celebrations or ritualistic preparation for combat. Others were purely for social entertainment. Folk traditions such as the American square dance and others of long history and ethnic origin, including the Bohemian polka, German waltz, Irish reel, and Jewish hora, continue to enjoy popularity today at social gatherings.

Popular music may function both as dance music and background music in social situations. From the Charleston and foxtrot of the 1920s, the Lindy and Jitterbug of the 1930s and the 1940s, the rock-and-roll dances of the 1960s—with colorful names like the Twist, Pony, Mashed Potato, Watusi, and Locomotion, to the breakdancing of the 1980s, popular dance tunes continue to be one of America's favorite forms of entertainment.

Some social dances have enjoyed an extended life through formal concert versions referred to as stylized dances. The minuet, allemande, courante, branle, bourree, gavotte, passepied, gigue, and sarabande are seventeenth- and eighteenth-century dances that have provided the rhythmic basis for instrumental compositions by Baroque composers. Nineteenth- and twentieth-century stylized dances include the mazurka, polonaise, waltz, foxtrot, tango, and polka.

Allemande
(ahl-MAHND)

Courante (koo-RAHNT)

Bourree (Boo-RAY)

Mazurka
(mah-ZOOR-kah)

Listening Guide
Stylized Social Dances

. . . .

J. S. Bach: Suite I for solo cello
  Prelude; Allemande; Corrente; Sarabande; Minuetto I; Minuetto II; Gigue

W. A. Mozart: Symphony No. 40 in G Minor
  III. Minuetto

F. Chopin: Polonaise in A♭ Major ("Heroic")

D. Shostakovich: The Age of Gold, suite for orchestra, op. 22-a
  IV. Polka (This work has also been transcribed for piano by the composer.)

Popular and folk styles that continue to appeal to audiences over a long period of time can eventually develop and take on characteristics of art music. American jazz is one such example. Music that was rooted firmly in folk and popular traditions grew to establish its own "standards"—works that are so effective in their expression that they transcend their initial cultural and chronological context to appeal to broad and diverse audiences. While jazz remains largely an unwritten form of music (due to its improvisational nature), you still can hear it performed in formal concert halls by highly trained and educated musicians. Today, jazz fits our definition of art music more closely than it fits the definitions for folk or popular music.

Music for Dramatic Support

Film Music

As a functional process, the main purpose of film music has been to enhance the dramatic, visual, and psychological aspects of the film. However, piano accompaniment to silent films began as a way to cover the noise of primitive film equipment as well as to convey a mood or even to identify villains and good guys with appropriate themes. As budgets permitted, instruments were added—to the point where some silent movie houses employed orchestras of 60 to 70 musicians. Scene changes often required abrupt orchestral cutoffs and the sudden beginning of a new piece of music. As an alternative to a large orchestra, theater organs of up to five manuals were

Figure 11.2
Console of a theatre organ built by the Wurlitzer Company.
B'Hend and Kaufmann Archives/ Wurlitzer Collection.

popular (fig. 11.2). These immense instruments could provide myriad sounds and were under the control of a single performer, making rapid changes of style and mood considerably easier.

Initially, the music for silent films was either improvised or borrowed from classical favorites. Since the music did not always match the action of the film, the result frequently was less than totally successful. One of the first works to be composed specifically for a particular film was a score by the well-known French composer Camille Saint-Saëns. In 1908 Saint-Saëns produced an original score for *L'Assassinat du Duc de Guise,* and a year later he adapted his score into a concert piece for strings, piano, and harmonium (a keyboard instrument similar to the organ but with thin metal reeds set in vibration by an airstream).

Figure 11.3
Sample of a musical "cue-sheet."

Source: Famous Players-Lasky Corporation.

(Musical "cue-sheet")

" ROSE OF THE WORLD "

No.	Min.	(T)itle or (D)escription	Tempo	Selections
		REEL No. 1		
1	1½	At screening	2/4 Allegro	Farandole — Bizet
2	1¾	T — Rosamond English	4/4 Moderato	[1] Rose in the Bud — Foster
3	1¼	D — Harry leaves boudoir	2/4 Allegro	[1] Farandole — Bizet
4	1	T — For two months, no word came	4/4 Allegro furioso	Furioso No. 1 — Langey (Battle music)
5	1¼	T — Then the survivors returned	4/4 Tempo di marcia	The Rookies — Drumm
6	1½	D — Rosamond and Berthune	3/4 Andante sostenuto	[1] Romance — Mildenberg (1st part only)
7	3	T — After a time	2/4 Allegretto	Canzonetta — Herbert
		REEL No. 2		
8	3	T — Surely you can help me?	6/8 Poco piu lento	En Mer — Holmes (From Letter D)
9	1¼	T — Before her lay	3/4 Andante sostenuto	[1] Romance — Mildenberg (1st part only)
10	2¼	T — Doctor finds body in queer state	4/8 Lento	Erotik — Grieg
11	1¾	T — So Lady G. sailed for the homeland	6/8 Andantino	Barcarolle — Hoffmann
12	3¼	T — The first day at Saltwoods	3/4 Moderato	Prelude — Damrosch (From *Cyrano*)
		REEL No. 3		
13	2	T — At last Rosamond sent for Major Berthune	3/4 Andante Cantabile	An Indian Legend — Baron
14	1½	T — It's a letter from Uncle Arthur	2/4 Allegretto	Air de Ballet — Borch
15	1	T — I am secretary of	3/4 Andante sostenuto	[1] Romance — Mildenberg
16	2	T — Then came agony	2/4 Allegro	[1] Farandole — Bizet
17	3	T — A little incident occurred	2/2 Agitato	[1] Implorations Neptune — Massenet
18	1½	T — What an inclosed note told	2/4 Molto allegro	Le Ville — Puccini (Battle music)
		REEL No. 4		
19	2½	T — Prompt, etc.	4/4 Risoluto	Cry of Rachel — Salter
20	2	T — The dregs of life	2/4 Allegretto	Canzonetta — Godard
21	2¼	D — Rosamond leaves table	3/4 Allegro	Appassionato — Berge
22	1	T — Have you noticed any derangement	3/4 Allegretto	Air de Ballet — Herbert
		REEL No. 5		
23	3	T — The breaking point	2/2 Agitato	[1] Implorations Neptune — Massenet
24	3¼	D — Jani enters with urn	6/4 Allegro	Flying Dutchman — Wagner (Overture — omit sailors' song)
25	1½	D — Doctor enters	4/4 Andante moderato	One Who Has Yearned — Tschaikowsky
26	1¼	T — Wounded, Harry escaped	6/8 Allegretto	Love in Arcady — Wood
27	1¼	T — The rainbow's end	4/4 Moderato	[1] Rose in the Bud — Foster

THE END

[1] Repeated Selections

(With kind permission of the " Famous Players-Lasky Corporation."

As the art of film scores progressed, film companies suggested specific music for their films, and catalogues of music were available to theaters in order to facilitate a variety of moods and dramatic effects. **Cue sheets** were developed to suggest appropriate musical selections as well as performance directions (fig. 11.3). These suggestions required quick transitions and significant modifications, if not butchering, of well-known classical works. Writers and producers soon began to identify specific musical needs for films at the beginning of production, and in the 1920s composers began to create original scores for individual films on a regular basis.

One interesting example of early original film music is the *Ballet Mécanique* by George Antheil. This composition, in part, earned the composer the nickname of "bad boy of music"—a title that he later used for an autobiography. In collaboration with the French artist Fernand Léger, George Antheil created this 1924 film score to be performed by eight player pianos, anvils, bells, automobile horns, airplane engines, and percussion. While the work was a pioneer in the use of nontraditional sounds in serious music, it retains only historical interest and is no longer performed.

On October 6, 1927, the era of silent films ended with the words "You ain't heard nothin' yet," spoken by Al Jolson in the film *The Jazz Singer*. As "talkies" took over, operettas and popular musicals flourished on screen. Animated cartoons quickly capitalized upon the popularity of musical scores, as exemplified by the use of "Turkey in the Straw" in the 1928 Disney film with Mickey Mouse, *Steamboat Willie.*

The extent to which music was used in early sound films varied from none at all to background music throughout. One popular musical scheme was to incorporate a theme song first played during the main titles at the beginning of the film and then used as **"source" music**—music that comes from a visible singer or performer on the screen. The use of theme songs continues today as record albums of the "original soundtrack" are released along with movies to capitalize upon the potential profits associated with a successful hit film.

Many "serious" composers became drawn to the combination of film and music in spite of the restrictiveness of close timing and having to work under the control of a film director. Eric Satie, Darius Milhaud, Arthur Honegger, Ralph Vaughan Williams, William Walton, Jacques Ibert, Francis Poulenc, Dimitri Shostakovich, and Aaron Copland each composed original background scores for motion pictures.

Darius Milhaud
(DAR-ee-uhs Mee-OH)

While Hollywood was sometimes able to lure famous names to film scoring, two of its most successful film score composers of the 1930s are far from household names today. Erich Wolfgang Korngold and Max Steiner both produced lush symphonic scores for numerous films at a time when limited technology required the simultaneous recording of music and film in order to synchronize the two. An error on the part of either musicians or actors meant redoing an entire scene. Korngold approached the task as if he were writing an opera and provided expressive themes to match each of the film's principal characters. Max Steiner is probably best known for two works—the 1933 horror film *King Kong,* in which the numerous sound effects were provided by an eighty-piece orchestra, and the epic film *Gone with the Wind.* Steiner's music for the latter was released as a commercial recording many years after the film first appeared.

As the art of film scoring became more sophisticated, synchronization of music with action became increasingly important. Thanks to a device called the **click-track** (invented by Max Steiner), composers were able to synchronize music and action with amazing accuracy. With film moving through the projector at 24 frames per second or 1,440 frames per minute, a series of holes punched at regular intervals on the edge of the film could produce an audible metronome for the conductor and musicians to follow. Music could be composed and recorded after the film was shot and still match actions and length of scenes with great precision.

The ability to edit scenes into neatly packaged lengths and add music after the film was recorded led to the utilization of groups of studio composers and orchestrators. Composition-by-committee was a fast and efficient method for creating film scores in extremely short time periods. Public demand for large numbers of movies encouraged this process, and the music departments of large studios produced film scores with assembly line ease, if not creativity.

Mood Music

Leitmotiv
(LAHYT-moh-teef)

The 1940s, known as the golden age of film music, saw a growth in the use of dramatic music to heighten the emotions portrayed on the screen. In the same way that Wagner used the *leitmotiv* to attach a melodic fragment to a character, idea, or object in opera, composers helped to identify characters in films with their own musical accompaniment. This form of "background" music, when skillfully manipulated, could closely mirror the actions and feelings portrayed on the screen. The symphony orchestra became the standard background and supporting timbre, and so composers already skilled in the medium were called upon to work in this lucrative business. Exemplary composers and their films include the following:

> **Alfred Newman**—The Mark of Zorro (1940)
> The Song of Bernadette (1943)
> **Bernard Herrmann**—Citizen Kane (1941)
> **Miklos Rozsa**—The Thief of Baghdad (1940)
> Rudyard Kipling's Jungle Book (1942)
> Spellbound (1945)
> The Naked City (1948)
> **Hugo Friedhofer**—The Best Years of Our Lives (1946)

More current original film scores that use orchestra include:

> **Bernard Herrmann**—Psycho (1960)
> **Jerry Goldsmith**—The Wind and the Lion (1975)
> **Maurice Jarre**—A Passage to India (1984)

The most prolific and successful film score composer to use the symphony orchestra since the 1940s is John Williams. Some of his best-known films include *Jaws* (1975), *Star Wars* (1977), *Close Encounters of the Third Kind* (1977), *The Fury* (1978), *Jaws 2* (1978), *Superman* (1978), *Dracula* (1979), *The Empire Strikes Back* (1980), *E.T.—The Extraterrestrial* (1982), *Return of the Jedi* (1983), *Indiana Jones and the Temple of Doom* (1984), and *Indiana Jones and the Last Crusade* (1989).

Concert Adaptations

Some composers have adapted their film scores to concert hall works. These suites or programmatic symphonies have found new and independent life beyond the original dramatic support of a film. Examples include the following:

S. Prokofiev: Lieutenant Kijé Suite (1934)

    I. The Birth of Kijé
   II. Romance
  III. Kijé's Wedding
  IV. Troika
   V. Burial of Kijé

Probably best known for his "Classical Symphony," Prokofiev wrote this suite based on his 1933 motion picture score for the film *Lieutenant Kijé.* The story of the film was a delightful satire on Soviet bureaucracy. In the film, Lieutenant Kijé was a fictional character created as the result of an error made by the Czar in reading a report. Since no one wished to point out the blunder, Kijé's career was further contrived by the Czar's staff, who conveniently used the character to take the blame for numerous other errors.

A. Copland: The Red Pony (1948)

This suite for orchestra was taken from the composer's background music for the film *The Red Pony.* The film, based on John Steinbeck's short story, depicted life on a California ranch. Copland's descriptions of the six movements are as follows.

    I. *Morning on the Ranch.* Sound of daybreak. The daily chores begin. A folklike melody suggests the atmosphere of simple country living.
   II. *The Gift.* Jody's father surprises him with the gift of a red pony. Jody shows off his new acquisition to his school chums, who cause quite a commotion about it. "Jody was glad when they had gone."
  III. *Dream March and Circus Music.* Jody has a way of going off into daydreams. Two of them are pictured here. In the first, Jody imagines himself with Billy Buck at the head of an army of knights in silvery armour; in the second, he is the whip-cracking ringmaster at the circus.
  IV. *Walk to the Bunkhouse.* Billy Buck "was a fine hand with horses," and Jody's admiration knew no bounds. This is a scene of the two pals on their walk to the bunkhouse.
   V. *Grandfather's Story.* Jody's grandfather retells the story of how he led a wagon train "clear across the plains to the coast." But he can't hide his bitterness from the boy. In his opinion, "Westerning has died out of the people. Westerning isn't a hunger anymore."
  VI. *Happy Ending.* Some of the title music is incorporated into the final movement. There is a return to the folklike melody of the beginning, this time played with boldness and conviction.

Ralph Vaughan Williams: Sinfonia Antarctica

for soprano, women's chorus, and orchestra

    I. Prelude
   II. Scherzo
  III. Landscape
  IV. Intermezzo
   V. Epilogue

Vaughan Williams' music was originally written to project the mood of explorers and depict the frozen landscape in Sir Robert Scott's ill-fated expedition as portrayed in the film *Scott of the Antarctic* (1948). Man versus nature, animals of the Antarctic, and the stark scenery find programmatic portrayal in this five movement symphonic adaptation of his original film score.

With the invention of the television, the 1950s saw a drop in movie theater attendance. Competition for additional revenue led the film industry to pursue theme music that could provide the market appeal of "popular music." Film producers today take their scores from many sources. Some still look to original compositions of theme music with the hopes of generating additional revenue through sales of soundtrack recordings. Modern recording techniques and the use of synthesizers have resulted in some scores being electronically written, produced, and performed by a single individual. The popularity of music videos has influenced motion pictures to the extent that some scores are simply collections of current hit songs by popular artists. Even traditional symphonic works have found new life as contemporary film scores.

Listening Guide
Functional Music—Film Music

. . . .

Commercially Successful Theme Songs
H. David/B. Bacharach: "Raindrops Keep Fallin' on My Head"

From the movie *Butch Cassidy and the Sundance Kid* (1970), this song (sung by B. J. Thomas) added more to the revenue of the composer than it did to the dramatic support or impact of the film.

Batman (1989)

Rock star Prince received most of the publicity for his soundtrack for this movie, but his songs were heard in only two of the film's scenes. Most of the background score was symphonic music written by Danny Elfman, lead singer and songwriter for a pop band called Oingo Boingo.

James Bond Films

The "James Bond Theme" by John Barry has been mixed with a commercially oriented theme song for each of the Bond films. A few examples include:

John Barry: Goldfinger (1964)—sung by Shirley Bassey
George Martin: Live and Let Die (1973)—sung by Paul McCartney
Marvin Hamlisch: Nobody Does It Better, theme from The Spy Who Loved Me (1977)—sung by Carly Simon
Bill Conti: For Your Eyes Only (1981)—sung by Sheena Easton
Michel Legrand: Never Say Never Again (1983)—sung by Melba Moore

"Borrowed" Classics

R. Strauss: Also Sprach Zarathrustra   2001 Space Odyssey (1969)
J. Strauss: Blue Danube Waltz   2001 Space Odyssey
G. Mahler: Symphony No. 3   The Gladiators (1971)
L. van Beethoven: Symphony No. 7, II.   Zardoz (1974)
J. S. Bach: Goldberg Variations   The Terminal Man (1974)
J. Pachelbel: Canon in D   Ordinary People (1980)
A. Vivaldi: The Four Seasons   The Four Seasons (1981)
S. Barber: Adagio for Strings   Platoon (1986)

Johann Pachelbel
(YOH-hahn PAHK-ay-bel)

Electronically Produced Scores

Composer/Performer	Film
Gil Mellé	The Andromeda Strain (1971)
Wendy Carlos	A Clockwork Orange (1971)
John Carpenter	Halloween (1978)
Wendy Carlos	The Shining (1980)
Vangelis	Chariots of Fire (1981)
Vangelis	Blade Runner (1982)
Wendy Carlos	Tron (1982)
John Harrison	Creepshow (1982)

Cultural Context

M usical *style* refers to the distinctive way in which all of the elements of music as a whole are treated in a composition or performance. Methods used to categorize musical styles are numerous and varied, but perhaps the most common is chronological classification by stylistic "periods." While the labels used for each of these "periods" are fairly standard, their time frames are somewhat arbitrary. Indeed, the exact years spanned by any of these musical eras depends almost entirely upon the writer who is citing it. The periods identified in this text are as follows:

Pre-Renaissance	1200 B.C.–A.D. 1400
Renaissance	1400–1600
Baroque	1600–1750
Classical	1750–1809
Romantic	1809–1900
Twentieth Century	1900–

Obviously, magical and far-reaching changes did not occur in musical styles at 12:00 midnight of December 31, prior to the beginning of any of these periods. Chosen for their convenience and proximity to a period of years when distinctive changes in music were taking place, these dates provide a framework for the comparison of those changes.

However, as noted above, identifying frames of time is not the only way in which musical styles can be categorized. Since classifications are based upon identifiable similarities, some of the following categories may be even more meaningful, depending upon the listener.

Stylistic Classification By	Selected Examples	Influences
Composer	Bach, Beethoven, Debussy	Personality and cultural time period
Nationality, race, or ethnic group	German, French, American, Creole, Black	Geographic proximity, language, folk music, and instruments
Musical medium	Symphonic, keyboard, instrumental, vocal	Technical capabilities and limitations of specific instruments
Form or type	Fugue, operatic, jazz	Characteristic musical elements
Function	Dance, funeral, sacred, secular	Purpose of the music and location of its performance

Yet another stylistic classification scheme is the one used by most commercial radio stations—often referred to as the station "format." While nonmusic formats are limited to sports, news, and "talk radio," possible music formats include rock/top 40, album rock, adult contemporary, black/urban, big band, country, classical, easy listening, oldies, new age, religious, and jazz.

What influences a particular style? As composers search for new forms of expressiveness, what guides them to create either something traditional or avant-garde? As you listen to the music identified in the final six chapters, you will be able to utilize information about the "cultural context" in which each composition was created as a significant guide to the expressive intentions of the composer. Remember, however, that a musical work can be expressive beyond the chronological boundaries of its creator. Therefore, you must use the information provided here *as well as* your imaginative perception in order to make the music become as meaningful as possible for you.

CHAPTER TWELVE

Pre-Renaissance

Preview of Terms and Concepts

While earliest signs of music can be found in Oriental civilizations dating from 5000 B.C., music of our Western culture can be traced more directly from the **ancient Greeks and Romans.**

With the development and growth of the Christian Church came efforts to preserve music through **notation. Monophonic chant melodies** provided most of the music approved by the early church. Soon, however, melodies were combined and **polyphonic textures** became common in both sacred and secular works.

Music in the fourteenth century, because of numerous innovations in rhythm, harmony, and melody, became known as the **Ars Nova** or "New Art."

D ue to the absence at that time of any means for preserving sound, very little is known about the origins of earliest music. Theories, however, have been constructed based upon pictorial representations, archaeological excavations of prehistoric instruments, and written descriptions of music. Most scholars agree that ancient music was monophonic and used primarily as a "magical power" in connection with rituals, dancing, working, and other group activities. Nevertheless, exactly what the music sounded like is unknown and will remain a matter for conjecture.

The earliest signs of music in higher civilization date back nearly 5000 years to Egypt, Sumeria and western Asia, and India and its neighboring countries, as well as Far Eastern countries—including China, Korea, and Japan. This Oriental heritage is richly depicted through sculpture and painting. Descriptions of instruments and their pictorial representations indicate the use of lyres (plucked strings), windblown pipes, and a variety of percussion.

Roots of Western culture can be traced more directly from the ancient Greek and Roman civilizations. (Even our word "music" comes from the Greek word *mousike*, meaning love of the arts.) The philosophy and art of the Greeks and subsequent political and religious domination by the Romans shaped the early development of Western music. A brief look at three main stages of early Western cultural development will provide a basic understanding of the musical materials that were brought forward to the Renaissance era that followed.

Greco-Roman Era
Ancient Greek civilization   1200 B.C.–146 B.C.
Roman domination   146 B.C.–A.D. 476
Early Middle Ages
Romanesque era   A.D.250–A.D. 1100
Late Middle Ages
Gothic era   A.D. 1100–A.D.1400

Greco-Roman Era (1200 B.C.–A.D. 476)

The music of ancient Greece held an important role in education, not as entertainment nor as a form of artistic expression, but because the Greek doctrine of *ethos* held music to be capable of *direct* influence upon emotions and character.

> . . . even in mere melodies there is an imitation of character, for the musical modes differ essentially from one another, and those who hear them are differently affected by each. Some of them make men sad and grave, like the so-called Mixolydian, others enfeeble the mind, like the relaxed modes, another, again, produces a moderate and settled temper, which appears to be the peculiar effect of the Dorian; the Phrygian inspires enthusiasm. The whole subject has been well treated by philosophical writers on this branch of education, and they confirm their arguments by facts. The same principles apply to rhythms; some have a character of rest, others of motion, and of these latter again, some have a more vulgar, others a nobler movement. Enough has

Court orchestra of Elam.
Barenreiter-Bildarchiv

been said to show that music has a power of forming the character, and should therefore be introduced into the education of the young. The study is suited to the stage of youth, for young persons will not, if they can help, endure anything which is not sweetened by pleasure, and music has a natural sweetness. There seems to be in us a sort of affinity to musical modes and rhythms, which makes some philosophers say that the soul is a harmony, others, that it possesses harmony. (*Poetics,* Aristotle)

In addition to this perceived power to mold character, music was believed by the Greeks to be effective in treating the mentally ill or weakening whole armies of men.

Inseparable from poetry and drama, Greek music was primarily monophonic vocal melodies, rhythmically controlled by six poetic meters.

Poetic Meter	Approximate Rhythmic Equivalent
Trachaeus	
Iambus	
Dactylus	
Anapaest	
Spondeus	
Tribrachys	

The earliest surviving pieces of Greek music include two hymns to Apollo, the sun god, and a drinking song, "Skolion of Seikelos," inscribed as the epitaph on a tombstone, which reads:

> As long as you live, be cheerful;
> let nothing grieve you.
> For life is short,
> and Time claims its tribute.

Modern notation

Ho- son dzes   phai-   nou,   me- den ho- los___   sy ly-   pou.

Pros o- li- gon es-   ti to   dzen,   to   te- los ho chro- nos   ap- ai- tei.___

Principal Greek instruments were lyres and pipes, probably used to accompany the voice by playing along on the same melody. Lyres varied in shape with four to eleven strings. Pipes, also called aulos, were made in pairs with oboe-like reeds, both of which were held in the mouth. One pipe probably provided a bagpipe-like drone as accompaniment to the melody of the other pipe.

With the Roman invasion of Carthage in 146 B.C. came increased emphasis on music for entertainment. The materialistic Roman society provided very few musical innovations except for the development of early brass instruments—loud trumpets and horns played in the outdoor amphitheatres. Choral music continued to be a preferred form, and large groups of slaves were trained to sing lyric poetry. Eventually, however, instrumental music, gesture, and dance were combined in an early form of ballet called *pantomimes*. These elaborate stage productions were enormously popular with the emperor, as well as with the general populace.

(a)

(b)

The Early Middle Ages: Romanesque Era (250–1100)

In spite of Roman persecution throughout the early years of this period, the Christian church developed and grew. With the conversion of the Roman emperor Constantine and the subsequent Edict of Milan in A.D. 313, Christianity became a legally recognized religion. Music, by this time, had become an integral component of Christian worship. It provided an interesting and expressive way to demonstrate and reaffirm one's religious faith.

As Christian music developed, Latin texts were set to ancient melodies and sung in unison by soloists, trained choirs, and congregations. Known as plainsong or plainchant, these unmetered melodies are characterized by flexible rhythm and a smooth flowing melody. Scales used as the basis for plainsong and other early music were based upon numerous systems that include more than just the major and minor scales with which you are most familiar. These systems, called **modes,** use different arrangements of half and whole steps, and the resultant music is described as **modal.** Pope Gregory the Great (c. 540–604) left his mark on this historic music by supervising the codification and organization of plainsong during the period 590 to 604. As a result, most plainsong today is referred to as Gregorian chant. It may be interesting to note that many of these chants are used today in the liturgy of some church services or as the melodic basis for some well known hymns.

(a) *Lyre player, ca. 470–450 B.C.;* (b) *aulos player, ca. 460 B.C.*

(a) H. L. Pierce Fund, Museum of Fine Arts, Boston, (b) Museo della Terme, Rome

Listening Guide
Gregorian Chant

. . . .

General characteristics:

Originally in Latin, although modern liturgies now use translations
Monophonic
a Cappella
(ah kah-PEL-lah
A cappella (voices without accompaniment)
Syllabic settings have one note for each syllable
Melismatic settings have many notes for each syllable
Modal—based on many different scale systems
Flexible, unmetered rhythms
Smooth, stepwise melodic movement
Narrow range (usually about one octave)

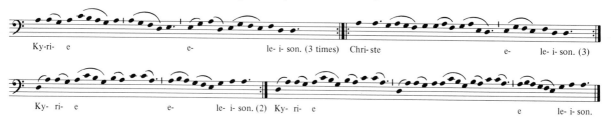

Ky-ri- e   e-   le- i- son. (3 times) Chri- ste   e-   le- i- son. (3)

Ky- ri- e   e-   le- i- son. (2) Ky- ri- e   e   le- i- son.

A church hymn based on Gregorian chant is "O Come, O Come Emmanuel" (*Veni, Veni Emmanuel*). Compare this familiar tune with the chant and characteristics shown above in the musical score for the Kyrie.

The liturgy of the Roman Catholic Church provided the most consistent usage of Gregorian Chant in settings of the *Mass* (the celebration of the Lord's Last Supper) and the *Divine Office*, also called *Canonical Hours* (eight services celebrated at specified times of the day).

Mass

Ordinary (remains the same)
    Kyrie
    Gloria
    Credo
    Sanctus
    Agnus Dei
Proper (varies according to the church year)
    Introit
    Gradual
    Alleluia
    Tract
    Offertory
    Communion

Canonical Hours	**Time of Day**
Matins	Between midnight and dawn
Lauds	Sunrise
Prime	6 A.M.
Terce	9 A.M.
Sext	noon
Nones	3 P.M.
Vespers	Sunset
Compline	After Vespers

In the *Divine Office* music was used mainly in the Matins, Lauds, and Vespers. Since the fourteenth century, musical settings of the *Mass* generally include just the five invariable sections of the Ordinary. A special version of the Mass is called the *Missa pro Defunctis* (Mass for the Dead) or more simply *Requiem Mass* (taken from the opening words *Requiem aeternam dona eis*—"grant them eternal rest"). The Requiem Mass omits the Gloria and Credo, and the Alleluia is replaced by a description of the Day of Judgment—*Dies irae* ("Day of wrath").

The earliest forms of polyphony date from the late ninth century when a second voice was added to plainsong melodies at the interval of a fourth below the original melody line, to create what is termed **parallel organum.** In this initial departure from monophony the two voices began and ended each phrase on a unison pitch and exhibited no rhythmic independence, as can be seen in the example that follows.

By the eleventh century, parallel organum had evolved into **free organum,** which included melodic independence through contrary and oblique motion. Most of the intervals used were fourths, fifths, and octaves, as the third was at this time considered a dissonance. The following example illustrates free organum.

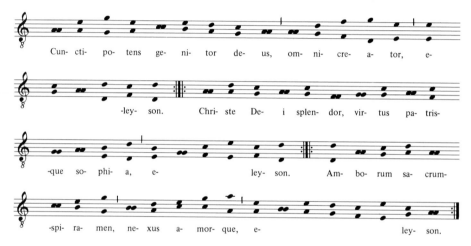

True polyphony was finally achieved in the first half of the twelfth century with the addition of the rhythmic independence that characterized **melismatic organum.** Here the rhythm of the plainsong melody was greatly elongated and the second voice moved freely above. The next example, that of melismatic organum, provides an excellent sample of polyphony.

for-   ma,   vir-   tus   pa-   tris-   que   so-   phi-

a,   e-   ley-   son.   Am-   bo-   rum   sa-

crum   spi-   ra-   men   ne-   xus   a-   mor-   que,   e-   ley-   son.

Secular music of this time did not have the sacred music's "advantage" of church support to organize and preserve melodies. Nevertheless, the entertaining and communicative properties of vocal music and dance ensured the utilization of music for secular as well as sacred purposes. Itinerant performers called goliards, jongleurs, and minstrels served not only as entertainers but also reporters of current events.

While no authentic examples of secular music are available from this early period, texts from the folk songs performed by these traveling musicians suggest several differences from the music used in the church. For one thing, the use of vernacular text (generally poems of love, political satires, or narratives of current events) rather than Latin most likely produced a metric rhythm with more regular phrases than sacred music exhibited. Instrumental accompaniments may have served to double voices, and also may have been used independently to accompany dance.

The Late Middle Ages: Gothic Era (1100–1400)

With the twelfth century came the development of an improved system of notation, which indicated both pitch and duration. As a result, not only were more musical examples preserved but also polyphonic texture became more practicable. The Cathedral of Notre Dame in Paris produced a school of polyphonic composition that influenced both sacred and secular music. From this school came Léonin, one of the first composers to be identified by name. In his *Magnus Liber Organi* ("Great Book of Organa") Léonin prepared a collection of two-part organa. This style was developed further by Léonin's successor, Pérotin, who incorporated additional rhythmic patterns and expanded the voices to three and four parts.

The most important musical form to come from the Notre Dame School was the **motet,** a three-voice composition that evolved during the twelfth and thirteenth centuries to include secular as well as sacred forms. The initial sacred form consisted of a slow-moving low voice called the tenor (meaning "held" from the Latin *tenere,* "to hold"), based upon a Gregorian chant but performed by an instrument; a second voice, called the duplum or motetus (meaning "having words"), and a third voice, the triplum, used Latin texts. With the secularization of the motet, however, the vocal lines evolved to include French language poems of love, and the slower moving tenor "chant" line was replaced with secular tunes.

Listening Guide
Motet

The tenor line in the motet which follows is based upon part of the Gregorian chant "Alleluia, Vidimus stellam," (above) which has been set to the repeated rhythm of a poetic meter.

Anonymous: En non Diu! Quant voi; Eius in Oriente

The Ars Nova

In the early fourteenth century, composer Philippe de Vitry wrote a treatise entitled *Ars Nova* ("New Art") in which he discussed musical innovations of the time, especially in notation, rhythm, and harmony. The name *Ars Nova* thus came into use as an appropriate description of the fourteenth century itself—emphasizing its distinction from the *Ars Antiqua*, or "Old Art," of the thirteenth century.

France and Italy—and their respective musical centers, Paris and Florence—led the musical innovations of the *Ars Nova*. Secular music flourished and grew even faster than the sacred music repertoire. As a result, musical trends included: (1) the use of duple meter in addition to triple meter; (2) the emergence of rhythmic diversity to replace rigid patterns based on poetic modes; (3) less frequent use of chant melodies as the basis for compositions; and (4) the acceptance of thirds and sixths as intervals of harmonic consonances.

Guillaume de Machaut (Gee-OHM day Mah-SHOH

Guillaume de Machaut (c. 1300–1377) was the greatest composer of the French *Ars Nova* period, as well as a poet, statesman, and cleric. Although he wrote many more secular motets and songs than sacred works, his *Notre Dame Mass* is particularly significant because it represents the first complete polyphonic setting of the "Ordinary" of the mass to have been written by a single composer.

Listening Guide
French Music of the Ars Nova

· ·

Guillaume de Machaut: "Agnus Dei" from the *Notre Dame Mass*

Rhythm. Triple meter; uses several repeated rhythmic patterns for unity
Melody. The tenor is based on a plainchant
Harmony. Sounds more modern through increased use of the 3rd as a consonance
Texture. Four-voice polyphonic
Timbre. a cappella
Text. Traditional from the Latin mass

Agnus Dei,	Lamb of God
qui tollis peccata mundi,	who takes away the sins of the world,
miserere nobis.	have mercy on us.

Francesco Landini (Fran-CHES-ko Lan-DEE-nee

Francesco Landini (1325–1397) was the best-known composer of the Italian *Ars Nova* period. The son of a distinguished painter, Landini was handicapped, due to an early childhood bout with smallpox that left him blind. Nevertheless, even in his own lifetime he enjoyed notoriety as a scholar as well as a virtuoso organist.

Listening Guide
Italian Music of the Ars Nova

· ·

Francesco Landini: Ballata, "Chi piú le vuol sapere"

> *Rhythm.* Duple meter
> *Melody.* Lyrical; no longer tied to plainchant
> *Texture.* Two-voice polyphonic
> *Timbre.* Tenor voice and viola da gamba
> *Text.* Secular poem

CHAPTER THIRTEEN

Renaissance

Preview of Terms and Concepts

Renaissance, from the Italian *renascimento* or French *renaître*, literally means "to be born again."

The period, from approximately A.D. 1400 to A.D. 1600, is frequently described—true to its name—as a time of **rebirth**—contrasting this era to the troubled time of plague and religious confusion that had immediately preceded it. This era also marks an important time of transition from the medieval to the modern world. As an incredible age of **intellectual and artistic awakening,** the Renaissance is marked by a rebirth of **ideas, imagination, scientific experimentation, geographic exploration, Greek and Roman classical ideals, language and literary skills, urban growth,** and **artistic expression of human feelings and emotions.**

I f you had lived in western Europe 400 to 500 years ago, what role would music have had in your life? During this period called the Renaissance (approximately 1400–1600)—not unlike the present day—music was a form of recreation and entertainment for everyone, regardless of their station in life. The lute was a popular instrument for peasants as well as for nobles; singing was also equally popular among all classes. As a peasant during the Renaissance, you would have enjoyed secular folk songs in your own language and dances with instrumental accompaniment at festivals and social gatherings. If you had been a member of the aristocracy or upper middle class, you probably would have had some training in singing or playing music, as these skills were considered essential to the well-rounded individ-

Woman playing the lute.
© Historical Pictures Service

ual. Music conservatories existed to provide instruction and degrees in music for the educated classes. Catholics had regular exposure to music with Latin text as part of their Mass, but they did not participate actively in this liturgical music as a congregation. Instead, the singing was left exclusively to the church choirs, which often were supported by a local ruler who also paid the singers to perform for secular ceremonies and festivities. After breaks with the Roman Catholic Church in the early sixteenth century, German and English Protestants enjoyed hearing sacred music performed in their own language and even singing metrical settings of psalms during worship service. Thus, to citizens of the era as well as to historical observers, the Renaissance was an exciting time for the development, support, and dissemination of both sacred and secular music.

Guillaume Dufay (c. 1400–1474) is considered the master of the Burgundian school. Although an ordained priest, he wrote secular chansons in French as well as sacred masses and motets.

Guillaume Dufay
(Gee-OHM Du-FAHY)

Guillaume Dufay.
© The Bettmann Archive

Cultural Centers

The signs of renaissance or rebirth first appeared in Florence, Italy, and spread to northern Europe. From Flanders (comprised of present-day Holland, Belgium, and northeast France), two important groups of composers emerged. The first of these was inspired by Philip the Good, Duke of Burgundy from 1419 to 1467, who supported such a fine collection of musicians that composers in his courts and chapels have been identified as the **Burgundian School.** The **Flemish School** developed next—named for an area of southern Belgium and northern France that became known for its composers of sacred masses and motets. Austria, Germany, England, and Spain followed, with styles largely based on the earlier Italian and French models.

Josquin Desprez
(Zshahs-KAN day PRAY)

Josquin Desprez (c. 1450–1521), sometimes referred to simply as Josquin, is not only recognized as a master of the Flemish school but also considered one of the greatest composers of all time. Josquin's recognition and popularity lie in the expressiveness of his compositions. His sacred works were largely contrapuntal in style and included about twenty masses (most based on a secular cantus firmus) and 100 motets. His secular works were more homophonic in style and included numerous chansons and other vocal works.

Josquin Desprez.
© The Bettmann Archive

Cultural Influences

Humanism

The dominant philosophical attitude of the Renaissance, at least for artists, scholars, and the elite, was **humanism.** Taking their inspiration from the fourteenth-century scholar Petrarch, who advocated the revival of ancient Greek and Roman classics, humanists were well-read and knowledgeable of language and literature. Humanism valued man's search for truth over religious dogma and measured all things in relation to man rather than God. Despite obvious conflicts with the Church, humanism well served the atmosphere of exploration and experimentation that flourished during the Renaissance. For artists in all fields—music, painting, sculpture, theater—humanism meant a search for new ways to express human feelings and emotions that had been avoided by the ascetics of medieval time.

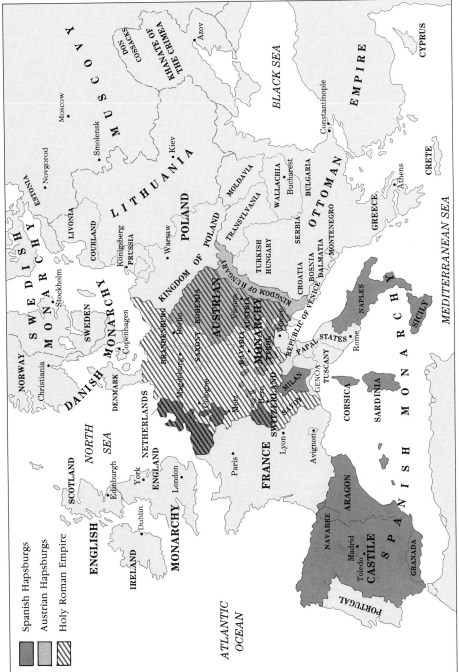

Spanish Hapsburgs
Austrian Hapsburgs
Holy Roman Empire

Anne Boleyn.
Engraving by S. Freeman, after
Holbein © The Bettmann Archive

Anne Boleyn (1507–1536) was the second wife of Henry VIII and mother of Elizabeth I. Her father's position as Ambassador to France allowed her several years of study in the French court. She evidently learned to play the virginals and the lute and is also thought to have composed songs with lute or keyboard accompaniment.

Religious Upheavals

As a period of intellectual and spiritual questioning, the Renaissance was a difficult time for the Catholic Church. Abuses of power and authority, especially associated with the sale of papal indulgences (monetary purchases of heavenly forgiveness), led to the Protestant Reformation, marked by Martin Luther nailing the Ninety-five Theses to the door of the Wittenburg Castle church on October 31, 1517. German Lutheranism and French Calvinism grew from this religious revolution. The English break from Rome, from which Anglicanism evolved, came in 1534 for political rather than theological reasons. The Catholic Church reacted to the Protestant Reformation with a Counter-Reformation of its own; and amid all the turmoil a rich new tradition of sacred music was spawned, which included special music for trained choirs as well as congregational singing.

Hans Hassler.
© The Bettmann Archive

Hans Leo Hassler (1564–1612) studied organ and composition with his father and then traveled to Venice in 1584 to become a student of Andrea Gabrieli. He developed a strong German style from his early training and Venetian influences. A fine organist, Hassler composed vocal and keyboard music for both Catholic and Protestant churches. His secular music included madrigals as well as some of the finest German songs of his time.

Printing

Johannes Gutenberg is generally credited with the invention, in 1454, of the first printing process to use movable metal type. Although block printing on wood probably started in China as early as the thirteenth century, it was Gutenberg who launched a revolution of communication by fastening cast metal type into a wooden press. This process enabled the mass production of books—a great improvement over the slow and error-ridden method of hand copying them. Such a technological advance was responsible for preserving and spreading ideas and, of course, musical scores.

Exploration

The combination of new navigational instruments, astronomical tables and sea charts, Spanish square-rigged ships, and the expertise of Italian mariners produced a wealth of geographic discoveries during this period. What began with explorations down the coast of Africa by Prince Henry the Navigator in 1415 resulted in the shattering of the medieval view of the earth as three landmasses.

(a) *Representation of the Gutenberg press;* (b) *sample pages from the "41-Line Bible" printed on the Gutenberg press.*

(a) © The Bettmann Archive, (b) The Newberry Library

(a)   (b)

Improvements in navigation spawned numerous worldwide explorations.

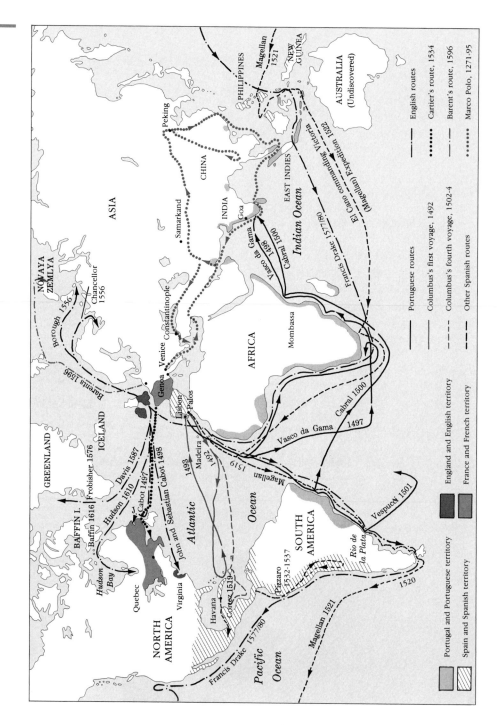

Table 13.1   Major discoveries and explorations of the Renaissance

Christopher Columbus	1492—Discovery and exploration of the New World
Vasco da Gama	Discovery of a sea route to India (sailing from Lisbon to Calcutta and back) 1497–1498
Amerigo Vespucci	Discovery of South America 1499
Vasco Nunez de Balboa	Crossing the Isthmus of Panama to discover the Pacific Ocean 1513
Ponce de Leon	Discovery of Florida 1513
Ferdinand Magellan	Circumnavigation of the globe 1519–1521
Hernando de Soto	Discovery of the Mississippi River 1541
Sir Frances Drake	Circumnavigation of the world by way of Cape Horn 1577–1580

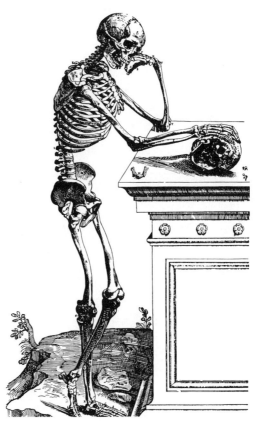

Sample diagram from "De fabrica corporis humani" (1542) by Andreas Vesalius.

Source: Saunders and O'Malley, *Illustrations from the Works of Vesalius,* The World Pub. Co.

Science

Modern Human Anatomy and the Circulation System

The dissection of corpses became a regular practice in the medical schools of Italy and led to a greater understanding of our nervous, muscular, skeletal, and circulation systems.

Figure 13.1
Comparison of the Copernican (top) and Ptolemaic (bottom) systems of astronomy.

Astronomy and Our Solar System

The work of Copernicus in the early 1500s led him to question the Ptolemaic view of the universe (fig. 13.1). Ptolemy in the second century A.D. had described a geocentric—earth centered—model of the heavens. This theory accommodated the belief in the earth as the center of creation and was embraced by the religious dogma of the time. A heliocentric or sun-centered universe was eventually described by Copernicus, who also identified more accurately the position of the other planets. This geocentric to heliocentric change—called the Copernican Revolution—required a significant shift in society's philosophical conception of the universe.

Revolution might be a better word than rebirth to describe the Renaissance. Considering the impact that the printing press, humanism, the Reformation, and geographical and scientific exploration had on the world, the changes in communication, ideas, religion, and science can be described as nothing short of revolutionary. This was an exciting and emotional period in history, and the music of the Renaissance reflects those emotions.

Thomas Weelkes (1575–1623), known for his madrigals (almost 100 of them), was an organist who also composed instrumental music and sacred works. His expressive choral music makes use of word-painting, rhythmic energy, and harmonic chromaticism.

Elements of Renaissance Music

Melody

Melody is the most important aspect of Renaissance music. Its melodic movement is primarily stepwise, or conjunct, and generally stays within a range narrow enough to fit a voice. Renaissance melodies for vocal works often use word-painting to help express the text.

Listening Guide
Renaissance Melody

. . . .

T. Weelkes: As Vesta Was Descending

This English madrigal comes from a collection published by Thomas Morley in 1601, called *The Triumphs of Oriana,* in honor of Queen Elizabeth. Oriana refers to the Queen, and all of the madrigals in this collection end with the same refrain: "Long live fair Oriana."

Voices (6) move mostly stepwise. The music is very expressive of the text through the prolific use of word-painting, which in this context is also called a **madrigalism.**

As Vesta was from	Four voices begin
Latmos hill	"Hill shaped" melody
descending,	Melody descends
She spied a maiden queen the	
same ascending,	Melody ascends
Attended on by all the	Other two voices added
shepherds swain,	
To whom Diana's darlings	
came running down amain.	Melody comes running down
First two by two,	Two voices
Then three by three together,	Three voices, changes to all six on "to-gether"
Leaving their goddess all	Solo soprano on "all alone"
alone, hasted thither,	
And mingling with the	
shepherds of her train	
with mirthful tunes her	Melody appears "mirthful"
presence entertain.	
Then sang the shepherds and	All voices together
nymphs of Diana,	
Long live fair Oriana!	Most repetitious line of all, as if the melody also "lives long"

Rhythm

Rhythm in renaissance music is controlled by meter, but is flexible through the use of shifting accents. Rhythmic independence of voices or instrumental parts contributes to polyphonic texture.

Andrea Gabrieli
(AHN-dray-ah
Gah-bree-EL-ee)

Andrea Gabrieli (c. 1520–1586), a student of the Netherlands composer Andrian Willaert, achieved a reputation as a fine organist at St. Mark's Cathedral in Venice. His vocal and instrumental compositions were used for both church and court events in the cathedral. These works are known especially for a polychoral tradition that uses both voices and instruments in antiphonal groups to produce an exciting stereophonic effect.

Listening Guide
Renaissance Rhythm

. . . .

A. Gabrieli: Ricercar on the Twelfth Tone

Switches between quadruple and triple meter with a faster tempo for the sections in triple meter. The four parts are rhythmically independent for most of the piece.

Timing	Meter	Rhythm
0'00"	4	Main rhythm (Characteristic of canzonas at this time.)
0'55"	3	Faster
1'15"	4	Brief return to four and original tempo with some syncopation
1'26"	3	Faster, identical to previous triple section
1'47"	4	Identical to brief section in four above, leads into return of opening melody
1'57"	4	Identical to first part of opening section. Strong cadence

Harmony

Harmony in renaissance music is still modal and, for the most part, a function of texture, created by simultaneous melodic lines in imitative polyphony. There was, however, a gradual shift throughout the period toward more control of the harmony, and the octaves, 4ths, and 5ths that dominated medieval harmony gave way to greater use of 3rds and 6ths.

Renaissance Harmony

· ·

T. Weelkes: As Vesta Was Descending

This work is modal and predominantly consonant with only the mildest of dissonances. The harmony is more interesting than that of medieval music but remains of secondary importance to the melodic line.

Texture

Polyphonic texture is most common in renaissance music, usually with imitation. Homophony is used for contrast.

Listening Guide
Renaissance Texture

· ·

A. Gabrieli: Ricercar on the Twelfth Tone

Timing	Texture	Description
0'00"	Polyphonic	Imitative, first between the two trombones, then the two trumpets, and finally with all four instruments; strong cadence
0'28"	Homophonic	Rhythmic independence decreases and this opening section cadences with homophonic texture
0'55"	Polyphonic	Thinner, mostly two and three instruments with imitative counterpoint in triple meter
1'15"	Polyphonic	All four instruments with imitative counterpoint in quadruple meter
1'26"	Polyphonic	Thinner, mostly two and three instruments with imitative counterpoint in triple meter
1'47"	Polyphonic	All four instruments with imitative counterpoint in quadruple meter
1'57"	Polyphonic	Imitative, first between the two trombones, then the two trumpets, and finally with all four instruments; strong cadence

Plate 5
Stained glass windows of Gothic cathedrals transform sunlight into brilliant colors to create special interior lighting for these magnificent structures. The chants and organa performed in these churches served an important role in the liturgy of worship and provide us with some of the earliest examples of musical notation.

Scala/Art Resource, N.Y. Sandro Botticelli, "Birth of Venus," after 1482. Tempera on canvas, 5'9" × 9'½" Uffizi Gallery, Florence.

Plate 6

The Renaissance humanists found inspiration in the ideals of the ancient Greeks and Romans. In this painting Botticelli depicts the mythological goddess of beauty as she floats across a stylized sea.

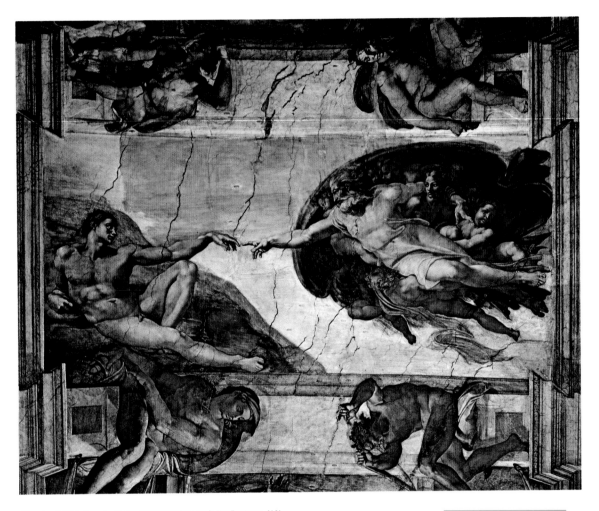

"Creation," Michelangelo, Sistine Chapel Ceiling, Scala/Art Resource, N.Y.

Plate 7
While Michelangelo considered himself first and foremost a sculptor, his painting of the ceiling in the Sistine Chapel is a monumental testimony both in quantity (44' × 128') and quality to his genius as a painter. This detail from the ceiling depicts the dramatic life-infusing moment of the creation of Adam.

Plate 8
The grandiose use of space and the elaborate details of this room (which was probably used to host important state functions) created a monument to the absolute monarchy of the Sun King—Louis XIV.

Versailles-78-Chateau. "La galerie des glaces," Caisse Nationale des Monuments Historiques et des Sites/S.P.A.D.E.M.

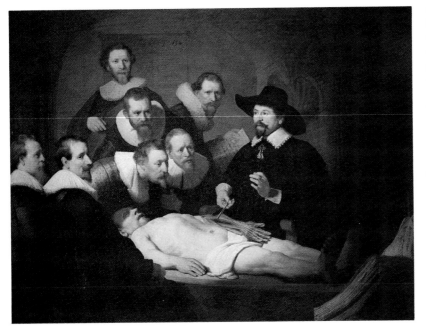

Plate 9
Scientific observation is dramatically pictured as Rembrandt's masterful use of light and shadow draws attention to the surgeon's hands as well as to the variety of expressions on the faces of the observers.

Plate 10
The balance of the three groups of figures in front of the three classical archs parallels the symmetry of musical form found in the music of Haydn and Mozart.

Plate 11
*Through delicacy of
color and typical use
of an outdoor setting,
rococo painter
Antoine Watteau
conveys the
pleasantries of
enjoying an afternoon
of music.*

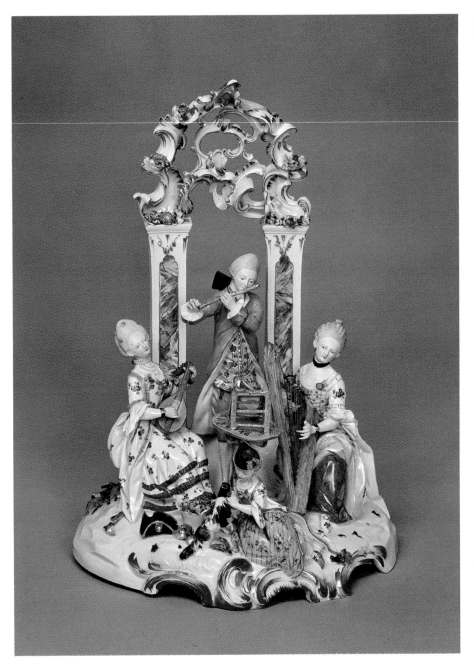

"Musikantengruppe," Fuldaer Porzellan. Modelleur: Vermatl. Wenzel Neu. Um 1770. Höhe 38.5 cm, Breite 27.5 cm. Staatliche Kunstsammlungen Kassel. Abteilung: Kunsthandwerk und Plastik, Landesmuseum.

Timbre

This was the "Golden Age of Vocal Music." Many of the existing instruments were still in relatively early stages of development, and there were no standardized groupings. Instrument choices were left up to performers, based upon what was available for a given performance with a pitch capacity to match the range of the score. During the first half of the Renaissance, instruments were generally used to double voices or were reserved for secular music. While they later came into use for service music in worship, the writing was still very similar to that for vocal music. The lute held a role and level of importance assigned to keyboard instruments of later centuries.

Listening Guide
Renaissance Timbre

. . . .

T. Weelkes: As Vesta Was Descending
A. Gabrieli: Ricercar on the Twelfth Tone

The Thomas Weelkes selection exemplifies vocal music with one on a part. As a secular work, female voices were appropriate; but sacred vocal music would use young boys with unchanged voices for the soprano and alto parts, since singing in church was not considered appropriate for women.

The Gabrieli ricercar represents instrumental music that could have been used as service music but was still written in a vocal style, as if it were a song without words. The instruments used in modern recordings of the ricercar are usually trumpets and trombones. The original composition did not specify instruments and would probably have been performed on whatever available instruments (possibly cornettos and sackbuts) fit the range of the parts.

Form

Most Renaissance music was organized into small sections that were unified more by melodic imitation than by repetition of entire sections. Melodies borrowed from preexisting chants or folk songs (called cantus firmus) were the basis for some very complex polyphonic compositions.

Listening Guide
Renaissance Form

. . . .

 A. Gabrieli: Ricercar on the Twelfth Tone

This piece is written in small sections based on imitative polyphony. Use either of the two previous listening guides for this selection and focus on how changes in meter and texture create an interesting alternation of sections.

Dynamics

Since dynamics were not specified in scores of this period, renaissance music tends to maintain constant volume throughout. The dynamic changes that do occur are largely the result of shifts in texture and/or timbre.

Listening Guide
Renaissance Dynamics

. . . .

 T. Weelkes: As Vesta Was Descending

Listen to the *subtle* dynamic shifts that result from changes in the number of voices present. (one to six voices)

As Vesta was from Latmos hill descending	Four voices begin
She spied a maiden queen the same ascending,	
Attended on by all the shepherds swain,	Other two voices added
To whom Diana's darlings came running down amain.	
First two by two,	Two voices
Then three by three together,	Three voices, changes to all six on "together"
Leaving their goddess all alone, hasted thither,	One soprano on "all alone"
And mingling with the shepherds of her train with mirthful tunes her presence entertain.	Return to all six voices
Then sang the shepherds and nymphs of Diana, Long live fair Oriana!	All six voices together continue to end

Functions of Music in the Renaissance

Music of the Renaissance provided spiritual inspiration and social entertainment, enhanced corporate religious worship, and furnished an artistic medium for individual expression. The challenges that faced Church doctrine were paralleled by challenges extended to its music, manifested by greater interest in polyphony and more congregational involvement in the liturgical music of the worship service. Nevertheless, the Catholic Church remained very influencial and supportive of the arts during this period in which sacred music flourished. At the same time, the philosophical impact of humanism, the technology of the printing press, and a general aura of exploration and experimentation all contributed to an environment in which secular music also could thrive and be preserved.

Sacred Music

The Roman Catholic liturgical Mass continued to dominate sacred music during the fifteenth century. The monophonic chant melodies of medieval times were used as the basis for more complex polyphonic settings of the Mass; and imitative counterpoint based on preexisting chants, folk songs, or motets was the principal unifying feature of the renaissance Mass.

Giovanni Pierluigi da Palestrina
(Jyoh-VAH-nee
Pee-ayr-loo-EE-jee dah
Pal-eh-STREE-nah)

Giovanni Pierluigi da Palestrina (c. 1525–1594) is considered the master of Renaissance Catholic Church music. His clear imitative counterpoint for unaccompanied voices was an acknowledged model for sacred music and more specifically the Catholic Counter-Reformation. Chant melodies provide the basis for most of his 105 masses, but not the majority of his motets.

Giovanni Pierluigi da Palestrina.
© Brown Brothers

With this increase in complexity came fears within the Catholic Church hierarchy that the text—the most important part of the Mass—was being obscured. The Council of Trent, which met from 1545 to 1564, very nearly banned polyphonic settings of the Mass until, as the legend goes, Giovanni Pierluigi da Palestrina demonstrated with his *Pope Marcellus Mass* (1555) that musical polyphony did not hamper textual clarity. The following example is recommended for listening because of its clarity of usage of the cantus firmus melody.

Listening Guide
Polyphonic Setting of the Mass

. . . .

G. P. da Palestrina: Missa Veni sponsa Christi
                    Kyrie

The title of this Mass makes reference to the chant melody, illustrated below, that provides
the cantus firmus on which the work is based.

Four-part unaccompanied voices, imitative polyphony
Three sections, each starting with staggered entrances of the four voices and ending
    with a strong cadence

Kyrie eleison.	Lord, have mercy upon us.
Christi eleison.	Christ, have mercy upon us.
Kyrie eleison.	Lord, have mercy upon us.

Other important sacred forms include:

Motet. A four- to six-voice polyphonic vocal work with a biblical text (usually
    from the Psalms) sung in Latin.
Chorale. A four-part setting of a hymn tune, used primarily by the German Lu-
    therans after the Reformation for singing by trained choirs. The melodies
    were sung in unison by the congregations. The texts were in the vernacular
    and usually set to older hymn tunes or even to secular folk tunes.
Anthem. An Anglican Church motet with English text. Following the break of
    England with the Roman Catholic Church, anthems were performed by the
    choir and soloists as part of the church service.

William Byrd (1543–1623), the greatest English composer of his time, is known primarily for his sacred vocal music and keyboard music for the organ and virginal. In addition to Catholic masses and motets, Byrd composed numerous anthems and psalms for the Anglican Church. His secular songs and madrigals lack the powerful originality found in his other work. Byrd was also active in London in the printing, publishing, and sale of music.

William Byrd.

Listening Guide
Renaissance Sacred Music

. . . .

Mass
G. P. da Palestrina: Missa Papae Marcelli
G. P. da Palestrina: Missa Veni sponsa Christi
G. Dufay: Missa, Se la face ay pale
J. Desprez: Missa Pange Lingua

Motet
J. Dunstable; Veni Sancte Spiritus
J. Desprez: Tu pauperum refugium
J. Desprez: Ave Maria
H. L. Hassler: Laudate Dominum

Chorale
J. Walter: Aus tiefer Not ("Out of the depths")
H. L. Hassler: O Haupt voll Blut und Wunden
              ("O sacred head now wounded")
M. Luther: Ein' feste Burg ("A mighty fortress")

Anthem
W. Byrd: Christ Rising Again
O. Gibbons: O Lord, Increase My Faith

Secular Music

The printing press was to secular music what the Catholic Church was to sacred music. In earlier years, although the Church had provided the motivation, organization, and resources to preserve sacred music, it had discouraged the secular use of music. With the printing press, however, came increased distribution of vocal and instrumental music for amateur as well as professional performances. Amateur performances were especially common among the aristocracy and upper middle class. While instrumental music eventually took on a more professional role when entertaining for the wealthy, dances and folk songs with texts in the vernacular continued to be popular with the masses at festivals and other social gatherings. Important renaissance secular forms include the madrigal, chanson, ricercar, and canzona.

Don Carlo Gesualdo
(Don KAR-loh
Jehs-WAHL-doh)

Don Carlo Gesualdo.
© The Bettmann Archive

Don Carlo Gesualdo (1569–1613), an Italian madrigalist, was notorious in Venosa, Italy, for both his chromatic harmony and the murder of his unfaithful wife. At its best, his chromaticism was profoundly moving and expressive.

Madrigal   This sixteenth-century vocal style began in Italy and later became popular in England. The voices, usually four or five with only one person on a part, were set in a polyphonic texture with occasional shifts to homophony for contrast. Madrigals were very expressive of their literary texts, frequently using a form of word-painting called madrigalisms. A special type of madrigal called the ballett (English) or balletto (Italian) incorporated a rhythmic refrain featuring nonsense syllables such as "fa-la-la."

Chanson   Chansons were secular songs, usually about love, but also capable of being humorous and even naughty as demonstrated by the translation of the following text by Josquin:

Faulte d'argent
Lack of money is an evil without equal.
If I say so, alas, I know well why!
Without the wherewithal one must keep very quiet.
But a woman that sleeps wakes up for cash.

Early examples of this form from the Burgundian School were polyphonic vocal compositions. Later, chansons evolved into songs with a more homophonic texture.

As instruments were increasingly used to accompany voices, it was only natural that instrumentalists found pleasure in performing any available music even without the benefit of its vocal text. When compositions were first written for instruments alone, it is not surprising that the resulting forms imitated vocal styles. Instrumental counterparts of the vocal motet and chanson are the ricercar and canzona, respectively.

Ricercar   These imitative polyphonic compositions were written first for instrumental ensembles and later for the lute and keyboard instruments. The renaissance ricercar eventually developed into the baroque fugue.

Canzona   Written for instrumental ensembles or keyboard, these lively polyphonic works characteristically employ the following rhythmic figure:

or

Listening Guide
Renaissance Secular Music

. . . .

Madrigal (Italian)
L. Marenzio: Madonna mia gentil ("My gentle lady")
D. C. Gesualdo: Io pur respiro ("In such anguish I still breathe")

Madrigal (English or Elizabethan)

T. Weelkes: As Vesta Was Descending
T. Morley: My Bonny Lass (A ballett with a "fa-la-la" refrain)

Chanson
G. Binchois: Files a marier ("Girls to be married")   **Binchois** (BEH-schwah)
J. Desprez: Faulte d'argent ("Lack of money")

Ricercar

A. Gabrieli: Ricercar on the Twelfth Tone
A. Willaert: Ricercar No. 7

Canzona
F. Maschera: Canzona (canzona for instruments)
G. Cavazzoni: Falte d'argens (organ canzona)

Expressiveness

In general, renaissance music saw more expressiveness of human feelings and emotions than earlier periods. The influence of humanism and broadened interest in literature brought new life to music previously controlled by the protective Catholic Church. Some of the ways in which musical elements became more expressive include:

1. *Vocal texts were written in the vernacular.* In addition to the use of word-painting and close ties to literature, texts became more meaningful when performed in the language of the people.
2. *Dynamic changes were subtle.* Although dynamic changes were not generally indicated in written music itself, the increased use of instruments and greater numbers of voices resulted in subtle dynamic variations based on differences in texture.
3. *Phrasing was vocally oriented.* Even instrumental works were based on phrase lengths appropriate for vocalists. These were extended, however, through the use of imitative counterpoint, which frequently omitted individual cadences and delayed stronger cadences by all voices or parts.
4. *Timbre was predominated by vocal music.* Instruments were used mainly to support vocal lines.
5. *Harmony became richer but remained modal.* Polyphonic melodic lines were still the most important harmonic tool, but composers began to pay greater attention to the resultant chords.
6. *Tension and release was achieved in subtle ways.* The active, independent rhythm of polyphonic texture was resolved at the cadence. Chords were seen as a means of expression rather than a coincidental by-product of simultaneous melodies. Contrasting sections were sometimes unified by a recurring theme or "cantus firmus." With the addition and subtraction of voices, dynamic increases and decreases were possible.

Table 13.2   Representative Composers in a Cultural Context

Guillaume Dufay c. 1400–1474 Burgundian School	1415—English victory at Agincourt
	1453—end of The Hundred Years' War
Josquin Desprez c. 1450–1521 Flemish School	1454—Johannes Gutenberg invents printing press
	1492—Columbus discovers America
	1512—Copernicus proposes theory of heliocentric universe
	1517—Martin Luther nails Ninety-five Theses to Wittenburg church door
Andrea Gabrieli c. 1520–1586 Venetian School	1519—Ferdinand Magellan circumnavigates globe
Giovanni Pierluigi da Palestrina c. 1525–1594 Italian sacred	
	1541—Hernando de Soto discovers Mississippi River
William Byrd 1543–1623 English sacred	1542—Andreas Vesalius first book of modern anatomy
	1545–64—Council of Trent meets to discuss Reformation and Counter-Reformation
Luca Marenzio 1553–1599 Italian madrigalist	1563—Church of England established
Hans Leo Hassler 1564–1612 German style	
Thomas Weelkes 1575–1623 English secular	1577–80—Sir Francis Drake circumnavigates globe via Cape Horn

CHAPTER FOURTEEN

Baroque

Preview of Terms and Concepts

The Baroque era, approximately 1600 to 1750, was marked by the **growth of opera** and the **development of instrumental music.** It was also an era during which the arts in general were characterized by restless activity and dramatic motion. Powerful emotional feelings were expressed through detailed ornamentation, dramatic contrasts, elaborate counterpoint, and lavish theatrical productions.

Significant baroque innovations include **the Doctrine of Affections, monodic style, concertato style, terraced dynamics, recitative and aria, functional harmony, basso continuo, melodic ornamentation,** and **idiomatic writing for voices and instruments.**

Monodic
(mah-NAHD-ik)

Louis XIV *(1665) marble sculpture by Gianlorenzo Bernini.*
Alinari/Art Resource, N.Y.

Bernini (Bur-NEE-nee)

T he period approximately from 1600 to 1750 was marked with restlessness and change. The Catholic Counter-Reformation, colonization of the New World, further geographic exploration of the world (including visual exploration of the universe), and the growth of absolute monarchies produced a complex time of new discoveries and ideas.

"Baroque," the term that has been applied to this period of about 150 years, initially carried a derogatory connotation. While its exact origin is uncertain (coming either from the Portuguese *barroco,* an irregularly shaped decorative pearl, or from the Italian *baroco,* a faulty syllogism in logic), the description was applied by eighteenth- and nineteenth-century critics who considered the art of this time period to be extravagant, melodramatic, gaudy, and grotesque.

When compared to the renaissance of Greek and Roman ideals that preceded it and the balanced and symmetrical elements of the Classical era to follow, Baroque characteristics do stand out as imaginatively active. Whether music, painting, sculpture, or architecture, baroque art is capable of displaying restless action and strong emotion. The decorative details found in architecture create a lively atmosphere within a grand space. The unposed actions of sculptures and paintings bring marble and oil to life, and the use of light and shadows in the latter create dramatic highlights.

The Night Watch, *oil on canvas by Rembrandt.*
Rijksmus. Amsterdam. Foto Marburg/ Art Resource, N.Y.

A general overview of the music of the Baroque, which encompasses composers ranging from Monteverdi to Bach, cannot totally do justice to each of the many extraordinary musicians of this time period. The broad stylistic characteristics described in this chapter can, however, provide a basis for discussion, comparison, and further study of those individual composers and compositions that you find particularly interesting.

Cultural Centers

The Baroque era was definitely a time of Italian dominance. Not only did the earliest signs of baroque innovation appear in Florence, Italy, but as the Baroque style spread to France, England, and Germany, the Italian influence remained strong.

Even when France became the artistic center for western Europe during the reign of Louis XIV (1643–1715), the key musical figure in the French court—Jean-Baptiste Lully—was Italian by birth. Many of the principal composers of England and Germany had either studied in Italy or at least had become proficient in the Italian styles. Italian opera became one of the chief exports of the country in both musical productions and stylistic influence.

Jean-Baptiste Lully
(Zhahn Ba-TEEST Loo-LEE)

The culmination of baroque style in the work of the famous German composer J. S. Bach represents the most significant musical contribution to this era from a non-Italian source. Bach's work was influenced by Italian as well as French, English, and other German composers. But his compositions were so innovative, superbly crafted, and personal, they made it clear that Italian dominance was finally ended.

Hall of Mirrors, Versailles Palace (1684).

Caisse Nationale des Monuments Historique et des Sites/S.P.A.D.E.M.

Jean-Baptiste Lully (c. 1632–87), an Italian by birth (Giovanni Battista Lulli), was the founder of the *Académie Royale de Musique* in Paris under Louis XIV, who became known for his superb orchestra and also founded the French opera. Lully was a very wise diplomat who worked his position in the court of France to his best advantage. In spite of his success, however, his own demise resulted from a somewhat unique hazard of his profession: Conductors at this time did not wave batons but beat out the time on the floor with a large staff; Lully died of an infection in his foot caused by accidentally striking his toe with his conducting staff.

Jean-Baptiste Lully.
© The Bettmann Archive

Cultural Influences

The Baroque era continued to be a time of geographic exploration, scientific discovery, and philosophical challenges to the old ways of thinking. Rationalism was the prevailing philosophy of the seventeenth century. Emphasis on observation and experience rather than superstition and the supernatural encouraged scientific advances in the following areas:

1. Improved navigation equipment, microscopes, and telescopes;
2. Invention of the barometer for measuring air pressure and the anemometer for measuring wind forces;
3. Confirmation by Galileo of Copernicus' theory of a heliocentric universe;
4. Increased importance of mathematics, especially through its role in exploration of the universe;
5. Publication by William Harvey, in 1628, of his finding on the circulation of the blood in the human body (*"Exercitatio anatomica de motu cordis et sanguinis"*);
6. Formulation and publication by Sir Isaac Newton, in 1687, of the laws of gravity and motion.

Politics also had an effect on the development of music. With the establishment of politically centralized states under absolute monarchies, national music styles became more distinct. The best example of this can be found in seventeenth-century France, where the statement attributed to King Louis XIV, "*L'Etat c'est moi*" ("I am the state"), was an accurate description of political reality. French music flourished under Louis XIV's reign, but always within tight control through his **Académie Royale de Musique,** established by Jean-Baptiste Lully. Nevertheless, royal patronage of the arts provided immense resources for the development of baroque music.

Elements of Baroque Music

Melody

Baroque melodies generally became **longer, more complex, and more dramatic** than their renaissance counterparts had been. Frequently used as a **unifying force** of compositions, melodies were also called **themes** or **subjects.** As compositions were now being written for specific instruments, melodies also became increasingly **idiomatic**—more characteristic of the technical capabilities of those instruments for which they were specified. **Melodic ornamentation** was common, even when not specified in the score, and performers became proficient in the art of improvising appropriate decorations of the melody.

Listening Guide
Melody as a Unifying Aspect of Composition

· ·

J. S. Bach: Passacaglia in C Minor

Passacaglia is a form of continuous variation in triple meter, built on a repeated bass line. This Bach organ piece uses the following 8 measure theme, which is stated 21 times. While this theme is used primarily as a bass line, Bach does move it into the upper voices, and partially disguises it in statements 12 to 16. Even though there are no breaks between restatements of the passacaglia theme, the regular repetition makes it easy to follow. (Each statement of the theme lasts approximately 22 to 24 seconds.) In addition to the unification provided by the theme, the accompaniment carries similarities from statement to statement.

Passacaglia
(pas-ah-KAHL-yah)

Statement	Key Elements and Their Changes
1	Theme with no accompaniment
2	Syncopated response to each long note in theme
3	Similar response as in #2, but each one moves lower in range
4	Two added moving melodies
5	Ascending accompaniment figures
6	Theme detached; three note accompaniment figures move in leaps
7	Theme connected again; ascending scales in accompaniment
8	Descending scales in accompaniment
9	Ascending and descending scales in accompaniment, more complex
10	Theme with ornamentation similar to the accompaniment figure
11	Theme separated; constantly moving accompaniment (mostly scalewise movements)
12	Theme in soprano; accompaniment descends and then ascends
13	Theme in soprano; much more active accompaniment, added voices
14	Theme in middle voice and decorated, almost hidden at times by active accompaniment
15	Theme in middle voice, mixed into arpeggios of accompaniment
16	Theme in middle voice; quieter, arpeggios continue to disguise theme; contrasts with build to climax, which follows
17	Theme in bass, returns to prominence; two measure rhythm figure in accompaniment begins to build
18	Faster moving accompaniment
19	Return to majestic accompaniment figures
20	Sustained and repeated accompaniment figures build texture
21	Climax of the work with strong cadence

(Left margin vertical labels: THEME IN BASS for statements 1–11; THEME IN BASS for statements 17–21)

Rhythm

Forward motion achieved through a steady beat and **driving rhythmic pattern** are characteristics of many baroque compositions. Rhythm in both the recitative and arioso is irregular, as it follows the natural movement of the words of the vocal text. Some instrumental forms, such as the toccata and fantasia for keyboards, imitate this more irregular rhythmic motion. Dance rhythms formed the basis for movements of suites, with contrasting tempos used to differentiate sections or movements from one another. These tempos were eventually designated with Italian terms, which gave at least approximate and relative speed indications.

Listening Guide
Baroque Rhythm

. . . .

 G. F. Handel: Messiah
Nos. 14–16 (Recitatives for soprano)

The nonmetric rhythm of the text in recitatives conforms to the irregular rhythm of speech. Just as we don't usually speak in rhyme and meter, recitatives provide a more speechlike presentation of large amounts of text.

> *No. 14.* There were shepherds abiding in the field, keeping watch over their flocks by night. And lo! the angel of the Lord came upon them, and the glory of the Lord shone round about them, and they were sore afraid.
>
> *No. 15.* And the angel said unto them, Fear not: for behold, I bring you good tidings of great joy, which shall be to all people. For unto you is born this day in the city of David a Saviour, which is Christ the Lord.
>
> *No. 16.* And suddenly there was with the angel a multitude of the heav'nly host praising God, and saying:
> ("Glory to God")

 J. S. Bach: Prelude and Fugue in C Major

The rhythmic precision of both the prelude and fugue in their own way is mathematical in character. The beat is steady, with a feeling of constant forward motion.

Harmony

The Baroque era marked three important changes in the development of harmony that still affect our music today:

1. A move from use of many church modes to **major** and **minor scale systems** to establish tonality;
2. Emphasis on chordal relationships in **functional harmony;**
3. A move toward the gradual the use of **equal-tempered tuning.**

    You will notice the use of "major" and "minor" in the titles of many compositions during this era. These two modes became (and remain today) the favored way to establish tonality, rather than relying on the many different church modes of Medieval and Renaissance times. Relationships of chords in major and minor keys became more important as increased use of dissonance helped create a stronger sense of pitch center in functional harmony. Changing pitch centers through modulations also became more common as musicians began to adopt the system of equal-tempered tuning. (Equal temperament divides the octave into twelve equal half steps—an acoustical compromise that made it more practical for a single instrument to play in all keys.) Harmony was an important source of expressive tension and release for baroque music.

Texture

While still **predominantly polyphonic,** baroque texture also made use of **homophony for contrast.** As a reaction against the complex polyphony of the Renaissance, composers of vocal music used homophonic texture in recitatives, monodies, and arias to help project the text clearly. Instrumental music continued to develop independently and enjoyed polyphony as an exciting form of expression. The bass line also played an important role in the texture, in that strength of both melody and bass line created an interesting spatial polarity between the two.

George Frideric Handel.
© North Wind Pictures Archive

George Frideric Handel (1685–1759) was a contemporary of J. S. Bach, but extended his study and composition far beyond his German heritage. A child prodigy who assumed the position of assistant organist in Halle at the age of twelve, Handel composed his first opera, *Almira,* at age nineteen. From 1706 to 1710 he lived in Italy, where he studied and composed Italian vocal and instrumental music. After a brief return to Germany, Handel moved to London, where he eventually became a naturalized citizen and remained until his death. His dramatic choral music, evidenced by twenty-six English oratorios and over forty operas, overshadowed his numerous keyboard and orchestral works.

Listening Guide
Baroque Texture

· ·

George Frideric Handel (FREED-rick HAHN-dl)

G. F. Handel: Messiah
    Nos. 14–16 (Recitatives)

Homophonic texture. Spatial polarity of soprano voice and bass line.

J. S. Bach: Fugue in G Minor

The melody upon which the fugue is based, called the subject, is stated in monophonic texture, which then becomes polyphonic with the gradual addition of three more voices. Usually, three of the four voices are sounding at once. The ending builds to a climax, with a return to the subject in the lowest voice (pedal) and the activity created by all four voices at once. All nine statements of the subject are identified below with other material shown by *x*'s.

Voices

1	¹Subject	xxxxxxxx	xxxxxxxxxx	xxxxxxxx	xxxxxxject	xxxxxxxxxx	xxxxxxxxxx	xxxxx⁸Subject	xxxxxxxxxxxxxxx
2		²Subject	xxxxxxxxxx		xxx		⁶Subxxxx	xxxxxxxxxx	xxxxxxxxxx	xxxxxxxxxxxxxx
3			³Subject	xxxxxxxx	xx⁵Sub	xxxxxxject			xxxxxxx	xxxxxxxxxxxxxx
4 (Pedal)				⁴Subject		xxxx xx		⁷Subject	xxxxxxxxxxxx	⁹Subject

Dynamics

Dynamic markings (as well as tempo indications) came into use for the first time during the Baroque period—indicating greater concern by the composers for musical expressiveness.

Since instruments were limited in their ability to achieve dynamic contrast, changes in dynamics generally were accomplished through changes of density—the number of instruments playing. Referring to the distinct levels of dynamics created by these abrupt shifts in density, the term **terraced dynamics** aptly describes this baroque style of dynamic expressiveness (see Chapter 7).

Timbre

Throughout the Baroque period, construction and design of existing instruments continued to improve and new instruments were invented. The harpsichord replaced the lute as the primary instrument for accompaniment. The popularity of instruments like the clavichord indicated the growth of music for the amateur performer, as this delicate instrument was so soft that it could only be played in small rooms and serve as an accompaniment for an equally quiet instrument. The viol family was gradually replaced by the violin family, with its louder, fuller sounding instruments. The clarinet and piano were initially developed during this period, but gained greater popularity in the classical era that followed.

(a) Woman Playing a
Clavichord *by Jan
Sanders van Hemessen;*
(b) *model of clavichord
action.*

(a) Jan Sanders van Hemessen oil on
panel, 26⁷/16 × 21³/4, Worchester Art
Museum, (b) Smithsonian Institution.

(a)

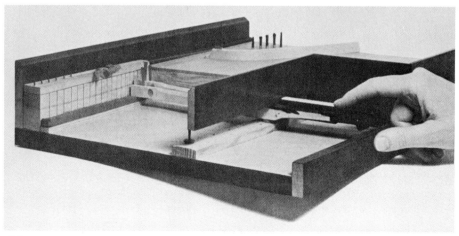

(b)

Modern attempts to re-create an authentic baroque timbre present several challenges. Many instruments used in the seventeenth century have developed and changed to the point where their contemporary counterparts sound quite different. Others have fallen totally into disuse. A comparison of recordings of baroque music using modern instruments versus authentic period instruments would quickly provide you with an aural understanding of the differences. The *Brandenburg Concerto* by Bach, in the listening guide that follows, will sound considerably different if a flute, modern oboe, trumpet with valves, and piano are used in place of the recorder, baroque oboe, clarino ("natural" trumpet), and harpsichord.

Clarino (Klahr-EE-noh)

While copies of baroque instruments can be constructed, the problem of authentic sound is more serious with the vocal parts of baroque operas. The seventeenth-century male **castrato voice,** achieved by castrating young boys with fine voices to preserve their soprano and alto range, is a difficult sound to copy today. The power and range of castrati was extraordinary, and many baroque operatic works are no longer performed because their production requires either females singing male roles or transposition of castrato parts to a lower male range.

An important form of baroque accompaniment is called **basso continuo.** Consisting of keyboard to fill in harmonies (organ or harpsichord) and a low melodic instrument to emphasize the bass line (cello or bassoon), this basic accompaniment timbre was used extensively in both vocal and instrumental music. Except for the solo keyboard works, you will hear the basso continuo used in almost all of the musical examples cited in this chapter.

Listening Guide
Baroque Timbres and Instrumental Techniques

· ·

J. S. Bach: Brandenburg Concerto No. 2, F Major, BWV 1047
       I. Allegro

Concertino. (Solo instruments) trumpet (clarino), oboe, flute (recorder), violin
Ripieno. (orchestral accompaniment) two violins, violas, cello, string bass, harpsichord
Stile Concertato. (concertato style) uses opposing forces (concertino and ripieno) for contrasts
Dynamics. terraced; changes in dynamics necessarily achieved through changes in density
Form. ritornello; uses a theme for structural unification
Melody. ornate
Harmony. functional (F major)
Texture. predominantly polyphonic with homophonic for contrast
Rhythm. steady beat with constantly running rhythm
Basso continuo. (harpsichord and cello) continues almost throughout
Idiomatic writing. not vocally oriented

Form

Musical organization in the Baroque used **sectional, continuous variations,** the **fugue,** and **free forms.** Many of these were then combined to create multimovement structures. **Melody** was very important in providing **unity** in most forms. **Contrasts** were achieved primarily through changes of **key, rhythm,** and **texture.**

The most common sectional forms were binary, ternary, and rondo. A form similar to rondo called **ritornello** was used mostly in **Concerto Grosso**—a concerto for orchestra and group of solo instruments. (Ritornello differs from rondo form in that the unifying theme returns in a different key in all but the final statement.)

Continuous variations include the **ground bass** and **passacaglia,** both of which are based upon a recurring melody. In the ground bass, the melody (sometimes referred to as the **basso ostinato**) is repeated over and over in the lowest voice with continuous variations in the upper parts. While the exact meaning of the term "passacaglia" has not always been clear, it generally refers to a set of continuous variations in triple meter with a ground bass that also moves into the upper voices.

The fugue is a contrapuntal procedure that develops a musical theme called the **subject** through an imitative polyphonic texture. The subject is usually stated by itself at the beginning of the work and then introduced through a polyphonic texture in each of the other voices to be used. Subsequent statements of the subject in various keys and with some variation are alternated with sections of free contrapuntal material.

Free forms, including toccata, fantasy, and prelude, were especially popular for keyboard compositions. Because of their openness of structure and rhythmic diversity, these works can even sound improvisational.

Multimovement structures such as sonata, suite, cantata, oratorio, and concerto combined smaller forms to add contrast to the larger structure.

> *Sonata.* The term sonata is used in several contexts. The Church Sonata (Sonata da chiesa) and the Chamber Sonata (Sonata da camera) were written for either a solo melodic instrument and continuo (solo sonata) or more commonly for two violins and continuo (trio sonata). Both are usually four-movement works with alternating slow, fast, slow, fast tempos. The Church Sonata was more serious in nature, and the Chamber Sonata more likely to have light, rhythmic dance movements.
>
> *Suite.* Keyboard suites consisted of four dances (Allemande, Courante, Sarabande, and Gigue), each usually written in binary form. Orchestral suites are similar, but freely substituted and added movements.
>
> *Concerto.* Two forms of concerto, the solo concerto and the concerto grosso, differed only as to whether a single instrument (solo concerto) or a group of instruments (concerto grosso) was featured. The concerto grosso generally used three soloists (called the concertino) who alternated with the full orchestra (called tutti or ripieno).

Cantata. The cantata (sacred or secular) was a vocal work that began as an alternation of recitatives and arias with accompaniment. Later, duets and choruses were added to create a grander choral work.

Oratorio. The oratorio is basically an opera without costumes, acting, or scenery. Most were based on biblical stories and also used recitative, aria, ensembles, and choruses.

Baroque Expressiveness

As with all fine art, baroque music is capable of symbolizing the realm of human feeling in a unique way. While music from this era grew out of a culture different from ours today, baroque music can still be meaningful to us. You don't have to be an aristocratic Italian to enjoy the opera of Monteverdi or a German Lutheran to be moved by the cantatas of Johann Sebastian Bach. Even the chronological distance of 350 years need not be a barrier to perceiving baroque music as a personally rewarding listening experience. By understanding the fundamental tools used by composers of this time and at least some of the context in which they were used, your own perception of baroque music can be enhanced and become personally meaningful.

Baroque music itself reflected a move toward a more personal kind of expression. Often this expressiveness was manifested in detailed ornamentation, dramatic contrasts, elaborate counterpoint, or lavish operatic staging. Each of the elements of music described in the first section of this chapter can contribute to a very complex composition. While this may lend itself to formal analysis and technical listening, you should also look for the expression of human emotional experience that transcends culture and time.

Think again about the general changes in musical elements that took place during the Baroque era. Which of these do you find significant in the music to which you listen?

Melody. A unifying factor; ornate; more dramatic

Harmony. Chords became more important; the use of equal temperament made modulations more practical; shift from modal tonalities to major and minor

Rhythm. Tempos were sometimes designated by the composer and used for contrasts between sections or movements; forward driving rhythms; irregular, speechlike rhythms

Timbre. Instruments began to be specified; basso continuo accompaniment; instrument construction improved

Texture. Predominantly polyphonic with homophonic for contrast; spatial polarity of melody and bass line

Form. Tended to sectionalize changes of tonality, rhythm, and texture; continuous forms also

Sometimes music is expressive through extramusical associations. Three such referential vehicles for baroque expressiveness were word-painting, descriptive program music, and the Doctrine of Affections.

Word-Painting

Baroque composers found the symbolism of word-painting to be an expressive and dramatic technique in vocal music. Words like "high" and "low" or "heaven" and "hell" suggested appropriate instrumental ranges. Shapes of objects were imitated by melodic contours. Pleasant or unpleasant feelings could be reinforced with either pleasing or dissonant harmonies, respectively.

Listening Guide
Word-Painting

. . . .

G. F. Handel: "Every Valley" from Messiah

Ev'ry valley, ev'ry valley shall be exalted,	
shall be exalted,	*long, rising line*
shall be exalted,	
shall be exalted,	*long, rising line*
and ev'ry mountain and hill	*melodic contour in shape of "mountain and hill"*
made low.	*low pitch*
the crooked straight,	
and the rough places plain,	*smooth alternation between two pitches*
the crooked straight,	*disjunct melodic line*
the crooked straight,	
and the rough places plain,	*smooth line*
and the rough places plain.	
Ev'ry valley,	
ev'ry valley shall be exalted,	*large upward leaps*
ev'ry valley,	
ev'ry valley shall be exalted	*large upward leaps followed by rising line*
and ev'ry mountain and hill made low;	
the crooked straight, the crooked straight,	
and the rough places plain,	*long, sustained pitch*
and the rough places plain,	
and the rough places plain,	
the crooked straight,	
and the rough places plain.	

Descriptive Program Music

Expressiveness through symbolism was not limited to vocal music. Descriptive program music that imitated natural sounds or physical movements was also a popular medium for baroque composers. Birds, running water, thunder and lightning, rain, high winds, gentle breezes, and physical movements like running, stopping, and falling have all found their way into imitative musical motion. Descriptive titles of compositions and their individual movements usually provide clues to the composer's expressive intentions.

Programmatic techniques *by themselves* cannot show to proper advantage the unique musical modes of expressiveness. Simple imitation of natural events and physical motions can be banal, unless the music provides additional room for personal, imaginative perception. Thus descriptive program music at its worst can be simplistic, shallow, and trite. At its best, however, this expressive technique can be inspiring and creative and continue to evoke a full range of emotional and unique experiences.

Antonio Vivaldi (c. 1678–1741) was a prolific Italian composer of vocal and instrumental music. "The red priest," *prete rosso,* of Venice (as he was known because of his red hair and priesthood in the Roman Catholic Church) was a virtuoso violinist who enjoyed a reputation for his compositions and performances all over Europe. For almost forty years Vivaldi was the Music Director of a Venetian conservatory for orphaned girls. His duties there included not only the preparation for weekly concerts but also the composition of new music for those performances. This high demand for new works, however, posed no apparent problem for such a creative mind. While known today primarily for his instrumental compositions, including almost 450 concertos, 23 sinfonias, and 75 sonatas, Vivaldi also wrote vocal works, including 49 operas, and numerous cantatas, motets, and oratorios.

Antonio Vivaldi.
© The Bettmann Archive

Antonio Vivaldi
(An-TOH-nee-oh
Vee-VAHL-dee)

Listening Guide
Descriptive Program Music

. . . .

A. Vivaldi: The Four Seasons

        Concerto grosso, Opus 8, No. 1, E Major, "Spring"
        Concerto grosso, Opus 8, No. 2, G Minor, "Summer"
        Concerto grosso, Opus 8, No. 3, F Major, "Autumn"
        Concerto grosso, Opus 8, No. 4, F Minor, "Winter"

These four solo concerto grossos for violin and string orchestra come from a set of twelve (Opus 8) published in 1725 entitled "The Test of Harmony and Invention." In addition to the descriptive title of each movement, the composer prefaced each concerto with a sonnet. He even went so far as to indicate points in the score that correspond with specific lines of the sonnet. Vivaldi's sonnet for the first concerto appears below, divided among the three movements as indicated by the composer.

Concerto grosso, Opus 8, No. 1, E Major, "Spring"

I. Allegro

A	Spring has returned and festively
B	Is greeted by the birds in happy song;
C	And fountains fanned by little Zephyrs
	Murmur sweetly in the constant flow
D	When skies are mantled all in black
	Lightning flash and thunder roar;
E	When these have done the little birds
	Return to carol their enchanting song.

Timing	Ritornello Sections	Sonnet Sections	Description
0'00"	A	A	Ritornello theme—full string orchestra with a lively melody; dynamic change to soft for contrast
0'28"	B	B	Solo violin with two additional solo violins in a spirited imitation of bird calls
1'00"	A		Abbreviated statement of the second half of ritornello theme
1'07"	C	C	Soft, smooth, running figures in the violins (Running scales at the end of this section foreshadow the coming storm—section "D.")

Timing	Ritornello Sections	Sonnet Sections	Description
1'30"	A		Abbreviated statement of the second half of ritornello theme
1'36"	D	D	Tremolos, running scales, jagged melodies, and hard accents imitate lightning and thunder
2'00"	A		Abbreviated statement of the second half of ritornello theme
2'08"	E	E	Bird calls in solo violins similar to "B"; full string orchestra enters briefly in the middle of this section with material from first part of ritornello theme
2'47"	A		First half of ritornello theme brings the movement to a close (3'05")

II. Largo e pianissimo sempre

An appropriately contrasting slow movement depicts a slumbering herdsman and his barking watchdog (imitated by the violas throughout).

F   While upon the flowering meadow
       Amid the murmuring leaves and boughs
       Sleep goatherd and his trusty dog.

III. Allegro: Rustic Dance.

The shepherds dance to the festive sound of bagpipes, complete with an imitation of the bagpipe drone in the lower strings.

G   To country bagpipes' festive sound
       Dance nymphs and shepherds underneath
       Beloved springtime's brilliant skies.

Doctrine of the Affections

The expression of affections or passions was a principal goal of baroque music. Not only was an environment enriched with music a sign of great wealth and power, but music itself was thought to possess the power to move and express emotions.

Affektenlehre was the German theory of musical affects that was widely accepted by baroque theorists and composers, who believed that a certain expressive vocabulary of melodic, harmonic, and rhythmic procedures could produce music capable of eliciting specific, predictable emotions and feelings. Attempts were even made to catalog these devices. René Descartes identified devices for six basic emotions or passions—surprise, love, hatred, desire, joy, sadness—combinations of which could theoretically produce additional feelings. Examples of similarly linked devices cataloged by Johann Mattheson in *Der vollkommene Capellmeister* (1739; "The Perfect Chapelmaster") include:

large intervals	joy
small intervals	sadness
rough harmony with rapid melody	fury
contrapuntal melodies	obstinacy

Such catalogs are very similar to those described in chapter 11 for use in composing early silent-movie scores. However, while silent movies progressed from musical fragment to musical fragment very quickly with frequent mood changes, baroque compositions generally expressed a single emotion or passion throughout an entire piece.

The Growth of Opera

The enhanced impact of combining drama and music has been recognized since the time of ancient Greece. Music was an integral part of Greek poetry, and the singing or reciting of epic poems accompanied by string instruments led to the development of Greek dramas and tragedies. During the Baroque era, the interest in reviving the ancient Greek tragedies led eventually to the development of opera.

Around the beginning of the seventeenth century a society of Italian poets and musicians, who called themselves the **Camerata,** met in Florence. One of the results of their study and experimentation was a new form of solo singing, which they called **monodies.** Based on the ancient Greek solo song, a monody consisted of a simple melodic line with sparse accompaniment. The rhythm of the melody was metrically free, to follow the accents and natural movement of the text in a reciting style.

Opera. A musical drama that uses costumes and scenery, along with arias, recitatives, and choruses to tell a story.

While monodies became very popular as independent solo songs, this "new" style of musical performance was most useful in operas, where it became the basis for the **vocal recitative.** By following the natural rhythmic inflection of words rather than strict metrical restraints, the recitative is both expressive and capable of clearly conveying a large amount of text in a very short period of time. Thus this vocal technique conveniently but musically advances the story line of the opera.

Claudio Monteverdi (1567–1643) was the musical bridge to the seventeenth century that Beethoven was to the nineteenth century. His polyphonic Italian madrigals are some of the best written, and *Orfeo* is considered to be the first great opera ever composed. Monteverdi's music is characterized by a dramatic use of harmony, enlarged role of instruments in vocal music, expressiveness of text, and the new monodic style.

Claudio Monteverdi.
© The Bettmann Archive

The first great composer of baroque opera was Claudio Monteverdi. While the story chosen for his first and best-known opera, *Orfeo,* was not innovative, his dramatic use of recitatives in the monodic style along with arias, ensembles, and choruses produced a significant change in musical trends.

The Greek mythological figure Orpheus was a gifted poet and musician whose melodious voice and harp could tame the animals of the forests. In Monteverdi's opera, Orpheus' joyous marriage to Euridice is destroyed when she dies from snakebite. The unhappy announcement of his wife's death elicits Orpheus' famous lament *"Tu se' morte"* ("You are dead, and I live"). His sorrow turns to resolve (see the listening guide that follows) as Orpheus plans to descend to the underworld and use his musical powers to rescue Euridice. Orpheus gains permission to make the journey, charms Charon, guardian of the crossing of the river Styx, and manages to free Euridice with the one stipulation that he not look back at her as he leads her to the world of the living. At the last moment, anxiety overcomes Orpheus; he turns to look at his beloved, and she is lost for the second time. The original story of Orpheus concluded with his death by decapitation because of his neglect. Since Monteverdi's opera was planned for performance at a wedding, this ending was not appropriate. Instead, the Greek god Apollo rescues Orpheus and takes him to the heavens where he can see the likeness of his fair Euridice in the heavenly constellations.

Listening Guide
Monodic Style

. . . .

C. Monteverdi: Orfeo, "Tu se' morta"

This recitative is a brilliant and expressive portrayal of Orfeo's reaction to the death of his wife Euridice and his gradual realization of the magnitude of his loss. His pain changes to resolve as Orfeo plans to enter the underworld to rescue Euridice.

Timbre. Tenor voice accompanied by small portative organ and bass lute
Texture. Homophonic
Rhythm. Vocal line is rhythmically free with no feeling of beat or meter
Word-painting. (primarily through register) found as follows:

earth. low register
heaven, sun. high register
deepest abysses. low, somber
stars. high register

Tu se' morta, mia vita,	Thou art dead, my life,
ed io respiro?	and yet I breathe?
Tu se' da me partita	Thou hast from me departed
Per mai piu, mai piu non tornare,	Nevermore, nevermore to return
ed io rimango?	and I remain?
Nò, nò che se i versi	No, no for if verses
alcuna cosa ponno	can do anything,
N'andro sicuro al più	Then I shall surely go
profondi abissi,	to the *deepest abysses,*
E intenerito il cor	And having softened the heart
del Rè del l'ombre	of the king of the shadows,
Meco trarotti	I will bring you back with me
a riverder le *stelle:*	to see the *stars* again:
O se cio negherammi	Or if this be denied me by
empio destino	cruel destiny,
Rimarro teco	I will stay with thee
in compagnia di morte.	in the company of the dead.
Addio, *terra;*	Farewell, *earth;*
addio *cielo, e sole,*	Farewell, *heaven, and sun,*
addio.	farewell.

By the end of the seventeenth century, opera had become dramatic entertainment for kings as well as for merchants and artisans. As public interest grew, Italian opera spread to other European cultural centers. The first Italian opera to be performed outside of Italy was composed by Francesca Caccini (1587–1630), the daughter of a member of the Florentine Camerata. France, England, and Germany imported Italian opera first, and then, to various degrees, created operatic forms that reflected their own nationalistic preferences.

Monodic Style. Expressive solo singing with sparse chordal accompaniment

Recitative. A vocal song in monodic style, found in operas, cantatas, and oratorios, that uses the natural rhythmic inflection of the text

Aria. Expressive solo song

Under the patronage of King Louis XIV, French opera achieved unequaled heights of lavishness. The French tradition of ballet greatly influenced opera, both by the addition of numerous dance scenes and through the dancelike rhythmic activity of many of the short solo songs. Jean-Baptiste Lully was the best-known composer of French opera from this period. Lully established opera in his own country as a distinctly French genre by adapting the Italian styles of recitative and aria to the French language, placing greater emphasis on dance, increasing use of the chorus, simplifying rhythms, and employing a more dramatic orchestral accompaniment for recitatives. The combination of dramatic settings of classical French tragedies with the successful adaptation of Italian opera to the French language pleased both Lully's audiences and his patron, King Louis XIV.

English and German audiences were more interested, initially, in supporting and patronizing the fashionable Italian opera than in developing their own nationalistic counterparts. Nevertheless, preexisting dramatic and musical forms in both countries eventually combined with the popular Italian operatic style to produce new ideas in musical expression.

In England opera was influenced by the masque—a popular form of theatrical entertainment that combined poetry, music, and dance. Henry Purcell's *Dido and Aeneas* is the best example of English opera composed at this time.

The German ***Singspiel*** (musical play) was the basis for that country's own operatic development. Emphasis was placed on spoken dialogue and strophic solo songs as opposed to the Italian recitative and aria.

Other Baroque Vocal Music

Oratorio

Two other forms of baroque vocal music that were influenced by opera are the oratorio and cantata. The oratorio is basically an opera without costumes, acting, or scenery. While most were drawn from biblical stories, oratorios were usually not liturgical works used in a church service. Instead, they were presented as entertainment in concert halls. Oratorios based specifically on the Crucifixion of Christ were called **Passions** and were written specifically to be performed at Good Friday services.

Messiah (1741)
by G. F. Handel

Composed in only twenty-four days, this magnificent oratorio by Handel is a testimony to the composer's prolific ability and musical craftsmanship. The oratorio format provided Handel with a dramatic way to present a sacred subject without violating the English ban on theatrical performances of biblical stories. A performance of this work in London so inspired King George II that he rose to his feet during the "Hallelujah" chorus. The audience followed the example of their King, and so today the tradition continues that a performance of this chorus brings the audience to their feet.

The text of the entire work is taken from passages of both the Old and New Testaments of the Bible. The three sections are based on different aspects of the life of Christ: the prophecy of Christ and his nativity (Advent and Christmas), the Passion story, and the Resurrection, respectively. The brief titles of the fifty movements listed below will give you some idea of the overall organization of the work.

Part I

Overture
Recit.: Comfort ye my people
Air: Every valley shall be exalted
Chorus: And the glory of the Lord
Recit.: Thus saith the Lord
Air: But who may abide the day of His coming?
Chorus: And he shall purify
Recit.: Behold, a virgin shall conceive
Air and Chorus: O thou that tellest good tidings to Zion
Recit.: For, behold, darkness shall cover the earth
Air: The people that walked in darkness

Part II

Chorus: Behold the Lamb of God
Air: He was despised
Chorus: Surely He hath borne our griefs
Chorus: And with His stripes we are healed
Chorus: All we like sheep have gone astray
Recit.: All they that see Him, laugh Him to scorn
Chorus: He trusted in God that He would deliver Him
Recit.: Thy rebuke hath broke His heart
Air: Behold, and see if there be any sorrow
Recit.: He was cut off out of the land of the living
Air: But Thou didst not

Part III

Air: I know that my Redeemer liveth
Chorus: Since by man come death
Recit.: Behold, I tell you a mystery
Air: The trumpet shall sound
Recit.: Then shall be brought to pass
Duet: O death, where is thy sting?
Chorus: But thanks be to God
Air: If God be for us, who can be against us?
Chorus: Worthy is the Lamb

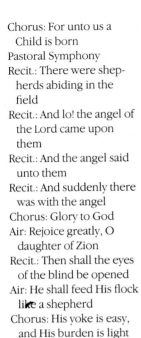

Chorus: For unto us a
Child is born
Pastoral Symphony
Recit.: There were shep-
herds abiding in the
field
Recit.: And lo! the angel of
the Lord came upon
them
Recit.: And the angel said
unto them
Recit.: And suddenly there
was with the angel
Chorus: Glory to God
Air: Rejoice greatly, O
daughter of Zion
Recit.: Then shall the eyes
of the blind be opened
Air: He shall feed His flock
like a shepherd
Chorus: His yoke is easy,
and His burden is light

leave His soul in Hell
Chorus: Lift up your
heads, O ye gates
Recit.: Unto which of the
angels said He
Chorus: Let all the angels
of God worship Him
Air: Thou art gone up on
high
Chorus: The Lord gave the
word
Air: How beautiful are the
feet of them
Chorus: Their sound is
gone out into all lands
Air: Why do the nations so
furiously rage
Chorus: Let us break their
bonds asunder
Recit.: He that dwelleth in
heaven
Air: Thou shalt break them
Chorus: Hallelujah!

Cantata

The cantata was a more versatile choral work written in both sacred and secular set-tings. Early forms of the cantata consisted of alternating recitatives and arias for solo voice with instrumental accompaniment—a format that resembled an independent scene from Italian opera. With the addition of duets and choruses the cantata as-sumed a unique place in vocal music development.

Cantatas written for the German Lutheran Church, especially those by J. S. Bach, are the most significant works of this genre. Through use of the vernacular (German) and reliance upon familiar chorales as the musical basis for many of these works, the church cantatas became a very meaningful part of the Lutheran church service. Bach wrote over 300 of these works, most of them for specific Sundays throughout the church year.

Johann Sebastian Bach.
© Three Lions, Inc.

**Johann Sebastian
Bach** (YO-hahn
Se-BASS-tee-ahn BAHK)

Johann Sebastian Bach (1685–1750) represents the culmination of the Baroque era. The magnitude of his compositional output and the quality of his contrapuntal art remain unsurpassed today. Johann Sebastian came from four generations of musicians in Germany, and many of his own children went on to be recognized as musicians in their own right. His musical education began with instruction on the violin from his father and organ lessons from a cousin; he also sang soprano in the school choir. Orphaned at age 10, he was taken in by his oldest brother, Johann Christoph. Even at this young age, Johann Sebastian was excelling at his studies, earning a modest income as a singer to help with household expenses, and taking a great interest in theology. After a period of study in Luneburg (1700–1703), Bach began his first of several court and church positions, which provided him with weekly performance opportunities and time to compose. While he wrote in virtually every sacred and secular form of his time except opera, Bach's greatest works grew out of his study of Lutheran theology and were inspired by his strong and personal spiritual beliefs.

> 1703–07—Organist in Arnstadt
> 1707–08—Organist in Mühlhausen
> 1708–17—Court organist and later chamber musician to the Duke of Weimar
> 1717–23—Chapelmaster at the Cöthen court
> 1723–50—Cantor of Thomas School in Leipzig

Bach's positions at Arnstadt, Mühlhausen, and Weimar were primarily as an organist, and so his compositions during that time were mostly organ works. While at Cöthen, however, Bach lacked an adequate organ and spent most of his time composing secular and instrumental music to provide entertainment for Prince Leopold. It was this position at Leipzig that Bach then held until his death that resulted in his greatest production of church music.

While employed in Weimar, Bach's fame as an organ virtuoso spread. His compositional genius, however, went largely unappreciated during his own lifetime. The complexity of his music sometimes confused and frustrated the church congregations for whom it was intended, and his independent nature caused tensions with the nobility and church elders who employed him. It was not until composers such as Haydn, Mozart, and Mendelssohn identified the genius of Bach's work that his compositions were recognized for their true significance.

Listening Guide
Sacred Cantata

. . . .

J. S. Bach: Cantata No. 140, Wachet auf, ruft uns die Stimme
                ("Sleepers Awake, a Voice is Calling")

The text of this work is based on the parable of the ten virgins—five wise and five foolish (Matthew 25:1–13). The virgins are likened to Christians who are watching for the coming of Christ (the Bridegroom). The parable teaches the need to be watchful and ready at all times, as the final day of Judgment is unknown.

> Then shall the kingdom of heaven be likened unto ten virgins, which took their lamps, and went forth to meet the bridegroom. And five of them were wise, and five were foolish. They that were foolish took their lamps, and took no oil with them: But the wise took oil in their vessels with their lamps. While the bridegroom tarried, they all slumbered and slept. And at midnight there was a cry made, Behold, the bridegroom cometh; go ye out to meet him. Then all those virgins arose, and trimmed their lamps. And the foolish said unto the wise, Give us of your oil; for our lamps are gone out. But the wise answered, saying, Not so; lest there be not enough for us and you: But go ye rather to them that sell, and buy for yourselves. And while they went to buy, the groom came; and they that were ready went in with him to the marriage and the door was shut. Afterward came the other virgins, saying, Lord, Lord, open to us. But he answered and said, Verily I say unto you, I know you not. Watch therefore, for ye know neither the day nor the hour wherein the Son of man cometh.

The melody upon which this work is based came from a hymn by Philipp Nicolai (1556–1608) and had probably been written around 1597. Three stanzas are presented, one at a time, in the first, fourth, and seventh movements. The melody is in bar form (AAB) and can be diagramed as follows:

Sections	A	A	B
Phrases	a_1 a_2 a_3	a_1 a_2 a_3	b_1 b_1 b_2 b_3 b_4 a_3

 I. Chorus

In this first movement the melody appears in long notes sung by the sopranos (and doubled by the horn), while the other voices and orchestra provide a very active accompaniment. The material in the orchestral introduction returns between the major sections and again at the end. Individual phrases are separated by two to four measures of orchestral material.

> *Timbre*. Two oboes, tenor oboe, horn, violino piccolo (small violin that sounds a minor 3rd higher than a regular violin), violin I, violin II, viola, continuo (organ), voices: soprano (melody doubled by horn), alto, tenor, bass.
> *Rhythm*. Triple meter; melody in long steady values, accompaniment (both instruments and voices) in faster moving, active note values.
> *Harmony*. E♭ major
> *Texture*. Mostly polyphonic
> *Text*. The cantata begins with a call to the virgins (Christians) to be ready and watchful for the Bridegroom (Christ). Word-painting is used at the word "*hoch*" (high)— the highest point of the melody—and at the word "*alleluja*"—where the most active and joyful vocal polyphony takes place.

A

16 measure
orchestra introduction

a_1

Wa-   chet   auf,   ruft   uns   die   stim-   me
(Sleepers awake, the voice of the watchman)

a_2

der   Wach-   ter   sehr   hoch   auf   der   zin-   ne.
(calls us from high on the tower.)

a_3

wach   auf,   du   stadt   Je-   ru-   sa-   lem
(awake you town of Jerusalem)

A

16 measure orchestra interlude
based on introduction

a_1

Mit-   ter-   nacht   heisst   die-   se   stun-   de
(Midnight is this very hour)

a_2

sie   ru-   fen   uns   mit   hel-   lem   mun-   de.
(they call to us with bright voices.)

a_3

wo   seid   ihr   klu-   gen   Jung-   frau-   en.
(where are you wise virgins?)

B

12 measure orchestra interlude
based on introduction

b₁

Wohl auf der Braut- gam kommt
(Take cheer the Bridegroom comes)

b₁

Steht auf, die Lam- pen nehmt
(Arise, take up your lamps)

b₂
("alleluja" begins in other voices)

Al- le- lu- ja.

b₃

Macht euch be- reit
(Prepare yourselves)

b₄

zu der Hoch- zeit
(for the wedding)

a₃

ihr mus- set ihm int- ge- gen gehn.
(you must go forth to meet him.)

16 measure orchestra conclusion
based on introduction

II. Recitative

Timbre. Dry recitative (recitativo secco) for tenor and continuo (organ)
Harmony. C minor
Rhythm. Follows natural rhythm of the text
Texture. Homophonic
Text. (syllabic) The coming of the Bridegroom (Christ) is announced

He comes, he comes, the Bridegroom comes!
Daughters of Zion come forth,
he is hurrying from on high
into your mother's house.

The Bridegroom comes, who like a roe and a
young hart leaping upon the hills,
brings you the wedding meal.

Wake up, bestir yourselves!
to receive the Bridegroom,
there, look, he comes along.

III. Aria Duet (soprano and bass)

Timbre. Soprano, bass, violino piccolo, continuo (organ)
Rhythm. $\frac{6}{8}$ meter
Texture. Polyphonic; conversational "give and take" of the two voices versus the independent violin line
Harmony. C minor
Text. This "love song" is shared by the Bridegroom (Christ) and his bride (the soul)

Soprano (Soul):	When will you come, my salvation?
Bass (Christ):	I am coming, your own.
Soprano (Soul):	I am waiting with burning oil.
	Throw open the hall to the heavenly banquet!
Bass (Christ):	I open the hall to the heavenly banquet.
Soprano (Soul):	Come, Jesus!
Bass (Christ):	Come, lovely Soul!

IV. Tenor Chorale

Timbre. Strings in unison, continuo (organ), unison tenor voices
Rhythm. Quadruple meter, moderate tempo, but the chorale melody moves along faster than in movement one
Texture. Polyphonic
Harmony. E♭ major
Text. Stanza two of the chorale

A	a_1	Zion hears the watchmen singing,
	a_2	for joy her very heart is springing,
	a_3	she wakes and rises hastily.
A	a_1	From heaven comes her friend resplendent,
	a_2	sturdy in grace, mighty in truth,
	a_3	her light shines bright, her star ascends.

B	b$_1$	Now come, you worthy crown,
	b$_1$	Lord Jesus, God's own Son,
	b$_2$	Hosanna!
	b$_3$	We follow all
	b$_4$	to the joyful hall
	a$_3$	and share in the Lord's supper.

V. Recitative

Timbre. Three-part strings, continuo (organ), solo bass voice
Harmony. E♭ major, with modulation to B♭ major
Rhythm. An accompanied recitative (recitativo accompagnato) in quadruple meter
Texture. Homophonic
Text. The Bridegroom welcomes his bride and pledges faithfulness.

Come enter in with me, my chosen bride!
I have pledged my troth to you in eternity!
I will set you as a seal upon my heart,
and as a seal upon my arm
and restore delight to your sorrowful eye.
Forget now, O soul, the anguish, the pain,
which you had to suffer; on my left you shall
rest, and my right shall kiss you.

VI. Duet (soprano and bass)

Timbre. Solo oboe, continuo (organ), vocal duet (soprano and bass)
Harmony. B♭ major
Rhythm. Quadruple meter
Texture. Polyphonic—similar to movement III
Text. The Bridegroom and bride celebrate their marriage.

Soprano (Soul):	My friend is mine!
Bass (Christ):	and I am thine!
Both:	Love shall separate nothing!
Soprano (Soul):	I will with you feed among heaven's roses,
Bass (Christ):	You shall with me feed among heaven's roses,
Both:	there fullness of joy, there rapture shall be!

VII. Chorale

Timbre. Orchestra doubles voices in four-part chorale
Texture. Homophonic
Rhythm. Duple meter
Harmony. E♭ major
Text. A continuation of the celebration

A	a$_1$	Gloria be sung to you
	a$_2$	with men's and angels' tongues,
	a$_3$	with harps and beautiful cymbals.

A	a_1	Of twelve pearls are the gates
	a_2	at your city; we are consorts
	a_3	of angels high about your throne.
B	b_1	No eye has ever sensed,
	b_1	no ear has ever heard
	b_2	such a delight.
	b_3	Of this we rejoice,
	b_4	io, io,
	a_3	forever in sweetest joy.

The Development of Instrumental Music

Instrumental music in the Renaissance had lacked a life of its own: Unspecified instruments either doubled voice parts or played compositions that were basically vocal works minus the text. With the development of baroque instrumental music, however, came new forms and compositional techniques that were *idiomatic*. That is, compositions were written for specific instruments with the unique capabilities of each instrument in mind.

Instrumental music became idiomatic.

Instrumental accompaniments no longer simply doubled voice parts but, rather, provided independent support for vocal solos and ensembles; and keyboard compositions took on technical runs and leaps that were not feasible for the voice. Many composers were also virtuoso performers who wrote for a new level of technical ability. J. S. Bach took organ performance to new heights through his playing and composing. Corelli did the same for violin as did Domenico Scarlatti for the harpsichord.

One style of writing to develop in conjunction with this new attitude toward instruments was called the "stile concertato" (concertato style), which was based on a concept of opposing forces—either vocal against instrumental or solo against ensemble. This approach provided an interesting method of contrast that highlighted the uniqueness of instrumental timbres and technical capabilities.

Listening Guide
Baroque Instrumental Music

. . . .

Concertato Style
H. Schütz: "Fili mi, Absalon" from Symphoniae sacrae I
  Bass voice is set against a trombone quartet.

J. S. Bach: Brandenburg Concerto no. 2
  Group of soloists (trumpet, recorder, oboe, violin) with string orchestra
  accompaniment

J. S. Bach: Violin Concerto No. 1
  Violin soloist with string orchestra

Keyboard Compositions
J. Pachelbel: Toccata in E Minor for Organ

J. S. Bach: Chromatic Fantasia and Fugue in D minor (BWV 903)

Violin
A. Corelli: Violin Sonatas Op. 5

J. S. Bach: Three Partitas for Violin Solo (BWV 1004–1006)

Functions of Music in the Baroque

Throughout the era music continued to serve the needs of patrons. Both the courts and the clergy vied for great musical extravagance as a display of wealth and power. Composers and performers found economic security in this system, but paid for this security in part through their loss of some measure of creative freedom. They were also subject to demands for the continuous production of new music for every court and church occasion. Salaries were not always high or paid on time but usually included in-kind payments of food, wine, and housing.

Due to the close relationship of church and state, court musicians and church musicians were interchangeable. Composers were expected to be prolific as well as sufficiently versatile to write music appropriate for the church, royal chambers, and even the theater. Not surprisingly, the musical output of this period was tremendous; but while special occasions required new music to be written, composers freely borrowed ideas from their earlier works or even other composers and quickly disguised and recycled old works for new occasions. Preservation of this musical abundance was made possible through a growing number of publishing houses and by students, who copied the manuscripts of their teachers as part of their music education.

Sacred Music

Composers continued to find sufficient inspiration in spiritual subjects to write music for use in worship services (liturgical) as well as compositions conceived for the concert hall but based on religious themes (nonliturgical). While old forms such as the mass, motet, and anthem continued to find acceptance in baroque church music, the dramatic influence of opera produced new sacred forms, which included the cantata, oratorio, and passion. These three genres incorporated theatrical elements with spiritual subjects to produce exciting and dramatic works for both the worship service and the concert hall.

The first known publication of instrumental sonatas to be composed by a woman was written by a nun from Novara, Italy, Isabella Leonarda (1620–1704). In addition to sonatas, Leonarda's more than 200 works included several masses, magnificats, and motets, all of which were intensely expressive of her personal faith and devotion to the Church.

The Baroque period was a pinnacle of development for Protestant church music. Where the Roman Catholic Church had previously dominated and controlled sacred music, the development and growth of Protestant religions resulted in a new source of patronage for composers and performers. The church cantata came to play a role in Protestant music parallel to that which the mass held in Catholic music. The departure from traditional Latin texts opened baroque music to new sources of inspiration. In addition to masses and motets composed in the vernacular, sacred music explored a broader range of biblical texts and developed new modes of musical expression.

Listening Guide
Sacred Music

. . . .

J. S. Bach: Jesu, meine Freude ("Jesus, dearest Master")
J. S. Bach: Mass in B Minor
J. S. Bach: Cantata No. 140 (see pp. 241–246)
G. F. Handel: Chandos Anthems
G. F. Handel: Messiah
J. S. Bach: St. Matthew Passion

Table 14.1   Representative Composers in a Cultural Context

	Italy	France	Germany	England
Founding of Jamestown colony (1607)	Claudio Monteverdi (1567–1643)		Michael Praetorius (1571–1621)	
Thirty Years' War in Germany (1618–48)	Girolamo Frescobaldi (1583–1643)		Heinrich Schütz (1585–1672)	
	Giacomo Carissimi (1605–1674)		Johann Hermann Schein (1586–1630)	
Mayflower Compact (1620)			Samuel Scheidt (1587–1654)	
			Johann Jacob Froberger (1616–67)	
Harvard College founded (1636)		Jean-Baptiste Lully (c. 1632–87)	Dietrich Buxtehude (1653–1707)	John Blow (1648–1708)
			Johann Pachelbel (1653–1706)	
English Civil War (1642–49)				
Reign of Louis XIV of France (1643–1715)	Arcangelo Corelli (1653–1713)			
	Antonio Vivaldi (c. 1669–1741)			Henry Purcell (1658–1695)
Commonwealth and Protectorate (1649–60)				
Restoration (1660)	Alessandro Scarlatti (1660–1725)	Jean Philippe Rameau (1683–1764)	Georg Philipp Telemann (1681–1767)	
	Domenico Scarlatti (1685–1757)			
			Johann Sebastian Bach (1685–1750)	George F. Handel (1685–1759)

Secular Music

Music for entertainment was found in small royal chambers as well as large theaters. Chamber music entertained, accompanied dance, and provided background music for social activities. Opera began as a princely pastime, but soon became a commercially successful form of entertainment for merchants and artisans. Audiences were drawn especially to hear virtuoso opera singers who enjoyed taking great liberties with the solo arias in order to show off their acrobatic vocal abilities, even at the expense of story continuity. Groups of wealthy merchants organized to create a form of collective patronage capable of supporting musical entertainments that were otherwise restricted to the nobility. Middle-class musicians enjoyed amateur performance through music clubs and private academies. While the Baroque era lacked the public concert halls of the Classical period that was to follow, opportunities to hear music continued to increase and reach a broader audience.

Listening Guide
Secular Music

J. S. Bach: Cantata No. 211 ("Coffee Cantata") (1732)

This operetta-like humorous work is about a concerned father who attempts to persuade his daughter to break her addiction to coffee. His threats and promises are in vain until he bribes her with a husband. The daughter, however, has the last word as she draws up a marriage contract that stipulates that her husband allow her to continue drinking coffee.

Strings and a flute accompany three singers—father, daughter, and narrator. The main story is given in recitative with expressive arias. The narrator provides an introductory explanation of the story and a summary near the end. All three voices join together in the final movement to accept the coffee craze as inevitable.

Additional Listening

Concerto Grosso
G. F. Handel: Concerto Grosso in C Major
J. S. Bach: Brandenburg Concertos (Nos. 1–6)
A. Corelli: Concerto Grosso Op. 6, no. 8 "Christmas Concerto"

Solo Concerto
G. P. Telemann: Concerto for Trumpet and Strings in D Major
G. F. Handel: Concertos for Organ and Orchestra

Sonata da Chiesa
A. Corelli: Sonata da chiesa in E Minor, Op. 3, no. 7
I. Leonarda: Sonate da chiesa, Op. 16

Sonata da Camera
F. Couperin: Concert Royal
J. S. Bach: Violin Sonata in E Major

Keyboard Suite
G. F. Handel: Suite No. 5 in E Major (harpsichord)
J. S. Bach: English Suites (harpsichord)

Orchestral Suite
J. S. Bach: Suite No. 3 in D Major for Orchestra
G. F. Handel: Water Music
G. F. Handel: Music for Royal Fireworks

Cantata

J. S. Bach: Cantata No. 80, Ein' feste burg ist unser Gott
  ("A mighty fortress is our God")
B. Marcello: Stravaganze d' Amore

Oratorio

G. Carissimi: Jephte
G. F. Handel: Judas Maccabaeus

Passion

J. S. Bach: St. Matthew Passion
J. S. Bach: St. John Passion

Italian Opera

A. Scarlatti: La Griselda
C. Monteverdi: L'Incoronazione di Poppea ("The Coronation of Poppea")
F. Caccini: La liberazione di Ruggiero d'al isola d'Alcina
G. F. Handel: Rinaldo

French Opera

J. B. Lully: Alceste
J. P. Rameau: Castor et Pollux

English Opera

H. Purcell: Dido and Aeneas
J. Blow: Venus and Adonis

Keyboard Toccata

J. S. Bach: Toccata and Fugue in D Minor (organ)
J. S. Bach: Toccata in F Major
J. Pachelbel: (see his toccatas for organ)

Fantasy

J. S. Bach: Fantasia in A Minor
J. S. Bach: Chromatic Fantasia and Fugue in D Minor
G. P. Telemann: Twelve Fantasias for Harpsichord

Prelude

J. S. Bach: The Well-tempered Clavier

Fugue

J. S. Bach: The Art of Fugue
G. F. Handel: Messiah (several choruses use fugues including No.7 "And He
  shall purify," No. 21 "His yoke is easy," No. 25 "And with His stripes we are
  healed," and No. 28 "He trusted in God."

CHAPTER FIFTEEN

Classical

Preview of Terms and Concepts

The Classical era, approximately 1750 to 1809, is characterized by **balance** and **symmetry.** Transitional styles (**rococo, sentimental, "storm and stress"**) began to appear in the first half of the eighteenth century, with new emphasis on **vocal-like melodies, homophonic texture,** and **changes in emotional intensity.** The **classical orchestra** and **piano** became important timbres for composers along with many kinds of instrumental **chamber music.** The techniques of **development** were used to construct longer sectional forms, which, in turn, were used to create **multimovement structures.**

While **Austria** and **Germany** became European artistic centers, **American music** began to develop important indigenous traits.

H ave you ever used the term "classical" to describe either a single piece of music or a general classification of musical works? If so, what did you mean? Were you describing: music based on the ideals of ancient Greece? music written between 1750 and 1809? music other than "popular" music? or popular music that has great lasting appeal (a "classic")?

These diverse, but frequently used, "definitions" demonstrate the confusion and lack of precision generated by the term "classical." Each of these meanings may be useful in a particular context; but, for purposes of clarification, the term "classical" in this text will be used specifically to identify a style of music composed primarily between 1750 and 1809. This era in musical history probably acquired its label because of stylistic similarities to the ancient Greek artistic ideals of **balance, clarity of form, objectivity,** and **emotional restraint.** Other more specific characteristics will be discussed in the following pages under each of the musical elements covered.

Framing a musical era within specific dates is a practice of convenience that suggests more precision than it should (fig. 15.1). The year 1750, for example, marks more accurately the end of the Baroque era (with the death of J. S. Bach) than the beginning of the Classical era. While on one hand stylistic elements of the Baroque continued to be used beyond 1750, on the other hand composers had already begun to look for new avenues of musical expressiveness, even when the Baroque era had still been at its height. The actual transition from Baroque to Classical is best seen in the "pre-Classical" works of selected composers between 1740 and 1770. (These new trend-setting composers included two of J. S. Bach's own sons—Carl Philipp Emanuel Bach and Johann Christian Bach.) The year 1809 is arbitrarily chosen as the end of the Classical era because it marks the death of Franz Joseph Haydn.

Transitional styles within "pre-Classicism" include rococo, sentimental style (*Empfindsamer stil*), and "storm and stress" (*Sturm und Drang*). Each of these is marked by significant changes from the Baroque, which helped to develop the classical style.

Rococo, from *rocaille* meaning "shell work," is a term that was originally applied to French art and decorative work and that characterized grace and elegance. Rococo music is light with a homophonic texture consisting of a melody with accompaniment. It represents a major departure from the heavy polyphonic texture of baroque music.

Figure 15.1
Styles overlap and trends of a new era appear in various composers before the end of the old era.

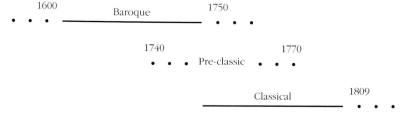

Two German styles—the sentimental style and "storm and stress"—provided additional movement away from the baroque with dramatic modulations and syncopated rhythms, which were a significant departure from that period's standard harmonic and rhythmic vocabularies. The sentimental style produced simple vocal-like melodies and numerous changes in mood. "Storm and stress," as the name implies, is passionate music, filled with emotional intensity.

The following examples of pre-classic styles will provide aural evidence of the transition from the Baroque era to the Classical era. A comparison of any of these selections to a familiar baroque work should help you to hear the trends that overlapped both eras and contributed to the development of eighteenth-century classicism.

The term "rococo" came from French decorative art, such as this delicate porcelain sculpture. "Musikantengruppe" Fuldaer Porzellan, Modelleur, Vermatl. Wenzel Neu Um 1770 38.5 cm × 27.5 cm. Staatliche Runstammlungen Kassel

Listening Guide
Pre-Classic Styles

. . . .

Rococo

D. Scarlatti: Sonata in C Minor, for harpsichord

Clear, homophonic texture

Francis Couperin
(FRAHN-swah
Koo-per-EHN)

F. Couperin: La Galante

Light, thin, polyphonic texture with many delicate ornaments

G. B. Pergolesi: La serva padrona ("The Servant-Mistress")

This comic opera originally was used as an intermezzo between acts of a serious opera created by the same composer. The small cast of three includes a soprano, bass, and one silent character. Explanatory recitatives connect the arias, which consist of short, repeated melodic phrases with unison introductions.

Sentimental Style

C. P. E. Bach: Sonatas für Kenner und Liebhaber ("Sonatas for Connoisseurs and Amateurs")

As keyboard sonatas with a singing, voicelike style, these works use chromatic harmony and sentimental musical "sighs" created by resolving an accented dissonance to an unaccented consonance.

Storm and Stress

C. P. E. Bach: Harpsichord Concerto in D Minor

Passionate intensity with many changes in emotions

Cultural Centers

Austria and Germany became the center of artistic activities during the Classical era. The cities of Mannheim, Vienna, and Berlin were especially notable for their support of the arts. The influence of Vienna was so great and it was home for so many composers that this period is sometimes referred to as the "Viennese Classical" era.

Many musicians supplemented their living in Vienna by opening schools to teach composition, singing, and instrumental performance. One such notable example is Marianne von Martinez, a pupil of Franz Joseph Haydn. In addition to her composing and teaching, she frequently performed duo keyboard works with Mozart.

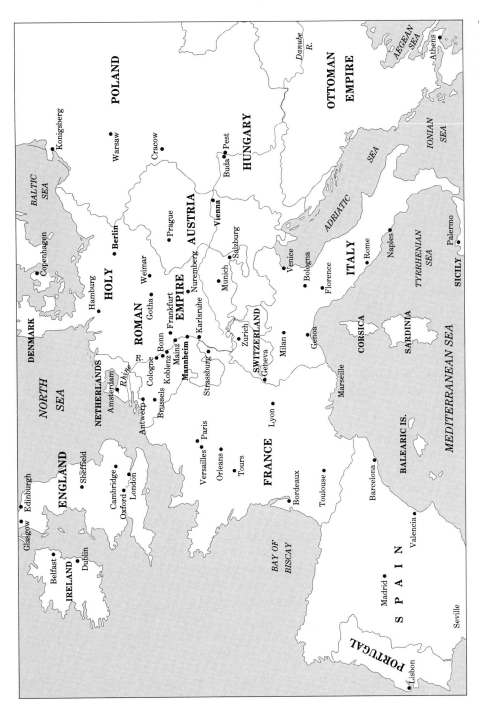

Austria and Germany became artistic centers during the Age of Enlightenment.

Cultural Influences

Known both as the "Age of Enlightenment" and the "Age of Reason," the eighteenth century was dominated by rationalism and an almost religious attitude toward empiricism. Scientific inquiry grew out of the early seventeenth-century emphasis on observation and experience. Significant inventions during this time include the lightning rod (1752), the water turbine (1775), the steam engine (1775), the threshing machine (1784), the seismograph (1785), the cotton gin (1793), the telegraph (1794), and muskets with interchangeable parts (1800).

The rise of the middle class in size, wealth, literacy, and power led to economic changes based on new technologies and political upheavals, which grew out of a struggle for individual freedoms and democratic ideals. Liberty and equality became important attainable goals, as evidenced by the American Revolution (1775–1783) and the French Revolution (1792–1801).

Elements of Classical Music

Melody

Tuneful melodies constructed of **shorter phrases**—usually four measures each—provided classical composers with the basic material for building larger structures. Contrasting melodies within a single piece provided variety, while smaller fragments of these melodies, called **motives,** were used in the process of **development** to expand a work through a combination of unity and variety.

Rhythm

While the strong bass pulse of the baroque basso continuo disappeared, classical **tempos remained steady.** Rhythms became **less complex** in order to complement the tuneful melodies. Variety within individual pieces was also achieved through **rhythmic diversity.**

Harmony

Classical harmonies were **comparatively simple** and moved more slowly than those of the Baroque era. Strong cadences were dependent on the dominant seventh to tonic relationship (V_7 to I), such as that shown in the example below. Modulations were used to help distinguish sections in form.

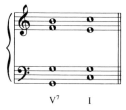

V⁷   I

Texture

With the emphasis on tuneful melodies, **homophonic texture** became favored, with polyphonic texture for contrast. An especially popular form of homophonic texture, which gave rhythmic activity to the accompaniment while still preserving the clarity of melody, was the **Alberti bass**—named after Domenico Alberti. The rhythmic animation of chords in this pattern created a light but interesting texture.

Dynamics

Composers began to use **dynamic markings** more regularly, along with the gradual nuances of **crescendo and diminuendo.** Melodic, rhythmic, and harmonic changes were often highlighted with dynamic contrasts.

Timbre

With the abandonment of baroque basso continuo came the establishment of the small **classical orchestra** (fig. 15.2), and the **piano** replaced the harpsichord as the preferred keyboard instrument. The dynamic flexibility of the piano offered greater expressive capabilities, although the instrument was to undergo additional improvements in the nineteenth century. The choice of instruments was no longer left up to the performers; composers conceived specific timbres for their compositions and wrote with those unique characteristics in mind.

Figure 15.2
While instrumentation varied, the orchestra of the classical period usually contained approximately 20 strings, 2 each of flutes, oboes, clarinets, and bassoons, and sometimes 2 trumpets, 2 horns, and 2 timpani.

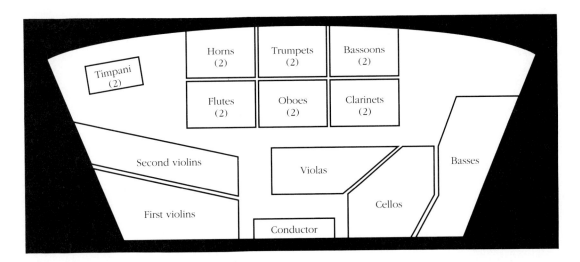

Form

The overall characteristics of **balance and symmetry** were naturally reflected in the broad scope of classical forms. Contrasting melodies were used in homophonic textures to create balanced **ABA forms,** and cadences clearly delineated individual cadences. Multimovement structures, including the **sonata, concerto, and symphony,** became standard ways to create large works.

Sectional forms, such as **sonata-allegro,** grew in complexity through the use of contrasting themes and motivic development. Because of its balance without sacrificing flexibility and room for creativity, sonata-allegro became the most common form for the first movement of sonatas, concertos, and symphonies. The diagram below should help to illustrate the balanced organization, contrasting themes, and use of development and modulations that made this form so useful and popular.

Exposition					Development	Recapitulation
(Intro)	First Theme	Transition	Second Theme	Closing Theme or Codetta	Material presented in the Exposition is used in new ways and various keys to create a climax.	F.T. trans. S.T. C.T. Coda
Keys	I (major) ---- modulation		V ---------------------		Various keys	I ------------------
	i (minor) ---- modulation		III ---------------------			i ------------------

1. The development section may be extensive or very minimal.
2. Early versions of the form frequently repeated the exposition. This repetition was later omitted by composers and is frequently ignored in modern-day performances of those earlier works.
3. Concertos used the "double exposition" as an introduction of themes in the orchestra (staying in the tonic key), followed by the repeat of the exposition with the soloist and normal modulation to a related key. A cadenza was also placed in the recapitulation right before the coda.
4. Treatment of the peripheral sections of the form—introduction, transition, codetta, and coda—varies greatly among composers. Sometimes these are very extensive, and in other cases these sections are omitted altogether.

Franz Joseph Haydn (1732–1809) lived from the peak of baroque music, through the complete life span of Mozart, and died after Beethoven's first six symphonies had already begun to exert considerable influence on nineteenth-century romanticism. With a catalog of compositions that includes over 100 symphonies, 82 string quartets, 52 piano sonatas, 23 operas, 4 oratorios, and numerous other masses, concertos, and chamber works, his prolific output reflects the variety of musical styles to which he was exposed and that he helped to shape during his long and active life. Haydn's early compositions, until about 1770, reflect pre-classic styles of rococo and sentimental. It was also during this period (1761 to be exact) that he began what would be thirty years of musical service under the patronage of the rich Hungarian Esterhazy family. With a full orchestra of musicians available at his call, Haydn became well known as a conductor, and was able to experiment with many different aspects of symphonic writing. He is thus known today as "the father of the symphony."

Franz Joseph Haydn.
Courtesy of the Free Library of Philadelphia.

The middle period of his life (1770–1795) included trips to London, where his symphonic composition reached classical perfection. After the death of his patron and during the final years (1795–1809), Haydn wrote mainly symphonic choral works—late masses and two oratorios—which even then showed signs of the approaching Romantic era.

Listening Guide
Synthesis of Classical Elements

. . . .

F. Haydn: Concerto for Trumpet and Orchestra in E♭
      I. Allegro
      II. Andante
      III. Allegro

Franz Joseph Haydn
(Frahntz YO-sef HAHY-dn)

Melody. Instrumentally oriented (especially the fast movements) but concise and contrasting within movements
Rhythm. Movements alternate tempos— I. Fast
                                      II. Slow
                                      III. Fast
Harmony. Not complex, but uses modulations within each movement
Texture. Homophonic
Dynamics. Considerable variation with many nuances
Timbre. Trumpet soloist with classical orchestra consisting of two flutes, two oboes, two bassoons, two horns, two trumpets, timpani, and strings; the timpani, trumpets, and horns are not used in the middle movement
Form. Clear, balanced forms
    I. Sonata-allegro form (with double exposition and cadenza)
    II. Ternary (AABA)
    III. Rondo (ABACABA)

Classical Expressiveness

The baroque concept of the expression of emotions known as "*Affektenlehre*" continued to influence music into the nineteenth century. While baroque composers limited each work or movement to a single affect or emotion, pre-classic and classical composers deliberately and frequently changed affects to create interesting contrasts. The importance of these affects and emotions can be seen in the writings of C. P. E. Bach.

> A musician cannot move others unless he too is moved. He must of necessity feel all of the affects that he hopes to arouse in his audience, for the revealing of his own humor will stimulate a like humor in the listener. In languishing, sad passages, the performer must languish and grow sad. Thus will the expression of the piece be more clearly perceived by the audience. . . . Similarly, in lively, joyous passages, the executant must again put himself into the appropriate mood. And so, constantly varying the passions he will barely quiet one before he rouses another. [from *Essay on the True Art of Playing Keyboard Instruments* by Carl Philipp Emanuel Bach, Translated and Edited by William J. Mitchell. By permission of W. W. Norton & Company, Inc. Copyright 1949 by W. W. Norton & Company, Inc. Copyright Renewed 1976 by Alice L. Mitchell.]

The concept of balance in classical music can also be seen in relation to the placement of climax. The musical climax of baroque works usually comes at the end, with an increase of motion into the final cadence. Tension is frequently lessened in the middle of the work. Classical works more often have their climax in the middle followed by a long section of resolution to relieve the tension and balance the beginning.

Wolfgang Amadeus Mozart.
The New York Public Library at Lincoln Center. Astor, Lenox, and Tilden Foundations. Music Division.

Wolfgang Amadeus Mozart (1756–1791) lived a short, tumultuous life. As a child prodigy who played keyboards and violin, he was paraded through European courts and musical centers by his father, Leopold. Although his life lasted only thirty-five years, he began composing at a very early age and his music matured very quickly. Mozart began to compose at age six, wrote his first symphony at age eight, and an opera by age twelve. His total musical output (more than 600 compositions) exceeded that of many composers who lived to be twice his age. He wrote out most of his compositions completely and accurately in one draft—without need of corrections or revisions.

Mozart's immense talent as a composer and performer seems not to have been balanced by good fiscal management or social sensibility. In spite of the popularity of Mozart's music, he died deeply in debt. Since this independent and irreverent genius had little success in the restrictive confines of the music patronage system, most of his music was written for commission. Yet, even those works that were meant as background music for social occasions were remarkable examples of melodic creativity structured to perfection with classical balance and clarity.

While Mozart did not provide opus numbers for his compositions, they were eventually cataloged by Ludwig van Köchel, who assigned numbers to each of the artist's works in chronological order. These "K" or Köchel numbers as they are called accompany each of Mozart's titles as a readily accepted way to differentiate works with the same or similar titles.

Listening Guide
Classical Expressiveness

· ·

 W. A. Mozart: Symphony No. 40 in G Minor, K. 550
          I. Molto Allegro

Wolfgang Amadeus Mozart (VULV-gahng AH-mah-DAY-oos MOHT-zart)

This movement in a very clear sonata-allegro form presents a variety of contrasting emotions in a balanced format. While this is absolute music and the attachment of an external program would be inappropriate, a definite progression of changes is evident. Even with many diverse elements, however, the movement is unified by a simple three-note motive.

motive (first three notes)

Timing		
	First Movement **EXPOSITION (repeated)**	
0'00" (2'00")	First Theme	Theme stays mostly in the violins; based on three-note motive; quick, concise, active; G minor (i); soft
0'32" (2'32")	Transition	Loud; more dramatic; modulates
0'50" (2'50")	Second Theme	B♭ major (III); melody shifts between strings and woodwinds; soft; smooth, connected, less active, relaxed
1'08" (3'08")	Closing Theme	Less lyrical, short motives; brings back motives from first theme; soft, with crescendo to loud, followed by abrupt changes in dynamics; ends with more rhythmic activity (exposition is then repeated)
4'00"	**DEVELOPMENT** First theme is developed:	Various keys; theme mostly passed between the violins and string basses; motive used in all instruments; begins and ends soft, dramatic climax in the middle

RECAPITULATION

5'20"	First Theme	Same as in exposition
5'50"	Transition	Extended; even more dramatic than the first time
6'30"	Second Theme	Except for the key (G minor), same as in exposition
6'50"	Closing Theme	Similar to presentation in exposition
7'45"	Coda	Based on First Theme motive; soft with sudden change to loud for ending and final cadence

III. Menuetto

While adhering to the traditional and predictable minuet and trio form, this delightful movement offers several interesting twists to keep the listener's attention.

Third Movement

Minuet

0'00"	A section in G minor
0'19"	A section repeated
0'38"	A_1 section, which is similar to A but more imitative
1'15"	A_1 repeated

Trio

1'52"	B section in G major (similar to the minuet)
2'18"	B section repeated
2'44"	C section
2'55"	B_1 like B but with horns
3'19"	C section repeated
3'32"	B_1 section repeated

Minuet

3'55"	A section in G minor (no repeat this time)
4'15"	A_1 section, which ends movement

American Music

The emotive power of music gave sacred music a prominent place in early America. While Europe was experiencing a rise in secular, instrumental music, the young American colonies produced mainly sacred vocal forms. The first book to be published in the New World was a metrical setting of the Old Testament psalms called the *Bay Psalm Book* (1640).

Choral Music

Most early American vocal music consisted of psalm-tunes, anthems, hymns, secular songs, and fuguing tunes. While the differences were not always clearly maintained, there are some common characteristics that give this music a uniquely American sound.

Psalm-tunes and **hymns** provided churches with a powerful way to unify a congregation in public worship. Favorite melodies carried strong emotional appeal, just as they do today. **Anthems** were choral pieces of greater difficulty meant for select choirs or sometimes congregations with music reading skills. **Secular songs** continued to be a source of entertainment as well as an outlet for expressing emotions such as love and patriotism. The various forms of vocal music ranged from one to four parts sung in a cappella style. When more than one part was used, the melody was usually found in a middle voice. Common voice classifications were as follows:

Treble. Highest women's voices; equivalent to what we call soprano today; this voice was sometimes omitted

Counter. Lower women's voices; modern day alto

Tenor. Highest men's voices; **carried the melody**

Bass. Lowest men's voices

The following tune by William Billings demonstrates the sound that results when the tenor voice carries the melody in a homophonic texture.

Listening Guide

Early American Hymn Tune

W. Billings: Chester

This strong and energetic hymn-tune reflects the militant and righteous text. Adopted by the Continental Army, the hymn became a favorite marching song.

Let tyrants shake their iron rod,
And slavery clank her galling chains
We fear them not we trust in God,
New England's God for ever reigns.

Howe and Burgoyne and Clinton too,
With Prescott and Cornwallis join'd,
Together plot our overthrow,
In one infernal league combined.

Burgoyne
(Ber-GOING)

When God inspir'd us for the fight,
Their ranks were broke, their lines were forc'd.
Their ships were shatter'd in our sight,
Or swiftly driven from our coast.

The foe comes on with haughty stride,
Our troops advance with martial noise,
Their vet'rans flee before our youth,
And gen'rals yield to beardless boys.

What grateful off'ring shall we bring?
What shall we render to the Lord?
Loud hallelujahs let us sing,
And praise his name on ev'ry chord.

Source: American Musicological Society, Inc., 201 S. 34 St., Philadelphia, PA 19104-6313.

The illustration below shows the song as it appeared in *The New-England Psalm-Singer*, followed by the piano reduction of the open score.

A fuguing tune was a hymn- or psalm-tune setting that used both homophonic and polyphonic textures. The melody would begin in a homophonic texture. Next, after a complete cadence, a phrase would be treated in imitative polyphony and then conclude in homophonic texture. While generally credited to early American music—especially William Billings—this form actually originated a century earlier in England. Eventually, more conservative forces in sacred music managed to discourage the use of fuguing tunes on the basis that they detracted from the clarity of the text.

William Billings (1746–1800) was the first distinctive composer of American music. The son of a poor Boston shopkeeper, William made a living most of his life as a respected leather tanner. Little is known of his early music education except that he did have a fine voice. At the age of 23 Billings began to organize and teach singing-schools. His interest extended beyond teaching, however, and his talent in sacred music composition led to the publication in 1770 of more than 120 original compositions in a book called the *New-England Psalm-Singer.* Over the next 24 years he published 5 additional collections of hymns and anthems—*The Singing Master's Assistant*, 1778; *Music in Miniature*, 1779; *The Psalm-Singer's Amusement*, 1781; *The Suffolk Harmony*, 1786; and *The Continental Harmony*, 1794.

Source: American Musicological Society, Inc., 201 S. 34 St., Philadelphia, PA 19104-6313.

This photo of the frontispiece of *The New-England Psalm-Singer* is typical of publications of that era.

Listening Guide
Early American Music: Fuguing Tunes

. . . .

W. Billings: "Sing to the Lord Jehovah's Name" from *The Singing Master's Assistant*
(1778)

Fuguing tune in two-part form
Four voice, a cappella style
Most fuguing tunes follow this same pattern.

Sing to the Lord Jehovah's name and in his strength rejoice. When his salvation is our theme, exalted be our voice.	Homophonic; triple meter; melody in tenor
When his salvation is our theme, exalted be our voice. (several repetitions)	Imitative polyphony; duple meter; slower; ends with strong cadence in homophonic texture (This entire second half may be repeated.)

W. Billings: Kittery

The title of this tune is taken from the name of a New England town. Since the same text was frequently sung to different tunes, independent titles were given to the tunes to make them more identifiable.

The text used here is a paraphrase of the Lord's Prayer.

Our Father who in heaven art, All hallowed be thy name,	Four-part hymn with melody in the tenor
Thy kingdom come, thy will be done Throughout this earthly frame.	Four-part imitative polyphony This last section is repeated in homophonic texture.

from *The Worcester Collection*
Modern Edition: G. Schirmer, Inc., No. 10309

Singing Schools

The New England colonists used the congregational singing of psalms as an integral part of their worship service. Since most people could not read music or "sing by note" as it was called, the practice of "**lining-out**" the text and melody was common. This consisted of a leader chanting or singing each line of the psalm, which was then repeated by the congregation. Lining-out was an expedient way to teach psalm-singing, but destroyed the natural flow of the melody. Schools for instruction in music-reading were a natural response to this problem. The **singing schools** that emerged served to teach music-reading, but they were equally important as a social form of entertainment. Frequently, a "public house" or tavern was used for the classroom, providing not only a large room to accommodate many students but also convenient access to refreshments following the lesson.

Leaders for these schools, "**singing masters,**" were hired and paid from student tuition and community sponsors. Additional income was earned by singing masters who composed new tunes and published them in collections to be used in the schools. Most of the songs in the collections were sacred. This assured the support of the churches who wanted trained choirs and a musically literate congregation. However, the use of rhythmic, dancelike tunes not commonly found in sacred music confirms that the singing masters were as much interested in keeping their students entertained as preparing them for service to the local churches.

"Framingham" from The Psalm-Singer's Amusement.

Source: Dacapo Publishing, Plenum Publishing Corporation, NY.

As the number of psalm-tune collections grew, so did the approaches to the teaching of note-reading. Most music books began with an introduction to music fundamentals that advocated a particular system to facilitate musical literacy. One of the most popular was a four-note system that used the syllables fa, sol, la, and mi represented by "**shaped notes.**"

Faw   Sol   Law   Me

The C major scale written with this notation would appear as follows:

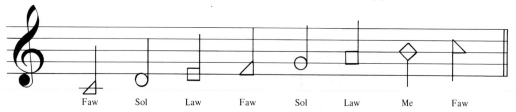

Faw   Sol   Law   Faw   Sol   Law   Me   Faw

By the second half of the nineteenth century, the system of seven syllables that originated in the eleventh century and is still used today (do, re, mi, fa, sol, la, ti, do) was accepted as a progressive and scientific improvement in music-reading and printing.

Instrumental Music

Due to its primarily secular nature, instrumental music was much slower to develop in America. While pianos and pipe organs were accepted because of their role in churches, band and orchestral instruments were at a disadvantage. They lacked the sacred requirement of conveying a text, the natural availability of the human voice, and the chamber music tradition of aristocratic European circles. A publication in 1800 by Samuel Holyoke called *The Instrumental Assistant* did provide instruction and literature for traditional band instruments. However, the expansion of instrumental music in America had to wait for the importation of European chamber music, the instrumental accompaniment of vocal works, and, most importantly for independent instrumental development, the composition of military marches.

Functions of Music in the Classical Era

While the New World colonists were struggling for survival and independence, many European countries were experiencing the expansion of a middle class that possessed more leisure time. Both sides of the Atlantic witnessed the growth of musical performance by amateurs, but for different reasons.

American music was still dependent upon church support. With musical participation in worship services by Puritan and Anglican congregations, a musically literate parish became a necessity. Music was primarily a means to worship God and only secondarily a form of social entertainment.

The growing European middle class with more leisure time encouraged increased instrumental musical performance by amateurs. Composers filled the need for solo and chamber music with works for a wide range of technical abilities. Some compositions were written specifically for instructional purposes, as were several well-known treatises on performance (Quantz–flute, C. P. E. Bach–Keyboards, Leopold Mozart–violin). Amateur performers also created a larger listening audience. Music that previously required patronage of nobility or the church achieved self-supporting status through public concert halls and opera houses. Where today's primary source of entertainment—television—presents most stories in half-hour or hour segments, eighteenth-century comic operas of three to four hours enjoyed great success by satirizing politics and the nobility.

Some composers began to augment their incomes through performances of their own music in the public concert halls. Ludwig van Beethoven began earning a living in Vienna in 1792 as a pianist and composer, and went on to be the first major composer to attain economic independence through royalties from his music and fees for his performances. While his early works, including the first two symphonies and early string quartets, were very much in the style of Haydn and Mozart, Beethoven's compositions after 1803 began to depart from classical molds and to forge the new musical expression of romanticism.

Ludwig van Beethoven (LUHD-vig fahn BAY-toh-ven)

Ludwig van Beethoven (1770–1827) stands astride the Classical and Romantic eras as one of the most significant musical innovators of all time. His childhood was difficult, as he suffered at the hands of his alcoholic father who wished to create a child prodigy after the style of Mozart. At age thirteen he was appointed to the position of assistant court organist in Bonn and a few years later moved to Vienna, where he spent most of the rest of his life.

As an admirer of Mozart and a student of Haydn, Beethoven's early works reflect the classical tradition. Even these first compositions, however, provided a glimpse of the significant changes that were to follow. His classical use of melody and form was mixed with innovations that included expansion of the sonata from three to four movements, dramatic modulations, replacement of the classical minuet with the more playful scherzo, and greater use of dynamics than his predecessors or colleagues indulged.

Ludwig van Beethoven.
Courtesy of the Free Library of Philadelphia.

Symphony

W. A. Mozart: Symphony No. 41 in C Major, K. 551
F. J. Haydn: Symphony No. 7 in C Major (rococo style)
F. J. Haydn: Symphony No. 46 in B Major (sentimental style)
F. J. Haydn: Symphony No. 49 in F Minor ("storm and stress" style)
F. J. Haydn: Symphony No. 104 in D Major (classical)
L. van Beethoven: Symphony No. 1, Op. 21, in C Major

Sonata

C. P. E. Bach: Piano Sonata No. 1 in F Minor
W. A. Mozart: Sonata in C Major for Piano, K. 545
F. J. Haydn: Sonata No. 7 in D Major for Piano

Concerto

W. A. Mozart: Concerto No. 3 in G Major for Violin and Orchestra, K. 216
W. A. Mozart: Piano Concerto No. 21 in C, K. 467
F. J. Haydn: Concerto in D Major for Harpsichord and Orchestra

Opera

W. A. Mozart: Don Giovanni
W. A. Mozart: The Magic Flute
W. A. Mozart: The Marriage of Figaro

Chamber Music

W. A. Mozart: Quartet No. 14 in G Major, K. 387
F. J. Haydn: Quartet in E Flat Major, Op. 33, No. 2
F. J. Haydn: Divertimenti, Op. 31

Choral Music

W. A. Mozart: Requiem Mass
F. J. Haydn: The Seasons (oratorio)
F. J. Haydn: The Creation (oratorio)

American Music

W. Billings: A Virgin Unspotted (Christmas anthem with rhythmic refrain)
W. Billings: "Adoration" (fuguing tune from *The Psalm Singer's Amusement*)

CHAPTER SIXTEEN

Romanticism

Preview of Terms and Concepts

Music of the Romantic era was **imaginative, revolutionary, emotional, full of contrasts,** and **strongly individualistic.** As support for the arts moved out of aristocratic salons and into large public concert halls, orchestras grew in size. Without musical training, audiences were amazed by and drawn to virtuosic solo performers. Operatic productions offered entertainment of sheer grandiosity, humorous farce, or tragic reality.

Composers were inspired by literature, nature, patriotism, distant places, the supernatural, and even the emotions and tragedies of real life. Vocal music and various referential forms of instrumental music flourished.

Delacroix
(Deh-la-KWAH)

F rom the "Age of Reason" we move to what might be termed the "Age of Imagination." While the diversity of the arts in the nineteenth century does not lend itself easily to generalizations, it is not difficult to recognize the imaginative spirit of the painters, sculptors, writers, and musicians that burst forth in dramatic new ways. Painters such as Delacroix created emotionally charged canvases with striking colors, dynamic lighting, and action-charged figures. Inspiration for paintings and sculptures frequently came from writers, including the German and English poets Johann Wolfgang Goethe and Lord Byron, respectively. Themes of liberty and equality became larger than life in the sculptures of artists like François Rude.

Nevertheless, music provided the medium best suited for the individualistic expression of the romantic soul. **Composers** found inspiration in literature, exotic locales, nature, the supernatural, and political and economic strife. **Performers** took their skills to higher levels of virtuosity and professionalism. The **listening audience** expanded beyond aristocratic patrons to include a wealthy middle class seeking entertainment. The breadth and complexity of romantic musical expression served composers, performers, and listeners in new and imaginative ways.

Because of the individualistic nature of nineteenth-century music, most surveys of romanticism organize their presentations by composer. However, the goal of this text is not to provide a comprehensive historical survey of music, but to help you

Liberty Leading the People, *1830, oil on canvas by Eugene Delacroix.*

Reunion des Musee Nationaux

to experience the expressiveness of a wide variety of music. Not every important composer can be adequately covered in this brief introductory effort, but if you understand the general concepts presented here, then you may wish to pursue a more in-depth study of particular composers or forms of music as listed at the end of the chapter.

Cultural Influences

"Revolutionary" also describes the nineteenth century in many respects. The ideals of liberty were strengthened in the aftermath of the American Revolution and the French Revolution. Technological advances led to the Industrial Revolution, which both solved and created social and economic problems. Other military conflicts included the War of 1812, between England and the United States, the Crimean War (1854–56), the United States Civil War (1861–65), and the Franco-Prussian War (1870–71). Many of these social, political, and economic upheavels were reflected in new and revolutionary artistic expressions.

Popularly referred as the "Marseillaise in stone," this stone relief on the Arc de Triomphe de l'Etoile in Paris is meant to stir strong patriotic emotions.

Francois Rude, La Marseillaise Haise (The Departure of the Volunteers in 1792) 1833–1836, Stone, *42' × 26' Arch of Triump, Paris, Photo Bulloz, Art Resource, NY*

One sign of change was the reaction of audiences to new works. Not all of the new modes of musical expression were readily accepted by listeners.

> Beethoven's compositions more and more assume the character of studied eccentricity. He does not write much now, but most of what he produces is so impenetrably obscure in design and so full of unaccountable and often repulsive harmonies, that he puzzles the critic as much as he perplexes the performer.*

Critics found many things about which they could complain, including the length of compositions.

> The *Heroic Symphony* contains much to admire, but it is difficult to keep up admiration of this kind during three long quarters of an hour. It is infinitely too lengthy. . . . If this symphony is not by some means abridged, it will soon fall into disuse.*

Generally, musical compositions became less predictable and seemingly more tolerant of disorder. **Greater tension and stronger climaxes** were achieved in new ways. Music became more **dramatic, emotional, and individualistic.** Some composers drew upon the **exoticism** of ethnic elements, unusual instruments, and unusual texts. Others created intensely **nationalistic works** with the help of folk melodies and dance rhythms. **Virtuosic performers** and the developing sophistication of instruments inspired composers to write works no longer playable by the amateur. Audiences were frequently drawn to public concerts to hear a renowned performer as much as to experience the works of a particular composer. With the decline of patronage, the successful marketing of music and musical performances became an important business.

One of the first and most significant compositions to clearly display the change from classical to romantic music was Beethoven's third symphony. Listen to the first movement of this work and note the numerous ways in which it differs from the Haydn and Mozart works studied in the previous chapter.

Ludwig van Beethoven
The Art and History Archives, Berlin

Ludwig van Beethoven (1770–1829) During the years from 1815 to 1820, Beethoven became almost completely deaf, causing him to be very reclusive, gloomy, and temperamental. Family problems and frequent quarrels with his two brothers added bitterness to his life and affected his music composition. In 1815, his brother Caspar Anton Carl died and left Ludwig and Caspar's widow, Johanna, joint custody of his nine-year-old son Karl. Since Beethoven felt that Johanna was a poor influence for Karl, he fought for complete custody of the boy. It took three years before Beethoven won the case, by which time his relationship with the boy had become quite strained.

These events in Beethoven's life, his total deafness in 1820, and his isolation from society made writing music a tremendous effort for him. Nevertheless, it was during this period that this great composer wrote his most abstract and sublime compositions. Although

---

*From Nicolas Slonimsky, *Lexicon of Musical Invective.* Copyright © 1969 University of Washington Press. Reprinted by permission.

he retreated to writing in the classical forms of his youth, the themes and motives used were worked out to their greatest depths, and meanings are quite obscure—keeping a romantic spirit in the music. These later period works include the *Missa Solemnis,* his *Ninth Symphony,* and the late string quartets. During the years from 1824 to 1826, when he wrote these famous string quartets, his health began to decline and relations with his nephew Karl deteriorated. Beethoven had begun to sketch a Tenth Symphony when Karl tried to commit suicide. This further unnerved the great composer. At the end of 1826, Beethoven caught a serious cold which developed into pneumonia and finally dropsy. He died on March 26, 1827.

Beethoven was the first entrepreneurial composer who did not have a patron. This was unusual because composers before his time normally required such support of a patron for living expenses. Patronage, of course, meant that a composer had to write music that was pleasing and acceptable to his patron and his audience so that he could continue to make money as a composer. Beethoven, however, did not want that kind of restriction and therefore took the risk of not making much money. His music was published and performed frequently enough, however, even from the beginning, for him to make a small income and remain independent. This income improved considerably during the composer's lifetime with the growth of his fame. Today, the continuing popularity of Beethoven's music is still evident in the frequent performances of his works and the numerous recordings available.

Listening Guide
Beginnings of Romanticism

. . . .

 L. van Beethoven: Symphony No. 3 ("Eroica")
I. Allegro con brio

Not only was this the longest symphony to have been composed up to this time, but Beethoven's use of themes to sustain the length was nothing short of revolutionary. The sonata-allegro form was expanded to include an unusual number of themes and motives. In addition to the first theme, second theme, and closing theme, the composer adds three additional themes or motives that create groups of themes, as opposed to clearly defined and expected sections. Even more surprising is the introduction of totally new themes in the development and the coda, and the use of the coda as a second development rather than a simple conclusion.

> *Melody.* Powerful, forceful themes
> *Rhythm.* Triple meter; the themes are rhythmically distinctive
> *Harmony.* Use of strong dissonances to create tension
> *Dynamics.* Many changes to extremes of loud and soft
> *Timbre.* Not essentially different from a classical orchestra (pairs of flutes, oboes, clarinets, and bassoons; three horns, two trumpets, timpani, and strings)

Texture. Primarily homophonic, but polyphonic sections and brief monophonic phrases provide contrast

Form. Sonata-allegro form—less clear and definitive; includes the following aspects of expansion from the classical format:

Exposition
Uses groups of themes

Development
Tremendous tension created through dissonances and distant modulations
Development of several themes
Introduces special new theme

Recapitulation
Continues to develop the themes rather than just present them in the tonic key

Coda
Introduces totally new theme
Brings back special new theme introduced in development
Much longer; equal in length to the other sections

Timing	Description
	EXPOSITION
0'00"	Two loud chords followed by introduction of the first theme in the cellos

0'17"	First theme repeated, and second half of it repeated twice; accented chords lead to . . .
0'42"	First theme in full orchestra
0'52"	New three-note motive (a) passed around in woodwinds and violins

	Unison orchestra statement of the motive leads to . . .
1'05"	Another new theme (b) in this group

1'15"	Transition

1'37"	Second theme

2'00"	Crescendo to closing theme

2'12"   Closing theme

ends with strong dissonance

DEVELOPMENT

3'00"   Begins softly
3'30"   "a" developed
3'45"   First theme in bass developed against transition material
4'35"   "a" returns
4'55"   Short fugal section
5'10"   Syncopation leading to strong dissonances
5'45"   Loud, strong dissonances
6'00"   Special new theme

6'20"   First theme returns
6'47"   Special theme returns for further development
7'10"   First theme in various keys builds to . . .
7'40"   Loud tremolos contrasted with sudden soft chords
8'08"   Soft tremolo versus woodwind chords
8'23"   Horn enters with soft statement of first theme

RECAPITULATION

8'28"   First theme in cellos
8'40"   First theme repeated in solo horn, then flute and violin; crescendo
            to . . .
9'07"   First theme in full orchestra
9'30"   "a" theme returns
9'46"   "b" theme returns
9'56"   Transition
10'17"   Second theme
10'42"   Full crescendo to . . .
10'55"   Closing theme
11'40"   Loud chords build to . . .
11'45"   Strong dissonance

CODA

12'05"   First theme with totally new counter theme
12'25"   Return of special new theme from development
12'55"   Closing theme material builds to . . .
13'30"   First theme in horns, then strings with countermelodies; continues to
               build to . . .
13'58"   First theme in full orchestra
14'30"   Accented chords; sudden change to soft statement of "b" theme
            Crescendo to ending with full chords (14'42")

Nineteenth Century Cultural Centers

With the shift of musical patronage from the aristocracy to free enterprise, audiences grew. Most large cities became cultural centers of some significance, depending upon the number of concert halls or opera houses each could support. Musicians continued to be mobile and rarely stayed in one country to study, compose, and perform. Franz Liszt, for example, was born in Hungary, studied in Vienna, gained fame in Paris as a concert pianist, was greatly influenced by the Italian violinist Paganini, and did considerable composing and teaching in Germany.

Germany and Austria produced numerous native composers and attracted many foreign-born talents to their fine conservatories and schools of music. Italy dominated opera with composers like Gioacchimo Rossini, Gaetano Donizetti, Vincenzo Bellini, Giuseppi Verdi, and Giacomo Puccini. Paris became an operatic center and was also supportive of virtuoso concert pianists such as Frederic Chopin, Franz Liszt, and the American, Louis Moreau Gottschalk. Russian composers were trained primarily in Germany, but made some attempts to infuse their music with their own

Rossini (Ros-SEE-nee)
Bellini (Bel-LEE-nee)

Louis Gottschalk
(Loo-EE Mo-ROH
Gott-SCHALK)

Europe in 1850.

nationalistic flavor. Nationalism was also strong in Poland and Bohemia, where operas drew upon a rich heritage of folklore, and instrumental music borrowed the melodies and rhythms of folk songs and dances.

During the nineteenth century, a greater number of women composers and performers gained recognition for their talent and ability. Polish pianist Maria Agata Szymanowska (1789–1831) performed and published her own piano works throughout Europe. Felix Mendelssohn's older sister, Fanny Mendelssohn Hensel, composed more than 400 lieder and piano pieces. Most of these were performed at private functions and never published. Clara Wieck Schumann enjoyed a very successful performance career both prior to and during her marriage to Robert Schumann. Her piano technique and musicianship won recognition from Chopin, Mendelssohn, and Liszt, and her composition of piano and vocal works was fully supported by her husband, who assisted in getting her works published.

America was still primarily an importer of art music at this point. As cities grew larger, concert halls were built and featured European symphonies and concertos. Orchestras founded during this century include the New York Philharmonic (1842),

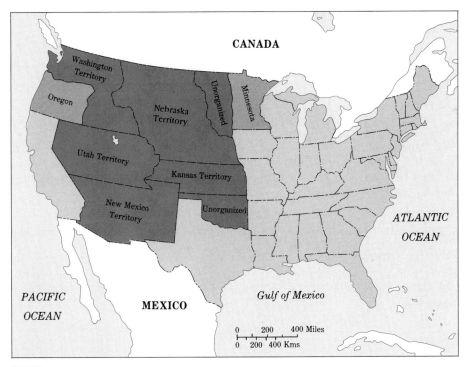

United States in 1860.

☐ Areas granted statehood prior to 1858

☐ Areas granted statehood in 1858 and 1859

■ Territories

the Boston Symphony Orchestra (1881) and the Chicago Symphony Orchestra (1891). Opera houses in these cities presented works from Italy, Germany, and France. In addition to the piano music of their native son Louis Gottschalk, music lovers in New Orleans reveled in the fashionable French opera. Throughout the United States, band concerts (which usually included orchestral and operatic transcriptions), minstrel shows, and the operettas of Offenbach were especially popular.

Elements of Romantic Music

Music of the Romantic era is characterized by **contrasts.** Not only were the musical elements manipulated in diverse ways, but the length of compositions ranged from simple pieces less than one minute long to complex compositions lasting several hours. Composers expanded their vocabulary of compositional resources to create not merely longer works but more personalized efforts of musical expression.

Melody

Melodic length ranged from short and fragmentary to long and flowing. Phrases were frequently **less balanced** and **symmetrical** than the idealized four-measure classical standard. **Increasing chromaticism** of melodies contributed to obscurity of cadences as well as greater harmonic tension. Melodies or parts of melodies provided the basis for **longer thematic development.** Melodies were also written with a particular timbre in mind.

Rhythm

Throughout the nineteenth century, rhythm became an increasingly more interesting, complex, and important musical element. Simple classical rhythms eventually gave way to **greater complexity, syncopation,** and **irregular patterns.** While tempos became more specific with the use of **metronomic markings,** they also became more flexible with the use of **rubato.**

Harmony

The use of **dissonance to increase tension** continued to grow. Harmonic resolutions were sometimes delayed, and tonalities or pitch centers were weakened with added chromaticism. Modulations became more frequent and also involved more distant keys.

Texture

Homophonic texture remained the most common, but more contrasts were created using polyphonic sections and monophonic phrases. Romantic texture can also be discussed in terms of levels of **density.** Lighter, more transparent homophonic textures found in solo songs as well as in some instrumental works contrast greatly with the thick, rich orchestral works that use both polyphonic texture in some sections and a greater number of instruments and instrumental parts.

Timbre

The three most important aspects of romantic timbre are the **improved and increased use of the piano, the greater use of percussion,** and **the growth of the orchestra.** Tone color was important to the elements of harmony and melody. The expressiveness of a melodic line was greatly enhanced by both the instrument playing the line and the timbre of the accompaniment.

The piano, invented by Cristofori in 1709, was initially built with a wooden frame. This limited the amount of tension that could be put on the strings and produced many intonation problems as the wooden frames were pulled out of shape. Around the turn of the century, however, iron frames and improved steel wires were developed. This stronger nineteenth-century piano had a better tone, greater dynamic capabilities, stayed more accurately in tune, and eventually increased in range from five to over seven octaves (fig. 16.1). All of these improvements, combined with the capability of dynamic range and nuance unique to this keyboard, made the piano one of the most popular instruments of the Romantic era—for composers, performers, and listeners alike.

Figure 16.1
Interior of modern piano.
© The Bettmann Archive

Figure 16.2
Timpani with pedals.
Courtesy of the Ludwig Drum
Company

Percussion instruments added unique expressive emphasis to the music of nineteenth-century orchestras. The timpani or kettledrums used in the classical orchestra were usually played in two pitches—the tonic and the dominant (fig. 16.2). With the expansion of romantic harmony to include modulations to more and distant keys came the need for additional pitches from the timpani. Not only were three or four of these instruments now used in an orchestra, but a pedal mechanism was added to facilitate changing pitches. Other percussion instruments common to romantic orchestras included the bass drum, snare drum, cymbals, and triangle. As composers became interested in the exotic music of other countries, Spanish, Turkish, and numerous Latin American instruments were added to the arsenal of sounds provided by orchestral percussionists.

Orchestras also grew in other ways. Flutes made of metal instead of wood became louder and more brilliant in sound. The brass section was enlarged and lower brass (trombones and tuba) were added. Improvements in the construction and design of valves enabled greater fluency of technique, better tone quality, and more accurate intonation for trumpets and French horns. As more and louder wind instruments entered the orchestra, the number of string instruments was also increased to keep a balanced sound. While the average nineteenth-century orchestra numbered between seventy and eighty members, some composers doubled or tripled that number for specific works. Hector Berlioz, Richard Wagner, and Gustav Mahler are all known for their monumental feats of orchestration for gigantic forces of instruments.

Berlioz' use of gigantic forces is humorously depicted in the nineteenth-century caricature by Gustave Dore.
© North Wind Picture Archives

With such large ensembles came greater responsibility as well as greater recognition for conductors. Many nineteenth-century composers were as well known for their conducting skills as they were for their compositions.

Dynamics

The nineteenth century also brought significant expansion in the range of dynamic contrasts. With the use of percussion and larger orchestras came the potential for **more dramatic,** louder levels of sound. Beethoven was especially fond of balancing moments of loud, crashing chords with sudden and unexpected silences. Many nuances and subtle changes in dynamics were also used to enhance the rise and fall of the melodic line.

Form

Classical forms continued to be used by nineteenth century composers, with sonata-allegro remaining one of the most popular methods of organization. Individual **sections expanded,** however, were no longer balanced and symmetrical, and became less clear. A comparison of the first movements of Mozart's fortieth symphony and Beethoven's third will quickly highlight some of the differences.

	Mozart	**Beethoven**
Exposition		
Approximate length of section	4′00″ (with repeat)	3′00″ (without repeat)
	First theme	Group of three themes
	Transition	Transition
	Second theme	Second theme
	Closing theme	Closing theme
Development		
Approximate length of section	1′20″	5′28″
	Built on a three-note motive	Develops several themes and introduces a new theme
Recapitulation		
Approximate length of section	2′25″	3′17″
	Both composers bring back material from exposition	
Coda		
Approximate length of section	0′17″	2′37″
	Brief conclusion	Further development and introduction of a new theme
Total time of first movement	8′02″	14′42″
Total time of entire symphony	27′30″	50′00″

The timings above give just one indication of the scope of the changes that Beethoven initiated. Because of the creative freedom possible, **development sections became longer.** Reworking of themes even took place outside the development sections and added both length and interest to the recapitulation and coda.

Free forms or through-composed works became popular, especially in character pieces for piano. Titles such as fantasy, nocturne, etude, and ballade are suggestive of moods rather than specific forms. Without the need for balance and symmetry, through-composed works oftentimes fit the expressive needs of the romantic composers.

Frederic Chopin (1810–1849) was a Polish-French composer and pianist who wrote almost exclusively for piano. He improved piano technique and created new sonorities on the instrument by an extended range in his compositions. As an infant, Chopin loved to hear his mother or sister play the piano. At age six, he began trying to play what he heard or to make up new tunes. Piano lessons began at age seven from a local piano and violin teacher, and during the same year he composed *Polonaise in G Minor* as well as a march that was later scored for military band. Frederic made his first public performance when he was eight, from which point he became known as a prodigy.

Chopin received his general education at the Warsaw lyceum and studied composition and theory with Jozef Elsner, the director of the Warsaw Conservatory. In spite of treatments for tuberculosis, Chopin continued to study at the Conservatory; and during breaks he went home with his friends and became acquainted with folk music in its natural surroundings. This exposure later proved to have a significant influence on his writing. Chopin completed a normal three-year course of study at the Conservatory in 1829.

After his graduation, he began touring as a concert pianist and made a debut in Vienna in August 1829. In September he fell in love with a singer at the Conservatory, but was too shy to develop a relationship. Instead, the composer transformed his feelings into the slow movements of his two piano concerti written at that time. The following year he performed both concerti in Warsaw. This was his last concert in his homeland; he never returned. As Chopin toured in western Europe, the Polish insurrection began, and he decided to stay in Vienna. At this time he set patriotic poems to music and wrote wild turbulent piano solos such as *Scherzo in B minor,* opus 20 and *Revolutionary Etude,* opus 10, no. 12. In April 1831, he made one public appearance in Vienna before moving to Paris in mid-September. At this time he met many other romantic composers such as Liszt, Berlioz, and Mendelssohn. Chopin made his first public appearance in Paris in February 1832. Because he played the piano with a more delicate touch, he was not as well-liked in large halls. He consequently turned to teaching rich and aristocratic pupils and played for intimate audiences only.

Chopin wrote various types of piano music, including nocturnes, etudes, preludes, waltzes, polonaises, mazurkas, ballades, fantasias, the berceuse, and the barcarole. His "singing" melodies were influenced by Italian operas and arias. Chopin's compositions were published in France, Germany, and England and were well-received by the critics. His music was banned in Poland by the reigning power, however, because its patriotic spirit so stirred the masses.

In July 1837, Chopin made his first trip to London, where he became acquainted with the novelist George Sand (Aurore Duderant). They began an affair that lasted for nearly ten years. During this time he spent most of his summers composing at Sand's country house in France. Otherwise, he stayed in Paris and continued teaching, using a method that stressed a flexible wrist and arm, new fingerings, and beautiful tone at all times. In April 1841, he again attempted to give a recital; but this was too much of a strain on his health, which had been declining rapidly. His relationship with Aurore Duderant ended, and in 1848, with the revolution in Paris, he lost much of his patronage. After brief travels and a few more performances, Chopin returned to Paris too ill to teach or compose. He died there of tuberculosis on October 17, 1849.

Oil painting of Frederic Chopin by Eugene Delacroix. 1838.

Oil on canvas, 18″ × 15″. The Louvre, Paris, Photo, Laurus-Giraudon/Art Resource, NY

Frederic Chopin
(FRED-er-rick
SHOH-pan)

Listening Guide
Use of Romantic Elements

. . . .

   F. Chopin: Polonaise in A♭ Major (Heroic)

Melody. Many contrasting melodies ranging from grand and rhythmic to delicate and melancholy

Harmony. Chromaticism used to increase tension

Rhythm. Powerful rhythms; frequent use of rubato

Dynamics. Wide range of dynamic contrast used

Texture. Primarily homophonic

Timbre. The piano, a favorite instrument for Romantic era composers, made great personal expressiveness possible for the performer; full range of the instrument is used

Form. Five-part rondo (Introduction A B A C A Coda)

Timing	Section	Description
0′00″	Introduction	Forceful, ascending sequence of chords seem to build up energy into "A"
0′30″	A	Powerful, rhythmic theme; ends with strong cadence
1′45″	B	Two new ideas presented, each repeated; leads directly into return of "A"
2′27″	A	Powerful, rhythmic; ends with strong cadence
3′08″	C	Begins with broad chords and descending scale pattern in left-hand accompaniment; contrasting, slower middle section; texture thins; seems to wander before finally returning to powerful "A" section
5′50″	A	Powerful, rhythmic; does not come to a stop but leads into coda
6′30″	Coda	Quick moving, active motion to end with abrupt harmonic shift right before the final cadence (6′53″)

Romantic Expressiveness

The chief artistic objective of nineteenth-century composers was the **personal expression of emotions.** The musical expressions of this era were more intense, passionate, and individualistic than at any previous time. Techniques of creating tension and release challenged listeners with more powerful climaxes, surprised them with unfamiliar sounds, and moved them with touching, personal sensitivity.

These changes, however, were not without their difficulties. The decline of aristocratic patronage—just as composers were becoming more individualistic—created some economic problems. The most creative and innovative compositions were not always met with immediate acceptance by audiences who had received little or no musical training. (Slonimsky's *Lexicon of Musical Invective* is a convincing and amusing testimony to this nonacceptance of the unfamiliar.) While this explosion of nineteenth-century individualism may have caused financial insecurity for some composers, newfound artistic freedom led to tremendous personal and creative expression.

Inspiration for this creative expression came from nature, literature, patriotism, the supernatural, exotic places, love, and a whole range of other feelings. Texts and stories from writers like Byron, Shakespeare, and Sir Walter Scott were enhanced with a new musical vocabulary. Absolute music continued to be produced, but romantic composers seemed to have a special affinity for vocal music and referential works. Whether absolute or referential, romantic music was deeply expressive of emotions.

Program Music

From simple descriptive titles to long, detailed narrations, nineteenth-century composers oftentimes provided significant insight into extramusical associations with their works. Titles and subtitles went beyond the simple identification of tempo, style, or form. Brief notations in the musical score or complete program notes provided by the composer gave clear documentation as to the source of creative inspiration.

Three nineteenth-century symphonic forms that are programmatic are the **tone poem,** the **concert overture,** and the **program symphony.** The tone poem and concert overture are single movement forms. They carry at least a descriptive title and probably additional programmatic information provided by the composer. The program symphony usually has a descriptive subtitle and at least four movements that are sometimes related by a common theme. (For a listening example of a tone poem, see *The Moldau* in the following section on nationalism.)

A subtitle may provide only a vague hint of what the composer had in mind. The *Symphony No. 3 in E♭* by Beethoven, for instance, carries the subtitle "Eroica" ("Heroic"). That term by itself may suggest certain emotions and guide the listener to hear the music within a particular context. Additional information can provide even greater insight. A well-known story surrounding this symphony tells of Beethoven's initial admiration of Napoléon as a champion of liberty and equality, which led to his dedication of the symphony to the French leader. When Beethoven heard that Napoléon had proclaimed himself Emperor, the composer in his anger tore in half the title page, which bore the dedication, and later gave the work the "Heroic" subtitle.

Hector Berlioz.

Courtesy of the Free Library of
Philadelphia

Hector Berlioz
(BAYR-lee-ohz)

Hector Berlioz (1803–1869) was born in a village in the French Alps. Since France was at war, Berlioz received his education from his father, a prominent physician of the time, who also gave the young boy his first informal music lessons. As Berlioz grew older, he figured out the elements of harmony by himself and began composing for local chamber-music groups by the time he was twelve. In May 1817, he began his formal music education by taking lessons first in singing and on flute and later on guitar, flageolet (an instrument similar to the recorder), and drum. In 1821, at his father's insistence, Berlioz began studying medicine in Paris. While there, however, he took every chance to see the Paris Opera and study the scores of Gluck. He was later accepted as a student of the professor of composition at the Conservatoire—Jean-François Lesueur. Berlioz quit medicine and continued his musical studies full time. In spite of many embittered disagreements with his parents, the young musician persevered and continued studying counterpoint with the influential Czech composer and teacher, Anton Reicha.

In 1830, Berlioz won the Prix de Rome, which required him to study three years abroad—two in Italy. This prize eased relations with his family but took him away from the great influences of Paris. Berlioz wrote in his *Mémoires* (published in 1870) how bored and unproductive he was in Italy compared to Paris, where he wrote many works, including the *Fantastic Symphony*. When he returned to Paris early, forfeiting part of his prize, he continued to write music and married Harriet Smithson, a well-known actress, in 1833. They had one child, Louis, before the couple separated permanently. It was during these years that he wrote the well-known symphonies *Harold in Italy* (1834), *Romeo and Juliet* (1839), and the *Funeral Symphony* (1840).

After 1840, Berlioz made many tours across Europe in an effort to have his music performed. These concerts spread his fame and influenced many other composers. Berlioz was also a well-known music critic for a Paris newspaper and wrote a famous treatise on orchestration in 1844. In his last years, he became quite famous abroad. However, in his private life, Berlioz fought illness and was saddened by the deaths of those closest to him, including his only son, who died in 1867 of yellow fever at the age of 33. Berlioz died in Paris on March 8, 1869.

Listening Guide
Romantic Programmatic Music

· ·

H. Berlioz: Symphonie Fantastique

Berlioz, an admirer of Beethoven, borrowed the great composer's idea of descriptive programs from Beethoven's sixth symphony (the "Pastoral") and extended the process to include fairly specific descriptions of an imaginative "Episode in the Life of an Artist."

This work is somewhat autobiographical. Berlioz fell hopelessly in love with the Irish actress Harriet Smithson. After finally convincing the young lady to marry him, reality could not possibly live up to the imagined bliss. The composer's tumultuous life continued to swing from deep personal miseries to great musical successes. The story provided by Berlioz for this symphony of gigantic proportions was most likely an expression of his imagination and his feelings surrounding this ill-fated love.

>   *Melody.* Berlioz uses a unifying melody, which he calls the *idée fixe* (fixed idea), to depict his beloved; the theme changes character in each of the five movements

>   *Timbre.* Inventive uses of traditional instruments as well as several innovative additions: two harps, English horn, E♭ clarinet, two ophicleides (predecessor of the tuba), four timpani, and a large battery of percussion
>   *Form.* Unusual extension of symphonic form to include five, rather than four, movements

Program as provided by the composer

A young musician of great sensibility and plentiful imagination, in deep despair because of hopeless love, has poisoned himself with opium. The drug is not strong enough to kill him but puts him into deep sleep with strange dreams. His sensations, emotions, and memories, as they filter through his fevered brain, are transformed into musical images and ideas. The beloved one herself becomes to him a tune, a recurring theme (the *idée fixe*) that continually haunts him.

1. *Reveries, Passions.* First he remembers the weariness of the soul, that indefinable longing, that sombre melancholia and those objectless joys that he experienced before meeting his beloved. Then the explosive love that immediately inspired him, his delirious suffering, his return to tenderness, his religious consolations.
2. *A Ball.* At a ball, in the middle of a noisy brilliant fête, he finds his beloved again.
3. *In the Country.* On a summer evening in the country, he hears two shepherds calling each other with their folk melodies. The pastoral duet in such surroundings, the gentle rustle of the trees swayed by the wind, some reasons for hope that had come to his knowledge recently—all unite to fill his heart with a unique tranquillity and lend brighter colors to his fancies. But his beloved appears anew, spasms contract his heart, and he is filled with dark premonition. What if she proved faithless? Only one of the shepherds resumes his rustic tune. The sun sets. Far away there is a rumble of thunder—solitude—silence.
4. *March to the Scaffold.* He dreams he has killed his loved one, that he is condemned to death and led to his execution. A march, now gloomy yet ferocious, now solemn yet brilliant, accompanies the procession. Noisy outbursts are followed without pause by the heavy sound of marching footsteps. Finally, like a last thought of love, the *idée fixe* briefly appears, to be cut off by the fall of an axe.
5. *Dream of a Witches' Sabbath.* He sees himself at a Witches's Sabbath, surrounded by a fearful crowd of spectres, sorcerers, and monsters of every kind, united for his burial. Unearthly sounds, groans, shrieks of laughter, distant cries, to which others seem to respond! The melody of his beloved is heard, but it has lost its character of nobility and reserve. It is now an ignoble dance tune, trivial and grotesque. It is she who comes to the Sabbath! A shout of joy greets her arrival. She joins the diabolical orgy. The funeral knell, burlesque of the *Dies Irae*. Dance of the Witches. The dance and the *Dies Irae* combine.

V. Dream of a Witches' Sabbath

Introduction. Wild shrieks and heinous laughter present an ominous beginning
Idée Fixe. The beloved's melody returns in the form of a diabolical dance
Dies Irae. Chimes lead to the Dies Irae ("Day of Wrath") theme, which becomes faster
and eventually changes into a rhythmic "burlesque parody" of the ancient melody
"Dance of the Witches' Sabbath." This section begins with a fugal statement taken from
part of the previous dance melody. The Dies Irae melody is combined with the
dance melody in a furious climax that brings this musical nightmare to a diabolical
end
(The form of this movement is freely composed with sections of varying length.)

Timing	Description
0'00"	Slow introductory section with ominous string tremolo and various instrumental "groans, shrieks of laughter" and "distant cries"
1'15"	Faster section; brief statement of the "idée fixe" as an "ignoble dance tune" in a solo clarinet

1'20"	Startlingly loud chord in the full orchestra is followed by a rhythmically chaotic "shout of joy" and "diabolical orgy"
1'30"	"Idée fixe"—The "ignoble dance tune" returns and builds to a frenzied climax that is resolved in sudden soft, long tones
2'40"	Bells toll to introduce fragments of the witches' dance theme

3'07"	Bells continue; the first half of the Dies Irae theme is played by: —tubas and bassoons; —faster version in trumpets and trombones; —rhythmic statement of the theme in woodwinds

3'44"	Second half of the theme receives similar treatment: —tubas and bassoons; —trumpets and trombones; —woodwinds

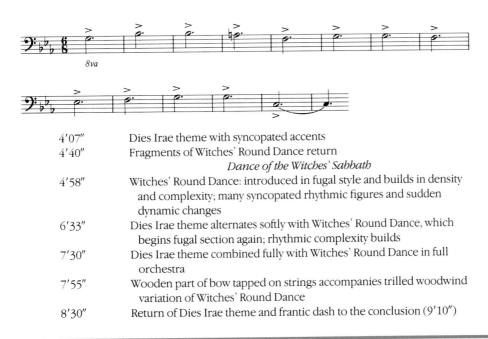

4′07″	Dies Irae theme with syncopated accents
4′40″	Fragments of Witches' Round Dance return

Dance of the Witches' Sabbath

4′58″	Witches' Round Dance: introduced in fugal style and builds in density and complexity; many syncopated rhythmic figures and sudden dynamic changes
6′33″	Dies Irae theme alternates softly with Witches' Round Dance, which begins fugal section again; rhythmic complexity builds
7′30″	Dies Irae theme combined fully with Witches' Round Dance in full orchestra
7′55″	Wooden part of bow tapped on strings accompanies trilled woodwind variation of Witches' Round Dance
8′30″	Return of Dies Irae theme and frantic dash to the conclusion (9′10″)

Peter Ilich Tchaikovsky (1840–1893) was a Russian composer born in Votkinsk on May 7, 1840. He showed musical ability at an early age, working with his sister when he was only four to compose a song for their mother. Tchaikovsky began taking piano lessons from a local teacher when he was five. As a young boy he enjoyed listening to such works as Mozart's *Don Giovanni* on the orchestrion—a kind of "player organ." In 1850 he became a student at the St. Petersburg School of Jurisprudence, where his studies included singing, piano, and harmony lessons. During this time his mother took him to see Glinka's *A Life for the Tsar*. This and other operas made a deep impression on him. When his mother died of cholera in 1854, he composed a short waltz in her memory. In 1859 Tchaikovsky graduated from the St. Petersburg School and took a job as a clerk in the Ministry of Justice.

In 1861 Tchaikovsky began his serious study of music by taking private harmony lessons. The following year he continued this study at the St. Petersburg Conservatory. Tchaikovsky resigned from the civil service in 1863 and began to study instrumentation with Anton Rubenstein. In 1864, Tchaikovsky completed his first orchestral score, an overture based on the play "The Storm" by Ostrovsky. He graduated the next year and became a professor of harmony at the Moscow Conservatory of Music—a position offered by Rubenstein's brother. A large annuity from a wealthy widow who admired his music allowed Tchaikovsky to resign his teaching position in 1878. This patronage continued until 1890 when the widow, Nadezhda von Meck, suddenly terminated both the money and her friendship. By this time, however, his finances were in good order because of his compositions and a pension. From 1887 to the year of his death, Tchaikovsky made various conducting tours in western Europe, England, and the United States. He was well received wherever he went and became well-known as a composer. In 1893 Tchaikovsky was awarded an honorary Doctor of Music degree at Cambridge.

Peter Ilich Tchaikovsky.
© North Wind Picture Archives

Peter Ilitch Tchaikovsky (EEL-yitch Chahy-KAWV-skee)

Tchaikovsky wrote the first of his six symphonies in 1866, the year after he graduated from the Conservatory. Because he was such a perfectionist in the orchestration of this and other works, he suffered mental crises at various times throughout his life. Not surprisingly, however, it is his orchestra writing for which he is most remembered. Some of his more popular compositions include the *Romeo and Juliet Fantasy Overture* (1869), *Piano Concerto No. 1* (1875), the *Symphony No. 4* (1877), *Violin Concerto* (1878), the *1812 Overture* (1880), and three ballets—*Swan Lake* (1876), *Sleeping Beauty* (1890), and *The Nutcracker* (1892). He also wrote solo songs, piano compositions, liturgical music, several symphony-fantasias, chamber works, and operas.

Because he had difficulty identifying with the characters, only one of his many operas, *Eugene Onegin,* was really successful. However, as he was writing this opera, he became acquainted with a girl, Antonina Milyukova, who was quite infatuated with him. Tchaikovsky identified her with the heroine in his opera and eventually married her, despite his homosexual tendencies. The marriage fell apart immediately, though, and another nervous breakdown and a suicide attempt followed.

Tchaikovsky's final composition, his *Sixth Symphony* (known as the "Pathétique"), had a pessimistic program based upon passion, love, disappointment, and death. He conducted its premiere performance on October 28, 1893, and took his own life a few days later on November 6. After many years of false speculation about his death, it was discovered that he had taken arsenic to avoid a scandal concerning the revelation of his homosexuality.

Listening Guide
Romantic Program Music (example 2)

· ·

P. I. Tchaikovsky: Romeo and Juliet Fantasy Overture

Tchaikovsky doesn't attempt to tell the story of Romeo and Juliet. The major characters and emotions are rather presented and unified with a traditional sonata-allegro form.

Shakespeare's tragedy contains many classic but powerful emotions that lend themselves to musical interpretations. In particular, the feud between the Montagues and Capulets, the well-intentioned mediations of Friar Laurence, and the devotion of Romeo and Juliet provide inspiration for three of the main themes in the work. The tragedy of the deaths of the young lovers is suggested in a dirgelike section of the coda and then is lifted to optimism (the lovers have defied fate and been reunited in death) in the final major chords of the work.

Love theme

Form. Sonata-allegro

Melody. Helps delineate the sections; varies from smooth, flowing, and lyrical to choppy and rhythmic

Timbre. Full nineteenth-century orchestra plus prominent use of harp

Harmony. Controlled dissonances for color and harmonic tension

Texture. Mostly homophonic, with polyphonic and monophonic for contrast

Rhythm. Diverse and interesting; themes are rhythmically distinctive; rhythm provides formal unification as well as motion and tension to help create the climax

Timing	Description
	INTRODUCTION
0'00"	Slow, hymnlike—"Friar's Theme"
0'27"	Soft layering of chords, gentle dissonances, followed by descending line and prominent harp arpeggios
1'42"	Friar's Theme: introduced and accompanied by quicker moving pizzicato line in strings, which gives a more agitated feeling
2'12"	Repeat of soft followup to the theme, but grows more intense
3'28"	More agitated and louder buildup of chords leads into louder, quicker, passionate statement of Friar's Theme
4'02"	Alternation of "opposing" woodwind and brass chords leads to . . .
	EXPOSITION
4'40"	Feud Theme (First Theme): rhythmic and jerky, loud; strings and woodwinds continue opposing roles
5'30"	Tension builds with fast-running string scales and unpredictable, hard-struck chords in the full orchestra
5'40"	Feud Theme in full orchestra leads to . . .
6'00"	Transition; soft, gets thinner and rhythmically static
6'40"	Love Theme (Second Theme): solo by English horn and viola followed by soft, pulsing string chords
7'40"	Long ascending scale into repeat of Love Theme, this time in the higher range of the flutes and oboes; accompanied by strings and pulsing French horn line; melody is extended to a climax that is resolved softly
8'42"	Soft conclusion of exposition with prominent harp chords; decreases to a single note in the violas
	DEVELOPMENT
9'45"	Feud Theme and Friar's Theme (from introduction) developed through various combinations; "opposing forces" evident in use of contrasting timbres and fragments of themes
11'30"	Climax with Friar's Theme in trumpet versus full orchestra playing the main rhythmic motive of the Feud Theme; running string line and unpredictable orchestral chords lead to . . .

	RECAPITULATION
12′00″	Feud Theme in full orchestra; even fuller than first presented in the exposition
12′20″	Moves more quickly than in the exposition to transition that now is based on material from Love Theme accompaniment; builds to . . .
13′00″	Loud, full, extended statement of Love Theme with fuller accompaniment and pulsing French horn line
14′00″	Soft transition section based on Love Theme; builds to . . .
	CODA—PART I
14′30″	Love Theme interrupted by the Feud Theme, which is then joined by the Friar's Theme; eventually reduces dynamics, all rhythmic action, and density to soft, but dramatic cadence
	CODA—PART II
15′55″	Funeral dirge suggested by the timpani; fragment of the Love Theme
16′35″	Soft woodwind chorale
17′20″	Harp arpeggios lead to final loud statement of fragment of Love Theme
17′55″	Crescendo in timpani brings the final cadence in triumphal major chords (18′10″)

Nationalism

Nationalistic music attempts to convey the spirit of a particular country—a process that always includes some aspect of folk art, either real or simulated. Actual folk songs, for example, can easily be incorporated into a symphonic work to create a flavor of the country from which they came. A similar effect can be produced by a skilled composer who simply writes melodies reminiscent of the folk songs of a particular region or country. Characteristic harmonies, rhythms of folk dances, and the use or imitation of folk instruments also create musical nationalism.

Extramusical associations can also produce an aura of nationalism. Folk stories or legends have been used as the inspiration or basis for an opera or programmatic work. Program music can also depict significant events or even landscapes.

Techniques Used to Create Nationalism in Music

Musical	**Extramusical**
Folk tunes (real or imitated)	Folk stories or legends used as inspiration or basis of an opera or programmatic work
Characteristic rhythms of folk dances	
Use or imitation of folk instruments	
Harmonies of folk tunes	Programmatic depiction of events or landscapes

Vocal music easily carries the message of national pride through a text. Instrumental music is more dependent upon descriptive titles or even extensive written programs provided by the composer. A wide range of musical and extramusical associations is found in the nationalistic works of nineteenth-century composers. Some of the best compositions are those that can endure multiple listenings even without awareness of the extramusical associations. However, the titles, written programs, and historical knowledge can greatly enhance your understanding and enjoyment of nationalistic works.

Bedrich Smetana (1824–1884) was born on March 2, 1824, in Litomysl, Bohemia (now part of Czechoslovakia). By age six, he was recognized as a superb pianist. His musical training continued in 1838 when Smetana went to Prague and studied piano and theory. While there, he began writing various compositions for piano, voice, and particularly string quartets; but these early works were poorly received. After completing his education, Smetana opened his own music school in Prague in 1848 and was married the following year. At this time he continued to compose various works, but wrote predominantly for his own instrument—the piano.

Smetana loved his homeland, but because of Austrian oppression in Bohemia, he accepted a position as conductor of the Göteborg, Sweden, orchestra from 1856 to 1861. It was during this time that Smetana began writing symphonic tone poems—a new form invented by Liszt. The family, including a young daughter, traveled back and forth to Bohemia as the orchestra toured, until 1858 when Smetana's wife became ill. She died the following year from tuberculosis. In 1860 Smetana married again, and the family was able to return to Bohemia the following year, when Bohemia won political freedom from Austria.

Smetana continued to teach in Prague and began composing operas. His best-loved comic opera, *The Bartered Bride,* premiered in 1866; and he was appointed conductor of the National Theater in Prague. Because of the folk rhythms and delightful folk melodies used in this opera, the work caused Smetana to become known as the first Czech national composer. Following his forced retirement in 1874 because of growing deafness, Smetana continued to write more nationalistic compositions such as *My Country*—a cycle of symphonic tone poems (which includes *The Moldau*) telling about the history of his homeland and *Evening Songs* (a cycle of patriotic songs). His last composition, a string quartet called *From My Life,* suggests in the last movement a piercing, whistling sound that he heard every evening as he was going completely deaf. During the last ten years of his life, Smetana suffered from severe mental depression, and with the encouragement of a friend, he committed himself to an asylum in Prague in late April 1884. He died May 12, 1884.

Bedrich Smetana.
© The Bettmann Archive

Bedrich Smetana
(BAYD-rik
SMEH-teh-nuh)

Listening Guide
Nineteenth-Century Nationalism

· ·

B. Smetana: The Moldau

This is a programmatic tone poem taken from a collection of six entitled *My Country*. Smetana's nationalistic intentions are evident in the musical depictions of his beloved countryside and the use of folklike rhythms and melodies.

Timing	Description	Smetana's Program
0'00"	Two flutes	Two springs
0'25"	Texture becomes more complex as clarinets are added	The springs join a brook that ultimately becomes the river Moldau.
1'07"	Broad, sweeping violin melody	The river Moldau flows through the forests and across the meadows.
2'05"	(River theme repeated)	
3'00"	Horn and trumpet fanfares	Hunting calls in the thick woods area
4'00"	Rhythmic folk dance	Merry feasts celebrated in the countryside
6'00"	Slow, muted strings with "swirling" woodwinds Soft horns added	Water nymphs dance in the moonlight; fortresses and castles of bygone days are reflected on the surface of the water.
8'40"	River theme returns in the violins	The Moldau swirls through the seething rapids near Prague.
9'30"	Intensity grows	
10'45"	River theme changes to major and moves much faster	The river flows past Vysehrad, where once stood a royal castle.
11'15"	Brass chorale	
12'05"	Decrescendo to end	The rivers disappears in the distance as it flows into the Elbe.
12'45"	Final two chords	

Listening Guide
Nineteenth-Century Nationalism (example 2)

· ·

J. Sibelius: Finlandia, op. 26

Although Sibelius lived well into the twentieth century (1865–1957), his music remained firmly entrenched in nineteenth-century romanticism. This single-movement tone poem was originally the fourth movement of a suite entitled *Finland Awakes*. First performed in 1899, the work was presented as part of a series of concerts used to raise funds to fight Russian oppression. Sibelius' composition musically suggests the tragedy of a country about to lose its freedom, the endurance of militant courage, and prayerful hope and strength. The melody was an original invention of the composer but sounded very much like a folk tune. As the work became identified with Finnish idealism and the struggle for independence, some writers suggested that *Finlandia* did more to bring about Finnish freedom than any speech, pamphlet, or published propaganda.

Melody. Distinguishes sections; vary from short and choppy to lyrical and expressive
Dynamics. Numerous dramatic changes
Harmony. Not harshly dissonant but used to help create tension and release
Texture. Mostly homophonic
Rhythm. Energetic, often syncopated
Timbre. Large orchestra; instrumental families help create contrasting sections
Form. Through-composed; basically an unfolding of ideas in a free and spontaneous
  nature

What emotions do you feel are suggested by each section?

Timing	Description
0′00″	Dramatic introduction with strong chords that crescendo and end with abrupt accents
1′05″	Woodwinds then strings continue in a choralelike setting
3′25″	Rhythmic brass fanfares and low rumbling pitches lead to a return of chords from the introduction
4′05″	Change of character—"marching" bass line followed by melody that grows out of the previous fanfare
5′50″	New melody introduced in woodwinds with string accompaniment— prayerful and optimistic (Words were later added to this melody to create a popular church hymn.)
6′40″	Strings repeat the melody with fuller, more confident sound
7′52″	Return of marchlike bass line and fanfares; tempo increases
8′30″	Final climax with full orchestra uses first phrase of the "prayerful" melody in a strong, forceful ending (9′00″)

Vocal Music

At its best, the combination of music and poetry in nineteenth-century music was a mutually beneficial relationship. Poems inspired creative images that led composers to produce many fine vocal settings. A great poem set to great music produces a whole that indeed is greater than the sum of its individual parts. Mediocre poetry can even be lifted to greatness with a superior musical setting. The reverse, however, is not true, as inferior music will only detract from poetry that could otherwise stand on its own.

Not every text set to music by romantic composers was of the highest quality. However, the partiality of romantic composers to literature, nationalism, and poetry produced a rich and varied repertoire of vocal works that included solo songs, choral masterpieces, and operas.

The popularity of the piano in this century, both as a solo instrument and as an accompaniment instrument, helped to make the solo song a natural form of musical expression. German songs, commonly referred to by the German word *lieder* (singular, *lied*), comprise a large portion of the performance repertoire of singers today. Composers such as Franz Schubert, Robert and Clara Schumann, Fanny Mendelssohn, Josephine Lang, Edvard Grieg, Bedrich Smetana, Antonin Dvorak, Johannes Brahms, and Hugo Wolf produced hundreds of individual songs. Many more were united by subject matter and melodic themes in collections called **song cycles.** The best of these works combined a poetic text and expressive melody with a complementary and equally important piano part that did more than merely accompany the vocal solo.

Franz Schubert
(Frahntz SHOO-bert)

Edvard Grieg (ED-vard Greeg)

Johannes Brahms
(Yo-HAHN-nes Brahms)

Franz Schubert.
Courtesy of the Free Library of Philadelphia

Franz Schubert (1797–1828) was an Austrian composer born near Vienna, the fourth of five children in a very musical family. As a young boy he often heard chamber music at home, played by his father and older brothers. (One of his brothers, Ferdinand, eventually became a composer of church music.) Franz started taking piano lessons from his brother Ignaz when he was six years old and studied violin with his father when he was eight. Later, he took lessons from the parish choirmaster in organ, music theory, singing, and violin. He did very well in the latter two and experimented with writing music, as well.

In October 1808, young Schubert won a scholarship to attend the boarding school attached to the imperial court in Vienna. There he studied music, while giving service as a chorister. Franz stayed in the orchestra and conducted when the regular conductor was gone. While he was at this school, he composed several works, including *Fantasia for Piano Duet* (1810), some of his first songs (of which he would eventually compose more than six hundred), several string quartets, and a few orchestral overtures. He was too shy to show these works, but his friends encouraged him to take them to Antonio Salieri, a composer at the court. Salieri was duly impressed and in 1813 agreed to give him lessons.

Schubert next attended a teacher-training school for about a year and took a job in 1814 at the same school where his father taught. He composed in any spare moment, experimented with forms, and wrote more chamber works, three symphonies, three masses, and four operas, as well as more songs. In 1816 Schubert began looking for other jobs in music at the university level. He was granted a leave of absence that December and continued to write two more symphonies, including the fourth—Tragic Symphony, a mass, and the first of his piano sonatas.

For the next several years Schubert spent most of his time composing and doing some occasional teaching. During the summers of 1818 and 1824 he taught music to the family of Count Esterhazy in Hungary, the same family Joseph Haydn had worked for years before. It was here that he grew to like Hungarian folk music and gypsy airs, which he eventually used in some of his works.

Schubert continued a full schedule of composing and produced a total of nine symphonies and twenty string quartets; his chamber music included an octet, two trios, two quintets, and incidental music; church music comprised a total of six masses, one hundred cantatas, psalms, hymns, etc., and the *German Requiem*; piano compositions numbered twenty-two sonatas, *Musical Moments,* eight impromptus, and many piano duets; vocal music included various operas, of which two still continue to be performed, and more than six hundred songs that he introduced and developed to their highest form.

In 1823 Schubert developed a venereal disease that caused him to retire from all endeavors except his composition. These were the years during which he produced his best opera, *Fierabras* (1823), the incidental music to *Rosamunde* (1823), and his song cycles *Die Schöne Müllerin* (*The Miller's Daughter,* 1823), *Die Winterreise* (The Winter Journey, 1827), and *Schwanengesang* (Swansong, 1828).

Throughout his life Schubert idolized Beethoven, and was finally able to meet this revered composer just one week before Beethoven died. The music that Schubert wrote after that point was even more profound than previous works and includes *Die Winterreise,* the *Piano Trio in E♭ Major,* his *Piano Sonata in C Minor,* his *String Quartet in C Major,* and *Schwanengesang.* Schubert died of typhoid fever on November 19, 1828, and was buried near Beethoven.

Listening Guide
Romantic Vocal Music—Solo Song

· ·

 F. Schubert: Erlking (1815)

The music for this dramatic poem by Goethe was written by Schubert when he was only eighteen. (The complete text and translation can be found in chapter 1.) The mystic qualities of the supernatural tale are enhanced by music that differentiates the three characters—the child, the father, and the Erlking.

> *Child.* The range of melody is generally higher; loud and pleading
> *Father.* Strong, comforting tones in a lower range; moderate dynamic level
> *Erlking.* Changes to major key; very soft and enticing

Tension is built throughout by a continuous rhythmic imitation of hoofbeats and rising modulations in key that come with each fearful cry of the sick child. Resolution is achieved when the rhythmic accompaniment ceases altogether and the final cadence returns to the original G minor key.

Choral music in the nineteenth century shifted away from the earlier emphasis on unaccompanied liturgical church works to nonliturgical and secular choral works accompanied by orchestra. Beethoven, Berlioz, Liszt, and Mahler all wrote symphonies that added a choral part. The oratorios and masses of baroque and classical composers became very popular concert hall works. In the United States, societies were formed for the purpose of performing choral music. The Handel and Haydn Society of Boston, America's oldest oratorio society, was founded in 1815 for the purpose of giving amateur singers an opportunity to perform great works of choral music. Concerts included music by composers such as Rossini, Mendelssohn, and Beethoven in addition to Handel and Haydn. Especially popular were Handel's *Messiah*, Haydn's *Creation*, and Mendelssohn's *Elijah*.

The garret scene of the opera, La Boheme.

G17, Julliard American Opera Center, Act IV. © Beth Bergman, 1990

The Mass and Requiem Mass continued to be inspirational forms for Romantic composers to re-create in their own individual styles. Berlioz' *Requiem* is a masterpiece of orchestration on a gigantic scale. A chorus of hundreds is joined by fifty violins, twenty violas, twenty cellos, eighteen basses, four flutes, two oboes, four cornets, twelve trumpets, sixteen trombones, six tubas, sixteen timpani, two bass drums, four gongs, and five pairs of cymbals. Brahms' *German Requiem* (*Ein Deutsches Requiem*, 1868) abandoned the traditional Latin text, which prayed for the dead, in favor of a text (in German) based on biblical verses that offered spiritual hope and comfort for the living. (See the Listening Guide on pages 312–313.)

Distinctly different operatic styles developed in several countries. Italy, France, and Germany expanded upon a strong heritage of operatic tradition. A lighter outgrowth of comic operas called **operettas** became popular in France, England, and the United States.

Italy, the birthplace of opera, began the nineteenth century still firmly entrenched in the classical style. As the century progressed, composers drew upon the chromatic harmony, rich orchestration, and lyrical melodies of romanticism to create more emotionally dramatic works. Operatic stories changed to portray reality (*verismo*). Whimsical stories of unbelievable characters and improbable disguises gave way to the somber pain of real-life situations. Rossini, Donizetti, Bellini, Verdi, and Puccini represent the most significant Italian opera composers of this time.

Listening Guide
Italian Realism

. . . .

G. Puccini: La Bohème
Act 3, "Mimi's Farewell"

Based on the French novel *Scenes from Bohemian Life* by Henri Mürger, this opera by Puccini became one of his best-known and most often performed. The premiere was greeted with little interest by the audience and a woefully inaccurate prediction by the critics that this opera, "just as it leaves no great impression on the mind of the spectator, will leave no great mark on the history of our opera."

The story has no great points of physical action, but rather gives insight into the lives of struggling artists in the Latin Quarter of Paris. A painter, musician, philosopher, and poet live a squalid existence in their garret studio. Rudolfo, the poet, meets Mimi, a neighbor, and they immediately fall in love. Mimi's failing health, Rudolfo's jealousy, and the poverty in which they live create a tragic scenario that ends with Mimi's death.

The following aria comes in Act III when the two lovers have agreed to separate. Mimi dislikes Rudolfo's jealousy, and Rudolfo despairs because he cannot even afford a fire to keep his dying beloved warm. Mimi sings a tender song of parting (although they later agree to remain together until spring).

Donde lieta usci	Back to the lonely nest
al tuo grido d'amore	I left so happily
torna sola Mimi	at your call of love
al solitario nido.	I'm returning alone.
Ritorna un'altra volta	Returning once more
a intesser finti fior!	to embroider artificial flowers!
Addio, senza rancor.	Goodbye, without bitterness.
Ascolta, ascolta, Le poche	But listen. Gather up
robe aduna che lasciai sparse.	the few things I left behind.
Nel mio cassetto stan chiusi	In my drawer is
quel cerchietto d'or,	that little gold ring,
e il libro di preghiere.	and my prayer book.
Involgi tutto quanto in un grembiule	Wrap them in an apron
e manderò il portiere . . .	and I'll send the porter for them . . .
Bada . . . sotto il guanciale	Oh . . . and under the pillow
c'è la cuffietta rosa.	there's my pink bonnet.
se vuoi . . . se vuoi serbarla	If you want to, keep it as
a ricordo d'amor!	a souvenir of our love.
Addio. Addio, senza rancor!	Goodbye. Goodbye, and no hard feelings.

Translation by Gwyn Morris, *Prelude to Modern Music.* Copyright © 1966. Reprinted by permission.

France was better known as a showplace for German and Italian composers than as a source of original French operas. Even the best operatic works of French composers were not immediately accepted by audiences. Berlioz' *Les Troyens* was not performed until after his death in 1890. Bizet's *Carmen* caused an uproar in 1875 at the Opéra-Comique Theatre of Paris. The family-oriented audience of this theater was offended by the sight of cigarette-smoking girls and the brutal stabbing of Carmen by her jilted lover.

Bizet (Bee-ZAY)

German romantic opera culminated in the **music dramas** of Richard Wagner, a composer whose innovations in melody, harmony, and rhythm set new directions for the twentieth century. Music drama was a unique combination of opera and drama created on such a formidable scale that most traditional opera houses lacked the resources to present these works. His greatest work, *Der Ring der Nibelungen* (*The Ring of the Nibelung*), is a cycle of four operas that requires four days to perform: *Das Rheingold* (The Rhine Gold, 1854); *Die Walküre* (The Valkyrie, 1856); *Siegfried* (1869); *Götterdämerung* (Twilight of the Gods, 1874).

The Festival Performance Hall in Bayreuth was designed by Wagner specifically for his music dramas (fig. 16.3). The unique arrangement of the orchestra extending under the stage permitted him to use more instruments than would have fit in a traditionally sized orchestra pit, maintain a balance of sound between the singers and instruments, and keep the audience close to the action on the stage.

Bayreuth (Bahy-ROYT)

Figure 16.3
(a) *Performance Hall in Bayreuth showing the orchestra extending back under the stage to give the audience a clear view;* (b) *view of the stage from inside Wagner's Festival Performance Hall in Bayreuth.*
(b) Courtesy Opera News

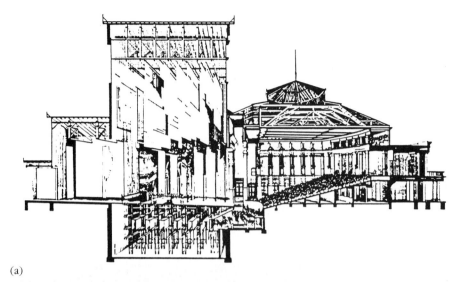

(a)

(b)

Wagner placed great emphasis on drama and relied upon the music as dramatic reinforcement. A special melodic motive called a "**leitmotif**" (leading motive) was frequently used to musically identify a character, object, idea, or emotion. These motifs added thematic unity to a work and furthered the drama, even without a word being sung.

Richard Wagner (1813–1883), in addition to being a major German composer of the late nineteenth century, was an important theorist and influential writer of the time. Best known for his distinct and complex style of opera, or "music drama" as he called it, his goal was the union of all the arts. Opera in Wagner's hands changed from a medium in which the voice held the primary role to one in which the orchestra played an equal and sometimes even more important part. Therefore, his operas require very full, well-trained voices to stand out against the large orchestra.

Richard Wagner.
© Three Lions, Inc. Publishers

Richard Wagner
(REE-kard VAG-ner)

Wagner commonly used the leitmotif in his works—a technique in which a work is unified by recurring brief melodic themes that represent ideas, characters, emotions, or objects. With his development of chromatic harmony, Wagner changed the nature of music more than any composer since Beethoven and led future composers to the development of Expressionism in the twentieth century.

In his early childhood, Wagner was influenced artistically and theatrically by his older sisters, who eventually became opera singers and actresses. He did poorly in school because he was impulsive and self-willed and did not like formal teaching techniques. He taught himself piano and composition and went to concerts, where he was inspired by the music of Beethoven, Mozart, and Weber. At the age of ten, Wagner studied Greek tragedy and enjoyed the plays and writings of Shakespeare, Goethe, and Schiller. Before he turned sixteen, he wrote *Overture in B♭* for piano and orchestra, which was performed by the Leipzig opera on December 24, 1830. Wagner began to show political tendencies at the age of eighteen when the July Revolution occurred in France. In 1831, he enrolled at Leipzig University, where he studied music under a teacher for only six months before deciding to study scores of the masters on his own, particularly the quartets and symphonies of Beethoven. He continued to compose diligently and in 1832 finished his *Symphony in C,* which was played by the university students in Prague the following year. He quit school that year and spent the summer as an operatic coach at Wüzburg. During that time, he composed his first opera, *Die Feen* (*The Fairies*), writing the plot, characters, text, symbolism, and music without collaboration of any sort. (Indeed all his operas were totally independent creations.) This first operatic work was, however, never performed during his lifetime.

From 1834 to 1848 Wagner continued to compose and conduct operas and worked with several struggling opera companies trying to raise their standards and keep them from going bankrupt. He married an actress, Minna Planer, in 1836, and the couple had to flee to London to avoid creditors. Successful premieres of two large-scale operas—*Rienzi* (1840) and *The Flying Dutchman* (1843)—eventually led to Wagner's appointment in Dresden as conductor of the court opera. With the production of *Tannhäuser* in 1845 he finally achieved widespread acceptance by critics and the public.

A few years later, in 1848, Wagner's involvement in an unsuccessful German revolution forced him to flee—first to Switzerland and later to Paris. While in exile over the next eleven years, he composed the remainder of what was to become *Der Ring des Nibelungen,* a cyclic opera consisting of four music dramas that last a total of eighteen hours. This epic endeavor was a return to Greek drama as Wagner saw it—to express national and human goals in symbolic form by way of myths. It was a new art of continuous vocal-symphonic texture, with leitmotifs interspersed to keep unity throughout the work. For the first several years of his exile he also wrote treatises such as *Oper und Drama*, completed in 1851. He conducted the London Philharmonic in 1855 and also composed prolifically. Included in his accomplishments were a piano sonata dedicated to Mathilde Wesendonk (the wife of one of his patrons and his partner in a love affair); the operas *Tristan und Isolde, Das Rheingold,* and *Die Walküre*; several additional songs, and the beginning of *Parsifal* (which would not be completed until twenty years later). He and Minna separated after she found out about Mathilde.

Turmoil continued to surround this great composer, as performances of *Tannhäuser* by the Paris Opera in 1860 resulted in politically instigated riots. After being allowed to reenter Germany, large debts forced him to leave a conducting position there. In 1864, Ludwig II, the young King of Bavaria and a fanatic admirer of opera, asked Wagner to go to Munich to work in the king's court. He remained there for eight years (except for a two year hiatus, from 1865–1867, when he was dismissed because of scandal) and fell in love with Cosima, the wife of the court director Hans von Bülow and daughter of Franz Liszt. Cosima and Wagner had three children before she divorced Bülow and married Wagner in 1870.

In 1870, preliminary plans were designed by Wagner for the construction of a festival theater at Bayreuth. Wagner societies were formed all over the world to raise money to complete this enormous opera house, and the composer himself spent much time and effort raising funds by conducting concerts. In 1874, King Ludwig again came to his financial rescue. The opera house was finally completed, and on August 13, 14, 16, and 17, 1876, the first performance there of the complete *Ring* produced a financial loss of 120,000 German marks. Most of the remainder of Wagner's life was spent conducting concerts in order to reduce this huge deficit. He died in 1883 of heart failure.

Listening Guide
German Opera and New Harmonic Directions

· ·

R. Wagner: Tristan and Isolde

The composition of this opera was inspired by Wagner's real-life love for Mathilde Wesendonk, the wife of a wealthy merchant. Based on a Medieval Celtic legend, the story centers on a love of such suffering, longing, desire and passion that it can only be resolved in death.

Plot

ACT I: On board a ship the knight Tristan is taking Princess Isolde back to Cornwall, where she is to marry his uncle, King Marke. When Isolde discovers that her previous fiancé was killed by Tristan, she orders her maid to prepare a cup of poison to kill both Tristan and herself. The maid substitutes a love potion, and the passionate love between the knight and princess develops.

ACT II: After Isolde's marriage to King Marke, Tristan realizes the futility of their situation. He feigns an attack on a jealous knight and is seriously wounded.

ACT III: The dying Tristan is carried back to his own castle in Brittany, where he refuses to die until Isolde is brought to him. "Liebestode" ("Love-Death") is the final passionate song of Isolde as she takes her own life and the two lovers are united in death.

"Prelude"

This orchestral introduction to the opera depicts the unresolved passion of the two lovers and foreshadows the tragic ending.

> *Melody.* The opening motive, heard in sequence three times, represents the unresolved longing of Tristan and Isolde. This motive returns at the end of the movement to lead into the first scene.
>
> *Harmony.* The intensely chromatic harmony is ambiguous and restless. The use of dissonances, upward movement, and lack of cadences creates a forward motion that is never totally resolved.
>
> *Rhythm.* $\frac{6}{8}$ meter, but the slow tempo and occasional pauses reduce the feel of a regular grouping.
>
> *Timbre.* Constantly shifting orchestral colors
>
> *Form.* Through-composed; somewhat unified by the opening motive, which influences the other melodic material and then appears again at the end.

London, along with Paris, Vienna, and New York, entertained large audiences with light and humorous operettas. Jacques Offenbach's farcical French wit (*Orpheus in the Underworld,* 1858), Johann Strauss' sentimental comedies in luxurious settings, enhanced by his popular Viennese waltzes (*Die Fledermaus,* "The Bat," 1874), and William S. Gilbert and Arthur Sullivan's stunning British satires (*The Mikado,* 1885) grew out of nineteenth-century comic opera traditions and remain popular today.

Niccolò Paganini.
© Historical Pictures Service, Inc.

Absolute Music

Many classical instrumental forms continued to dominate the nineteenth century, especially in the development of the symphony and the concerto. Virtuosic solo players, larger orchestras, and greater dramatic contrasts produced a concert hall repertoire that dominates symphony orchestra seasons even today.

Violin and piano concertos flourished. Some of their popularity may be attributed to the great violin virtuoso Niccolò Paganini (1782–1840) who toured Italy, France, Austria, England, and Scotland, demonstrating new techniques of violin performance. These included the use of harmonics, pizzicato effects, new fingering methods, and innovative tuning techniques. Romantic era composers who wrote violin concertos include Beethoven, Brahms, Mendelssohn, and Tchaikovsky. The technical proficiency of Paganini opened new musical doors for composers. This child prodigy of the violin even inspired composers such as Liszt to push piano concertos to new heights.

The symphony also relied on classical form when not tied to an extramusical program. Brahms, Tchaikovsky, Mendelssohn, Schumann, and Schubert all wrote symphonies based on purely musical ideas, but explored the romantic vocabulary of musical elements to pour new life into old forms.

Listening Guide
Romantic Absolute Music

. . . .

J. Brahms: Symphony No. 3 in F Major
     I. Allegro con brio

Melody. Broad themes with wide ranges

Harmony. While this movement is in F major, the opening F A♭ F suggests F minor and instigates considerable harmonic ambiguity that continues throughout. This F A F motive was used in several of Brahms' works and stood for the phrase *"Frei aber froh"* (free but joyful).

Rhythm. Compound meters of ⁶₄ and ⁹₄; feeling of two or three large beats in each measure of ⁶₄ and ⁹₄, respectively; considerable use of syncopation and hemiola, a technique that occurs with a rhythmic ratio of 3:2

Usual grouping

Use of hemiola

Texture. Great variety of textures ranging from dense chords to the thin texture of a chamber ensemble

EXPOSITION

Two opening chords create ambiguity as to whether the symphony is in F major or F minor

First theme—First and second phrases continue the major/minor ambiguity

New melodic material leads into a transition of arpeggios that modulate to A major

Second theme is in $\frac{9}{4}$ meter; presented first in the clarinet, then in the oboe and
viola

Closing of exposition returns to first theme; exposition may be repeated

DEVELOPMENT

Begins with strong, syncopated chords:

Develops the first and second themes in a variety of timbres; many dynamic
changes and plenty of syncopation in the accompaniment parts

A quiet statement of the first theme reappears to lead into the Recapitulation

RECAPITULATION

Opening two chords transformed into four chords that finally establish the return
to F major

After the first theme, transition, and second theme, there is further development of
the themes

CODA

Based mainly on the first theme; ends quietly

Functions of Music in the Nineteenth Century

Sacred Music

The declining patronage of the Church did not mean that composers abandoned sacred music. Biblical texts, spiritual themes, and traditional forms of church music,
such as the mass, requiem, and oratorio, continued to be sources of artistic inspiration. As you would expect from individualistic nineteenth-century artists, these sacred creative expressions were usually of a deeply personal nature. Composers shed
some of the restrictions of early liturgical forms in favor of more personally meaningful expressions of religious belief and conviction. Even though most of these sacred
works were conceived for the concert hall, they have also found acceptance in liturgical settings.

Johannes Brahms.
© Art and History Archives, Berlin

Robert and Clara Schumann.
© The Bettmann Archive

Johannes Brahms (1833–1897) was born on May 7, 1833, in Hamburg, Germany. He grew up with his two brothers in a rather poor home, but had a happy family life despite his father's meager income. At age seven Brahms began piano lessons and learned rapidly, developing into a brilliant pianist. At the age of thirteen he joined his father's work, playing in taverns, restaurants, and clubs to help earn money. He also brought in some income working as an "arranger" for a music publisher.

When Brahms was twenty, he accepted an offer to go on tour with the Hungarian violinist Remenyi and, through Remenyi's connections, was able to meet Franz Liszt and Robert Schumann, both well-known composers of the time. Schumann was quite impressed with Brahms' work and helped him to get his first works published—three piano sonatas and a piano trio. In 1854, a nervous disorder triggered a suicide attempt by Schumann, who was consequently placed in an asylum. This left Schumann's wife Clara at home with six children and a seventh on the way. Brahms had already been acquainted with Clara, but from this time throughout the rest of his life, the two remained especially close.

When Schumann died in 1856, Brahms began working on the largest of all of his works—*The German Requiem.* The work was not completed until twelve years later after his own mother's death, but its eventual publication hastened the acknowledgment of Brahms as one of the leading German composers of the time.

Brahms' very productive composing career included a total of three hundred songs, two piano concertos, various types of chamber music, four symphonies, numerous piano duets, various works for solo instrument and piano, and several choral compositions. Because of the popularity of his compositions, Brahms was able to earn a good income from his writing alone, but he did accept several other jobs conducting various orchestras and choruses. The Philharmonic Society of London awarded him a gold medal in 1877, and the University of Breslau gave him an honorary Doctor of Music degree in 1879. It was for this occasion that Brahms wrote the *Academic Festival Overture.* In 1896, Brahms wrote *Four Serious Songs* with thoughts of his dear friend Clara Schumann whose physical well-being was deteriorating rapidly. She died in May of that year. Brahms traveled forty hours on a train to Bonn for her funeral and came back quite ill himself. Doctors diagnosed an advanced state of liver disease that was incurable. That summer he wrote one more work for organ—*Chorale Preludes.* Brahms died the following year on April 3, 1897, in Vienna, and he is buried near the graves of Beethoven and Schubert.

Listening Guide

Non-Liturgical Sacred Music

· ·

J. Brahms: German Requiem
          IV. How Lovely Is Thy Dwelling Place

This work was written for baritone and soprano solos, chorus and orchestra. Rather than using the traditional Latin text, which prays for the souls of the dead, Brahms drew upon German texts from the Old and New Testaments of the Lutheran Bible. These verses of hope and optimism focus on consoling the living, as clearly established by the first movement, which begins, "Blessed are they that mourn: for they shall be comforted" (Matthew 5:4).

The fourth movement, one of the most popular sections of this work, is frequently used as a choral anthem. The melodies are strong and sweeping. The powerful rise and fall of these long melodic lines is supported by dynamic changes. The most active and rhythmic section climaxes on "praising Thee evermore" with the polyphonic complexity of a fugal setting. The ending returns to the first line of text to give a sense of completion and comfort and allows the movement to stand on its own, even without the entire *Requiem*.

Wie lieblich sind deine Wohnungen,
  Herr Zebaoth!
Meine Seele verlanget und sehnet sich
  nach den Vorhöfen des Herrn;
mein Leib und Seele freuen sich in
  dem lebendigen Gott.
Wohl denen, die in deinem Hause
  wohnen, die loben dich immerdar.

How lovely is thy dwelling place,
  O Lord of Hosts!
My soul longs and faints for the
  courts of the Lord;
my body and soul rejoice in
  the living God.
Blessed are those who dwell in thy
  house, praising Thee evermore.
Psalm 84:1,2,4

Secular Music

Outside of the church and concert hall, music provided popular entertainment as well as new opportunities for employment of performers, publishers, and teachers. Bands, which entertained the public with original marches, operatic airs, and orchestral transcriptions, grew out of the military tradition of using instruments to signal everything from ceremonial and daily movements to actual battle commands. Music instruction gradually assumed a more respected place in society. Numerous conservatories and schools of music were founded. (In America Lowell Mason [1792–1872], who pioneered the teaching of music in the public schools, started out as a banker who also wrote music. His first collection of hymns did not carry his name, for fear that being known as a musician would hurt his position as a banker.) Some composers were able to make a living selling their music and performing concerts, but many continued to teach and even compose etudes and practice pieces specifically for their students. The publication of these pedagogical works created another source of income for teachers. The best of these "instructional" compositions, such as Chopin's etudes, were even appropriate for concert performance.

American Music

As a country still busy pioneering its Western frontiers, you might expect nineteenth-century America to have engendered little more than the usual selection of folk music that accompanies such work and social interaction, but concerts in the more sophisticated art-music tradition were also surprisingly common. In the metropolitan areas of nineteenth-century America, especially along the eastern seaboard, both European and American artists enjoyed profitable concert tours. Music societies were organized to perform masterpieces of choral and orchestral music. Virtuoso performers were admired more for their technical feats than for the artistic values of the music they performed. In the 1850s, through the shrewd marketing of P. T. Barnum,

the famous Swedish soprano Jenny Lind (1820–1887) toured extensively in the United States, where she earned more than $1,000 a concert. The native American pianist Louis Moreau Gottschalk, whom Chopin called a "king of pianists," turned down a similarly lucrative offer from Barnum. In addition to the hundreds of concerts he did perform in America, however, Gottschalk toured France, Spain, and South America.

Along with this adulation of the virtuoso, Americans possessed a strong "do-it-yourself" drive. Amateur performers created a tremendous demand for printed music, which enterprising sheet music publishers readily filled. Songs and piano music represented most of these compositions.

With the proliferation of sheet music, an attractive title page was frequently used to help make a song more competitive in the marketplace.

Piano Music

The piano was an instrument of versatility and romantic expressiveness and played a unique and important role in the culture of nineteenth-century America. Solo piano recitals by artists such as William Mason (son of Lowell Mason) and Louis Moreau Gottschalk entertained audiences from New York to Chicago and all the way down to New Orleans. Piano manufacturing in the United States grew quickly, and builders such as D. H. Baldwin, Steinway and Sons, Chickering, Knabe, and Mason & Hamlin produced fine instruments for concert halls as well as for American homes. Household instruments, usually located in the parlor, were used to entertain the family with popular and operatic airs, transcriptions of marches, dance tunes, and sets of themes and variations. One measure of the significance of the piano in the American home is a report that by the beginning of the twentieth century there were more pianos and harmoniums (small reed organs) in the U.S. than bathtubs.

Parlor Songs

I remember the days of our youth and love,
When we sat 'neath the green oak tree;
When thy smiles were bright as the skies above,
And thy voice made music unto me.
Never more will come those happy, happy hours,
Whiled away in life's young dawn;
Never more we'll roam thro' pleasures' sunny bow'rs,
For our bright, bright summer days are gone.
(From *Our Bright Summer Days Are Gone* by Stephen Collins Foster)

Sentimentality, self-pity, and nostalgic longing for better times or faraway places were all conventional ways of eliciting a strong emotional response with parlor songs. What these songs lacked in substance they made up for in immediate appeal and in their encouragement of group singing. An attractive melody, simple accompaniment, and modest vocal range brought the parlor song, or household song as it was sometimes called, within reach of the amateur performer. Stephen Foster, composer of about 150 of these songs, is still remembered for tunes such as *Jeanie with the Light Brown Hair, My Old Kentucky Home,* and *Beautiful Dreamer.*

Stephen Foster (1826–1864) was born on July 4 in Lawrenceville, Pennsylvania (now a part of Pittsburgh). He was the tenth of eleven children and grew up in a prominent family that was active in political and commercial affairs. With a natural talent for music he played flute, violin, and piano.

From 1846 to 1850, Stephen worked as a bookkeeper for one of his brothers in a commission business in Cincinnati. Although he was good at his work, he was most interested in the songs of the Negro deckhands on the Ohio riverboats, and he began writing music and verses for minstrel performers who could sing his songs in public. While he was in Cincinnati, Foster met W. C. Peters, a publisher who eventually made a fortune from the songs Stephen had given him. At this point, Foster had no interest in the royalties, but he gained much fame as a songwriter.

Soon, however, royalty contracts became a prosperous source of income. Foster married and moved to Allegheny, Pennsylvania, where he wrote some of his finest songs—"Old Folks at Home" (1851), "My Old Kentucky Home" (1853), and "Jeanie with the Light Brown Hair" (1854). Although he was paid a fair income, his debts began to accrue, and he often had to sell the rights to his songs in order to make a living. Eventually, Foster moved to New York with his wife and his daughter, Marion, but his songs began to decline in quality. Money problems followed and were accompanied by his turn to heavy drinking. Destitute and alcoholic, he was abandoned by his family. In January 1864, Stephen Foster, suffering from what was probably tuberculosis, had a bad fall. He died a pauper three days later on January 13 at the age of thirty-seven.

Stephen Foster.

Listening Guide
Parlor Song

. . . .

S. Foster: Gentle Annie

First published in 1856, this tender song is said to have been inspired by a tragic accident. A young girl was sent on an errand at night in a storm. Because she had her head covered with a shawl for protection from the rain, the child was killed when she did not see a horse and carriage as she crossed the street. Foster offered personal condolences to the family and soon after wrote this touching verse and chorus.

> Thou wilt come no more, gentle Annie,
> Like a flow'r thy spirit did depart;
> Thou art gone, alas! like the many
> That have bloomed in the summer of my heart
> Chorus:
> Shall we never more behold thee;
> Never hear thy winning voice again
> When the Springtime comes, gentle Annie,
> When the wild flow'rs are scattered o'er the plain?
>
> We have roamed and loved mid the bowers,
> When thy downy cheeks were in their bloom;
> Now I stand alone mid the flowers
> While they mingle their perfumes o'er thy tomb.
> (Chorus)
> Ah! the hours grow sad while I ponder
> Near the silent spot where thou art laid,
> And my heart bows down when I wander
> By the streams and the meadows where we stray'd.
> (Chorus)

Orchestral Music

Where European orchestras were primarily associated with opera houses, the American public was more prone to support independent symphony orchestras in public concerts through subscription sales and box office receipts. The first permanent orchestra still in existence today came out of the New York Philharmonic Society established in April 1842. While the New York Philharmonic is recognized today as one of the finest orchestras in the world, the ensemble in its early years consisted of amateurs who played primarily for their own enjoyment. The first concert, performed on December 7, 1842, in the Apollo Rooms of New York City, included the *Symphony No. 5 in C minor* by Beethoven, *Overture in D* by Kalliwoda, *Overture to "Oberon"* by

Weber, *Quintet in D minor* by Hummel, and vocal selections from the works of Weber, Rossini, Beethoven, and Mozart. By 1855 the seventy-piece ensemble performed
a season of four concerts, and each member received a total payment of $65.00.

With relatively few performing orchestras in America (the second one—The
Boston Symphony—wasn't founded until 1881), not many American composers
were motivated to produce symphonic music. Anthony Philip Heinrich (1781–1861),
called the "Beethoven of America," was a Bohemian by birth. A composer of songs
and piano music as well as orchestral concertos and symphonies, Heinrich was acknowledged as an eccentric nationalist whose numerous works received relatively
few performances. His most significant contribution to American music is the use of
the native American Indian as the basis for programmatic orchestral works. One of
his largest works was a three-movement symphony called *The Mastodon*. The titles of
the movements clearly indicate the programmatic connections: "Black Thunder, the
patriarch of the Fox tribe"; "The Elkhorn pyramid, or the Indians' offering to the
spirit of the prairies"; and "Shenandoah, a celebrated Indian chief."

Other American orchestral composers were also drawn to the romantic ideals
of nationalism and programmatic writing. George Chadwick (1854–1931), John
Paine (1839–1906), Edward MacDowell (1861–1908), and Horatio Parker (1863–
1919) were German-trained musicians who attempted to infuse their orchestral and
other compositions with American nationalism. This was usually accomplished
through programmatic works inspired by a geographic area, based on folk traditions
of literature, song, and dance, or drawn from the music of the American Indian and
Negro cultures. While these works received few performances, they expressed many
unique aspects of the evolving American culture and pioneered a new voice in orchestral music.

Popular and Folk Traditions

Nineteenth-century America was occupied with settling new frontiers and resolving
the issue of slavery—which culminated in the Civil War (1861–65). Where large metropolitan areas could support an opera house and sell subscriptions to a season of
orchestra concerts, small towns were more likely to host a traveling form of vaude-
ville and music hall entertainment (called the minstrel show) and possibly form a
village band.

The minstrel show was a unique form of American entertainment that traced its
roots to the songs of the British music hall comedians. White singers blackened their
faces with burnt cork to impersonate Negroes, usually in a very patronizing way. Instrumental accompaniment usually included the banjo, fiddle, bones, and tambou-
rine. With the addition of dances, skits, and parodies, companies of minstrels traveled the entire country and even gained popularity in England.

Stephen Foster wrote a number of minstrel songs for the Christy Minstrels, one
of the best-known traveling shows of its time. Because of the low esteem in which
minstrel shows were held, one of Foster's most popular tunes, *Old Folks at Home,*

was sold to Christy for fifteen dollars on the condition that Foster's name not appear on the music. The composer later changed his mind when this tune became one of his best-selling compositions.

Minstrel songs are characterized by a rhythm conducive to swinging dance steps and banjo strumming (accents on the after-beats in $\frac{2}{4}$), simple harmonies, texts of humor or nonsense, and words written in a Negro dialect. *Oh! Susanna,* by Stephen Foster, not only played well at minstrel shows, but became even more popular with the "forty-niners" going to California in the gold rush of 1849.

> I come from Alabama with my banjo on my knee;
> I'se gwan to Lou'siana My true lub for to see.
> It rain'd all night de day I left, De wedder it was dry;
> The sun so hot I froze to def, Susanna, don't you cry.

Village bands also grew from English roots as adaptations of the British military band. From earliest times, music has been used to lift the spirits of troops, provide a rhythmic cadence for marching, and stir patriotic fervor in both the soldier and the admiring public. British military bands originally consisted of drums and fifes (flutes). Troops on horseback used bugles (trumpets without valves) and kettledrums to give commands and sound various signals. Eventually, woodwind instruments were added, and these bands played entertaining concerts in addition to providing functional music for ceremonies and drills.

Militia units of the American colonies copied the idea of British bands, and prior to the American Revolution they even gave formal concerts in the northern colonies. During the Revolution, the fife and drum were particularly useful; the drummers sounded calls that were joined by the fifers for marching and ceremonies.

Plate 13
Winslow Homer, a self-taught nineteenth century American painter, worked primarily in oils and watercolors to capture many different aspects of life, from formal dances to the Civil War. Homer is best known for his depiction of the boats and rugged sailors found along the Eastern seaboard.

"Breezing Up," Winslow Homer, National Gallery of Art, Washington, gift of the WL and May T. Mellon Foundation (Dated 1876, canvas, 0.615 × 0.970)

Plate 14
Delacroix's highly emotional painting was inspired by Dante's Divine Comedy.

Delacroix, "Dante and Vergil in Hell," Paris, Louvre. Giraudon/Art Resource, N.Y.

Plate 15
*Tension is created
through color, shape,
and perspective.*

Munch: ''Il Grido.'' Oslo, Gall. Nazionale. Scala/Art Resource, N.Y.

Pablo Picasso, "Accordianist," Summer 1911, oil on canvas, 51¼" × 35¼" Collection, the Solomon R. Guggenheim Museum.
Photo: David Heald © 1990. The Solomon R. Guggenheim Foundation.

Plate 16
Distortion of familiar objects through "cubism" was one way twentieth century artists forced the viewer to look at things in new ways.

Claude Monet's ''Impression: Sunrise'' exhibited 1874 Scala/Art Resource, N.Y.

Plate 17
Applied originally as a derisive term, ''Impressionism'' gained its name from this painting by Claude Monet.

River Vltava and St. Vitus Cathedral, Prague, Czechoslovakia © Spectrum Colour Library.

Plate 18
The Bohemian countryside, as seen from the Moldau River and the majestic castle of Vysehrad in Prague provided inspiration for Smetana to compose one of his most frequently performed programmatic and nationalistic works— "The Moldau."

As the musicians returned home after the war, larger bands were formed; but they retained many military characteristics, including the use of distinctive uniforms and the playing of fast marches called quicksteps.

Two band leaders who grew to great public fame with tours of the United States and Europe were Patrick S. Gilmore (1829–1892) and John Philip Sousa (1854–1932). As leader of the Twenty-second Regiment Band of the New York Militia, Gilmore became known as an outstanding conductor whose band played with great precision and musicianship. Sousa, remembered today for the more than one hundred marches he wrote, also composed ten comic operas, fifty songs, several suites and dances, and numerous band arrangements and transcriptions. Sousa was leader of the United States Marine Band in Washington from 1880 to 1892 and later formed his own band, which he conducted until his death. With an ensemble that carried as many as eighty-four musicians, Sousa was able to achieve timbral contrasts which paralleled the symphony orchestra. Although he was known as the "March King," Sousa's orchestral transcriptions and programming genius introduced a greater variety of music to the American public through the concert band than had any previous medium.

A typical Sousa program included instrumental and vocal solos, marches, and orchestral transcriptions, as well as numerous encores.

Source: Hawthorn Books, Inc., New York, NY.

Listening Guide
Nineteenth-Century American Band Music

John Philip Sousa: Stars and Stripes Forever

Rhythm. Strong, steady marching tempo in $\frac{2}{4}$ meter
Timbre. Strong contrasts of brass, woodwind, and percussion
Form. Typical sectional organization that builds to a climax at the end through repetition of sections and the gradual increase of activity
Dynamics. Many changes in dynamics and strong dynamic accents
Melody. Instrumentally oriented; provides contrasts between sections

Short four-measure introduction
First Strain. Main melody in woodwinds; several dynamic changes punctuated with accents
(Repeated)
Second Strain. Brass melody; steady; loud throughout
(Repeated)
Trio. Soft woodwind melody
Bridge. Loud rhythmic brass figures; decrescendo to . . .
Trio. Soft woodwind melody with piccolo countermelody
Bridge. Same as before
Trio. Repeat of trio melody with piccolo countermelody, this time with full band and additional trombone countermelody

Additional Listening

Solo Piano

F. Liszt: Hungarian Rhapsody No. 2 in C♯ Minor
        Variations on the Bach Prelude "Weinen, klagen"
        La Campanella
L. M. Gottschalk: Bamboula
        Le Bananier
        Le Banjo
R. Schumann: Fantasiestücke
L. van Beethoven: Sonata in F minor, op. 57 ("Appassionata")
J. Brahms: Variations and Fugue on a Theme by Handel
F. Chopin: Ballade in G minor, op. 23

Orchestral

F. Mendelssohn: Symphony No. 5 ("Reformation")
L. van Beethoven: Symphony No. 6 ("Pastoral")
P. I. Tchaikovsky: Symphony No. 6 ("Pathetique")
J. Brahms: Variations on a Theme of Haydn
        Academic Festival Overture
H. Berlioz: Harold in Italy
        Roman Carnival Overture

Vocal

Art Songs
F. Schubert: "Gretchen am Spinnrade", op. 2
        Heidenröslein, op. 3, no. 3

Song Cycles
F. Schubert: Die Schöne Müllerin (The Fair Maid of the Mill), op. 25
F. Schubert: Die Winterriese (The Winter Journey)
R. Schumann: Dichterliebe (The Poet's Love), op. 48
R. Schumann: Frauenliebe und Leben (Woman's Life and Love), op.48

Choral
F. Liszt: Christus
C. Franck: Les Béatitudes

Parlor or Household Songs
S. Foster: My Old Kentucky Home

Opera
C. M. von Weber: Der Freischütz
H. Berlioz: Les Troyens
C. Gounod: Faust
G. Verdi: Rigoletto
        La Traviata
R. Leoncavallo: Pagliacci

Operetta

J. P. Sousa: El Capitan

W. Gilbert and A. Sullivan: H.M.S. Pinafore

                                    The Gondoliers

                                    Trial by Jury

Nationalism

F. Chopin: Mazurka in A Flat Major, op. 59, No. 2

P. I. Tchaikovsky: Nutcracker Suite

J. Sibelius: The Swan of Tuonela

A. Dvořák: Slavonic Dances

B. Smetana: Má Vlast ("My Country")

I. Albeniz: Iberia (piano suite)

               Spanish Dances (eight dances for orchestra)

E. Granados: Spanish Dances

E. Grieg: Peer Gynt Suites

Program Music

P. I. Tchaikovsky: 1812 Overture

M. Mussorgsky: A Night on Bald Mountain

P. Dukas: The Sorcerer's Apprentice

S. Rachmaninoff: Isle of the Dead

C. Saint-Saëns: Danse Macabre, op. 40

F. Mendelssohn: Fingal's Cave Overture

R. Strauss: Till Eulenspiegel

              Thus Spake Zarathustra

              Don Quixote

              An Alpine Symphony

J. Sibelius: Swan of Tuonela

CHAPTER SEVENTEEN

Twentieth Century

Preview of Terms and Concepts

Attempts to describe the diversity of twentieth-century music result in the creation of numerous categories that can only suggest some of the directions composers have gone. Musical labels of this century include: **impressionism, expressionism, primitivism, neo-classicism, neo-romanticism, new nationalism, minimalism,** and **electronic music.** Popular idioms include many **developments in jazz and rock.**

General trends in the use of musical elements include greater freedom of melodic line, the harmonic "emancipation of dissonance," the rhythmic release from the "tyranny of the barline," and the evolution of totally new timbres.

Twentieth-century music continues to express human emotions. While the unique timbres and musical vocabulary of this century reflect technological changes, many of the human interests and concerns, sources of inspiration, and creative energies remain the same. **Music is expressive.**

T he accelerated speed of change is probably the most significant characteristic of twentieth-century society. Previous eras have been described in this text as ages of "asceticism," "rebirth," "enlightenment," "reason," and "imagination." While we are still too close to the twentieth century to have a clear and objective perspective, a fairly accurate attempt to name it might be the "Age of Accelerated Change and Diversity."

This diversity and pluralism of twentieth century society is clearly reflected in the arts. With a multitude of "isms" and "ists" we have attempted to categorize styles of art music sufficiently to enable adequate descriptions of the various composers and their characteristics.

With the increase in leisure time, the development of mass communications, and the growth of the lucrative business of marketing printed and recorded music, popular music idioms have also grown at a speed unparalleled in previous centuries. Folk songs, popular songs, musical theater, dance music, and music videos all serve a growing population with time and money to spend on the arts. Artists idolized for their performance and compositional skills rise to public acclaim and fall to obscurity with lightning speed. Only a small percentage of artists make sufficient adjustments with the times to remain "hot" for more than a few years.

Cultural Influences

Rapid and far-reaching changes in this century have taken place in politics, science, economics, and sociology. Music, as an artistic expression of human experience of all kinds, has not only reflected these changes but also contributed to many of them. As you can see by the following examples, these areas are interrelated and interact with music on many levels.

In this century virtually every country on this planet has been affected either directly or indirectly in this century by political conflicts ranging in size from small internal protest movements to massive world wars. These violent struggles carry social and economic impacts beyond the borders of the nations directly involved. Even with limited economic resources available to musicians in wartime, the arts have provided meaningful avenues to expression of the many powerful emotions associated with the social and economic tragedies of war. Many times these emotional musical expressions have been used to rally large populations around a revolutionary cause.

Advances in science and technology have had effects on everything from the economy to our social relationships. **The world has become smaller through advances in transportation.** In 1907 the S.S. Lusitania broke the transatlantic record by steaming from Queenstown, Ireland, to New York in five days, forty-five minutes. Today the Concorde supersonic passenger plane can cross the Atlantic in about $3^{1}/_{2}$ hours. The Ford Motor Company produced the first Model "T" in 1908 and eventually sold 15 million of them. Today new car sales in the United States number more than 11 million every year.

Mass communications developed with the technical ability to broadcast audio and video signals. Radio signals were first transmitted in 1895. By 1912 this "wireless" technology was used in an often life-saving capacity for ship-to-ship and ship-to-shore telegraphic communication. Experiments in voice broadcasting led to the licensing of AM stations after World War I and FM and TV broadcasting in the 1930s. The broadcast of TV on a commercial basis began with ten stations in 1942 and had grown to 1,017 by 1988, plus another 325 noncommercial stations. Radio stations in 1988 numbered 10,244. Cable television broadcasts began as early as 1940 and now reach more than one-half of all American households.

Radio and TV ownership has grown quickly. In 1949 approximately 40,800,000 homes had radios and 1,600,000 homes had TVs. This grew to 88,100,000 and 88,600,000, respectively, for 1987. Not only have radio stations grown in number, but the formats of stations have expanded to include options such as album rock, adult contemporary, black/urban, big band, country, classical, easy listening, jazz, news, new age, news/talk, oldies, public, rock/top 40, religious, sports, Spanish, and, most recently, Asian.

	1949	**1987**
Homes with radios	40,800,000	88,100,000
Homes with televisions	1,600,000	88,600,000

Twentieth-century electronic technology as applied to sound recording produced several significant innovations, as Table 17.1 clearly illustrates.

Table 17.1   Progress of Sound Recording Technology

1918	78 rpm recordings were first made available commercially. People no longer had to go to major metropolitan areas to hear artists such as Enrico Caruso and Jenny Lind.
1934	Reel-to-reel tape recorder that used cellulose acetate tapes coated with ferric oxide allowed manipulation of sound.
1948	33$\frac{1}{3}$ rpm recordings increased recording time from four minutes per side to twenty minutes per side. This allowed longer works to be put on record.
1963	Cassette tape recorders increased convenience and portability of taped music.
1984	Compact disc players provided a significant improvement in sound quality and increased single side playing time from 23 minutes to 75 minutes.
1988	Digital Audio Tape (DAT) began making its way into U.S. markets against fears that it would result in mass illegal duplication of compact discs.
19??	With the speed of change in this area, additional advances undoubtedly will have been made by the time this book is published.

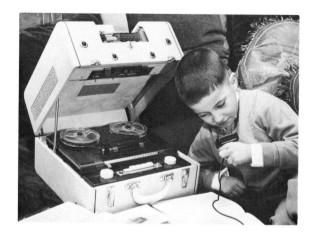

The methods for storage and reproduction of musical sound have changed considerably and improved dramatically over the past fifty years.

Twentieth-Century Cultural Centers

With the shrinking of the world through mass communications and air travel, musicians are no longer exclusively dependent for their public recognition upon live audiences in a handful of European capitals. Composers and performers have been able to travel extensively to study, perform, and teach. Music publication and distribution along with continually improved recording techniques have made new artistic works available almost instantaneously to an international audience. Established cultural meccas, such as Paris and Vienna, and countries steeped in rich artistic tradition, such as Italy, Germany, Russia, and England, have continued to produce as well as attract large numbers of composers, performers, and listeners. However, the ease of travel in a modern world has encouraged mobility for those in search of broader cultural exposure, and since the beginning of the century it is the rare artist who spends an entire lifetime in a single country or even continent. Numerous **composers** have come to the United States seeking greater freedom of expression. New universities and schools of music have trained **increasing numbers of performers,** and growing metropolitan areas have provided a large population from which to attract supportive **listeners.** National styles influenced by folk musics have helped provide some composers with a sense of geographic foundation and distinction in an increasingly cosmopolitan world.

Elements of Twentieth-Century Music

Generalizations about the basic tools used to construct music in the twentieth century have become increasingly difficult to identify. While influenced by each other, vast differences exist between art music and popular idioms. The musical diversity of the nineteenth century has expanded exponentially in the twentieth century. The accelerated rate of change in our society has brought an equally rapid turnover in musical styles. The synopses that follow may appear vague or even contradictory at times, but they will help provide a basic framework for further discussion and for your own observations regarding current trends.

Melody

During the first third of the twentieth century, the classical regularity of four and eight measure phrases and the romantic expansiveness and repetition of melodic line gave way to **greater freedom, conciseness, angularity,** and even **fragmentation.** Melodic movement, which encompasses large intervals and wide ranges, created a more **instrumentally oriented line.** The previously dominating presence of melody was sometimes replaced by other elements, even to the point of total omission. Rhythm, timbre, and harmony each became capable of achieving the level of interest and dominance previously reserved for melody.

In most popular idioms melody remains important and usually the unique characteristic by which a selection is identified. In some cases rhythm may be a more powerfully dominating force, but it is less likely to be unique.

Harmony

One of the most significant developments in twentieth-century music has been referred to as the "**emancipation of dissonance.**" The increased chromaticism of
nineteenth-century composers that culminated in the harmonic innovations of
Richard Wagner have continued to generate new systems of harmonic organization.
Some of the ways in which the general trend toward greater dissonance has manifested itself include:

1. Common usage of 9th, 11th, and 13th chords.

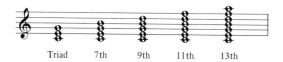

Triad   7th   9th   11th   13th

2. *Bitonality.* The use of two pitch centers at the same time
3. *Polytonality.* The use of two or more pitch centers at the same time
4. *Atonality.* The absence of a pitch center
5. *Twelve-tone technique.* A system of atonal composition that gives equal emphasis
   to each of the twelve notes of the chromatic scale. Twelve-tone composition
   was pioneered by Arnold Schoenberg. Because of the fundamental tone row
   or *series* of pitches, this was also described as a **serial technique** or **serialism.** Schoenberg's student, Webern, extended the serial concept to include
   rhythm, timbre, and dynamics. The result was a highly structured, almost
   mathematical approach to composition.

   In addition to these techniques of creating dissonance, functional harmony has
become weakened through the use of scales other than major and minor modes settled on during the baroque era. Whole tone (all whole steps) and pentatonic (five-
note) scales, for example, lack half-steps that help create the sense of direction in
functional harmony. Ancient church modes have also been revived to create unique
and exotic-sounding harmonies.

Whole tone scale   Pentatonic scale

Rhythm

A renewed emphasis on rhythm has become evident in aspects of timing and duration, use of accents, and metrical relationships. On the broader rhythmic plane, **music has been released from the "tyranny of the barline."** Shifting accents, syncopation, mixed meters (changing meter as frequently as every measure), and
asymmetrical meters (such as those based on groupings of fives and sevens) have
created both a freedom and complexity not common to the traditional meters of $\frac{2}{4}, \frac{3}{4}$,
$\frac{4}{4}$, and $\frac{6}{8}$. Experimental methods of timing have abandoned metric organization and

steady beat altogether. Rhythmic complexities have created new challenges for virtuoso performers and new frontiers for performances enhanced by electronic technologies.

Listening Guide
Twentieth-Century Elements

· ·

 C. Ives: The Unanswered Question

Notes provided by Ives for the performance of this "Cosmic Landscape" indicate the composer's program and offer several options for instrumentation and rhythmic flexibility.

> *"The Answers."* Flute quartet (or two flutes, oboe, clarinet)
> *"The Perennial Question of Existence."* Trumpet (or English horn or oboe or clarinet)

> *"The Silences of the Druids Who Know, See, and Hear Nothing"* (off stage, or at least separated from the trumpet and flutes) Violin I and II, viola, cello (either as a quartet or whole string orchestra)

The strings remain soft, slow, and steady through the composition. The trumpet "question" is always played in the same quiet but determined way. The flutes are rhythmically independent, playing at a quicker tempo than the strings and requiring a separate conductor. Each of the six flute entrances is marked with a faster tempo and consists of more complex rhythmic activity and dissonant harmony.

Flute Entrances

Tempo	Dynamics
Adagio	*p*
Andante	*mp*
Allegretto	*mf*
Allegro	*f* (crescendo) *ff*
Allegro molto	*f* (crescendo) *ff* (crescendo) *sf*
Allegro accellerando to Presto (and later "con fuoco")	*ff* (crescendo) *ffff*

Ives' description of the climax and ending is as follows:

"The Fighting Answerers," as the time goes on and after a "secret conference," seem to realize a futility, and begin to mock "The Question"—the strife is over for the moment. After they disappear, "The Question" is asked for the last time, and "The Silences" are heard beyond in "Undisturbed Solitude."

Timbre

Traditional timbres have continued to evolve and totally new timbres have been created. The symphony orchestra, staple of nineteenth-century tone color, has remained important but with greater emphasis on clarity. **The large orchestra has become more transparent,** operating like an ensemble of multiple chamber groups. **The band has developed a repertoire** separate from its original nineteenth-century military heritage, attracting major composers who consider concert or symphonic bands worthy of serious compositions independent of the traditional arrangements and orchestral transcriptions. **Chamber music has flourished** at the demand of economic conditions and individualistic composers not wishing to be confined to conventional instrumental combinations. **Percussion instruments have assumed a larger role** in both conventional ensembles and innovative chamber groups. **Vocal works have become increasingly difficult** as composers use more dissonant harmonies and write instrumentally oriented melodies with wide ranges and large intervals.

New timbres have developed from two sources—**nontraditional performance techniques** used on traditional instruments and **electronically generated or altered sounds.** As composers explore new sounds, many unusual requests appear in musical scores: The whole world has become a percussion instrument. String players tap their instruments with their bows; brass players tap on their bells and "pop" their mouthpieces; woodwinds clatter their keys; and musically trained percussionists comb junkyards for accurately pitched brake drums. Singers are not exempt from this sound exploration as composers request vocalizations previously unknown in artistic performance. Even instrumentalists are now called upon to create vocal sounds with the simultaneous performance of their instruments. The definition of musical timbre has expanded dramatically as composers seek fresh and unique vehicles of expression.

The application of electronic technology to music is the single most significant development to take place in twentieth-century timbre. Variations include the simple amplification of traditional instruments, electronic alteration of conventional sounds, the creation of totally new sounds, and the digital duplication of traditional sounds. Popular music, even to a greater extent than art music, has taken advantage of this new technology.

Texture

Considering the variations in melody and harmony described earlier, you can imagine the diversity possible in the relationship of these two elements. Generally, there is a **return to greater polyphony,** sometimes assisted by the complex rhythms that reinforce independence of melodic lines. When other elements are more dominant, a nonmelodic texture that emphasizes rhythm or timbre is possible. **Melody remains strong in most popular music.** With the equally strong presence of an amplified bass, a polarity of melody and bass line develops similar to that found in baroque basso continuo.

The Ensoniq EPS electric keyboard and synthesizer.
Courtesy of the Ensoniq corporation

Krzysztof Penderecki (b. 1933) was raised in a devoutly Roman Catholic home, where as a young boy he studied piano and violin. In 1951 he entered the university in Krakow to study art, literature, and philosophy as well as to continue violin lessons at the school's Conservatory. His study of composition led to a greater determination to pursue a musical career, and so, in 1954 Penderecki entered the State Academy of Music in Krakow to study music composition full time. After graduation, the young composer stayed at the Academy as a member of the faculty to continue his teaching and composition.

Prizes that he won in composition competitions—for *Strophes* (1959), *Emanations* (1958), and *Psalms of David* (1958)—brought regional fame. In 1961 his *Threnody* was quickly recognized as an outstanding work by the *Tribune Internationale des Compositeurs* in Paris, and the premiere of *St. Luke Passion* in 1962 brought international acclaim.

Krzysztof Penderecki.
Courtesy of David Cope

Listening Guide
Twentieth-Century Elements

. . . .

Penderecki
(PEN-de-retz-kee)

K. Penderecki: Threnody: To the Victims of Hiroshima (1959–61)

On August 6, 1945, the United States dropped an atomic bomb possessing the power of more than 20,000 tons of TNT on the Japanese city of Hiroshima. In addition to the immediate and complete destruction of over four square miles of the city, the killing of 70,000 to 80,000 people, and the injuring of another 70,000, this destructive force—more than 2,000 times the power of any previous explosion—changed the world forever.

Sometimes the elements of music, as we have defined them, fail to adequately describe what a composer creates. Through the use of extended performance techniques, which include a chromatic scale further divided into quarter tones (half of a half-step), very dense pitch clusters, extreme instrumental ranges, percussive striking of string instruments, and durations indicated by seconds rather than conventional rhythm, Penderecki has created a nine minute sound experience unlike anything previously heard.

Melody. None
Harmony. Very dissonant, but not based on scales and chords; quarter tones in dense clusters create blocks of simultaneous pitches that are not perceived as identifiable chords (see score and performance directions)
Texture. Nonmelodic; no melody or accompaniment to relate to each other
Rhythm. Durations and timings are based on blocks of time indicated by seconds in the score
Timbre. 52 strings (24 violins, 10 violas, 10 cellos, 8 string basses), but the nontraditional performance techniques result in percussive timbres and at times a sound that even resembles electronic music
Form. No traditional form; the work does build to a climax at approximately 6'30", which is tenuously resolved through a long decrescendo that eventually fades into silence

Tension is created through:	**Release occurs with:**
Crescendos and loud, dense pitch clusters	Decrescendos and softer dynamic levels
High piercing violin pitches	Lower pitches in cellos and basses
Glissandi from unisons into dissonant clusters	Unison pitches (around 2'00")
Lack of steady beat or predictable entrances	Long steady decrescendo
The climax occurs around 6'30" as all 52 instruments create random-sounding noises that increase in volume	The climax is tenuously resolved through a 30 second decrescendo on the final pitch cluster

Abkürzungen und Symbole
Abbreviations and symbols

(a) *Special symbols used by Penderecki to indicate specific sounds created* Threnody.

Source: Deshon Music, Inc. & PWM Editions, Miami, FL.

Erhöhung um einen Viertelton
sharpen a quarter-tone

Erhöhung um einen Dreiviertelton
sharpen three quarter-tones

Erniedrigung um einen Viertelton
flatten a quarter-tone

Erniedrigung um einen Dreiviertelton
flatten three quarter-tones

höchster Ton des Instrumentes (unbestimmte Tonhöhe)
highest note of the instrument (no definite pitch)

zwischen Steg und Saitenhalter spielen
play between bridge and tailpiece

Arpeggio zwischen Steg und Saitenhalter (4 Saiten)
arpeggio on 4 strings behind the bridge

auf dem Saitenhalter spielen (arco), Bogenstrich über den Saitenhalter (in einem Winkel von 90° zu dessen Längsachse)
play on the tailpiece (arco) by bowing the tailpiece at an angle
of 90° to its longer axis

auf dem Steg spielen (arco), Bogenstrich über das Holz des Steges
senkrecht zu dessen rechter Schmalseite
play on the bridge by bowing the wood of the bridge at a right
angle at its right side

Schlagzeugeffekt: mit dem Frosch oder mit der Fingerspitze auf die
Decke klopfen
Percussion effect: strike the upper sounding board of the violin
with the nut or the finger-tips

mehrere unregelmäßige Bogenwechsel
several irregular changes of bow

molto vibrato

sehr langsames Vibrato mit ¼ Ton-Frequenzdifferenz durch
Fingerverschiebung
very slow vibrato with a ¼ tone frequency difference produced
by sliding the finger

sehr schnelles, nicht rhythmisiertes Tremolo
very rapid non rhythmisized tremolo

ordinario	ord.
sul ponticello	s. p.
sul tasto	s. t.
col legno	c. l.
legno battuto	l. batt.

(a)

(b) *Score for the final 54 seconds of* Threnody.

Source: Deshon Music, Inc. & PWM Editions, Miami, FL.

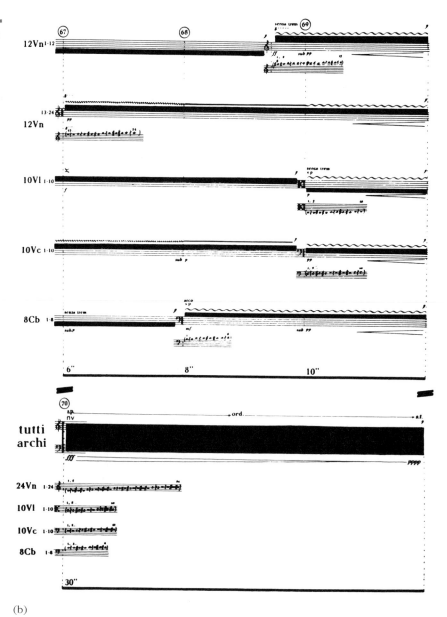

(b)

Dynamics

You may have thought that dynamic contrast had reached its limits in the nineteenth century, but this was not so. With the use of electronic amplification, new levels of loudness have been attained. Intensity of sound in today's rock concerts may reach

120 decibels or greater. With the threshold of pain being about 130 decibels, prolonged exposure to sounds of 100 decibels or greater can produce permanent hearing damage. To the other extreme, silence couldn't get any softer, but it could last longer. Beethoven's innovative moments of rest were brief when compared to the ten to fifteen seconds or more of silence used by twentieth century composers to create contrast, heighten tension and suspense, or provide respite and resolution.

Form

Traditional forms continue to be used by twentieth-century composers but in more concise or condensed versions. The formal harmonic relationships have been altered to meet the contemporary needs, and unnecessary repetitions have been eliminated. Entirely new methods of organization avoid symmetrical structures and are less clearly defined. Emphasis is on diversity rather than unity. Some organizational processes have allowed for spontaneous composition through improvisation as well as composition or performance decisions based on elements of chance.

Twentieth-Century Expressiveness

The individualism of the previous century has continued to thrive since 1900. The presence of so many "isms" attests to our futile attempt to categorize diversity. We are still, chronologically, too involved in this century to identify with certainty all of the most significant musical events. Moreover, with the ever-increasing rate of change, the years surrounding the transition from the twentieth to the twenty-first century may well yield a range of musical trends that previously would have required decades to develop.

In some ways the music of this time period is no different from any other; twentieth-century music has continued to be expressive of the realm of human emotions. However, this realm has expanded to reflect societal concerns not previously addressed, at least in such an open and honest fashion. The tragedy of war has been stripped of its heroic shrouds and depicted as a chaotic and grotesque waste of human lives. The depression, loneliness, fear, and hopelessness that accompany economic strife, an increasingly mechanistic society, and threats of the nuclear age have found powerful voices in all of the arts. Composers have borrowed musical ideas from around the Western and non-Western world to create eclectic styles no longer identifiable with a single country or culture. Music has evolved with societal changes to become an even more diverse expression of human emotions.

Concise insights into these diverse and expressive modes have been provided to varying degrees by the descriptive titles or labels that have been applied to distinctive trends in twentieth-century musical composition—sometimes by the critics and sometimes by the composers themselves. (Additional jazz styles will be discussed later in the chapter.)

Impressionism	New nationalism
Expressionism	Neo-romanticism
Primitivism	Minimalism
Neo-classicism	Electronic music

Impressionism

One of the most influential styles of music to contribute to the transition from the nineteenth to the twentieth century emanated primarily from a single French composer—Claude Debussy. The term "impressionism" was first applied in a critical manner to painters who employed a technique of vague forms, shimmering colors, and subtle distinctions of light and shadow. Claude Monet's *Impression: Sunrise* (1872) typifies this style and was instrumental in providing critics at an 1874 exhibition with the initially derogatory label.

The poetic "impressions" of symbolist poets like Paul Verlaine and Stéphane Mallarmé were infused with a musical quality that had a profound influence on Claude Debussy, even more so than the impressionist painters he so greatly admired. As a young man whose originality clashed with the musical discipline of the Paris

Impression: Sunrise *by Claude Monet (1872).*

Art Resource, NY

Conservatory of Music, Debussy greatly admired the works of Wagner and was soon exploring a new vocabulary of shifting and unexpected harmonies. Based upon Mallarmé's poem *L'Après-midi d'un faune,* Debussy's *Prélude à l'Après-midi d'un faune* (Prelude to the Afternoon of a Faun) is a landmark in musical impressionism. By de-emphasizing form and clarity of meaning in favor of atmosphere, nuance, and color, Debussy created aurally what the impressionist painter had done visually. While the Frenchman Debussy is the principal composer of impressionistic music and generally credited with its creation, other composers who were influenced by Debussy include Maurice Ravel (French), Frederick Delius (English), and Charles Tomlinson Griffes (American).

Claude Debussy.
© The Bettmann Archive

Claude Debussy
(Klohd Day-byoo-SEE)

Claude Debussy (1862–1918) in his later years followed his signature with "musicien français." Indeed, his break from German and Italian musical traditions created a distinctly French style that set new directions for twentieth-century music.

To the dismay of his father, who wished his son to become a sailor, Claude began to study piano at age seven. Four years later he entered the Paris Conservatory, only to spend his next eleven years there in constant conflict. Debussy's rebellious creativity and love of unorthodox harmonies produced great friction with his teachers and resulted in very little recognition of his performance or compositional ability. Ultimately, in order to win the coveted Prix de Rome, the young composer temporarily succumbed to more traditional influences with his cantata *L'Enfant Prodigue* (*The Prodigal Son*).

After an unhappy stay in Rome, Debussy returned to his beloved Paris, where he enjoyed regular association with literary circles of symbolist poets, including Maurice Maeterlinck and Stéphane Mallarmé. The mood and vague images in symbolist poetry influenced Debussy's musical creation of sensuous timbre, clear textures, subtle rhythmic motion, and nontraditional harmonies.

Some of Debussy's best works followed his return to Paris. His only opera, *Pelléas et Mélisande,* based on a play by Maeterlinck, premiered in 1902 to mixed reviews but soon played to sold-out audiences. Orchestral works, including *Prélude à l'Après-midi d'un faune* (*Prelude to the Afternoon of a Faun,* 1894); three *Nocturnes* (1899)—*Nuages* (*Clouds*), *Fêtes* (*Festivals*), and *Sirènes* (*Sirens*), and three symphonic sketches called *La Mer* (*The Sea,* 1905), continue to be programmed frequently. Debussy's piano compositions represent some of the most important pieces for that idiom in the twentieth century. These include two sets of *Images* (1905–1907), the *Children's Corner* (1908) written for his daughter "Chouchou," and two books of *Preludes* (1910–1913).

The outbreak of World War I deeply affected the composer at a time when his health was already failing. In spite of good royalties, a divorce left him financially strapped. An operation for cancer in 1915 left Debussy greatly weakened, and he managed to compose only a few more compositions before his death in 1918.

Listening Guide
Musical Impressionism

. . . .

C. Debussy: Prélude à l'Après-midi d'un faune
(Prelude to the Afternoon of a Faun)

Mallarmé's poem is a vague depiction of a warm summer day in a wooded area and the daydreams of a mythical figure—half man, half goat—and his sensual encounter with three nymphs. Debussy's work is a tone poem that creates a mood rather than telling a story.

> *Timbre.* Strings, two harps
>> Three flutes, two oboes, English horn, two clarinets, two bassoons
>> Four French horns
>> Antique cymbals (small, delicate sounding)
>> Constantly shifting orchestral colors that rarely use all instruments at once; Debussy exploits nuances and shadings rather than large forces and dramatic contrasts
>
> *Melody.* Passed among several solo wind instruments, especially flute, oboe, clarinet, and horn; flowing and expressive
> *Dynamics.* Delicate and subdued; remains relatively soft for most of the piece
> *Rhythm.* $\frac{9}{8}$ and $\frac{3}{4}$ meters serve to organize the durations, but fail to give a strong feeling of grouping or regular accent
> *Harmony.* Many dissonant chords that create more harmonic color than functional direction; no clear tonal center
> *Texture.* Homophonic, thin and transparent
> *Form.* Loosely A A$_1$ B A$_2$
>> The "A" sections are marked by the return of the opening flute melody (A$_1$—varied and expanded; A$_2$—slower, longer values)

Listening Guide
Musical Impressionism (Example 2)

. . . .

 C. Debussy: Prelude No. 8 (Girl with the Flaxen Hair)

The piano prelude, as written by Debussy (he wrote twenty-four in all), no longer served to introduce another work. Each of these brief but complete impressionistic miniatures is a rich and poetic independent composition. The titles were placed by the composer at the end of each prelude so as to emphasize the primary importance of the music.

"The Girl with the Flaxen Hair" is inspired by the poem of the same name by Leconte de Lisle.

La Fille aux Cheveux de Lin

Sur la luzerne en fleurs assise
Qui chante dès le frais matin?
C'est la fille aux cheveux de lin,
La belle aux lèvres de cerise.

L'amour, au clair soleil d'été
Avec l'alouette a chanté.

Ta bouche a des couleurs divines,
Ma chère—et tente le baiser!
Sur l'herbe en fleur veux-tu causer,

Fille aux cils longs, aux boucles fines?

L'amour, au clair soleil d'été
Avec l'alouette a chanté.

Ne dis pas non, fille cruelle!!
Ne dis pas oui!!! J'entendrai mieux
Le long regard de tes grands yeux
Et ta lèvre rose, O ma belle!!

L'amour, au clair soleil d'été
Avec l'alouette a chanté.

Adieu les daims, adieu les lièvres
Et les rouges perdrix!! Je veux
Baiser le lin de tes cheveux,
Presser la pourpre de tes lèvres!!!

L'amour, au clair soleil d'été
Avec l'alouette a chanté.

The Girl with the Flaxen Hair

Seated on the alfalfa in bloom
Who sings about the fresh morning?
It is the girl with the flaxen hair,
The beauty with the cherry lips.

Love, to the clear summer sun
Together with the lark has sung.

Your mouth has divine colors,
My dear—and tantalizes to kiss it!
What do you desire to talk about on the
     blooming grass,
Girl with the long eyelashes, with the
     delicate locks?

Love, to the clear summer sun
Together with the lark has sung.

Don't say no, merciless girl!!
Don't say yes!!! I will understand better
The slow glance of your spacious eyes
And your rosy lips, Oh my beauty!!

Love, to the clear summer sun
Together with the lark has sung.

Farewell deers, farewell hares
And the red partridges! I desire
To kiss the flaxen of your hair,
To press the purple of your lips!!!

Love, to the clear summer sun
Together with the lark has sung.
(Translation by Arline Cravens)

Melody. Simple, tuneful, based on a pentatonic scale that suggests the character of a folk song

Harmony. Diatonic with gentle dissonances to emphasize points of melodic and rhythmic stress

Texture. Homophonic

Rhythm. Flexible use of rubato reduces metrical control

Dynamics. Follow the rise and fall of the melodic line and emphasize moments of harmonic stress

Timbre. Debussy achieves an amazing wealth of delicate tone colors from the solo piano

Form. ABA_1 The middle section is very brief (five measures) but animated and contrasting with the opening material; the return of A is in longer rhythmic values (augmentation)

Other Trends

Expressionism was primarily a German style that explored emotional extremes through distorted images. Psychological and sometimes violent subject matter in painting and the harsh dissonance of atonal harmony and other serial techniques in music were used to express the pain and anguish of the oppressed and the horrors of war.

Listening Guide

Expressionism

. . . .

A. Schoenberg: A Survivor from Warsaw, op. 46 (1947)
(Cantata for narrator, men's chorus, and orchestra)

This single movement work lasting about six minutes is one of the most realistic and ghastly expressions of horror ever written. Schoenberg's text is delivered by a narrator speaking from the perspective of a Jew in a World War II Nazi concentration camp. An emotionally powerful scene is re-created as the Nazis shout orders in German, the old and sick are beaten, and the prisoners are forced to line up and count off before being led to the gas chamber. The climax arrives with the chorus singing a traditional Hebrew prayer, "Hear, O Israel." This song of supplication grows into a shout of defiance, bringing the work to its dramatic conclusion.

The pain and anguish of this event are expressed through the use of:

1. Schoenberg's twelve-tone technique;
2. Harsh dissonances;
3. *Sprechstimme* (a mixture of singing and speech);
4. Complex rhythms that fail to provide a steady pulse (except for the singing of the prayer at the climax); and
5. Special instrumental techniques and timbres—including tremolos, glissandi, mutes, and flutter-tonguing.

Text

I cannot remember everything. I must have been unconscious most of the time; I remember only the grandiose moment when they all started to sing, as if prearranged, the old prayer they had neglected for so many years—the forgotten creed!

But I have no recollection how I got underground to live in the sewers of Warsaw so long a time.

The day began as usual. Reveille when it still was dark—get out whether you slept or whether worries kept you awake the whole night: you had been separated from your children, from your wife, from your parents, you don't know what happened to them; how could you sleep?

They shouted again: "Get out! The sergeant will be furious!" They came out; some very slow, the old ones, the sick men, some with nervous agility. They fear the sergeant. They hurry as much as they can. In vain! Much too much noise, much too much commotion and not fast enough!

The Feldwebel shouts: *"Achtung! Still gestanden! Na wird's mal, oder soll ich mit dem Gewehrkolben nachhelfen? Na jut; wenn Ihr's durchaus haben wollt!"* ("Attention! Stand still! Well, are you going to listen, or do I need to use a riflebutt? OK, you asked for it!")

The sergeant and his subordinates hit everyone: young or old, strong or sick, guilty or innocent—it was painful to hear the groaning and moaning.

I heard it though I had been hit very hard, so hard that I could not help falling down. We all on the ground who could not stand up were then beaten over the head.

I must have been unconscious. The next thing I knew was a soldier saying, "They are all dead!" Whereupon the sergeant ordered to do away with us.

There I lay aside half conscious. It had become very still—fear and pain—then I heard the sergeant shouting: *"Abzählen!"* ("Count off").

They started slowly, and irregularly: One, two, three, four, *"Achtung."* The sergeant shouted again: *"Rascher! Nochmals von vorn anfangen! In einer Minute will ich wissen wieviele ich zur Gaskammer abliefere! Abzählen!"* ("Attention! Faster! Start again, from the beginning! In one minute I want to know how many I'm going to deliver to the gas chamber! Count off!")

They began again, first slowly: one, two, three, four, became faster and faster, so fast that it finally sounded like a stampede of wild horses, and all of a sudden, in the middle of it, they began singing, the Shema Yisroel.

Shema Yisroel Adonoy elohenoo Adonoy ehod. Veohavto es Adonoy eloheho behol levoveho oovehol nafsheho oovehol meodeho. Vehoyoo haddevoreem hoelleh asher onohee metsavveho hayyom al levoveho. Veshinnantom levoneho vedibbarto bom beshivteho beveteho oovelehteho baddereh ooveshohheho oovekoomeho. (Hear, O Israel, the Lord our God, the Lord is One. And you shall love the Lord your God with all your heart, and with all your soul, and with all your might. And these words, which I command you this day, shall be in your heart. And you shall teach them diligently to your children, and speak of them when you sit in your house, and when you go out, and when you lie down, and when you rise up.")

A renewed interest in primitive cultures on the part of painters such as Matisse and Picasso spilled over into music. Chantlike repetitions, wildly erratic rhythms, percussive effects, clear folklike melodies, and clashing dissonances created a musical primitivism.

Pablo Picasso's Guernica, *1937, oil on canvas, 11'6" × 25'8"*

© 1990 Artists Rights Sedety, Inc., NY/S.P.A.D.E.M. On extended loan to the ARS, NY from the artist, Pablo Picasso.

Igor Stravinsky.

Courtesy of the New York Public Library at Lincoln Center. Astor, Lennox, and Tilden Foundations, Music Division.

Igor Stravinsky (EE-gor Strah-VIN-skee)

Igor Stravinsky (1882–1971) was one of the most influential composers of the twentieth century. Born in a small Russian town near St. Petersburg, Stravinsky began piano lessons at the age of nine, and later studied instrumentation with Rimsky-Korsakov. His father, a well-known bass-baritone with the St. Petersburg Opera, insisted that Igor study law and keep music as a hobby. By age twenty-four, however, Stravinsky had completed his studies in law, married his cousin, and decided to pursue musical composition full time.

Continued study with Rimsky-Korsakov led to Stravinsky's first symphony and song cycle, which were performed in St. Petersburg in 1908. The following years produced almost instantaneous recognition of the young composer's talent with his production of three masterpieces of music for ballet—*The Firebird* (1909), *Petrouchka* (1910–1911), and *The Rite of Spring* (1912–1913). The initial criticism of Stravinsky's ballets was harsh but short-lived. Orchestral suite versions of these works have become a staple of the current concert repertoire.

With the outbreak of World War I Stravinsky moved to Switzerland, and his compositions evolved toward the neo-classical style. In 1919 he went on to Paris, where he eventually became a French citizen. *L'histoire du soldat* (*The Soldier's Tale*, 1918), *Pulcinella* (1919), *Symphonies of Wind Instruments* (1920), and *Octet* (1923) clearly established the composer's move toward an economy of ensemble size, clarity, and transparency of texture and a return to traditional structures.

Opportunities to conduct and perform his own music as a pianist took Stravinsky throughout Europe and eventually brought him to America. In 1945 he became a naturalized citizen of the United States. His opera *The Rake's Progress* (1951) marked the end of his neo-classical composition; and, at the age of seventy, he made one last major stylistic transition to serialism. *Canticum sacrum* (1956), *Threni* (1958), and *Requiem Canticles* (1966) attest to the composer's creativity and musical intensity, which continued up to his death in 1971.

Listening Guide
Primitivism

· ·

I. Stravinsky: The Rite of Spring

The composer's original inspiration for this work came to him in 1910.

> "I saw in imagination a solemn pagan rite: Sage elders, seated in a circle, watched a young girl dance herself to death. They were sacrificing her to propitiate the god of spring." (I. Stravinsky, *An Autobiography* [New York, 1936; 1962], p. 31)

The first performance of this ballet score in Paris on May 29, 1913, resulted in one of the most well-known riots in musical history. A review in the *Musical Times* of London on August 1, 1913, spoke for many listeners.

> "The music of *Le Sacre du Printemps* baffles verbal description. To say that much of it is hideous as sound is a mild description. There is certainly an impelling rhythm traceable. Practically it has no relation to music at all as most of us understand the word."

Part I: The Adoration of the Earth

1. Introduction
2. Omens of Spring: Dance of the Youths and Maidens
3. Ritual of Abduction
4. Spring Rounds
5. Games of Rival Tribes
6. Procession of the Wise Elder
7. Adoration of the Earth
8. Dance of the Earth

Part II: The Sacrifice

1. Introduction
2. Mysterious Circles of the Young Girls
3. Glorification of the Chosen Maiden
4. Evocation of the Ancestors
5. Ritual of the Ancestors
6. Sacrificial Dance

Part II: Sacrificial Dance

> *Rhythm.* This is the dominant element with irregular, jarring patterns that create a forceful primitiveness; complex rhythms are played by the orchestra almost as if it were a single unified instrument; the meter changes almost every measure (as seen in the following ten measures)

Harmony. Dissonant
Melody. Consists mainly of short fragments
Timbre. Very large orchestra
Form. A B A$_1$ C A$_2$

Timing	Section	Description
0'00"	A	Jarring, irregular percussive rhythm played by most of the large orchestra
0'25"	B	Dramatic drop in volume, single chord repeated in a less jarring but irregular pattern; provides basis for sudden loud, harsh interjections by piercing, muted brass
1'50"	A$_1$	Return to opening—almost identical to A, but ¹/₂ step lower
2'18"	C	Five timpani become an active and dominant force, along with gong and bass drum; complex rhythms eventually settle into duple meter and give the only sustained feeling of regular pulse in this movement; brass, woodwinds, and strings interject short motives; brief reference to A (6 measures) quickly returns to the chaotic rhythms of C
3'30"	A$_2$	Returns to material from opening but begins softly and in a lower pitch range; timpani become much more active than in previous statements of A; frenzied push to end with crescendo

Another reaction to the highly programmatic and emotional works of romanticism was **neo-classicism.** Composers modeled nonreferential works after Mozart and Haydn, using traditional forms with modern harmonies.

Listening Guide
Neo-Classicism
. . . .

S. Prokofiev: Symphony No. 1 in D, op. 25 (Classical Symphony)
    I. Allegro (Sonata allegro form)
    II. Larghetto (Ternary form)
    III. Gavotta (AABBA)
    IV. Finale (Sonata allegro form)

If Haydn had been alive in 1916, perhaps he would have written a symphony that sounded like this. At least that is what Prokofiev was hoping to accomplish. The form and orchestra are eighteenth century, but the harmonies and melodic movement are much more modern.

I. Allegro

Exposition

Introduction. Short two measure fanfare
First Theme. Violins; repeated in a slightly higher key
Transition. Beginning in the flute, then oboe, bassoons, and cellos; repeated
Second Theme. Bold leaps in the melody (violins) with the bassoon playing an accompaniment of broken chords; repeated
Closing Theme. Brass, making a definite end to the section

Development

First Theme. In minor, violins
Transition
First Theme. Developed briefly
Second Theme. Bold leaps; then in syncopated rhythm
Fragment of the Closing Theme

Recapitulation

Fanfare. As at the beginning
First Theme. Violins
Transition. Woodwinds
Second Theme. Violins; repeated
Coda. Material from opening fanfare

Some composers failed to make a clean break with nineteenth-century ideals of musical expression. Rather than compose as a reaction against romanticism, musicians such as Samuel Barber and Howard Hansen extended those ideals with subtle changes influenced by twentieth century developments. **Neo-romanticism or new romanticism,** as this style is described, usually retains significant elements of nineteenth-century timbre and form.

Listening Guide
Neo-Romanticism

· ·

S. Barber: Adagio for Strings

Originally the slow second movement of Barber's String Quartet no. 1, op. 11, this transcription by the composer has become one of his best-loved pieces.

> *Melody.* Lyrical and smooth
> *Harmony.* Dissonance used to create tension for the climax
> *Rhythm.* Slow tempo, with a feeling of rhythmic freedom
> *Timbre.* String orchestra
> *Texture.* Homophonic and polyphonic, but not really an attention drawing element
> *Form.* Freely based theme and variations
> (A A$_1$ A$_2$ A$_3$ A$_4$ coda)

Another carryover from nineteenth-century romanticism can be found in the nationalistic compositions of composers like Ernest Bloch, Zoltan Kodaly, Charles Ives, Aaron Copland, and Manuel de Falla. Borrowed or simulated folk songs and dances provide obvious musical ties to a particular country. Choral works, ballet scores, and programmatic music are based on folk tales and other nationalistic literature. Twentieth-century harmonies, rhythms, and methods of formal organization provide a modern sound for otherwise traditional genres. Operas and ballets may have additional contemporary elements added through innovative methods of staging and costume design.

Listening Guide
New Nationalism

· ·

M. de Falla: El Amor Brujo (Love, the Magician)
           "Danza Ritual del Fuego" (Ritual Fire Dance)

Falla's ballet score is an interesting mixture of folklore and art music. Combining what is essentially a classical orchestra (two flutes, piccolo, oboe, two clarinets, bassoon, two French horns, two trumpets, timpani, piano, bells, strings) with gypsy dances and an ancient folktale, this Spanish composer has created a fresh but truly nationalistic twentieth-century sound. At times the orchestra imitates a giant guitar, and at other times the percussive tapping of feet found in a rhythmic "Zapateado" (folk dance). But even without ever borrowing a single folk melody, Falla has produced a vibrant expression of nationalistic pride.

As a ballet score written for folk dancers, Falla's story was based on an old gypsy tale. A beautiful gypsy girl, Carmelo, falls in love with Candelas but is haunted by the ghost of her dead lover. Carmelo persuades Lucia, an attractive friend, to flirt with the ghost and divert his attention while the two young lovers exchange the perfect kiss of love. This breaks the spell of the ghost and love is able to triumph over witchcraft.

The "Ritual Fire Dance" was performed at midnight by Candelas in an attempt to defeat the evil spirits. Mysterious trills, a truly Spanish-sounding melody, powerful ostinato rhythms, and a dramatic climax make this an exciting movement that has also become popular in the form of a piano transcription.

Characterized by a steady beat, limited harmonies, short melodic fragments, and hypnotic repetition, **minimalism** is a style that has left some critics either bored or outraged. This very distinctive sound was influenced by classical Indian music and seeks to create a mood rather than present a diverse sequence of events. Listening to a minimalist work with the same expectations as a movement in sonata allegro form would be frustrating and disastrous.

Listening Guide
Minimalism

· ·

T. Riley: In C (1964)

This very early minimalist work consists of fifty-three musical fragments that can be played by any combination of musical instruments. Every player performs each fragment an unspecified number of times and the work ends whenever all of the players are finished. The one persistent and unifying factor throughout is what the composer calls "the pulse"—the top two C's on a piano played together in steady eighth notes throughout. The rest of the work consists of a slowly shifting timbre of overlapping melodic motives.

Electronic Music

Twentieth-century inventions of the tape recorder, synthesizer, and computer have supplied composers with new timbres and novel methods of sound manipulation. In the 1940s, German and French composers in radio station studios began experimenting with altering recorded sounds on magnetic tape. Both acoustical and electronically generated sounds were taped and then changed by splicing the tape, changing tape speeds, playing the sound backward, combining sounds, and filtering sounds electronically. The results produced taped compositions that had been constructed and totally controlled by the composer without being subject to different interpretations by performers.

In 1958 the general public was introduced to this new form of composition at the Philips Corporation pavilion at the Brussels World's Fair. Edgard Varèse, a composer who had previously searched for new sonorities with orchestral and percussion instruments, finally fulfilled a dream. His *Poème électronique* combined acoustical and electronically produced sounds to be coordinated and played through 425 loudspeakers spread around the entire pavilion.

By 1959, using facilities at Columbia University, Milton Babbitt, Otto Luening, Vladimir Ussachevsky, and Roger Sessions had developed an electronic music synthesizer, which greatly facilitated the process of electronic sound manipulation. Because the synthesizer obviated the need to spend tedious hours on secondary tasks such as splicing magnetic tape, composers could focus more on the artistic construction and control of their new sounds and less on the technical difficulties of working with this new medium.

Listening Guide
Electronic Music

· ·

E. Varèse: Déserts (1950–1954)
E. Varèse: Poème électronique (1956–1957)
M. Babbitt: Composition for Synthesizer (1961)
M. Babbitt: Philomel (1964)

Even these early pioneers of the synthesizer could not have anticipated the revolutionary and pervasive changes in electronic sound production that followed. From the first synthesizer in the 1950s, which filled an entire room, to the portable units now used routinely by virtually every popular music group, electronic technology has defined new directions in music composition, performance, recording, and reproduction. The most significant recent advances are those that involve computer technology and the digital processes of sound production. With the MIDI (Musical Instrument Digital Interface) technology of the 1970s, electronic music has become available to a much larger audience of composers and performers. Indeed, computer controlled sound synthesis has created an entirely new field of composition.

What was once an important distinction in electronic composition—the use of basic sounds from acoustical sources versus electronically generated sounds—has become less significant with recent technological advances. Acoustical timbres can now be "sampled," stored, and reproduced digitally with amazing clarity and accuracy.

Until the 1980s, records and tapes reproduced music by what is described as an *analog* process—the creation of an electrical analogy. Like all sound, music creates sound pressure waves. In the analog process these are picked up by a microphone

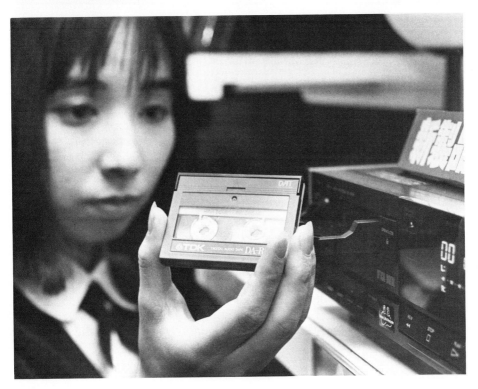

Figure 17.1
*Compact disc (CD)
player and digital audio
tape (DAT) player.*

1) © AP/Wide World Photos, Inc.
2) © Reuter/Bettmann Newsphotos

and converted to an electrical signal that is, in effect, an electrical "impersonation"—or analog of an acoustical event. The electromagnetic head of a tape recorder or cutting stylus of a record master then creates another analog in the form of either magnetic signals on tape or waves in the groove of a record.

With the development of computers that could process enormous quantities of numerical information in speeds measured by fractions of a second, a whole new era in storage of musical sound began. In digital recording, the microphone serves the same function of creating an electrical analog; but this analog is measured thousands of times each second, and then the information is converted into numbers stored in a binary code used by computers. Compact disc (CD) players and digital audio tape (DAT) players are simply computers that convert information from digital back to analog (fig. 17.1). CD players use a laser beam to read pits on the surface of the disc without ever touching it. DAT players use magnetic heads to read highly magnetized areas on a tape containing the same digital information. By adding special filters and an error detection system, called "oversampling," the computer can produce a very high-quality sound that eliminates noise and can't be matched by the old method of dragging a needle through grooves in vinyl.

Functions of Music in the Twentieth Century

The balance of sacred and secular functions of music has continued to shift away from liturgical church music toward secular music for entertainment.

The Business of Music

With the decline of church patronage in the eighteenth century and the end of aristocratic patronage in the nineteenth century, composers who were not of independent means found it increasingly important to sell their art through ticketed performances or printed scores in order to survive financially. Patronage of the arts has returned to some extent during this century in the form of research missions of universities and commissions and artist support programs of local, state, and national "arts councils." Many composers have found teaching in colleges and universities to be a profession that is personally gratifying as well as economically supportive of their creative research in the form of new music composition. The availability of musicians and ensembles at these institutions also provides a convenient lab for trying out musical innovations.

Local, state, and regional arts councils, which number close to 2,000 in the United States, offer a variety of programs that directly support composers and performers. Composers may also benefit from grants to performing ensembles that enable the ensembles to commission new works. The National Endowment for the Arts spent more than 14.5 million dollars in 1986 on programs that gave support to composers and performers. Many arts council programs also provide special music listening opportunities for schools and communities that could not otherwise afford them.

The patron of twentieth century popular music is the entertainment industry. Over the course of almost thirty years, money spent on sound recordings alone has increased from $360 million in 1958 to more than $4.5 billion in 1986. According to a 1986 survey by the National Association of Recording Manufacturers, jazz and "classical" recording sales that year each accounted for only about 6 percent of the total market compared to the pop/rock category that held 53 percent of recording sales.

Changes in society and technology during this century have certainly contributed to these trends. Increased leisure time combined with the availability of money to spend on nonessential items has been a boon to the entertainment industry. Inexpensive and portable radios provide constant access to music of all kinds for the mere cost of batteries or electricity (and the inconvenience of listening to the commercials). Portable tape and compact disc players allow the more particular listener to limit his or her music selection to a specific artist or style. Popular music composers and performers have expanded their income sources from simple concert performances to include marketing of music videos and sound recordings, radio and television commercials, and film scores.

Beethoven, one of the first composers to make a living by selling his music to the public through publications and performances, had few options and a limited audience compared to composers and performers today. The following excerpts from a letter Beethoven wrote in 1801 to the publisher F. A. Hoffmeister reveal the business side of music almost two hundred years ago.

> And for the time being I am offering you the following compositions: a septet (about which I have already told you, and which could be arranged for the pianoforte also, with a view to its wider distribution and to our greater profit) 20 ducats [a ducat was worth approximately $2.25]—a symphony 20 ducats—a concerto 10 ducats—a grand solo sonata (Allegro, Adagio, Minuetto, Rondo) 20 ducats. . . . Perhaps you will be surprised that in this case I make no distinction between sonata, septet and symphony. The reason is that I find that a septet or a symphony does not sell as well as a sonata. That is the reason why I do this, although a symphony would undoubtedly be worth more . . . I am valuing the concerto at only 10 ducats because, as I have already told you, I do not consider it to be one of my best concertos—if you treat all the works as one item you will not, I believe, find my demand excessive. At least I have endeavoured to make the prices as moderate for you as possible. . . . The total sum for all four works would thus be 70 ducats [$157.50]. The only currency I can cope with is Viennese ducats. How much that sum amounts to in your thalers and gulden does not concern me, because I am really an incompetent business man who is bad at arithmetic—
>
> Well, that tiresome business has now been settled. I call it tiresome because I should like such matters to be differently ordered in this world. There ought to be in the world a *market for art* where the artist would only have to bring his works and take as much money as he needed. But, as it is, an artist has to be to a certain extent a business man as well, and how can he manage to be that—Good Heavens—again I call it a tiresome business—

What Beethoven had to do for his own music business has now grown into a multibillion dollar industry that, besides composers and performers, includes music arrangers and copyists; talent agents; concert promoters; audio engineers; record producers; commercial and graphic artists; music wholesalers, distributors and retailers; copyright and business lawyers. Music, through the entertainment industry in the twentieth century, functions as a major source of economic development and employment.

American Music

Jazz

One of the most significant stylistic developments in American music is jazz. With musical roots in the instruments and harmonies of Europe and the African emphasis on rhythm, the eclectic American culture provided fertile ground for the development of this truly unique and indigenous art form.

As with other musical styles, a look at the elements of music will tell you quite a bit about how to identify the characteristic sounds of jazz. Yet even more basic to this idiom is not *what* is created but *how* it is created. Jazz is essentially based on the process of spontaneous musical composition called **improvisation.** Working within a basic framework that usually includes an established meter, key, sequence of chords, basic melody, and formal organization, performers become the composers. The range of freedom allowed within these elements may vary among various jazz styles. Smaller ensembles allow greater flexibility as the members can hear each other clearly and immediately follow new musical directions. A larger group must be more dependent upon an established plan that allows for specific sections of improvisation set within a formal composition. In either case, improvisation adds a uniquely creative spark to jazz.

The standard elements of music are used by jazz musicians in distinctive ways. The following general characteristics will provide a basis for comparison of the many different jazz styles.

Melody   The melody in a jazz tune frequently operates as a **basic theme** upon which performers improvise their "variation." Sometimes parts of the melody are passed back and forth between a soloist and the larger ensemble or between two soloists in a pattern called **call and response.** This technique evolved from a work-song tradition of Africans and slaves. Singing, which provided a rhythmic way to work together in a group, was conducted between a leader who gave the "call" and the group that followed with a "response." This technique can also be found in churches where the congregation responds to the minister in an energetic and emotional interchange.

Jazz melodies are vocally influenced. **Field hollers,** a form of outdoor signals used by slaves, were first imitated by instruments through pitch inflection techniques called note bending (lowering the middle of a pitch), scoops (starting a note by sliding up into it), slides (moving in a smooth glissando between two pitches), and fall-offs (letting the pitch drop at the end). These inflections are all ways for the performer to add emotional emphasis to a melody.

Harmony   Jazz harmony began very simply with three chords (I, IV, V) and has progressed to become as complex as any other twentieth-century style (fig. 17.2). Harmonic color is added to melodies by flatting the third, fifth, and seventh notes of the scale, producing what are called "blue notes."

Figure 17.2
C scale with "blue notes."

Rhythm   Syncopation in one form or another is present in all jazz. Accents on normally unaccented beats may occur in the basic beat

in melodic phrases

or in the "**swing**" of eighth notes as they are traditionally played in jazz:

Timbre   Jazz ensembles may range from small three- to four-piece ensembles to "big bands" of sixteen to twenty players. Almost all are divided into:

> *Rhythm section.* piano, bass, drums
>   (piano may be replaced or augmented by guitar or banjo)
> *"Horns."* trumpet (or cornet), trombone
> *"Reeds."* alto, tenor, and baritone saxophones
>   (these players sometimes double on clarinet)

Texture   Jazz texture is most commonly homophonic—soloist with accompaniment. Polyphonic texture can be found in the group improvisation of New Orleans Dixieland or parts of special arrangements where the more complex texture is written out for the instruments.

Form   Forms used extensively in jazz include the **twelve-bar blues** and the **sixteen or thirty-two-bar chorus.**

Twelve-bar blues

Three lines of text (a a₁ b) supported by three chords.

	Line 1 (a)	Line 2 (a₁)	Line 3 (b)
bars	1 2 3 4	5 6 7 8	9 10 11 12
chords	I--------------------	IV---------I---------	V-(IV)-I----------

Sixteen- or thirty-two-bar choruses are usually divided into four- or eight-measure sections, such as A A B A (also called song form) or A B A B. These choruses may be repeated as often as the performers dictate, either through musical arrangements or spontaneous decisions made during improvisation.

Jazz solo improvisation and the use of blue notes, pitch inflections, and interesting rhythms all contribute to making this idiom very personally expressive for the individual performer. Many musical decisions are left in the hands of the soloist as he or she spontaneously creates a new composition with each performance.

Listening Guide
The Elements of Jazz

. . . .

B. Smith: Lost Your Head Blues

> *Melody.* The basic melody is slightly altered with each verse. Call and response between the voice and cornet occurs on each line. Both the voice and cornet use note bending, scoops, slides, and falloffs
>
> *Harmony.* E♭ major; I, IV, and V chords; blue notes added to the melody
>
> *Rhythm.* ⁴⁄₄ meter; the eighth notes "swing" and syncopation is found throughout; compare the swing and syncopation of the first line of melody (the bottom line illustrated below) to this "straight" version (shown in the top line of the illustration)

Bessie Smith.
Courtesy of Columbia Records

LOST YOUR HEAD BLUES by Bessie Smith. © 1925 FRANK MUSIC CORP. © Renewed 1953 FRANK MUSIC CORP. International Copyright Secured. All Rights Reserved. Used by permission.

Timbre. Rhythm section (piano, bass, drum)
   Voice
   Cornet
Texture. Homophonic
Form. Twelve-bar blues

Jazz Styles

The twentieth century has witnessed a progression of diverse jazz styles, many of which were born out of dissatisfaction with an earlier kind of jazz. Significant differences to look for include: the role of improvisation; the target audience—general listener, musically educated listener, dancers; and the size of the performing ensemble.

Early Jazz

Out of Creole dance tunes, African rhythms, black work songs and gospel hymns, marching bands, European dances and marches, and the cultural melting pot of the American South came three important early forms of jazz—**blues, ragtime,** and **New Orleans Dixieland.** The influence of these styles for voice (blues), piano (ragtime), and instruments (Dixieland) is still felt almost one hundred years later in today's contemporary jazz.

Blues

Yesyounevermissyourwaterwaterwater baby till your well's gone dry
Yesyounevermissyourwaterwaterwater baby till your well's gone dry
Yes you never miss your loved one son, until she says goodbye.
L. C. Williams

"Singing the blues" is an expression commonly understood to mean being sad and dejected. What began as a simple unaccompanied vocal medium, grew quickly to incorporate instrumental accompaniment. Twelve-bar blues has become established as one of the standard jazz forms upon which thousands of jazz and popular tunes are based.

Source: *THE BLUE LINE* compiled by eric Sackheim. copyright © 1975 Grossman Publishers.

Listening Guide
Blues

. . . .

Characteristics. Originally a vocal medium
   Twelve-bar form—in choruses
   $\frac{4}{4}$ meter
   Three chords (I, IV, V)
   Text—three lines (a a b)
   Melody uses "blue notes" for color and expression
   Call and response pattern usually established between the singer and a solo
      instrument on each line of text
Notable performers. Ma Raney, Bessie Smith, Leadbelly, Joe Williams

New Orleans Dixieland

Maybe New Orleans wasn't the only town where Dixieland was played, but this city became known as the "birthplace of jazz" because of the enormous number of famous musicians who got their starts here. During the first two decades of the twentieth century, Dixieland bands developed from collaborations of black musicians who played in marching bands and club bands. Led by a cornet (or trumpet), the bands included a clarinet playing an actively moving countermelody, a trombone emphasizing but ornamenting the bass line, and a rhythm section of banjo, tuba, and drums. The resulting jubilant sound was achieved through **group improvisation, a strong "marching" beat,** and **very active syncopated rhythms** in the cornet, clarinet, and trombone.

   Sometimes these bands returned to the streets with their Dixieland sound. Funeral traditions in the South included walking to the cemetery from the church accompanied by a dirge—a slow and mournful tune played by the band. As a demonstration of the belief that the deceased had gone on to a better life in the hereafter, these same musicians returned from the cemetery playing in a very up-tempo Dixieland style. Concert performances of tunes such as "Just a Closer Walk with Thee" reflect this alternating character of dirge and Dixieland.

Listening Guide
New Orleans Dixieland

. . . .

Characteristics. Steady four-beat pattern
"Horns"—cornet (lead)
clarinet (countermelody)
trombone (elaborate bass line)
Rhythm section—banjo, tuba, drums
Group improvisation
Choruses—8, 12, or 16 bars
Many syncopated rhythms
Notable performers. Kid Ory, Joe "King" Oliver, Charles "Buddy" Bolden

Ragtime

Because piano "rags" are totally composed and then played from a written score without improvisation, some people do not consider ragtime music a form of jazz. Whether or not ragtime music is truly jazz, however, is inconsequential. The march-like steady left hand and improvisatory sounding syncopated right hand produce a wonderfully exciting jazz sound.

Sedalia, Missouri, became a center for ragtime pianists in the late 1890s. Pianists who had no place in New Orleans Dixieland bands (because they had evolved from pianoless marching bands) created this new solo style of playing that retained the syncopated, rhythmic vitality of jazz.

Ragtime, and specifically the rags of Scott Joplin, made a strong comeback in 1973, thanks to the popularity of the motion picture *The Sting*. "The Entertainer" and "Maple Leaf Rag" in particular have enjoyed a well-deserved revival.

Scott Joplin.

Scott Joplin (1868–1917), the "King of Ragtime," was born in Texarkana, Texas. His father, a railroad laborer, had been released from slavery about five years before Scott was born. His mother, a freeborn Negro who helped to support the family by taking in laundry, was a singer and could play banjo as well.

Young Scott first tried his hand at music by playing guitar and bugle, but the piano soon captured his interest. Free lessons from a local teacher who recognized Joplin's talent quickly had the youngster making low wages but good tips in saloons, gambling halls, and brothels. In 1885 the seventeen-year-old moved to St. Louis, where the riverboat traffic of a growing port created a great demand for musical entertainment. Here Joplin heard many other pianists and banjo players who influenced his playing and composing.

After living in Chicago for a brief time, Joplin eventually settled in Sedalia, Missouri, where he continued to teach, play in local clubs, and compose piano rags. Although two publishers rejected his *Maple Leaf Rag*, another composition called *Original Rag* was published in 1898. When *Maple Leaf Rag* was finally published the following year, Joplin's best-known tune became an instant success. Royalties made it possible for him to quit playing nightclubs and spend more time composing. In addition to numerous piano rags, Joplin produced two operas—*A Guest of Honor* (1903) and *Treemonisha* (1911)—and several marches, waltzes, and songs.

The last ten years of Joplin's life were spent in New York where he continued a full schedule of composing and teaching. At first his numerous publications produced a comfortable living. This financial security, along with his marriage in 1909 to Lottie Stokes, led to some of the most satisfying and productive years of his life. However, Joplin's preoccupation with composing his second opera, *Treemonisha,* produced great disappointment. The opera received only one very dismal performance in Harlem in 1915. The lack of interest in *Treemonisha,* by publishers as well as the general public, left Joplin broken both physically and mentally and led to his death two years later.

. . . .

Characteristics. Piano idiom
    Written down rather than improvised
    Steady, marchlike left-hand accompaniment
    Syncopated right-hand melody
    Sectional, with repeats (that is, AABACCDD)
    Characteristic rhythm—(16th, 8th, 16th)
Notable composers. Scott Joplin, William Krell, Tom Turpin, James Scott, Joseph Lamb
Notable performers. Jelly Roll Morton, Scott Joplin, Joshua Rifkin

Hot Jazz

In 1917 the Storyville district of New Orleans, known for its jazz clubs and brothels, was closed. The 1919 enactment of the Volstead Act enforcing prohibition further encouraged musicians to move north to Chicago, Detroit, Kansas City, and New York and west to Los Angeles. This migration of jazz musicians brought about stylistic changes and involved more white musicians in jazz. The carefree "Roaring Twenties" produced a new demand for entertainment by talented jazz soloists. A new emphasis was put on the soloist, and the piano once again became part of the rhythm section. The guitar replaced the banjo in the rhythm section, and the saxophone was added to the horn section. These changes resulted in a stronger, more driving style known as **hot jazz** or **Chicago Style Dixieland.**

    With the growth of radio stations and recordings, musicians such as Louis Armstrong, who got their start in New Orleans, became nationally recognized artists for the first time. The group improvisation of New Orleans Dixieland was replaced by emphasis on these star soloists who were recognized for their individual styles.

. . . .

Characteristics. Emphasis on solo rather than group improvisation
    Driving rhythm
    Piano added to rhythm section
    Guitar replaced banjo in rhythm section
    Saxophone added to horn section
Notable performers. Louis Armstrong, Bix Beiderbecke, New Orleans Rhythm Kings, Freddie Keppard

Beiderbecke
(BAHY-der-bek)

Swing

In 1929 the stock market fell, money became scarce and many small clubs could no longer afford to pay musicians. One economic solution that provided the public with an affordable social activity was the construction of huge ballrooms and the contracting of large bands to play dance music. Bands led by Fletcher Henderson, Duke Ellington, and Count Basie, which had organized in the 1920s, suddenly found a special popularity in what has become known as the **Swing Era.**

Big bands of sixteen to eighteen musicians were organized into three sections—brass (trumpet and trombone), reeds (saxophones), and rhythm (piano, bass and drums)—and required more written music. The spontaneity of small combos could not be controlled with three times as many musicians. Solo improvisation continued to be a part of swing, but within the context of carefully written arrangements.

Because of the emphasis on ballads, many of these bands carried a vocalist or even a small vocal ensemble. Some of the most popular singers of the 1950s (Frank Sinatra, Ella Fitzgerald, Sarah Vaughn, Mel Torme) got their start with big bands of the thirties and forties. These talented vocalists were also capable of improvisation in an instrumental style through **scat singing**—a technique that uses nonsense words

Duke Ellington.
Courtesy of the Institute of Jazz Studies

and syllables to create interesting sounds and vocal colors as the singer is free to imitate the agility of a trumpet or saxophone. This captivating form of improvisation begun by Louis Armstrong in the 1920s is still widely used by jazz vocalists and ensembles today.

Listening Guide

Swing

. . . .

Characteristics. Big Bands—Sixteen to eighteen musicians

Brass — trumpets (four)
— trombones (four)
Reeds—saxophones (four–five) (double on clarinet)
Rhythm section (piano, bass, guitar, drums)
Singer(s)
Band leader
Played from written arrangements
Utilized call and response technique between sections
Music primarily for dancing
Strong steady beat (for dancing)
$\frac{4}{4}$ meter with accents on 2 and 4

Syncopated rhythms—but smoother than those found in earlier styles
Notable performers. Fletcher Henderson, Duke Ellington, Benny Goodman, Paul Whiteman, Count Basie, Tommy Dorsey, Jimmy Dorsey, Glenn Miller, and Artie Shaw

---

Bop

Bop (or bebop as it is sometimes called) was a reaction against the constraints of the big band arrangements and performing for dancers. The creative urges of younger players in the 1940s and the 1950s led them to look for opportunities to play exclusively for listeners (rather than dancers) and improvise more solos without being restricted to an arrangement, strong dance rhythm, or a singable tune. The result was smaller combos of four or five players, including piano, bass, drums, trumpet, and/or saxophone.

Charlie Parker.

Courtesy of the Institute of Jazz
Studies

The rhythm section instruments that previously provided just the basic harmonies and steady pulse also gained new freedom with bop. Without the need to serve dancers, the drums became more active and complex; the piano became less constant and added chordal punctuations; and the bass player kept a quick steady pulse while creating an interesting bass line.

A small group and more opportunity for improvisation also allowed for greater experimentation with chromatic harmonies. Bop tunes were almost always organized around a melody, eight or sixteen bars long, that was played in unison by the melody instruments at the beginning and end of the piece. The middle consisted of many choruses improvised on the melody by any or all of the instruments.

Bop was not an overnight commercial success. While the complexities of the rhythm, melody, and harmony made this style more immediately rewarding for the performers themselves and their small group of followers, the larger listening audience still looked to jazz for dance tunes or ballads with which they could hum along.

Listening Guide
Bop

. . . .

Characteristics. Music for listening, not dancing

Small combos (four–five players)
$$\left.\begin{array}{l} \text{piano} \\ \text{bass} \\ \text{drums} \end{array}\right\} \text{greater rhythmic freedom}$$
trumpet and/or saxophone
(The trombone was used eventually, as players became technically proficient enough to play the very fast and complex melodic patterns.)
Complex rhythms
More chromatic harmonies
Form—unison melody (called the head), many improvised choruses, unison melody

Notable performers. Charlie Parker (alto sax), Dizzy Gillespie (trumpet), Thelonious Monk (piano), Max Roach (drums)

Cool Jazz

Reactions to styles continued with the development of cool jazz as an alternative to bop. While retaining an emphasis on combos and improvisation, cool jazz opened the door to new jazz timbres. Instruments not previously used in jazz bands, such as strings, oboe, flute, and French horn, were suddenly improvising very melodic solos. The flugel horn—a form of trumpet with a large conical bore—became very popular with its mellow brass timbre. Unusual meters and polyrhythms were explored. Classically trained musicians became interested in jazz and brought old forms and techniques to improvisation and arrangements.

Listening Guide
Cool Jazz

. . . .

Characteristics. Music for listening—more broadly appealing than bop
New jazz timbres—strings, French horn, flugel horn, oboe, flute
Smoother melodic sound
Exploration of polyrhythms and unusual meters
Notable performers. Miles Davis, Stan Getz, Dave Brubeck

Eclectic Jazz Styles

Jazz continues to change and evolve. Improvisation and rhythmic vitality remain central to the spirit of innovations; but creative musicians never cease to explore new techniques and timbres, and even continue to borrow from traditional sources.

Orchestral composers influenced by the spirit of jazz have created **symphonic jazz.** Even though the aspect of improvisation may be missing, characteristic rhythms and jazz timbres have provided composers like George Gershwin and Leonard Bernstein with fresh material for the symphony orchestra medium.

Free-form jazz is a fairly controversial extension of the directions taken by bop. Besides seeking escape from dance tunes, free-form jazz has abandoned steady beat, meter, and preconceived chord progressions. The melodic characteristics of this music, although not bound to traditional meters and harmonies, have a strong tie to the earlier jazz styles of unaccompanied blues singing. Even if free-form compositions are not easily accepted by traditional jazz listeners, they can be recognized as powerfully emotional and highly individual forms of expression.

An extension of cool jazz that has borrowed compositional techniques from other musical idioms is called **third-stream music.** Using nontraditional jazz timbres, such as the symphony orchestra, composers in this idiom have freely mixed the old with the new. Jazz improvisation, harmonies, and rhythms are combined with symphonic forms and musical elements borrowed from or characteristic of Bach and Mozart. Third stream produces an eclectic style of jazz with a very wide range of sounds not easily characterized by a single example.

The mixture of jazz and rock music has produced a style called **fusion.** The rock characteristics of a driving beat, electric bass guitar, and electronic keyboards have combined with improvisation and jazz "horns and reeds" (trumpet, trombone, saxophone) to create a **crossover** between the two styles. In record industry terms this means that the music appeals to more than one market of record buyers and usually increases sales.

New mixtures of styles continue to appear, usually with mixed reactions. **New Age music,** while sometimes referred to as "yuppie elevator music," began as a California fad; but it has developed a growing national and international audience and acquired numerous composer/performer converts from rock, bop, and cool jazz. The diversity of New Age music includes (but is certainly not limited to) mesmerizing repetitions, electronic "soundscapes," a return to acoustical instruments, a reduced range of dynamic differences, less complex rhythms, and Asian and other non-Western influences.

Listening Guide
Eclectic Jazz Styles

. . . .

Symphonic Jazz

G. Gershwin: Rhapsody in Blue

G. Gershwin: An American in Paris

L. Bernstein: Symphony No. 2, for piano and Orchestra ("Age of Anxiety")

Bernstein
(BERN-stahyn)

Free Form

O. Coleman: Free Jazz

J. Coltrane: Ascension

M. Davis: Bitches Brew

Third Stream

G. Schuller: Transformation

G. Schuller: First Symphony

D. Sebesky: The Rite of Spring (a reconstruction and arrangement of the composition by Igor Stravinsky, for jazz soloists and symphony orchestra)

J. Loussier: Play Bach Jazz

F. Hand: Jazzantiqua

Fusion

Albums by Chicago; Blood, Sweat and Tears; Herbie Mann; Chick Corea; Weather Report; and Chuck Mangione

New Age

Look for works on Windham Hill records as well as specific artists such as George Winston (piano), Andreas Vollenweider (harp), Paul Winter (saxophone), Suzanne Ciani (electronic keyboard), William Ackerman (guitar)

Rock and Roll Music

Rhythm and Blues + **Country and Western** = **Rock and Roll**

(jazz + gospel + blues)   (folk songs & ballads)

Black   White

Take out the papers and the trash
Or you don't get no spending cash
Just tell your hoodlum friends outside
You ain't got time to take a ride
Yakety yak
Don't talk back.*   (Yakety Yak, 1957)

The combination of black and white styles of music with youthful rebellion and a large audience (commonly known as the baby boom generation) created a phenomenal new American popular art form. "Rock and Roll," a phrase coined by disc jockey Alan Freed in 1951, became the term to describe this music that combined the rhythmic energy and strong beat of black rhythm and blues with the folk-song melodies and traditional harmonies of southern white country and western music. While Freed has been credited with putting this term in its current musical context, "rocking and rolling" and "rocking and reeling" had been used since the beginning of the century to describe two rather divergent activities—the excitement and energy of black gospel music and, as a socially acceptable metaphor, sexual activity.

Because of the sexual overtones of its lyrics and dance movements, the initial reaction of most adults to rock and roll was to equate it with juvenile delinquency. To make things worse, the audience response to much of the music, such as that of Little Richard, was physical, not intellectual. With songs like "Tutti-Frutti" or "Good Golly Miss Molly" most people weren't content merely to find gems of melody to hum all day. Instead, the energy of Little Richard's performance—screaming, kicking, and pounding out chords on a piano—aroused the audience to an equally frenzied celebration of good times. Rock and roll finally became somewhat more acceptable to parents when it was marketed through the "clean-cut" image projected by the television show *American Bandstand* and neatly groomed, well-mannered young singers like Pat Boone, Paul Anka, and Frankie Avalon.

While not as straightforward as the equation above might suggest, the development of rock-and-roll music did grow out of the mixture of musical styles. One of the ways in which the music of blacks and whites intermixed in the early fifties was through **"cover" records**—the practice of re-recording the hit singles of another group. Many white singers (including Perry Como, the Crew Cuts, Pat Boone, and Elvis Presley) recorded black singles that reaped profits for themselves and for the original composers of the tunes but left the original artists out of the picture. Black covers of white songs frequently included older tunes of the thirties from the big bands and American popular songs.

What Does Rock Express?

Where commonalities among earlier songwriters were primarily racial or regional (that is, black music, white music, urban music, country music), rock musicians and fans were bound by the common factor of age. The subjects of rock-and-roll lyrics and the feelings they expressed naturally reflected the values of this new grouping. They included:

Adolescent fears and tragedies (for example, death, lost love, loneliness)
Adolescent freedoms (for example, cars, summer vacation, the beach)
Feelings of love and infatuation
Sexual desires
Patriotism and social awareness—an expression of social protest and political activism
Rebellion against authority (for example, parents, teachers, government)

How Does Rock Express These Things?

Vocal inflection. the very personal and nontraditional vocal styles developed by individual pop artists molded uniquely to the kinds of sentiments reflected in the lyrics (imagine "Hound Dog" sung by an operatically trained baritone)
Repetition. of both the short and simple phrases of the lyrics and the relatively few chords in the harmony
Rhythmic energy provides a strong dance beat as well as all the rocking, rolling, and reeling connotations
Amplified instruments (loud dynamics)
Use of a "hook." something to grab the listener's attention quickly
for example—catchy refrain that is easily remembered and promotes singing along
—strong rhythm that encourages a physical response
Physical movements in live performance. (Bill Haley and Elvis Presley introduced this with their athletic, sensual, and erotic movements)

With a full range of emotions to express and a large audience of young pocketbooks to tap, rock and roll was shaped by creative and innovative performers and by powerful record companies that promoted their artists with cunning and vigor. Some of the most significant dates in the development of the idiom are shown in Table 17.2.

Table 17.2	Significant Dates in Rock and Roll
1947	Fender Electrical Instrument Co. formed in Los Angeles Fender, Gibson, and other companies expanded the market (which had been dominated by electric Hawaiian guitars) to cater to country and rhythm-and-blues artists.
1948	33⅓ and 45 rpm records were introduced. Previously, 78 rpm records were the industry standard. While the 33⅓ rpm record introduced by Columbia gave classical works the playing time they needed, 45 rpm records (introduced by RCA Victor) were inexpensive and easy to carry around—making them ideal for the pop songs of teens.
1949	Chess Records founded by Leonard Chess in Chicago Over the years this company promoted artists such as Chuck Berry, Muddy Waters, and Bo Diddley.
1950s	Singers such as Elvis Presley and Jerry Lee Lewis incorporated a black rhythmic drive in their white country music sound.
1950	Sun Records founded by Sam Phillips in Memphis The artists promoted by this company included Elvis Presley, the Rhythm Kings featuring Ike Turner, and Jerry Lee Lewis.
1951	Disc jockey Alan Freed is credited with coining the phrase "rock and roll," although the terms "rocking and reeling" and "rocking and rolling" had been used earlier in the lyrics of black music. The term came into popular use as a substitute for "rhythm and blues" in order to market black songs to the white audience.
1955	The film *Blackboard Jungle* thrust Bill Haley's song "Rock Around the Clock" (recorded one year earlier) into popularity.
1956	On September 9, Ed Sullivan televised a performance of Elvis Presley showing the performer from the waist up only. (Presley's gyrating pelvis was considered too lurid for television.)

Elvis Presley.
© AP/Wide World Photos, Inc.

1957   In August, *American Bandstand* began national broadcasting from Philadelphia. Predominantly white teenagers, governed by a dress code set by the television station, were used to market rock and roll as an acceptable media for "clean-cut" youth. The exposure of this show helped Philadelphia become a major recording center, in spite of limited resources in musical talent.

Late 1950s   The success of a given song became linked to the artist or group who performed it. (Previously, any number of groups could record and sell the same pop song with equal success.)

1962   Motown Records, the first black owned and operated record company in America, was founded by Berry Gordy, Jr. in Detroit. Black artists began to be trained and packaged for mass promotion to predominantly white audiences. Motown went on to promote artists such as Mary Wells, the Miracles, the Marvelettes, Martha and the Vandellas, Marvin Gaye, the Supremes, and the Four Tops.

1964   The Beatles "invade" America. They appeared on *The Ed Sullivan Show* on February 9, and by April they were responsible for the top five songs on the singles chart.

The Beatles on The Ed Sullivan Show in 1964 was the start of the "British Invasion" of American popular music.

© UPI/Bettmann Newsphotos

1960s   The civil rights movement, Vietnam War, and the drug culture motivated a broad range of social protest songs.

1967   *Sergeant Pepper's Lonely Hearts Club Band* album was released by the Beatles with innovations that included a studio-created sound that could not be reproduced in live performances. Also "new" were the unification of all cuts on the album (using the concept of a music-hall presentation) and the incorporation of unconventional timbres for a rock-and-roll album (for example, large symphony orchestra, harp, harpsichord, sitar) as well as numerous sound effects.

Listening Guide
The Development of Rock and Roll
. . . .

Gospel

Religious popular music that grew out of the spiritual. Sometimes referred to as "religious blues," the main characteristics include vocal melisma (singing many pitches on each syllable of text) and falsetto, simple lyrics, call and response, and an inspirational and evangelical tone.

Mahalia Jackson: "Precious Lord"
Blind Willie Johnson: "Let Your Light Shine on Me"
Rosetta Tharpe: "Shout, Sister, Shout" (1942)
Pilgrim Travelers: "Standing on the Highway"
Blackwood Brothers: "Have You Talked to the Man Upstairs" (1954)

Blues

Based on a twelve-bar form with a simple two-line text (aab), this genre of melancholy song has had significant influence on both rock and jazz.

Leadbelly: "How Long Blues"
B. B. King: "Three O'Clock Blues" (1951)
Lightin' Hopkins: "Please Don't Go Baby" (1954)

Rhythm and Blues

Originally called "race music," this popular music marketed initially to blacks was a more rhythmic and up-tempo style of singing the blues.

Dominoes: "Rocket 88" (1951)
Chuck Berry: "Maybellene" (1955)
Platters: "Only You" (1955)

Country and Western

Also called the "Nashville sound" or the "white man's blues," C & W developed from the folk music of the American rural South.

Hank Williams: "Why Don't You Love Me" (1950)
Eddie Arnold: "There's Been a Change in Me" (1951)
Webb Pierce: "In the Jailhouse Now" (1955)
Tennessee Ernie Ford: "Sixteen Tons" (1955)
Elvis Presley: "Heartbreak Hotel" (1956)

Early Folk Music

Simple melodies that encourage "singing along" and the use of acoustic instruments characterize this music. Most of the tunes and texts exist in several versions due to the oral tradition of this music rather than preservation through notation and printing.

Woody Guthrie: "This Land Is Your Land"
The Weavers: "Goodnight Irene" (1950)
Pete Seeger: "Little Boxes" (1964)
Burl Ives: "Mr. In-Between" (1962)

White Covers

White performers recorded black hits but with a more subdued and restrained style.

Perry Como: "Ko Ko Mo" (1955) (originally by Gene and Eunice)
The Crew Cuts: "Sh-Boom" (1954) (originally by the Chords)
"Earth Angel" (1955) (originally by the Penguins)

Black Covers

A rhythm and blues feel was added to older white tunes to create a fresh and more energetic sound.

Fats Domino: "Blueberry Hill" (1956)
Platters: "Smoke Gets in Your Eyes" (1958)
Ray Charles: "Georgia on My Mind" (1960)

Rock and Roll

From all of the influences above came this phenomenon of popular music. Part of the appeal of rock and roll was that the untrained musician could, with a few simple guitar chords and an uninhibited vocal technique, imitate a favorite singer and actually make music.

Bill Haley and His Comets: "Rock Around the Clock" (1955)
Little Richard: "Tutti-Frutti" (1955)
Chuck Berry: "Roll Over Beethoven" (1956)
Jerry Lee Lewis: "Great Balls of Fire" (1957)
Elvis Presley: "Jailhouse Rock" (1957)
Buddy Holly: "Peggy Sue" (1957)

American Nationalism

Since the nineteenth century, many composers had attempted to convey an American nationalistic spirit by programmatically painting musical soundscapes of the Western frontier and borrowing or imitating American Indian music and traditional folk songs. In the twentieth century, jazz and popular music provided new resources for composers striving to create uniquely American forms of art music. Whether patriotism or simply the search for fresh musical ideas has been the motivating force, the result has been many diverse and profoundly personal expressions of American nationalism. A brief look at the music of two composers will provide an overview of just some of the directions taken in this century.

Charles Ives.
© The Bettmann Archive

Charles Ives (1874–1954), the son of a New England bandmaster, was one of the most extraordinary American composers who ever lived. His compositional techniques included many complex rhythmic and harmonic innovations. In spite of all his creativity and innovative compositional style, however, Ives drew most of his inspiration from New England Americana. Village bands, revival meetings, barn dances, folk tunes, religious hymns—as well as the many social and political events typical of rural New England—found their way into the unique musical vocabulary of Charles Ives. His desire to re-create the spirit and sound of amateur music-making led to intentional writing of "wrong notes" and "inaccurate rhythms." There was no way his music could have been mistaken for that of a European composer.

Ives recognized at an early age that his radical compositions would not be accepted readily by the public. Rather than sacrifice his musical freedom and write to please popular tastes, he learned the insurance business and eventually founded his own firm of Ives and Company. Success came quickly. Within three years his company became Ives and Myrick, an insurance organization that not only provided Ives with financial security for the rest of his life but also first created the idea of "estate planning," a basic concept in the life insurance business today.

With financial security, Charles Ives was free to compose as he wished. Most of his works were not performed until many years after they were written, and Ives refused to publish and sell any of his works. Content to write and then perform with a few friends who accepted his eccentric ways, Ives maintained his musical independence.

Near the end of his life, Ives's creativity finally began to be recognized and appreciated. By this time, however, the composer had become a recluse who refused to attend performances of his own works or even acknowledge critical acclaim for his music, which had been written many years earlier.

Charles Ives was a man clearly ahead of his time. As a student of music, Ives studied all of the "rules" of traditional composition then proceeded to break virtually every one of them. This was not done as an exercise in being contrary, but was the result of experimentation, creative freedom, and honest expression of American culture as experienced in the small towns of New England.

For some time musicologists had admired the scores of Charles Ives. Their innovations included polyrhythms, polytonality, atonality, quarter tones, and tone clusters, seemingly years before Schoenberg, Stravinsky, and others established these techniques as conventions of twentieth-century composition. Recent discoveries now suggest that Ives possibly antedated many of his works and simply was influenced by some of these composers. (See "Charles Ives: Some Questions of Veracity" by Maynard Solomon. *Journal of the American Musicological Society*, Vol. XL Fall, 1987, No. 3, pp. 443–470.) Even if this is true, Ives's compositions are innovative and strikingly different from anything else written in the first half of the twentieth century.

The vast majority of Ives's instrumental works are progammatic and nationalistic. The texts of his vocal works reflect diverse views of Americana and heartfelt patriotism. One favorite technique used by Ives, which gave many of his compositions a readily identifiable nationalism, was the direct quoting of folk songs and patriotic songs such as "Columbia, the Gem of the Ocean," "America, the Beautiful," "Turkey in the Straw," "Camptown Races," as well as ragtime rhythms and old church revival hymns. Charles Ives had a vision of his music as a part of the universe and not just the mere reflection of New England folkways, as presented in his highly individualistic approach to music.

> If the Yankee can reflect the fervency with which his gospels were sung—the fervency of Aunt Sarah, who scrubbed her life away for her brother's ten orphans, the fervency with which this woman, after a 14-hour work day on the farm, would hitch up and drive 5 miles through the mud and rain to prayer-meeting—her one articulate outlet for the fullness of her unselfish soul—if he can reflect the fervency of such a spirit, he may find there a local color that will do all the world good. If his music can but catch that spirit by being a part with itself, it will come somewhere near this idea—and it will be American, too. In other words, if local color, national color, any color, is a true pigment of the universal color, it is a divine quality. And it is a part of substance in art, not of manner.*

Listening Guide
Nationalism of Charles Ives

. . . .

C. Ives: Fourth of July (1912–13)

Although frequently programmed independently, this is the third of four movements from the *Holiday Symphony*. (The other movements are "Washington's Birthday," "Decoration Day," and "Thanksgiving.") Ives has created an imaginative work based on a man's recollections of his childhood Fourth of July holiday. Those memories are not complete, contiguous, nor totally accurate.

> I remember distinctly, when I was scoring this, that there was a feeling of freedom that a boy has, on the Fourth of July, who wants to do anything he wants to do, and that's his one day to do it. And I wrote this, feeling free to remember local things etc., and to put [in] as many feelings and rhythms as I wanted to put together. (Ives, *Memos*, p. 104)

> Parades, a baseball game, food, the village band, drunks, and an annual fireworks display—which accidentally sets fire to the Town Hall—are all recalled through a cacophonous collage of sounds.

> It's a boy's '4th—no historical orations—no patriotic grandiloquences by "grownups"—no program in his yard! But he knows what he's celebrating—better than most of the county politicians. And he goes at it in his own way, with a patriotism nearer kin to nature than jingoism. His festivities start in the quiet of the midnight before, and grow raucous with the sun. (Ives, *Memos*, p. 104)

---

*From Henry and Sidney and Cowell, *Charles Ives and His Music.* Copyright © 1969 Oxford University Press. New York, NY. Reprinted by permission.

Aaron Copland.
Courtesy of the American Symphony
Orchestra League

Aaron Copland
(KOH-pland)

Aaron Copland (b. 1900) was the fifth child of Russian-Jewish immigrants who had fled to America in search of freedom and opportunity. His father's business, a department store in Brooklyn, provided both a comfortable income for the family and a source of educational funds and personal income for young Aaron to spend on music. Piano lessons began at age eleven and eventually opened up many other musical worlds, as the young student became interested in playing transcriptions of great orchestral works. In 1916, after several attempts at musical composition, Copland tried to complete a mail-order harmony course. When this proved to be a waste of time and money, his parents agreed to pay for lessons in basic harmony and composition. Subsequent studies with Rubin Goldmark provided a basic, but musically conservative, foundation in musical composition.

Public library musical scores and numerous New York City concerts expanded Copland's musical education, but his most important educational opportunity came in 1921 when he went to France. While there, his first publication came when Debussy's publisher, Jacques Durand, bought the rights to "The Cat and the Mouse," a piano piece that Copland had written in 1919. While this composition and a few others began to draw attention to Copland's talents, his biggest break came when his teachr, Nadia Boulanger, asked him to write a work for organ and orchestra for her to premiere in New York. Copland's *Symphony for Organ and Orchestra* received mixed reviews at the first performance in January 1925. One month later a performance of this work by the Boston Symphony Orchestra led to a close and valuable friendship with the conductor of that orchestra, Sergey Koussevitzky. This association continued to be a productive one for many years.

With the help of a wealthy patroness and Guggenheim Fellowships for 1925 and 1926, Copland was able to devote all of his time to composition without financial concerns. Additional study in Europe and Latin American countries followed, but Copland's American heritage remained strongly evident as he built a significant and successful compositional repertoire. His dramatic *Music for Theater* (1925) and *Concerto for Piano and Orchestra* (1926) demonstrated his interest in elements of jazz. Two ballets, *Billy the Kid* (1938) and *Rodeo* (1942), explored the American spirit of the pioneer West. *Lincoln Portrait* (1942) for narrator and orchestra provided a stirring profile of the great American president. Another ballet, *Appalachian Spring* (1944), recalled "folksy" scenes of early nineteenth-century pioneer life in the hills of Pennsylvania. His suite for orchestra, *The Red Pony* (1948), was adapted from the composer's background music for a motion picture by the same name. In the 1950s Copland began to turn toward serialism in works such as *Piano Fantasy* (1957), *Connotations* (1962), and *Inscape* (1967).

Throughout his life as a pianist, composer, and conductor, Aaron Copland was also an influential teacher and author. He has written numerous articles on music and his three books, including *What to Listen for in Music* (1939), *Our New Music* (1941), and *Music and Imagination* (1952), have provided significant insight into music of all styles from a composer's point of view.

Composer, pianist, and conductor, **Aaron Copland** explored musical styles in jazz, absolute instrumental idioms, music for film, radio, and the theater, and several popular and folk idioms including folk music of the American West. Copland's works exude a patriotism and sense of personal pride in the diverse heritage of his country. His earliest music is heavily influenced by jazz, drawing upon the rhythms of ragtime, the fox trot, and the Charleston as well as the melodic and harmonic characteristics of the blues. They include large-scale works like *Symphony for Organ and Orchestra, Music for the Theatre, Concerto for Piano and Orchestra,* and *Symphonic Ode* and also smaller works—"Nocturne" and "Ukelele Serenade" for violin and piano and two piano pieces, "Sentimental Melody" and "Blues."

In a more functional vein, Copland wrote music with instructional value for young performers and film, radio, and theater works with broad appeal for the general public. His children's opera, *The Second Hurricane,* and orchestral piece, *The Outdoor Overture,* are both uniquely American contributions to the repertoire of high-school players. Film scores include *Of Mice and Men, Our Town, The City, North Star, The Heiress,* and *The Red Pony.* An orchestra suite completed in 1942, *Music for Movies,* is based on excerpts from three of the composer's film scores. Copland's music for the ballet and opera is richly flavored with folk music of the American West. The opera, *The Tender Land,* and ballet scores, *Billy the Kid, Rodeo,* and *Appalachian Spring,* draw extensive inspiration from folk tunes and scenes of the American cowboy.

Listening Guide
Nationalism of Aaron Copland

. . . .

A. Copland: Lincoln Portrait, for narrator and orchestra (1942)

Written during World War II, this work served an important function of proclaiming basic ideals of democracy in a concise and appealing way. The text is taken from excerpts of Lincoln's own speeches and letters, which are as timely today as they were 150 years ago. Copland said of the work:

> In the opening, I hoped to suggest something of the mysterious sense of fatality that surrounds Lincoln's personality, and near the end of the first section, something of his gentleness and simplicity of spirit. I was after the most universal aspects of Lincoln's character, not physical resemblance. The challenge was to compose something simple, yet interesting enough to fit Lincoln. . . .
>
> The first section opens with a somber sound of violins and violas playing a dotted figure that turns into a melodic phrase by the eighth bar; the second subject is a transformed version of "Springfield Mountain."
>
> The second section is an attempt to sketch in the background of the colorful times in which Lincoln lived. Sleigh bells suggest a horse and carriage of nineteenth-century New England, and the lively tune that sounds like a folk song is derived in part from "Camptown Races." In the conclusion, my purpose was to draw a simple but impressive frame around the words of Lincoln himself—in my opinion among the best this nation has ever heard to express patriotism and humanity. (Copland and Perlis, *Copland, 1900 through 1942,* pp. 342–3)

What Does the Future Hold?

Composers will create new sounds and methods of organization as well as innovative combinations of the old ones.

Performers, through greater technical virtuosity and with the help of improved instruments, will provide composers with an even wider range of skills from which to draw upon and present listeners with exciting performances of both the new and old.

Listeners (both casual and critical) will continue to fashion labels to describe and categorize the styles. The majority of listeners will continue to have difficulty accepting innovations in art music.

Technology will create changes in life-styles that directly affect the **composer, the performer,** and **the listener.**

Yet in ten years (from any date), whether we are listening to Bach or the most recent popular release, the best music will continue to be that which is

Imaginative itself and evokes the listener's imagination;
Expressive of human values and emotions;
Meaningful and powerful enough to move us.

Music is expressive.

Additional Listening

Impressionism

C. Debussy: Three Nocturnes
C. Debussy: La Mer (The Sea)
M. Ravel: Pavane pour une infante défunte (Pavane for a Dead Princess)
M. Ravel: Jeux d'eaux (Fountains)
C. Griffes: The White Peacock

Expressionism

P. Schoenberg: Pierrot lunaire, op. 21
A. Berg: Wozzeck

Serialism

A. Webern: Variations for Orchestra, op. 30
A. Webern: Symphony for Chamber Orchestra, op. 21
M. Babbitt: All Set
K. Stockhausen: Kontrapunkte No. 1
I. Stravinsky: Threni (Tears), Lamentations of the Prophet Jeremiah, tone poem for orchestra, op. 112

Neo-Romanticism

J. Sibelius: Tapiola
D. Shostakovitch: Twenty-four Preludes for Piano, op. 34
H. Hanson: Symphony No. 2, op. 30 ("Romantic")
A. Copland: El Salón México

Neo-Classicism

D. Shostakovitch: Symphony No. 5
I. Stravinsky: Octet for Wind Instruments
I. Stravinsky: The Rake's Progress

Nationalism

R. Vaughan Williams: The Lark Ascending
A. Copland: "Hoedown" from Rodeo
D. Milhaud: Suite Française
G. Gershwin: Porgy and Bess

Minimalism

S. Reich: Tehillim
S. Reich: The Desert Music
S. Reich: Four Organs
P. Glass: Einstein on the Beach
M. Oldfield: Tubular Bells
B. Eno: Discreet Music
K. Stockhausen: Stimmung

Jazz (General Collections)

Smithsonian Collection of Classic Jazz, Columbia Special Products, P6 11891
Atlantic Jazz (12 volumes), 15-Atlantic 81712-1
Leonard Feather Presents Encyclopedia of Jazz on Records (five volumes), 2-MCA 4061-3
Jazz (eleven volumes), Folkways Records, 2801-11

CHAPTER EIGHTEEN

Non-Western

. . . .

Preview of Terms and Concepts

Non-Western music refers to any musical style that has not been derived from western European traditions. Examples include the music of the American Indian, Latin America, Africa, Oriental countries, and most other Far Eastern countries. Scholarly study of this music is usually conducted by **ethnomusicologists** who combine the study of music with anthropology to examine non-Western music in relation to its culture.

Attempting to study non-Western music using just a knowledge of Western musical elements can present some problems. Some of the basic materials for non-Western music frequently include **scales with intervals smaller or larger than the half- and whole-step intervals** to which our ears have become accustomed; a texture called **heterophony,** which is comprised of the simultaneous performance of a melody and one or more variations on that melody; and a **different classification of instrumental timbres.**

Almost all non-Western music study requires an examination of the **function** of the music. In most non-Western cultures music is a functional part of daily life and integral to work, play, and ritual ceremonies.

A ll of the music presented in previous chapters of this text comes out of what is called the "Western" cultural tradition. This term is used to describe music that is based on the European style, the roots of which can be traced to ancient Greek and Roman civilizations. Outside of this Western tradition various existing musical forms have been termed folk, ethnic, world, or primitive; but since none of these terms encompasses *all* of the diverse musical styles outside of the western European tradition, it is more efficient to label this vast body of music as a whole by describing what it is *not*. Hence the term "non-Western" provides a convenient label for many musical styles that otherwise share few common features.

Non-Western music includes any style that has not been derived from western European traditions.

Because of its enormity and diversity of styles, a comprehensive survey of non-Western music is beyond the scope of this chapter. Instead, the three examples provided here can only give a brief glimpse of the rich musical treasures and cultural insights available through the study of non-Western music. Hopefully, this approach will provide some interesting points of departure for further study, which can be pursued through the resources listed at the end of the chapter.

The more complete study of non-Western music has commonly occurred in the context of examining other cultures. From the combination of two scholarly disciplines—musicology (the study of music) and anthropology (the study of man)—has come the interdisciplinary study called **ethnomusicology.**

Ethnomusicology is the study of music in relation to its culture. From its late nineteenth-century inception up until 1950, this area of study was referred to as comparative musicology. Using a combination of the methods and materials of musicology and anthropology, ethnomusicology is not limited to non-Western music. Our own western European traditions are also worthy of study in relation to our own culture. However, most ethnomusicologists look beyond their own cultural backgrounds to examine the music of non-Western cultures.

Ethnomusicology is the study of music in relation to its culture.

Elements of Non-Western Music

While listening to non-Western music through "Western ears" can be a refreshing and inspiring experience for some, others will find it difficult and frustrating, since many of the musical elements most familiar to us may be absent. Few first-time listeners will immediately wish to purchase recordings of African drumming, native American Indian tribal songs, or Balinese gamelans to play for casual enjoyment. Nevertheless, the study of non-Western music may provide some unique insights into a particular culture you wish to study or a country you may plan to visit. Comparing the functions of music in non-Western cultures to your own experiences can also be an interesting and revealing process. An awareness of some of the differences between Western and non-Western music can help to prepare you for a listening experience that may not create an immediate appreciation but may help you to keep your ears and mind open to sampling new sounds.

Melody

While some non-Western music may not use melody at all, the concept of melody as a "succession of pitches" remains viable in non-Western music. However, the basic materials for melody—scales—may be quite different from those used by Western composers. Non-Western scales may use as few as two pitches or as many as fifty or even more pitches within what we call the "octave." Scales with five pitches are common and are called **pentatonic.**

Texture

Monophonic texture dominates non-Western music. The next most common relationship of melody to harmony is a simple variation on polyphonic texture called **heterophony** (fig. 18.1). Found almost exclusively in non-Western music, this consists of a melody and one or more slight variations on that melody performed simultaneously.

Heterophonic texture is the simultaneous performance of a melody with one or more slight variations on that melody.

Figure 18.1
Graphic representation of heterophony.

Harmony

Usually of less importance in non-Western music is the element of musical harmony. In many cultures harmony, as we know it, does not even exist. Single, unaccompanied melodic lines, melodies accompanied with rhythm instruments, or non-melodic textures of rhythm instruments are more common than our Western forms of homophonic and polyphonic combinations of melody and harmony. Even music with harmony may not have tonality as we know it. By using different scales, systems of tonality other than the major and minor result.

Timbre

Instruments may provide the most noticeable difference in non-Western music. Since instruments made in other cultures may not fall into our classifications of brass, woodwind, string, and percussion, four other categories are frequently used to classify non-Western instruments. The four categories and their Western counterparts include:

> *Aerophones.* (woodwind and brass)—instruments that produce a sound with a vibrating column of air (flutes, whistles, single and double reed pipes, horns and trumpets)
> *Membranophones.* (percussion)—instruments with a stretched skin that is struck (drums of all sizes and shapes)
> *Idiophones.* (percussion)—instruments that vibrate when struck or scraped (xylophones, rattles, bells, notched sticks, gongs)
> *Chordophones.* (strings)—string instruments that may be bowed, struck, plucked, or scraped (lutes, lyres, harps, fiddles, zithers)

Functions of Non-Western Music

As discussed in chapter 11, music in Western society certainly can be functional. Patriotic anthems are played before sports events; sacred music enhances religious worship; film scores heighten the drama of a visual image; "Hail to the Chief" signals the arrival of the president of the United States; and background music influences work and shopping habits. However, in spite of its expanding functional role, music in Western culture also continues to be created and produced for listening through concerts, recordings, and radio and television broadcasts designed for pleasure and the appreciation of an art. This is not the case for non-Western music.

One of the most significant characteristics of non-Western music is its greater **emphasis on function.** That is, music is less likely to be treasured for its beauty and more likely to be valued for its power to address the supernatural, its magical ability to heal or bring good fortune, its practical ability to help a group work rhythmically together, or its psychological role in preparing a people for conflict. In many cultures music is an integral part of daily life and inseparable from work, play, and ritual activities. In the cultural examples that follow note the wide variety of ways in which music serves the people who create it.

> Within its own culture, Non-Western music is more likely to be treasured for its function than for its beauty.

Music of Native North Americans

From the Eskimos of the Arctic region to the Apaches of the Southwest, the music of native North American Indians is abundant and diverse. Vocal and instrumental music has been and remains today an integral part of Indian life. Singing is found in all of the various tribes, and instrumental styles have been shaped in the different regions of the continent by the availability of materials with which to make instruments. Common to almost all regions is the use of a monophonic vocal melody accompanied by drums, rattles, and rasps. Many song texts include "nonsense" syllables called **vocables,** such as "hey-ah" or "yu-way." This places emphasis on the melodic contour and rhythmic characteristics of the song rather than specific meaning carried by a text.

Most Indian music is tied to religious ceremonies. Rituals that incorporate singing, playing, and dancing frequently concern food (that is, growth and harvest of crops and hunting of game), healing the sick, and seeking sacred power from supernatural spirits for protection and guidance.

The percussive sounds of drums, rattles, and rasps provide a steady rhythmic accompaniment for almost all Indian ceremonies. Animal hide stretched across the end of a section of a hollow log and then struck with either the hand or a single stick accompanies dancing and singing. Rattles are not only played by musicians but also are attached to the legs of dancers to provide rhythmic accompaniment. Hollow gourds filled with small pellets, strings of shells, or teeth, and notched sticks rubbed together provide many subtle variations in timbre.

In addition to the percussion of idiophones and membranophones, a few wind instruments (aerophones) in the form of flutes and whistles have also served important roles in several areas of Indian culture. While flutes were used primarily to woo young women, they could also serve as secret "alarms" to warn villagers of impending enemy attacks without letting the enemy realize they had been discovered. Higher-pitched whistles were also used to heal the sick, assist with magic, and accompany some dances.

Indian flutes are usually made of a soft, round stick of wood that is split lengthwise, hollowed out, and then glued with resin and tied back together. A solid stopper at the top end is formed to create a whistle, and four to six finger holes are placed to fit the hand of the player rather than to create a specific scale. Variations in this design might use bamboo or animal bones. Quills, feathers, and simple paintings might be added for decoration.

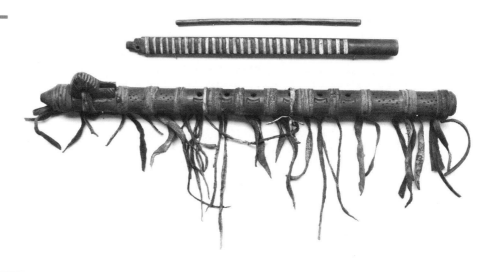

Vertical Dakota flute.

Courtesy of the Museum of the American Indian Heye Foundation, N.Y.

Listening Guide
Music of the North American Indian

Sioux Indian Love Song

The young man wishing to court an Indian maiden would make his own flute, learn to play it, and then make up his own song to play. The "courting flute" was played outside the young woman's lodge, but shyness and protective parents kept the girl from going out to respond. The song in the recording provided is based on four notes, consisting of scale tones one, two, three, and five of our E♭ major scale plus the lower octave of the fifth.

While limited in tonal resources, the melody, in a feeling of $\frac{6}{8}$ meter, has several interesting and subtle variations on a simple motive.

Music of Africa

Music is an integral part of the African life-style. Rituals marking milestones—for individuals or for entire communities—are celebrated with music. Birth, the appearance of the first tooth, the onset of puberty, marriage, death, the change of seasons, healing, teaching values, planting, growing and harvesting crops, preparing for war, courtship, warding off evil spirits, festivals of various deities, and entertainment at spontaneous social gatherings are all occasions for music-making.

African melodies are usually based on five-, six-, or seven-note scales, but not with the same kind of precise intervals employed in Western music. Most African melodies have a text. Since many African languages are tonal languages—that is various pitch levels are associated with particular words—the melodies usually follow the melodic contour of the text. Melodies are usually sung in unison—sometimes with an octave between the voices of the men and women or even parallel intervals close to fourths and fifths in Western music.

Polyrhythms—the simultaneous combination of two or more different rhythmic patterns—are common in African music. A simple way to demonstrate the resulting effect is to clap two rhythmic patterns in two different meters at the same time:

This is a very simple example compared with the complicated rhythmic structures possible in African music.

A vocal form of "call and response" is found in many African songs.

A	B	(repeated numerous times)
leader	chorus	
call	response	

The leader in such a song will improvise—sometimes a narrative of past or current events; the choral "response" usually remains the same throughout. Call and response may also be heard instrumentally—between the master drummer and the secondary instruments.

As the popularity of call and response might suggest, there is more repetition in African music than in Western music, which tends to prize variation. Indeed, beauty in African art in general is less concerned with variation and thematic development and better determined by how well a particular function is performed.

Besides the voice, the most common African instruments are drums, xylophones, rattles, strings, and the mbira. Because the African language is tonal, high- and low-pitch drums can create sounds that actually simulate that language. "Talking drums" that imitate the natural rhythm and tonal inflection of speech can thus be used for sending messages over long distances.

Xylophones range in size from a few pitches to as many as thirty different pitches. Some are made from logs. Wooden keys are laid across hollow banana trunks, which provide excellent resonance. In other designs the "keys" are placed on a wooden frame with a gourd under each key for a resonator.

The **mbira,** sometimes referred to as a thumb piano or hand piano, consists of several metal strips or "reeds" attached to a hollow box or to a soundboard attached to a resonator (such as a hollow gourd) shown in figure 18.2. The strips of metal are stroked gently with the thumbs to create a delicate and pleasant sound. Because of its delicate sound, this instrument is commonly used without accompaniment.

Figure 18.2
African mbira.
Courtesy of the Woodfin Camp &
Associates, Inc.

Other instruments include simple strings such as the lyre, harp, musical bow (shaped like a hunting bow); flutes and whistles; trumpets made from animal tusks and horns, as well as shells, gourds, wood, or metal; rattles; and notched sticks.

Listening Guide
Music of Cameroon, West Africa

· ·

 Song of the Grass Ceremony

Located on the central West coast of Africa, the United Republic of Cameroon has dense tropical rain forests and vast woodlands teeming with wildlife. Most of the country's economy is based on the export of coffee, cocoa, bananas, cotton, timber, and palm kernels, all of which are produced on large plantations as well as on small private farms.

This song comes from the Bafut, a tribe in the grassy highlands. It celebrates the re-thatching of the king's house with fresh grass and repeats in the simple A B—call and response form between the leader and chorus. The voices are accompanied by a small drum and a musical rasp made from a notched palm stem that is scraped with a brass bracelet in a rhythmic pattern.

Cameroon

Music of Indonesia

The Republic of Indonesia consists of more than 13,000 islands in the Pacific Ocean, of which only 4,000 are named and only 1,000 are inhabited. Indonesia's terrain includes volcanic mountains, dense tropical rain forests, and coastal plains. The Republic's motto—*Binneka Tunggal Ika* ("Unity in Diversity")—hints at the complexity of its population, which encompasses more than three hundred ethnic groups and two hundred and fifty languages.

Yet from among this complexity of cultural heritages, one form of music stands out as the best known of Indonesia—the **gamelan** of Java and Bali. Gamelan refers to an ensemble that consists mostly of percussion instruments—drums, gongs (from Hindu origins), and xylophones made of wood or bronze. Other instruments sometimes found in the ensemble include a small bamboo flute played vertically, zitherlike string instruments that are plucked, and a two-stringed bowed instrument from Persia. The louder instruments are used when played outdoors and the soft instruments when played inside the courts and temples.

Map of Indonesia.

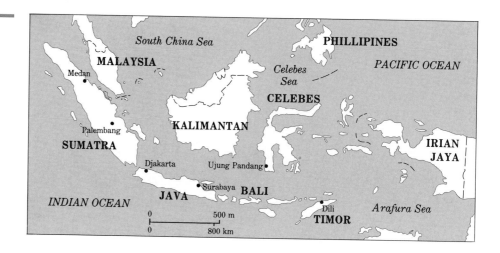

There are two tuning systems for gamelans—an older five-note scale called the **slendro** and a more modern seven-note scale called the **pelog.** Besides having different numbers of pitches, these scales use different intervals between pitches. Since tunings vary not only among but also within the ensembles, a sense of "out-of-tuneness" results, creating a shimmering effect as the various tunings clash gently. None of these tunings can be represented accurately with Western notation. However, *approximations* of the two scales can be described as follows:

Slendro. The five notes are spaced relatively equidistant (approximately 1¼ step apart) within an octave. This scale is said to be capable of expressing feelings of great happiness or great sadness.

Figure 18.3
Western approximation of the slendro scale.

From Jennifer Lindsay, *Javanese Gamelan.* Copyright © 1979 Oxford University Press, New York, NY. Reprinted by permission.

Pelog. The seven notes are spaced in unequal intervals ranging in size from slightly larger than one-half step to almost a minor third. This scale is said to be capable of expressing feelings of majesty as well as tenderness.

Figure 18.4
Western approximation of the pelog scale.

From Jennifer Lindsay, *Javanese Gamelan.* Copyright © 1979 Oxford University Press, New York, NY. Reprinted by permission.

Listening Guide
Balinese Gamelan Music

. . . .

Kebjar Hudjan Mas

Gamelan orchestra.
© George Holton/Photo Researchers, Inc.

Bali, a small mountainous island east of the island of Java, is known for its wood carving, its loyalty to Hinduism (amidst an otherwise Islamic domination of Indonesia), and its multitude of gamelan orchestras. These instrumental ensembles accompany plays, pantomime, dancing, and religious rituals and can be found in every village.

Gamelan music itself is sectional, with gongs delineating changes in sections. A principal melody and steady drumbeat provide unity. Layers of other sounds, sometimes with several ostinato patterns, provide rhythmic accompaniment and create homophonic and heterophonic textures based upon the principal melody. A leader usually controls both tempo and dynamics by playing a double-headed drum called a kendang.

In the title of this piece, *Kebjar*, which literally means "to burst into flames," refers to an exciting virtuosic style normally used to accompany a dramatic dance. Bursts of virtuosity are alternated with traditional ostinato patterns accompanied by a steady drumbeat to produce a wide range of emotions that are interpreted freely by the dancer.

Timing	Descriptions
0'00"	Heterophonic melody
	—steady drumbeat added
	Pause
	Return of opening figure
	—steady drumbeat added
	Pause
0'24"	Unmetered melodic fragments
0'54"	Ostinato patterns and steady drumbeat
	Pause
1'12"	Several short segments with pauses
1'40"	Longer, more continuous section based on ostinato patterns
	—several changes in dynamics
2'25"	Sudden burst of syncopated rhythm
2'35"	Change to freer movement with drum
	Pause
3'00"	Longest section—based on ostinato patterns
	—starts slightly slower and more deliberately
	—ostinato patterns in metallic instruments with steady drumbeat
	—several changes in dynamics
	—feeling of quadruple meter
(3'38")	—some exchanges back and forth between metallic instruments and drums
6'05"	Sudden increase in dynamics and rhythmic activity to the end (6'28")

Additional Reading

Baker, Theodore. Translated by Ann Buckley. *On the Music of the North American Indians.* Leipzig: Breitkopf & Hartel, 1976.

Collaer, Paul. *Music of the Americas.* London: Curzon Press, 1968.

Collins, John. *Musicmakers of West Africa.* Washington, DC: Three Continents Press, 1985.

Densmore, Frances. *The American Indians and Their Music.* New York: The Womans Press, 1926.

Haserich, Royal B. *The Sioux: Life and Customs of a Warrior Society.* Norman: University of Oklahoma Press, 1964.

Kebede, Ashenafi. *Roots of Black Music.* Englewood Cliffs: Prentice-Hall, Inc., 1982.

Lindsay, Jennifer. *Javanese Gamelan.* New York: Oxford University Press, 1979.

May, Elizabeth, ed. *Music of Many Cultures.* Berkley: University of California Press, 1980.

Merriam, A. P. *The Anthropology of Music.* Northwestern University Press, 1964.

Nettl, Bruno. *Music in Primitive Culture.* Cambridge: Harvard University Press, 1956.

———. *Theory and Method in Ethnomusicology.* London: The Free Press of Glencoe, 1964.

———. *The Study of Ethnomusicology.* Urbana: University of Illinois Press, 1983.

O'Brien, J. P. *Non-Western Music and the Western Listener.* Dubuque: Kendall/Hunt Pub. Co., 1977.

Warren, Fred. *The Music of Africa.* Englewood Cliffs: Prentice-Hall, Inc., 1970.

Additional Listening

(Most of these albums include additional descriptive information.)

Music of Southeast Asia, Ethnic Folkways Album No. P423.

Music of Indonesia, Ethnic Folkways Album FE4406.

Music from the Morning of the World, Nonesuch Explorer Series H-72015.

Folk Instruments of the World, Follett Educational Corp., Album L24.

Music from Distant Corners of the World, Nonesuch Explorer Series, H7-11.

Gamelan Music of Bali, Lyrichord, LLST 7179.

Music of Indonesia, Vol. 1, Ethnic Folkways Library Album FE4537AB.

Music of Indonesia, Vol. 2, Ethnic Folkways Library Album FE4537CD.

Folk Music of the Western Congo, Ethnic Folkways Album FE4427.

Music of the World's Peoples, Ethnic Folkways Library Albums FE4504, 4505, 4506, 4507, 4508.

Music of the Cameroons, Ethnic Folkways Album FE4372.

Music of the Sioux and the Navajo, Ethnic Folkways Album FE440.

a cappella. A style of choral singing without accompaniment.

absolute music. Instrumental music that has no extramusical associations.

accelerando. Gradual increase in tempo.

accent. Emphasis or stress on a particular note or beat.

adagio. "At ease," Italian term for a slow tempo.

aerophone. Any instrument that produces a sound with a vibrating column of air.

allegro. "Cheerful," Italian term for a fast tempo.

allegretto. A little slower than allegro.

andante. "Walking" tempo.

antecedent and consequent. A pair of musical phrases that complement each other in a "question and answer" type relationship.

appreciation. Preference accompanied by an awareness of salient characteristics.

aria. A formal composition for solo voice and instrumental accompaniment.

arpeggio. The notes of a chord played consecutively rather than simultaneously.

atonal. Absence of tonality; music that has no pitch center.

augmentation. The statement of a theme in longer rhythmic values than originally presented.

baritone. Male voice with a range between that of the tenor and bass.

bar line. Vertical line used on the staff to separate measures.

bass. Classification of the lowest range of a man's voice.

basso continuo. Form of instrumental accompaniment found primarily in the Baroque period. Usually consists of a keyboard instrument and a low melodic instrument.

basso ostinato. See *ground bass*.

beat. Steady pulse in music.

bebop (or bop). Style of jazz originating in the 1940s that featured complex improvisation by small combos.

binary form. Two-part sectional form (usually A B or A A B).

bitonality. The simultaneous use of two different pitch centers.

blues. A form of black popular music that developed from field hollers and work songs. It is characterized by a twelve-measure harmonic progression, the use of "blue notes" (lowered 3rd, 5th, and 7th steps of the scale), and a melancholy mood.

cadence. A rhythmic pause that has a feeling of complete or partial rest at the end of a musical phrase.

cadenza. A virtuosic section of music near the end of a concerto for the unaccompanied soloist.

cantabile. An indication for instrumental music to be performed in a "singing" style (smooth and connected).

cantata. A sacred or secular work for voices, usually accompanied by orchestra, consisting of movements such as arias, recitatives, duets, and choruses.

chamber music. Instrumental music for small ensembles with one player on a part.

chanson. The French word for song.

chorale. A hymn tune, usually associated with the German Protestant Church.

chord. Three or more pitches sounded together.

chordophone. A classification for string instruments that may be bowed, struck, plucked, or scraped.

chorus. A large group of singers. This also refers to a piece of music written for such a group.

chromatic. Using pitches outside of the seven-note diatonic scale.

coda. "Tail," a final section of a composition.

codetta. "Little tail," the final section of the exposition in sonata-allegro form.

col legno. "With the wood," a technique of playing a string instrument with the wood part of the bow rather than the hair.

compound meter. The accented grouping of beats in multiples of discernible three-count subdivisions.

concertino. A group of soloists in baroque concerto grosso.

concerto. A composition for soloist with orchestral accompaniment.

concerto grosso. A baroque composition for a group of soloists with orchestral accompaniment.

connotation. The process of conveying meaning through personal associations.

consequent. See *antecedent and consequent.*

consonant harmony. The stable and harmonious sounding together of two or more pitches.

continuo. Short for "basso continuo."

counterpoint. See *polyphony.*

crescendo. Gradually louder (<).

decibel. A unit of measure for loudness of sound.

decrescendo. Gradually softer (>).

denotation. The process of conveying meaning through shared experiences or universally understood signs.

development. The reworking and expansion of a theme.

diatonic. Using a scale that consists of seven different pitches within an octave and that is constructed with two half-steps and five whole-steps.

diminuendo. Becoming softer.

diminution. The statement of a theme in shorter rhythmic values than originally presented.

dissonant harmony. The unstable or disagreeable sounding together of two or more pitches—which creates tension.

double stop. The simultaneous playing of two or more pitches on a violin or similar string instrument.

duet. A vocal or instrumental composition for two performers of equal importance.

dynamics. The volume (loudness or softness) of musical sound.

equal temperament. A system of tuning which divides the octave into twelve equal half-steps.

etude. A study piece used to practice a particular technique. Artistic and musical etudes are frequently used for concert performance.

exposition. The first section of sonata-allegro form.

figured bass. A kind of musical shorthand for keyboard used in the seventeenth and eighteenth centuries. It consists of a bass line and numbers to indicate the harmonies to be filled in by the performer.

form. The organization of musical sound events.

forte. Loud (f).

fortissimo. Very loud (ff).

fugue. A contrapuntal procedure that develops a theme called the subject, through imitative polyphonic texture.

gamelan orchestra. A non-Western musical ensemble that consists mostly of percussion instruments; found primarily in Java and Bali.

glissando. A smooth sliding between pitches.

ground bass. A melodic phrase that is repeated over and over as the bass line of a composition. (Also called basso ostinato.)

half-step. The smallest interval commonly used in Western music. (Also called a semitone.)

harmony. Two or more pitches sounded together.

heterophony. A form of non-Western musical texture consisting of a melody and one or more slight variations on that melody performed simultaneously.

homophony. A musical texture consisting of a melody with accompaniment.

idiophone. Any instrument that vibrates when struck or scraped.

imitation. The immediate repetition of a melody or a melodic contour in another voice of a polyphonic texture.

improvisation. The spontaneous composition of music by a performer.

interval. The distance between two pitches.

key. The pitch center of a composition.

key signature. The flats or sharps placed at the beginning of a composition to indicate the tonality of the work.

keynote. (Tonic) the main note—pitch center—of a particular tonality.

largo. Extremely slow tempo.

lento. Very slow tempo.

libretto. The text of an opera, oratorio, or similar vocal composition.

lied. German art song (plural is lieder).

maestoso. Majestic.

Mass. The ritual of communion celebrated in the Catholic Church.

mazurka. A Polish dance in triple meter.

mbira. An African instrument that consists of metal strips or "reeds" attached to a hollow box or to a sound board attached to a resonator. Also called a thumb piano.

measure. The grouping of beats in musical notation marked by vertical lines called bar lines.

melody. The succession of pitches and time values with a sense of cohesiveness.

membranophone. Instrument with a stretched skin that is struck.

meter. Grouping of beats.

metronome. A mechanical or electrical device used to provide a steady beat at various speeds—usually measured in beats per minute.

mezzo. Medium.

mezzo forte. Medium loud (mf).

mezzo piano. Medium soft (mp).

microtone. An interval smaller than a half-step.

moderato. Moderately.

modulation. A change of pitch centers.

molto. Modifier used with dynamic, tempo, or stylistic terms—means "very."

monophony. A musical texture consisting of a single melody without accompaniment.

motive. A short melodic figure used as a unifying aspect of a musical instrument.

movement. A self-contained section of music that is part of a larger work such as a symphony, concerto, or sonata.

mute. A device used to dampen or soften the sound of a musical instrument.

non-melodic texture. Musical sound without a melody.

non-Western music. Any musical style that has not been derived from western European traditions.

octave. An interval measured as the distance from the first to the eighth tones of a diatonic scale.

opera. A musical drama that includes acting, costumes, scenery, and usually the singing of all parts with orchestral accompaniment.

opus. "Work," op.—the abbreviation of this term—is used with a number to more accurately identify a work or group of works by a particular composer.

oratorio. A vocal work similar to opera but without costumes, acting, or scenery.

Ordinary. The section of the Roman Catholic Mass that remains the same from day to day (Kyrie, Gloria, Credo, Sanctus, Agnus Dei).

ostinato. A rhythmic or melodic pattern that is repeated over and over.

overture. An orchestral composition that usually serves as an introduction to an opera or musical. Some overtures are written as independent concert pieces.

pelog. A seven-note scale used by modern gamelan orchestras.

pentatonic scale. Five-tone scale.

phrase. A musical sentence. Part of a melody with a complete thought and usually marked by a cadence.

pianissimo. Very soft (pp).

piano. Soft (p).

pitch. The highness or lowness of sound.

pizzicato. Plucking a string as opposed to bowing it.

plainsong.   Gregorian chant.

polyphony.   A musical texture with two or more melodies playing simultaneously that are rhythmically independent and of relatively equal interest.

polyrhythm.   The simultaneous performance of two or more different rhythms or meters.

polytonality.   The simultaneous use of more than one pitch center.

preference.   Choosing one thing over another.

prestissimo.   Extremely fast tempo.

presto.   Very fast tempo.

program music.   Instrumental music that is descriptive of some extramusical object or idea.

Proper.   The sections of the Roman Catholic Mass with texts and chants that vary with the seasons of the Church year (Introit, Gradual, Alleluia, Tract, Offertory, Communion).

quartet.   A composition for four instruments or voices.

quintet.   A composition for five instruments or voices.

ragtime.   A style of American popular music primarily for piano with a steady marchlike accompaniment figure in the left hand and strong syncopated rhythms in the melody of the right hand.

recapitulation.   The third main section of sonata-allegro form, which contains much of the same material as the first section (exposition).

recitative.   A vocal style that imitates the natural rhythmic and melodic inflections of speech.

Requiem Mass.   A musical setting of the Mass for the Dead.

rhythm.   The duration of sound and the illusion of movement of that sound in time.

ripieno.   Refers to the full orchestra in baroque concerto grosso.

ritardando.   A gradual slowing in tempo.

ritornello form.   "Return form," usually found in the baroque concerto grosso where a theme played by the full ensemble alternates with freer material played by a soloist or group of soloists.

rondo form.   Sectional form usually in five or seven parts (A B A C A or A B A C A B A).

rubato.   "To rob," a slight fluctuation in tempo for expressive purposes.

scale.   A series of pitches arranged in order (low to high or high to low).

simple meter.   A grouping of beats with note values divisible by two.

slendro.   Five-note scale used by older gamelan orchestras.

sonata.   A composition for piano, or for solo instrument with piano accompaniment, that has three or four movements.

song cycle.   A set of songs unified by subject matter and melodic themes.

Sprechstimme.   "Speech song," a type of vocal production that mixes speech and song.

strophic.   Form used for a song in which each stanza is sung to the same music.

swing.   A jazz style of playing eighth notes with a triplet feel.

symphony.   Large multimovement work for orchestra.

syncopation.   An accent in a normally unaccented place.

tempo.   Speed of the beat.

ternary form.   Three-part sectional form, usually A B A or A A B A.

terraced dynamics.   Sudden change in dynamic levels commonly found in baroque music, usually created with changes in numbers of instruments playing.

texture.   The relationship of melody to other melodies or harmony in music.

theme.   A melody used for development and unification of a composition.

theme and variations.   A sectional form based upon a melody and variations on the melody. Usually diagrammed $A A_1 A_2 A_3 A_4$.

through-composed.   A vocal free form with a continuous changing of ideas and moods and no significant repetition of material.

timbre.   Tone color, the characteristics of musical sound that enable distinction between different voices, instruments, or combinations of instruments.

toccata.   "Touch piece," a composition usually written for keyboard to demonstrate brilliant technique.

tonality.   Pitch center.

tone color.   See *timbre*.

tonic.   (Keynote), the main pitch in a particular tonality. (The first note of the scale in a key.)

transcription.   A composition that has been rewritten for a different instrument or ensemble with essentially no other changes in musical elements.

tremolo. The quick repetition of the same tone on a string instrument.

trio. Chamber ensemble of three players.

tutti. An indication in orchestral parts for all instruments to play rather than just the soloist.

twelve-tone technique. A twentieth-century method of composition that arranges the twelve pitches of the chromatic scale into a series (called a row) upon which the entire work is then based.

value. A choice made freely from alternatives, which is cherished and affirmed to others through repeated actions.

verismo. "Realism," a school of nineteenth-century Italian opera that drew upon everyday life for realistic stories.

vibrato. Slight fluctuation in a musical pitch that adds "warmth" to the sound.

vivace. Quick, lively.

whole-step. The interval comprised of two half-steps (or a major second).

whole-tone scale. A scale consisting only of whole-tones.

word-painting. The musical expression of a word or phrase by imitating the object or action with musical elements (for example, the music rises on the word "exalted").